Exchange Rates and Economic Policy in the 20th Century

Modern Economic and Social History Series

General Editor: Derek H. Aldcroft

Titles in this series include:

The Seaside, Health and the Environment in England and Wales Since 1800
John Hassan

Disillusionment or New Opportunities? The Changing Nature of Work in Offices, Glasgow 1880–1914
R. Guerriero-Wilson

Raleigh and the British Bicycle Industry
An Economic and Business History, 1870–1960
Roger Lloyd-Jones and M.J. Lewis with the assistance of M. Eason

Battles for the Standard
Bimetallism and the Spread of the Gold Standard in the Nineteenth Century
Ted Wilson

The British Footwear Industry
Peter R. Mounfield

Trade Unions and the Economy: 1870–2000
Derek H. Aldcroft and Michael J. Oliver

The British Electronics Industry
Technical Promise and Market Failure, 1930–2000
John F. Wilson

The Skilled Compositor, 1850–1914
An Aristocrat Among Working Men
Patrick Duffy

Lancashire Cotton Operatives and Work, 1900–1950
A Social History of Lancashire Cotton Operatives in the Twentieth Century
Alan Fowler

Industrial Clusters and Regional Business Networks in England, 1750–1970
John F. Wilson and Andrew Popp

Exchange Rates and Economic Policy in the 20th Century

edited by
ROSS E. CATTERALL and
DEREK ALDCROFT

Routledge
Taylor & Francis Group
LONDON AND NEW YORK

First published 2004 by Ashgate Publishing

2 Park Square, Milton Park, Abingdon, Oxon OX14 4RN
711 Third Avenue, New York, NY 10017, USA

Routledge is an imprint of the Taylor & Francis Group, an informa business

First issued in paperback 2017

British Library Cataloguing in Publication Data
Exchange rates and economic policy in the twentieth
century. – (Modern economic and social history)
1.Foreign exchange rates 2.Economic policy 3.Economic
history – 20th century
I.Catterall, Ross E., 1948– II.Aldcroft, Derek H. (Derek
Howard), 1936–
332.4'56'0904

US Library of Congress Cataloging in Publication Data
Exchange rate regimes and economic policy in the twentieth century / edited by
Ross E. Catterall and Derek H. Aldcroft.
p. cm. -- (Modern economic and social history)
"Original versions of the papers in this volume were presented in Session E5 ... at the Twelfth International Economic History Congress, held in Madrid in Aug. 1998"--Pref.
Includes bibliographical references.
ISBN 1-84014-264-2
1. Foreign exchange. 2. Foreign exchange rates. I. Catterall, Ross, 1948– II. Aldcroft, Derek Howard. III. Modern economic and social history series.

HG3851b.E918 2001
332.4'56--dc21

2001022924

ISBN 978-1-84014-264-8 (hbk)
ISBN 978-1-138-26728-2 (pbk)

Typeset in 10/12 Sabon by IML Typographers, Birkenhead, Merseyside

Contents

List of Figures vii
List of Tables ix
Preface xi
General Editor's Preface xiii

Introduction 1
Ross E Catterall

1. Exchange rate regimes and economic performance in the inter-war years 17
Derek H. Aldcroft

2. Exchange rate crises and US financial markets during the 1930s 71
Scott Sumner

3. The political economy of money supply, exchange rate and inflation targets since Bretton Woods 103
Michael J. Oliver

4. European monetary union: does recent economic history in the UK suggest that exchange rates pose significant trade barriers? 130
Allan Webster

5. The cart before the horse? Australian exchange rate policy and economic reform in the 1980s 172
Kieron Toner

6. Stabilisation and adjustment in Greece, 1990–99 202
Costas Karfakis

7. Riding the exchange rate roller-coaster: speculative currency markets and the durability of exchange rate regimes 228
Ross E. Catterall

8. The elusive case for flexible exchange rates 254
George Zis

9. Unilateral euroisation in transition countries: the case of southeastern Europe 296
Angelos Kotios

Index 321

List of figures

5.1	Australian unemployment rates (1973–97)	175
5.2	Australian GDP growth rates (1973–97)	175
5.3	Australian consumer price inflation (1973–97)	176
5.4	Australian exports to selected countries (1973)	181
5.5	Australian Dollar/SDR exchange rate (1973–97)	183
5.6	Growth of Australian deposit money banks' foreign liabilities (AS$ millions) (1973–97)	185
5.7	Australian share price index (1973–97)	186
5.8	Australian industrial production 1973–97	187
5.9	Australian terms of trade (1973–97)	190
5.10	Australian discount rate (1973–95)	196
6.1	Consumer price inflation	204
6.2	Real money and velocity growth	208
6.3	Real short-term interest rates	208
6.4	Real effective exchange rate	209
6.5	Inflation, output growth and real money	211
6.6	Inflation and unemployment	211
6.7	Entrepreneurial capital	213
6.8	Changes in net domestic and foreign assets	214
6.9	Inflation persistence	220
6.10	General government fiscal deficit	221
6.11	General government primary balance	221
6.12	General government debt	222
6.13	Productivity, real wages and real unit labour costs	222
6.14	Profitability index	223
7.1	The first 18 months of the euro–eurozone interest rates and the USD value of the euro, January 1999–June 2000	231
7.2	Annual GDP growth rates for the EU, 1992–2001	231
7.3	EU growth rates, quarter 1, 2000–quarter 2, 2003	245
7.4	British pounds per euro, January 1999–December 2003	246

List of tables

1.1	Volume of gross domestic product	23
1.2	Volume of exports	24
1.3	Indices of manufacturing production	25
1.4	European trade and currency fluctuations, 1922–27	27
1.5	Range of fluctuation of gold value of selected currencies, 1931–37	31
1.6	Yearly range of quotations of certain currencies in Switzerland, 1931–36	32
1.7	Great power trade blocs	34
1.8	Fluctuations in GDP/GNP and exports, 1929–37/8	50
1.9	Fluctuations in industrial/manufacturing production, 1929–1937/8	51
2.1	Annualized changes in the world (physical) monetary gold stock and related crises, 1929–39	73
2.2	The relationship between US industrial production, the gold ratio, the world monetary gold stock and the deposits of failed US banks, January 1927–April 1933, monthly	75
2.3	The relationship between variations in the real value of the Cowles index of stock prices and the world monetary gold stock, January 1927–April 1933, selected periods, monthly	78
2.4	The relationship between the Dow Jones industrial average and the dollar price of French francs, 17 April 1933–1 February 1934, daily	83
2.5	The relationship between commodity prices and the dollar price of French francs, 17 April 1933–1 February 1934, daily	83
3.1	Average inflation performance in inflation-targeting countries	125
3.2	Average GDP growth in inflation-targeting countries	126
4.1	Simulations of trade policy equivalents for 1989	151
4.2	Simulations of trade policy equivalents for 1990	156
4.3	Simulations of effective protection of capital for 1990	162
4.4	Effective protection of capital simulations for alternative policy barriers to trade	168
5.1	Manufacturing, share of GDP and employment, selected countries and groups	188
5.2	Composition of Australian exports	189
6.1	Intermediate targets and indicators	205

6.2 Interest rates 207
6.3 Aggregate expenditure 210
6.4 Instrumental variable estimates 216
6.5 Inflation equation 219
7.1 Maastricht tests for EMU membership 240
7.2 The range of differences across the EU countries (percentages) 242
7.3 EU countries' position on the world competitiveness scoreboard 242
9.1 The EU–Balkans contractual relations 299
9.2 SEE external trade, 2000 301
9.3 Monetary integration with the EU, 1998 302
9.4 Exchange rate regimes in SE Europe 303
9.5 Selected economic indicators, 2000 307

Preface

The original versions of the chapters in this volume were presented in Session E5 on 'Exchange Rates and Economic Policy in the Twentieth Century' at the Twelfth International Economic History Congress held in Madrid in August 1998.

The editors would like to thank the authors for their collaboration and for preparing the final versions of their papers for publication. We should also like to express our sincere thanks to Ashcroft International Business School of Anglia Polytechnic University for their generosity in funding the costs of the editors' attendance at the Congress in Madrid.

REC
DHA

Modern Economic and Social History Series General Editor's Preface

Economic and social history has been a flourishing subject of scholarly study during recent decades. Not only has the volume of literature increased enormously but the range of interest in time, space and subject matter has broadened considerably so that today there are many sub-branches of the subject which have developed considerable status in their own right.

One of the aims of this new series is to encourage the publication of scholarly monographs on any aspect of modern economic and social history. The geographical coverage is worldwide and contributions on non-British themes will be especially welcome. While emphasis will be placed on works embodying original research, it is also intended that the series should provide the opportunity to publish studies of a more general and thematic nature which offer a reappraisal or critical analysis of major issues of debate.

Derek H. Aldcroft
University of Leicester

Introduction

Ross E. Catterall

Background to this volume

The initial basis for this volume was a collection of papers presented at the Congress of the International Economic History Association held in Madrid in August 1998, but subsequently the original papers were extensively revised and reworked to reflect further research, and new papers were added to provide a more extensive view of exchange rates and economic policy in the 20th century. These revisions have helped to create a volume which is not only backward-looking in the sense that it analyses exchange rate issues of the past, but also a volume which it is hoped will help readers derive new insights into key factors affecting future exchange rate management and policy.

The original versions of the papers presented in Madrid centred on empirical issues of exchange rate behaviour and performance in the period since the First World War through to the late 1990s. Subsequently, these papers were revised and extended, and new chapters were added covering more theoretical issues: issues of the durability of European economic and monetary union and country convergence, and a consideration of the alternative exchange rate strategies open to new aspirants to the European Union membership (especially in south-eastern Europe). With the addition of these new chapters, the euro increasingly became an object of focus. At the Madrid Congress in August 1998, when earlier versions of some of the papers were presented, the formal launch of the euro was still to come. However, in many European countries the event was excitedly anticipated as a revolutionary change in international finance, and especially important in propelling an integrated Europe forward in terms of international trade in goods and services, prestige and economic growth. Some also saw it as an important milestone along the way to political union in Europe. In the opening session of the Congress, the Spanish Minister of Finance stressed the great significance for Europe and the global economy of the single currency project. This euro-enthusiasm was reflected in the Spanish banks at the time, many of which bore posters announcing 'Hola euro, adios peseta'.

Of course this euro-enthusiasm was by no means universal. The UK and Swedish governments choose not to participate in the euro project, at least for the time being. In a subsequent referendum, on 14 September

2003, the Swedish electorate rejected Euroland membership by a vote of 56 per cent to 42 per cent, with more than 81 per cent of electors turning out to vote. Likewise, Denmark had resoundingly rejected the euro in a national referendum three years earlier, although more recently Danish public opinion appears to have moved more in favour of the new currency. In Britain, the official position of Tony Blair's Labour government remains that a referendum on euro membership will be held when the UK economy is sufficiently convergent with that of Euroland. To demonstrate this convergence, and show net economic benefits from membership, the economy has to pass five 'tests' laid down by the Treasury. Passing the tests would indicate that higher growth, greater economic stability and more employment would result from the UK being a participant in the single currency. In contrast to Sweden, Denmark and the UK, the Greek government, showed its enthusiasm for economic and monetary union by pursuing a rigorously disinflationary policy in the latter part of the 1990s, resulting in its meeting the European Union's Maastricht convergence criteria in June 2000, and formally joining as the twelfth member of the Euroland club on 1 January 2001.

To the clear dismay and consternation of many euro enthusiasts, despite an almost flawless launch of the euro in 1999 and a similarly almost flawless transition into a circulating currency amongst the 12 Euroland members on 1 January 2002, the initial performance of the currency after its launch (at least in terms of its nominal value against the US dollar) caused disappointment. Starting out at around one euro to 1·17 US dollars, the currency fell to a low point of 82·5 US cents in October 2000, and was not much above this in the middle of 2001. Latterly, with a deceleration in US economic growth, there has been a recovery of the euro's position. Beginning in early 2002, the euro began to appreciate against the US dollar, getting back to the 1·17 level in early summer 2003, although doubts remain of whether this level can be sustained in the longer term.

Although euro-enthusiasts felt dismay and disappointment about the initial performance of the currency, these were perhaps rather misplaced sentiments as a weaker euro had bestowed considerable competitive advantages on a Europe blighted by high unemployment blackspots and a poor recent growth record. The experience of the first four years of the euro underlines the volatile nature of foreign exchange markets. Sometimes this volatility results in benefits to countries in terms of international competitiveness, but at other times trade and employment levels can be threatened by sharp currency appreciations. The causes and impacts of this volatility are discussed in Chapter 7.

One of the aims of this volume is, by analysing the historical experience of exchange rates and economic policy in the 20th century, to inform and enlighten the debate over exchange rate policy in the 21st century. The entry of the euro into circulation on 1 January 2002 and the contemporaneous abolition of 12 national currencies is a clear new direction in 21st-century exchange rate policy. No previous monetary union has ever resulted in the disappearance of so many major trading currencies, or involved such a large percentage of global economic activity, or been associated with a high degree of economic and political policy coordination. Previous monetary unions, largely 19th-century creations, were much more limited in their scope and most lacked coordinated economic policy and any degree of political union. (One partial exception is the German monetary union established after 1857. This centralised economic and political policy in Prussia and the Prussian Central Bank, and created, by 1875, the Reichmark to replace the dual currency system established in 1857.) It is the coordination of economic policy and aspects of political decision making which are both a source of strength of, and a threat to, Euroland's new monetary arrangements. They provide eurosceptics with ample ammunition to challenge EMU on the basis that it threatens national economic and political sovereignty, and is simply a step too far for them to accept.

There is no doubt that the European single currency project has altered the international financial architecture and encouraged emulation elsewhere in the world. The arrival of EMU has sparked off new interest in cooperative monetary arrangements and has encouraged other countries in both hemispheres to think in terms of creating monetary unions (Wyplosz, 2001). For example, the idea of NAMU – a North American Monetary Union – has been canvassed in the USA, Canada and Mexico, the North American Free Trade Area (NAFTA) members. Canadian academics and policymakers have considered unilateral US dollarisation to replace the Canadian dollar, and discussions on this topic have taken place with the US monetary authorities. Latin American countries have also debated the question of US dollarisation, or, alternatively, the creation of their own single currency. The possibility of a monetary union encompassing Asia and Australasia has been raised, and Africa too has shown interest in cooperative monetary arrangements. There has been talk, for example, of a new common currency for Kenya, Tanzania and Uganda, and countries with historical ties to France have contemplated a link with the euro (Honohan and Lane, 2000, p. 1).

So far, many of the discussions regarding potential monetary unions have only been exploratory in nature. However, the states of the Arabian Gulf, with their own embryonic variant of economic integration through the Gulf Cooperation Council (GCC) have declared it as their aim to establish a single currency in the area by 2010. In their 22nd summit in

Muscat on 21 December 2001, leaders of the GCC signed an agreement for the establishment of a customs union for the GCC states that came into effect in January 2003, rather than 2005 as agreed previously. The agreement contained clauses relating to the establishment of a monetary union of GCC states and the creation of a single currency, and set out a timetable with a view to launching a single currency on 1 January 2010. This interest in monetary unions cannot as yet be seen as an affirmation of the durability of the euro project; rather it reflects Eichengreen's hypothesis (1999) that, in a world of high capital mobility, the only sustainable exchange rate regimes are the so-called 'corner solutions' of free-floating or immutably fixed exchange rates (monetary unions, immutable or orthodox currency boards and dollarisation). If the growth of interest in monetary unions leads to the formation of new unions which prove successful, another outcome might be in prospect: that the merger of monetary unions may occur, creating a possibility that during the 21st century Keynes' vision of a global single currency may be realised. Much depends on how Europe's evolving monetary arrangements are judged as the century unfolds.

A volume of this kind cannot hope to provide a comprehensive coverage of the debate over monetary unions or the history of exchange rates in the 20th century. Indeed there is always the danger that there will be a lack of integration of the various chapters, and insufficient glue or dovetailing between the themes covered. Moreover, the literature on exchange rates, both empirical and theoretical, is immense and growing rapidly, yet theoretical explanations of exchange rate behaviour remain somewhat inadequate. As two leading researchers have commented, understanding exchange rate volatility 'remains a high-priority task for international finance scholars' (Flood and Rose, 1999, F671). The purpose of this introduction is to provide some of the cohesion necessary between the individual chapters in this book, and to provide a background canvas of the exchange rate scene on which the specific chapters represent the foreground. In other words, this introduction attempts to create a more 'joined-up' volume, linking some of the key themes addressed to overall developments in exchange rate regimes and policies.

The overall historical perspective is naturally backward-looking. The majority of the chapters are about the empirical observation of economic policy and performance under various types of exchange rate regime during the 20th century. But the volume is very much forward-looking as well, raising questions as to what can be learnt from the 20th-century experience for exchange rate regime construction and management in the 21st century. Critical issues raised and discussed in one or more chapters include the following:

a. the interaction between the exchange rate regime chosen and overall macroeconomic performance;
b. the necessity of structural reform to make any system of fixed or pegged exchange rate viable;
c. the political economy of the selection of exchange rate targets and the predisposition of politicians to select over-ambitious targets;
d. the use of exchange rate targets as a means of inflation control and supply side improvement;
e. elements of the theory of exchange rate determination and the political economy of monetary unions;
f. the long-run durability of monetary unions, especially European economic and monetary union;
g. the unpredictable and somewhat mysterious behaviour of exchange rates;
h. the consideration of whether exchange rate volatility represents a serious barrier to international trade;
i. the impact of speculation on the foreign exchange market and economic policymaking, especially in terms of exchange rate regime selection;
j. key questions regarding the exchange rate strategies that new members, and indeed those who so far have remained apart from EMU, might best follow.

The broad canvas of 20th-century exchange rate history

Throughout the 20th century exchange rate regimes were high on the agenda of economic policymakers. Views of their impact and role changed during the century, but they were always a critical object of concern. Popularly a country's exchange rate may be seen as a reflection of the economic virility of an economy, and as a matter of prestige. But the rate chosen undoubtedly has profound economic impacts. The rate is, at least in theory, an outcome of the competitiveness of the economy in engaging in international trade with other nations, but it is in itself also a key determinant of that international competitiveness. Countries which over-ambitiously aim for high exchange rates may fail to create favourable structural change (which could result from a moderately, but not excessively, high exchange rate). In consequence they may experience the debilitating impact of low investment, deindustrialisation and mass unemployment. Thus the rate chosen is an important influence on economic growth, competitiveness, trade, investment, consumption, saving, money supply, expectations, industrial structure and structural change, employment, confidence in financial markets, the government's budget and the price level. Every macroeconomic aggregate is affected, and so is the microeconomy through the impact on the growth of firms, industries, regions and the size and composition of the workforce.

As the exchange rate has often been 'administered' to the economy rather than selected by the invisible hand of market forces, policymakers have faced a great challenge in selecting an appropriate rate, and considerable odium (and often political defeat) when they have been perceived as making the wrong decision. Thus, not only does the exchange rate affect all dimensions of economic life, it also has a considerable impact on politics and the political complexion of government. But the process is much more complex than this: there are two-way feedbacks. The condition and performance of any economy will also affect the exchange rate itself (although not always clearly and predictably owing to the behaviour of speculators causing over-tracking of nominal exchange rate movements). The political ideology of the ruling party will naturally be a key factor in the exchange rate regime chosen, and it is also likely to be a determinant of the vigour with which it pursues and maintains a particular exchange rate target. Exchange rates are very much issues of political economy, as becomes apparent throughout the chapters in this volume.

In the period covered by this volume the following types of exchange rate regimes can be identified:

Exchange rate regimes: a typology

Basically fixed regimes: pegged exchange rates

1. Vis-à-vis a single currency: economies that peg their exchange rate to major international currencies with no or rare parity adjustments (including currency board arrangements); economies that announce a pre-arranged schedule of exchange rate adjustments against the currency of the peg (the exchange rate changes, but at a fixed pace).
2. Vis-à-vis a currency basket: economies that peg their exchange rate to a basket of currencies of their main trading partners or to standardised currency composites such as the European currency unit (ECU) or IMF Special Drawing Rights (SDRs).
3. Within pre-established margins: economies that peg their exchange rate to a single currency or a currency basket within certain (typically narrow) margins (for example, the European Exchange Rate Mechanism – ERM – the precursor of the euro).
4. Fixed but adjustable peg: the arrangement that prevailed under the Bretton Woods par value system, where nominally devaluations were permissible only in cases of 'fundamental disequilibrium' in the

balance of payments. However, in practice speculation and other factors (such as competitive pressures) might force realignments.

5. A single currency: a hybrid where the members of a trading bloc or zone create a single currency to be used among its members so that exchange rate fluctuations between them cease to exist. However, the single currency itself will either move in one of the manners outlined below against other currencies (such as the European single currency) or, in theory, it could be fixed vis-à-vis some other currency or indicator.

Basically flexible regimes: adjustable and flexible exchange rates

1. Indicators: economies that adjust their currencies automatically to changes in selected indicators, such as developments in the real effective exchange rate, or movements in inflation indicators.
2. Managed float: economies that adjust their rates frequently on the basis of judgments made following developments in variables such as reserves and the payments position. Such managed floats have often been camouflaged by governments and constitute what have become known as 'dirty floats'.
3. Independent float: a genuinely free float where governments allow free markets and market forces to determine the exchange rates for their currencies.

The typology set out above broadly follows that used by the IMF (Guitián 1992, p. 16; IMF, 1995) in classifying exchange rate regimes. Examples of the various types of regime will be found throughout the volume, and one of the purposes of this introduction is to outline how various types of regime have emerged. What are frequently referred to as two 'corner solutions' exist. One is the genuinely free independent float; the other is the hard peg provided by an immutable currency board or by a monetary union. Other arrangements which occupy the middle ground are susceptible to speculative attacks, which can often prove fatal to the existing exchange rate regime.

Throughout the 20th century, exchange rate disasters have occurred because the wrong parity or the wrong type of regime has been selected or maintained, and then perhaps defended too long against enormous speculative odds. The fact that, in the post-gold standard world, a 'fixed' exchange rate does not remain fixed compounds the difficulty for policymakers in maintaining 'fixed' rates. The markets learned rapidly that so-called 'fixed' exchange rates were in fact targets for tilting at, unless genuinely immutable underpinnings existed. Successful speculation offered the prospect of large short-term gains, usually at the expense of dislocating national economies, and even perhaps global economic growth.

Policymakers 'administering' exchange rates to an economy, rather than leaving them to be determined by market forces, have both a considerable challenge and wide-ranging economic power to affect a nation's progress. With justification, when their decisions are perceived as ill-judged and damaging, they face considerable opprobrium and the prospect of political defeat.

The modern international exchange rate system does not have a long history. Effectively, it began in the later 19th century with the general spread of the gold standard system. This was not only applicable to the advanced industrialising countries. By 1914, India and a number of other far eastern countries had linked their currencies to gold. In Latin America, silver and bimetallic standards were replaced in Argentina, Brazil, Chile, Mexico, Peru and Uruguay. The gold standard club grew, from nine countries in 1880, to 22 in 1890, 29 at the turn of the century and 42 by 1912. Silver was effectively demonetised and, on the eve of the First World War, only a few countries such as China, Ethiopia, Persia, Honduras and San Salvador clung to the silver standard. For most areas of the world a gold-backed system of fixed exchange rates now existed (Palyi, 1972, p. 8). It was a genuinely fixed 'corner solution' providing countries maintained a fixed parity between their currency and gold, free convertibility of currency into gold existed, and there were no restrictions on the import and export of gold.

This system was not to remain in being for long. Just as the wars with France had led to the suspension of the original British gold standard in the early 19th century, and the wars and revolutions which plagued Europe between 1848 and 1871 broke the links between precious metals and currency issues in many countries, so too did the war of 1914–18 undermine the international gold standard. The vast expansion of government spending in affected European countries forced governments to turn to the printing presses to finance war-related procurements. This ended, it was assumed temporarily, the system of international fixed exchange rates. It also created new problems of inflation and differential rates of inflation which meant that prewar exchange rates were rendered inappropriate once peace had returned. Although attempts were made to resurrect the prewar system during the 1920s, and Britain made its valiant but misguided attempt to restore the prewar parity with the US dollar, the new dominance of fiat money over gold as a circulating medium of exchange meant that devaluation was now a practical possibility for policymakers operating under a so-called 'fixed' exchange rate regime. Policymakers were now operating in the middle ground between the two opposing corners.

The experience of floating by some countries in the first half of the 1920s and the possibility that nominally fixed exchange rates might be devalued, paved the way for destabilising capital flows and speculative currency attacks in the foreign exchange markets, which were a key element of the 1931 financial crisis. Once it was clear that currencies, and hence exchange rates, were not tied irrevocably to something relatively inelastic in supply such as gold, the stage was set for speculative foreign exchange attacks. These speculative attacks have grown enormously in scale since the inter-war years and their genesis, development and impact on economic policy are discussed in Chapter 7. However, the occurrence and magnitude of such attacks are difficult to predict in advance, as their relationship to macroeconomic fundamentals, especially in the short run, is uncertain. Different aspects of the relationship between economic aggregates and the behaviour of the exchange rate are also considered in other chapters in this volume.

Before there was a general return to fixed exchange rates after the Second World War, many governments had experimented with floating rate regimes of one sort or another, because they lacked the confidence to select a fixed parity and doubted whether this was even possible in the highly volatile environment that existed. The inter-war period as a whole includes free floating in the early 1920s, fixed exchange rates under the gold exchange standard, 1925–31, and managed floats in the 1930s. In Chapter 1, Derek Aldcroft examines the inter-war experience from an international perspective and assesses the impact of different exchange rate regimes on national economic performance. Although the picture is somewhat clouded by the overall volatility of the international environment and also on account of the short periods during which regimes operated, Aldcroft indicates that, from a medium-term perspective, economies with managed floats generally fared better than those which clung to fixed exchange rate regimes. Countries which did not have fixed exchange rates were much better able to absorb price and other shocks than those that did. Moreover, the former generally achieved superior macroeconomic performance compared to the latter in the 1930s.

A different perspective is offered on exchange rate crises and economic aggregates by Scott Sumner in the second chapter. He examines how US exchange rate crises of the 1930s affected American financial markets and the level of aggregate demand. He argues that, although many countries devalued their currencies in the 1930s, no country revalued its currency in terms of gold. As a result, during most exchange rate crises, speculators could anticipate either a devaluation or no change in the value of a currency. As the opportunity cost of holding gold was extremely low during this period (as a result of the low nominal interest rate), exchange rate crises often led to dramatic switches from threatened currencies to gold hoarding. This would reduce aggregate demand and depress affected economies. In the case of the USA, where Sumner analyses the affects of exchange rate crises on financial markets, he concludes that such crises 'probably did not trigger the Great Depression. But they almost certainly did play a role in depressing aggregate demand during 1931–32 and again during 1937–38'.

Following the chaotic experience of the inter-war years, it is scarcely surprising that arguments for a global fixed exchange rate regime won the day at the Bretton Woods Conference in 1944, and agreement was reached that IMF members would maintain their exchange rates within plus or minus 1 per cent of declared parities. It was generally accepted that floating exchange rates created additional uncertainty for firms and made them reluctant to engage in international trade. A fixed exchange rate system was held to lower exchange volatility, reduce risk to international traders and simplify their profit-maximising calculations. In addition, intensified competition between producers in different locations through the expansion of international trade would also yield benefits of specialisation in areas which had comparative advantages. This was seen as further integrating the international economy and having beneficial effects on its growth. However, this rosy scenario did not accord with reality. Trading partners often had markedly different levels of productivity and wage growth, inflation and structural change. The single most obvious manifestation of these differences was through inflation rates, and policymakers needed a safety valve for their uncompetitive economies. Devaluation provided this safety valve, and over time it became a frequently used escape route for economies with persistent trading difficulties, which could be argued to meet the International Monetary Fund's (IMF's) test of 'fundamental disequilibrium' in their balance of payments. However, the use of this safety valve often left economies with an endemic inflationary problem. Other ingenious devices such as adjustable pegs, crawling or creeping pegs, only accommodated inflation and inefficiency, and further reduced the alleged fixity of the exchange rate regime, again encouraging currency speculation which could prove seriously destabilising to affected economies.

The growing pretence of a global fixed exchange rate system finally broke down in the early 1970s, which interestingly coincided with the end of the postwar growth boom for most economies. Although the Bretton Woods system had been far from perfect, it did exert some pressure on governments to refrain from pursuing highly expansionary policies and thus acted as a check to inflation worldwide. Under its 'fixed' exchange rate system, balance of payments deficits could only be financed temporarily, and ultimately governments had to introduce deflationary policies (or devalue) to correct the imbalance. Devaluation in one form or another became the 'political solution', especially where high unemployment was deemed to threaten electoral success.

Slower global economic growth after 1973, coupled with higher unemployment, presented a new threat to politicians, and the way out was seen to lie in floating the exchange rate. Under floating, the balance of payments constraint was absent, at least in theory. Governments now felt they could pursue an expansionary policy in the belief that a depreciation would automatically eliminate any balance of payments deficits (assuming appropriate price elasticities for exports and imports). However, this approach only stoked up inflation further, especially after the dramatic rise in oil prices which occurred after the first oil price shock of 1973–4. Economies with poor productivity records could mask their inefficiencies with an exchange rate depreciation, at least until the international financial system declined to support them further with an inflow of debt capital.

Serious and persistent inflationary problems ultimately led to a reaffirmation, especially in Europe, of the desirability of some form of fixed exchange rate regime, or at least challenging exchange rate targets for managed floats. The conviction grew that only with a fixed exchange rate discipline or at least tough exchange rate targets could serious inflation be prevented or lessened, and the supply side of economies be improved. Greater exchange rate fixity would prevent populist governments from pursuing unduly expansionary monetary and fiscal policies. Pushful trade unions would not be able continually and successfully to demand real wage increases that outstripped productivity growth, as the impact would be a reduction in exports and employment. Inefficient producers would no longer be 'featherbedded' by exchange rate depreciation. No longer would a depreciating exchange rate automatically compensate for excess inflation relative to key trading partners. As Michael Oliver discusses in Chapter 3, the problem was now 'how to control inflation in a world without monetary rules', especially as hitting money supply targets proved an elusive goal for policymakers in most countries.

Europe did of course try to develop its own regional rules for the coordination of monetary matters following the demise of the Bretton Woods system of fixed exchange rates. At the beginning of 1972, the six members of the European Economic Community (EEC) created the 'snake', an exchange rate regime that required them to keep their exchange rates in a constrained band or 'tunnel'. The system was soon joined by the UK, Ireland, Denmark and Norway. Each member had a bilateral central rate with every other currency involved and the authorities of each country undertook to keep its currency within 2·25 per cent of this central rate. The whole snake was to fluctuate by no more than 4·45 per cent against the US dollar. The new system quickly came to be known as a 'Deutschmark zone', dominated by the strong West German economy. But the arrangements were short-lived. Within a year or so, the dollar peg had been removed and the weaker currencies – sterling, the Italian lira and the Norwegian krona – left the 'snake' as a result of intense speculation against sterling and the US dollar. France also pulled out in 1974.

By 1979, the system had metamorphosed into the European Monetary System (EMS), with France again a member, although she was involved in several realignments of the system and devaluations of the franc against the Deutschmark. The EMS was based on a weighted average 'basket' of all EEC currencies, establishing the European currency unit (ECU) as a reserve asset for central banks, which replaced part of their excessive dollar reserves. Weaker economies (initial members in this category were Italy and the Republic of Ireland, but later Portugal, Spain and Britain would also be included) could allow their currencies to depart from the basket average by up to 6 per cent either way, but for the stronger core countries the margin of deviation was only 2·25 per cent.

The EMS worked reasonably well so long as the US dollar did not exhibit too great short-run instability and as long as its members remained content with the iron rule of the Bundesbank in controlling inflation. The Bundesbank's austerity forced them to follow similar counter-inflationary policies to remain within the necessary parity bands. (This inevitably involved raising interest rates to exceed West German levels, a process heightened when the dollar was under pressure and the USA tightened the monetary screw.) Under the Plaza-Louvre Accords regime, finalised by the Louvre meeting in Paris early in 1987, the G7 (USA, Germany, Japan, France, Britain, Canada and Italy) countries effectively took some of the pressure off the EMS and the dollar. It was agreed that the dollar had depreciated enough and it would be managed, principally by the G3 (Germany, Japan and the USA) to ensure greater stability, which would buy up the dollar when it was weak. This system worked reasonably well. The dollar exhibited much greater stability from 1987 to 1992 than it had done in the 14 years from 1973 to 1987 (McKinnon, 1993, p. 34).

Although management of the value of the US dollar was relatively successful, the success of the European Exchange Rate Mechanism (ERM, a part of the EMS) also depended strongly on the preparedness of the EU countries to maintain parities by using interest rates to control domestic inflation and encourage foreign capital inflows. Attempts at disinflation could severely dislocate the domestic economy by creating severe industrial difficulties and unemployment. Nowhere was this effect greater than in the case of the UK. Britain was only formally in the ERM (at a central rate of 2·98 DM to the pound) during a short period in 1991–2, but tracking the Deutschmark at a rate of around 3 DM to the pound had begun somewhat earlier, with the British Chancellor, Nigel Lawson, using interest rates to further this end from 1986. The speed of disinflation was remarkable. The headline inflation rate fell from 10·9 per cent in October 1990 to 4·5 per cent in December 1991, and to 1·7 per cent in January 1993 (Lamont, 1999, p. 387). But interest rates were as high as 14 per cent in October 1990 and, although declining to 10·5 per cent in 1991, remained at 10 per cent or above until sterling was forced out from the ERM in September 1992. In October 1990, official unemployment had been 5·8 per cent, but it moved up to almost 11 per cent at the start of 1993. As can be seen from Costas Karfakis's chapter on Greece's progress to the EMU, this is the kind of problem that the Greek government faced as part of its successful attempt to become part of European economic and monetary union (EMU) in 2001.

This experience underlines the points made earlier about the key impact that exchange rate choice can have on all economic variables, both macroeconomic and microeconomic. The structural impacts of exchange rate choice, especially for the export sector, are clearly apparent in the case of the European economies, both in the ERM period and during the inter-war years. In Chapter 5, Kieron Toner convincingly argues the case for resolving serious structural difficulties, which affect export competitiveness, prior to attempting to settle an exchange rate regime or parity. Using the examples of policy mistakes from Australia in the 1980s, he argues that the Australian government failed to do this, leading to a crisis for economic policy as an attempt was made to put 'the cart before the horse'. Allan Webster's chapter, however, offers a different view on the structural impacts of exchange rate policy. The proposition that exchange rates cause trade barriers by engendering additional transactions costs and risks associated with currency volatility is examined. Webster concludes that the anti-trade impact of exchange rates and rate movements is small and that monetary union is likely to have less beneficial microeconomic impacts than the reform of Europe's common agricultural policy or the reform and harmonisation of taxes and subsidies.

Despite the severity of the 1992–3 crisis for the European monetary system and its virtual destruction of the ERM itself, the EU continued to press on with its grand plan for a single European currency as being the final act of creating a genuinely integrated single market among existing EU members. In order to level the playing field for trade and investment,

12 countries have so far proved willing to give up their national monetary sovereignty and to subject their economies to the interest rate policy determined by the European Central Bank in Frankfurt. Denmark, Sweden and the UK currently remain apart from the single currency. In the last chapter of the volume, Angelos Kotios considers whether the new entrants to the EU (especially in south-eastern Europe) need formally to join the single currency. He considers the possibilities offered by 'de facto' rather than 'de jure' euroisation, which does not necessarily involve giving up national monetary sovereignty. His discussion offers interesting alternative possibilities for the UK and Sweden as well.

In putting this volume together, the editors have attempted to create an international perspective on critical issues concerning exchange rates and economic policy in the 20th century and to lay the foundation for the continuing debate on these issues, which is likely to continue well into the 21st century. A critical part of this debate is of course based, not only on empirical observations of actual exchange rate experiences, but also on the theoretical foundations of exchange rate economics. In the penultimate chapter of the volume, George Zis attempts to bring these two strands together by considering the theoretical case made for flexible exchange rates and the empirical evidence about their actual behaviour and impacts in the period after 1983. His conclusions emphasise again that, whatever exchange rate regime is chosen, its selection is unlikely to be based on purely objective economic criteria, but rather on political factors and aspirations.

Political factors are a critical factor in Europe's creation of a single currency and the desire to expand the number of the economies which are members of Euroland. As well as promoting the growth of trade, income and welfare, euro-enthusiasts believe the new monetary order will help to engender collaboration and cooperation, peace and security throughout an (enlarged) European Union. Eurosceptics fear there is a hidden agenda of creating full political union on the heels of EMU. They find particularly unacceptable the loss of political and economic sovereignty which arises from the operation of a single monetary policy from the European Central Bank headquarters in Frankfurt. Former British Prime Minister Margaret Thatcher has declared repeatedly that 'Britain should not contemplate giving up the pound'. According to Lady Thatcher, the European 'political–bureaucratic elite ... in Britain as elsewhere in Europe believes it has an overriding mission to achieve European [political] integration by hook or by crook'. She further believes that the 'abolition of the pound in favour of the euro would constitute a major loss of Britain's power to govern herself and thus an unacceptable blow to democracy'. Furthermore, the alleged economic benefits of the single currency are either 'non-existent, or trivial, or can be achieved by other means' (Thatcher, 2002, p. 388). She also challenges a frequently articulated view that Britain's membership of Euroland is inevitable, as Britain will fail to prosper outside the single currency. She argues that the trade benefits of membership are insignificant and the growth of trade in NAFTA shows that free trade rather than a single currency is necessary for prosperity. Moreover, if the world wants a single currency it already exists – 'it is called the US dollar' (ibid., p. 386). William Hague, UK Conservative Party Leader from 1997 to 2001, also attacked the inevitability argument on similar grounds, claiming: 'It was inevitable that the *Titanic* was going to set sail, but that doesn't mean you had to be on it' (quoted in Marshall, 1999, p. 355).

EMU has been a central preoccupation of policymakers in Europe for several years now, but problematically the single currency appears to have only lukewarm support among their electorates, even among the 12 Euroland members. In part, this is because, since its inception at the beginning of 1999, the euro's performance has not been impressive, at least as far as public perceptions are concerned. It fell 15 per cent against the US dollar during its first year, and then below one-to-one parity with the dollar in 2000 (a total fall of 30 per cent), although it subsequently recovered lost ground. In addition, the introduction of the euro into circulation is believed in several member states to have intensified inflationary pressures as prices in the new currency have been 'rounded-up'. Above all, legitimate doubts exist about 'the one size fits all' monetary policy being administered by the European Central Bank. For example, higher interest rates to dampen inflation could have seriously damaging consequences for the weakest Euroland economies, which in turn might pressurise the ECB not to raise interest rates sufficiently to combat inflation in the stronger economies. This might damage the international credibility of the euro, reducing its international value and further stoking up inflation through higher cost imports. Alternatively, despite the outcry from weaker economies, the ECB might attempt to bolster the strength of the euro through higher interest rates, raising the level of unemployment generally. In a world where pursuing exchange rate targets has contributed to a sustained and significant reduction in inflation levels (the prime concern of the ECB), it is understandable that popular concerns should shift to the level of employment rather than the inflation rate. If the ECB fails to establish clear credibility for itself and the euro, increased interest rates remain a potential threat to prosperity in some member states, especially if Euroland members remain economically divergent rather than convergent. The issue of the convergence of the European economies is made more problematic by the EU's completion of the first stage of eastward enlargement with 10 new accesion members on 1 May 2004. Some of the new EU members have aspirations to join the single currency at an early date. Other countries toying with the idea of monetary union as the 21st-century 'solution' to exchange rate dilemmas will doubtless have much to learn from the European experience. It is by no means certain that monetary union will be chosen as the universal path.

References

Eichengreen, B.J. (1999), *Toward a New International Financial Architecture: A Practical Post-Asia Agenda*, Washington, DC: Institute for International Economics.

Flood, R.P. and K.R. Rose (1999), 'Understanding exchange rate volatility without the contrivance of macroeconomics', *Economic Journal,* 109, FF660–72, November.

Guitián, M. (1992), 'The choice of an exchange rate regime', in R.C. Barth and C. Wong (eds), *Approaches to Exchange Rate Policy: Choices for Developing and Transition Economies,* Washington, DC: IMF Institute.

Honohan, P. and P.R. Lane (2000), 'Will the Euro trigger more monetary unions in Africa', Working Papers, no. 176, UNU World Institute for Development Economics, Helsinki, March.

IMF (1995), *Issues in International Exchange and Payments Systems,* Washington, DC: IMF.

Lamont, N. (1999), *In Office,* London: Little, Brown & Company.

Marshall, M. (1999), *The Bank: The Birth of Europe's Central Bank and the Rebirth of Europe's Power*, rev. edn, London: Random House Business Books.

McKinnon, R.L. (1993), 'The rules of the game: international money in historical perspective', *Journal of Economic Literature,* 31.

Palyi, M. (1972), *The Twilight of Gold 1914–36,* Chicago: University of Chicago Press.

Thatcher, M. (2002), *Statecraft: Strategies for a Changing World,* London: HarperCollins.

Wyplosz, C. (2001), 'A monetary union in Africa: some European lessons', *Future Directions for Monetary Policies in East Asia,* Sydney: Reserve Bank of Australia.

CHAPTER ONE

Exchange rate regimes and economic performance in the inter-war years

Derek H. Aldcroft

Introduction

The inter-war years are remarkable in many ways, not least for the variety of exchange rate experiences. In contrast to the prewar period when the gold standard had reigned supreme in the major countries, the inter-war period saw several different regimes. Following the general abandonment of the gold standard during or shortly after the war, there was a period of free floating, with very little government intervention, when many currencies often fluctuated quite violently, but generally in a downward direction against the dollar, which emerged from the war as the strongest currency and one that became the yardstick for the subsequent stabilisation of other currencies. The floating period lasted until about the mid-1920s, though there was no clean break since stabilisation was a haphazard and uncoordinated affair, each country stabilising its currency as and when it thought fit to do so, which in practice meant when it had brought its internal finances under control. By 1925, when Britain and the Dominion countries returned to gold, there was a sufficiently large number of countries back on the gold standard (or rather the gold exchange standard) to refer to a fixed exchange rate regime. This system lasted until the early 1930s, when it disintegrated under the impact of the Great Depression and financial crisis of these years. A short period of floating ensued, when currency fluctuations were as violent as those of the early 1920s, to be replaced by a mixed system of semi-managed currencies within regional currency zones or blocs, such as the sterling area, the gold bloc, the Reichsmark bloc and the dollar and yen zones.

This is an ideal period to compare economic performance under alternative exchange rate regimes, namely free floating of the early 1920s, fixed exchange rates of the period 1925–30, and the managed regional floats of the 1930s. Less attractive from a comparative point of view is that the periods are rather short and distorted by extraneous events such as the aftermath of war and the Great Depression.

The free float of the 1920s

Contemporaries were understandably alarmed by the instability of exchange rates in the first half of the 1920s, and believed that no sound recovery of trade and output was possible until they had been stabilised. As the League of Nations (1920, p. ix) commented in one of its early reports: 'Everywhere currency and exchange disorder is hampering trade and retarding reconstruction. In some countries it is a prime factor amongst those which are causing a breakdown of the economic and social system.' Free floating was associated, rightly or wrongly, with currency depreciation and inflation and unsound finance. It was also deemed to induce excessive speculation in the exchanges, causing exchange rates to over-track from their true equilibrium levels. Such speculation was considered to be inherently destabilising, though recent research has cast some doubt on the veracity of this assumption (Aldcroft and Oliver, 1998, ch. 1). Be that as it may, for contemporaries, getting back to a fixed exchange rate system was not simply a nostalgic wish for the good old days, but a pragmatic response to unstable conditions. In virtually every discourse on the economics of postwar Europe, stabilisation was the key word; inevitably this presaged a rapid return to what was seen as the golden Eldorado of before the war, since the gold standard and all that went with it was seen as 'the very anchor of the sociopolitical tradition and thus of stability' (Barkai, 1993, pp. 3–5). Even the iconoclast Keynes saw the wisdom of stabilising the exchanges as soon as possible in order to encourage trade and investment. Though he rejected the old-fashioned gold standard as a 'barbarous relic', and was not in favour of a managed gold standard with the USA since this would have left Britain in thrall to that country, he advocated, through the pages of *The Manchester Guardian* in the spring of 1922, an early stabilisation of the key currencies in Europe, providing that no attempt was made to restore the old parities of those currencies which had depreciated by more than 20 per cent (Moggridge, 1992, pp. 377–8, 382–3; *Manchester Guardian*, 6 April 1922; Keynes, 1971, pp. 138–40; 1977, pp. 354–69; 1978, p. 40).

The debate, where there was such, was not about 'if' but 'when' the return was to be made, since there was no question in contemporary minds that the golden parities had proved their worth, and that they would prove equally efficacious in the postwar world was never for one moment questioned. For most European countries stabilisation was easier said than done. The majority had little hope of regaining their prewar parities, much as they would have cherished such a step. Distortions of the cost and price structure during the war period were too great to allow this; and, more to the point, they had risen much faster than costs and prices in America (back on gold in 1919), whose currency was the obvious comparator for stabilisation purposes. Furthermore, prices kept rising after the war in many European countries since national finances were in a chaotic state and often they deteriorated further in the period of postwar reconstruction. Consequently, exchange rates continued to weaken and inflation proceeded apace. With one or two exceptions, most European countries experienced inflation of varying degrees of intensity in the early 1920s. In several cases, Germany, Austria, Hungary, Poland and Russia, it slid into hyperinflation, with currencies becoming worthless and being replaced by new units of account. Moderate to severe inflations occurred in France, Belgium, Italy, Greece and the Balkans. Only the Anglo-Saxon countries (the UK, Netherlands, Switzerland and Scandinavian countries) eradicated inflation at an early date before it became serious by taking firm macroeconomic action, and eventually managed to stabilise their currencies at the prewar parities.

Although at the time the general European experience was regarded as disastrous, with the hard-line Anglo-Saxon countries being commended for their fiscal and monetary prudence despite the unemployment caused thereby, there has since been some reassessment of the relative costs and benefits incurred under the floating rate regime. It has been argued, for example, that inflation and currency depreciation were not always detrimental; that they boosted output, exports and employment, so that real variables, as opposed to nominal magnitudes, responded better in inflationary countries than they did under the tough policy regimes of the Anglo-Saxon countries (Laursen and Pedersen, 1964; Eichengreen, 1986b). The latter in fact suffered a severe contraction in 1920–22, partly as a result of the counter-inflationary measures, while their subsequent performance was said to be constrained by the pressure to return their currencies to the prewar parities (Broadberry, 1984).

For the purpose of this exercise it seems appropriate therefore to compare the real performance of three groups of countries: (1) the Anglo-Saxon: the UK, Sweden, Norway, Denmark, Switzerland and the Netherlands; (2) the hyperinflationary countries: Germany, Austria, Hungary and Poland (Russia is ignored here because of its special domestic factors); (3) the moderate to severe inflators: the selection here is confined to France, Belgium, Italy and Greece. Though the major focus is on the floating period, it will be appropriate to extend the period of comparison through the fixed rate years of the later 1920s in view of the implications which policy had in the longer term.

Countries returning to parity were clearly at a disadvantage vis-à-vis those countries experiencing continuous inflation and currency depreciation. The elimination of inflation at an early stage in the Anglo-

Saxon countries through severe macroeconomic retrenchment meant that they experienced a sharp downturn in the early 1920s, caused by a combination of internal compression and a decline in exports as the worldwide postwar boom collapsed and exchange rates became overvalued. The need to maintain a tight policy stance to bring about the internal price adjustment necessary to restore currency parities also meant that subsequent growth potential was somewhat constrained. Thus the UK, Switzerland and the Scandinavian countries had a rather chequered economic performance in the run-up to stabilisation (UK, 1925; Switzerland, 1924; Sweden, 1924; Denmark, 1926; Norway, 1928). The Netherlands, however, appears to have escaped almost unscathed, although it is perhaps misleading to make judgement solely on the basis of the pre-stabilisation years. Once return to gold was completed, most of these countries, apart from the UK, performed quite creditably (see below).

When judging the hyperinflationary countries, the main point to bear in mind is the post-stabilisation effects. For a time these countries enjoyed some benefit from inflation and currency depreciation. Output and employment were more buoyant in the early 1920s than was the case in the Anglo-Saxon countries. In all cases there was a noticeable stimulus to investment, even though it may have been prompted by the desire at times to convert cash into hard assets to avoid the ravages of inflation. But the good times did not last. Inflation was driven to such extremes that currencies eventually became worthless; in time the beneficial effects of inflation dwindled and in the final stages they became negative. Economic activity then seized up and real earnings declined dramatically. Thus, when new currencies were introduced, there followed a post-stabilisation setback, with rising unemployment, while many of the former gains proved ephemeral. Even the investment boom was something of a mixed blessing since many of the assets created in the inflation period were not always in the best interests of long-term economic growth. Finally, there were some serious political and social consequences arising out of inflation, especially in Germany (Aldcroft, 1997, ch. 3).

The moderate to severe inflators (France, Belgium, Italy and Greece) appear to have got the best bargain. There were some lasting benefits without the disasters suffered by the second group of countries. Inflation and currency depreciation played an important role in the reconstruction and recovery of the French economy. The decline in the value of the franc helped to modify the impact of the recession of 1921, which was much less severe than in the counter-inflationary countries. It gave a sharp boost to exports and the tourist trade. Exports rose by no less than 56 per cent between 1922 and 1926, by which time they were around one-third higher than in 1913 (Maddison, 1982, pp. 250–51). Nor did the stabilisation of the franc pose a serious problem, since France adopted a rate which under-valued the currency. Belgium's experience was somewhat similar, though the recovery effort was not as impressive. One factor accounting for the difference was the poor record in exports which languished badly in the first half of the decade, still well below the 1913 volume in 1925, despite currency depreciation on a par with that of France (van der Wee and Tavernier, 1975).

The Italian and Greek experiences are less clear-cut partly because of the intervention of other factors. The Italian record was somewhat mixed despite inflation and a depreciating exchange until the lira was stabilised at an over-valued level in 1927. The expansion of total output was not especially impressive, but manufacturing surged ahead strongly for most of the decade, no doubt influenced heavily by the policy promotion effects of the new fascist state. In the case of Greece it is particularly difficult to distinguish the influence of inflation and currency depreciation from that of other factors. Until the mid-1920s, Greece suffered quite severe inflation and exchange depreciation due to lax fiscal and monetary policies arising from the war and political instability. Industrial production showed an impressive rate of growth of 7·5 per cent a year between 1921 and 1927. While inflation and currency decline no doubt imparted a short-term stimulus to industry, one should also bear in mind that manufacturers benefited from heavy tariff protection together with a sharp fall in real wages after 1921 as a result of the depressing effects on the labour market of a large increase in the country's population arising from the influx of expatriates, many of whom were urban workers, following defeat by Turkey in Asia Minor (over 1·5 million Greeks, or one-quarter of Greece's population, were exchanged for some 400 000 Turks resident in Greece). It should also be noted that industrial expansion subsided somewhat when the authorities moved to stabilise the currency in 1927–8 (Lazaretou, 1996, pp. 649–50, 664; Herschlag, 1968, p. 24; Pentzopoulos, 1962, p. 18).

How do the three groups of countries compare, taking the decade overall? It is important to look at the 1920s as a whole since performance in the aftermath of inflation did not always match that of the inflation period, while early stabilisers could later reap some benefit from their financial rectitude. The record seems to confirm these suppositions. The hyperinflationary countries had the worst record overall through the period 1913–29. Exports failed to recoup their prewar levels; manufacturing performance was easily the weakest on average, and the same was true for GDP growth. Austria and Poland were probably the two worst cases. By contrast, the Anglo-Saxon countries, apart from the UK, performed quite creditably. On average output, manufacturing and export growth were much better than in the case of the hyperinflationary countries, and compared favourably with that of the moderate inflators (see Tables 1.1–1.3).

On balance, therefore, countries which experienced very severe inflation and loss in currency value had a distinctly desultory economic performance over the long haul compared with many of the confirmed stabilisers. The performance of the moderate inflators was commendable but by no means exceptional. The Netherlands and the Scandinavian countries, for example, had a better overall performance on average than either France or Belgium (Tables 1.1–1.3). Accordingly, the conclusion would appear to be that inflation and currency depreciation were not necessarily a winning combination in the recovery effort.

However there may even have been a better alternative, namely stabilisation at an early date but with an undervalued currency. Czechoslovakia and Finland, both of which experienced substantial inflation in the immediate postwar years, with sharp fluctuations in exchange rates in 1921 and 1922, soon adopted tight macro policies and by 1923 inflation had been brought under control and the exchanges stabilised at one-seventh and one-eighth, respectively, of their prewar levels (League of Nations, 1925, p. 53). Keynes (1923, pp. 146–7) criticised the harsh policy in Czechoslovakia, which for a short time caused an industrial setback and serious unemployment, but also recognised that the country was better placed than most other European nations to reconstruct her economy on the basis of a sound and fixed currency. In both cases the strategy was subsequently vindicated since in manufacturing production they outpaced most other countries. Spain, the only country other than Turkey with a floating rate throughout the 1920s, also performed quite well.

The new gold standard

Though there were still a number of stabilisations to be effected, most countries were back on fixed rates in the latter half of the 1920s, so one can speak legitimately of a fixed exchange rate standard. However, the new regime was very short, 1925–31 at best, and for purposes of comparison even shorter since, after 1929, the ravages of the Great Depression make comparisons somewhat meaningless. Effectively therefore we are dealing with the period 1925–9.

During these years things were much more stable and congenial to economic progress than they had been in the chaotic postwar years. Reconstruction in Europe was nearing completion by the middle of the decade and ‘real progress began to take the place of a painful struggle to

Table 1.1 Volume of gross domestic product (1913=100)

	1918	*1919*	*1920*	*1921*	*1922*	*1923*	*1924*	*1925*	*1929*
Austria	–26·7	–38·2	–33·6	–26·5	–19·9	–20·7	–11·5	5·5	5·1
Germany	-18·0	–27·7	–21·4	–12·5	–4·8	–20·9	–7·4	3·0	21·3
Belgium	–32·2	–20·8	–7·5	–5·9	3·3	7·0	10·5	12·2	25·5
France	–36·1	–24·7	–12·9	–16·5	-1·5	3·6	16·6	17·1	34·4
Italy	33·3	11·0	1·3	–0·2	4·9	11·3	12·4	19·8	31·1
Finland	-33·0	–19·1	–9·5	–6·5	3·4	11·0	13·9	20·4	45·6
Denmark	–6·2	5·9	10·9	7·7	18·6	31·1	31·5	28·5	53·0
Netherlands	–9·3	12·4	15·8	22·9	29·6	32·8	42·5	48·5	77·4
Norway	–3·7	12·6	19·7	9·8	22·6	25·3	24·7	32·4	58·6
Sweden	–15·5	–10·3	–5·4	–8·9	–0·3	5·0	8·3	12·3	35·9
Switzerland	–10·6	–4·7	1·5	–1·0	8·5	14·8	19·1	27·8	54·5
UK	–13·2	0·9	–5·2	–12·9	–8·2	–5·5	–1·6	3·2	11·9

Source: calculated from Maddison (1995, pp. 148–50).

Table 1.2 Volume of exports (percentage changes since 1913)

	1918	*1919*	*1920*	*1921*	*1922*	*1923*	*1924*	*1925*	*1929*
Austria	—	—	—	—	—	—	–24·4	–17·9	–13·7
Germany	–85·0	–80·3	–53·3	–55·6	–38·7	–47·1	–49·2	–34·7	–8·2
Belgium	—	—	—	—	—	—	—	–27·2	7·2
France	–72·0	–55·5	–14·0	–17·0	–14·0	3·0	19·0	24·0	47·0
Italy	–51·1	–24·9	5·5	–29·3	–19·2	–6·3	17·3	27·4	22·7
Finland	–88·6	–48·8	–22·4	–27·6	2·7	8·7	24·9	38·9	61·4
Denmark	–60·1	–61·4	–22·1	–12·8	–3·4	23·2	42·5	38·4	81·0
Netherlands	–76·2	–18·7	–12·6	–17·0	–6·6	3·7	24·6	34·9	71·2
Norway	–38·9	–32·9	–9·5	–24·0	–2·2	4·5	10·8	21·8	67·1
Sweden	–34·9	–33·5	–24·2	–40·9	–18·8	–20·3	–4·2	6·0	56·1
Switzerland	—	—	—	–37·4	–29·9	–25·6	–12·7	–10·3	0·7
UK	–62·3	–45·3	–29·3	–50·7	–32·0	–25·3	–24·0	–25·3	–18·7

Source: calculated from Maddison (1991, pp. 316–18).

Table 1.3 Indices of manufacturing production (1913=100)

	1920	*1921*	*1922*	*1923*	*1924*	*1925*	*1926*	*1927*	*1928*	*1929*
Austria	48·0	64·0	76·0	81·0	82·0	95·0	95·0	106·0	116·0	118·0
Germany	59·0	74·7	81·8	55·4	81·8	94·9	90·9	122·1	118·3	117·3
Hungary	—	64·0	80·0	56·6	66·6	76·7	83·4	98·7	108·0	113·9
Poland	35·1	46·8	73·9	71·2	56·8	63·1	58·9	76·1	86·1	85·9
Belgium	67·3	55·8	80·6	92·1	104·4	100·0	117·4	127·7	137·4	139·9
France	70·4	61·4	87·8	95·2	117·9	114·3	129·8	115·6	134·4	142·7
Italy	95·2	108·1	119·3	140·7	156·8	162·8	161·2	175·2	181·0	164·0
Denmark	127·8	106·9	112·6	125·1	136·2	126·4	126·4	127·9	138·3	160·6
Netherlands	—	109·9	115·2	117·4	127·5	141·8	147·4	159·9	174·5	187·3
Norway	101·9	71·8	90·0	99·8	107·2	117·0	104·2	106·5	118·2	131·2
Sweden	97·2	74·7	87·2	96·8	100·9	112·7	123·5	126·8	136·0	150·8
Switzerland	94·5	71·4	76·9	86·7	93·3	95·5	90·0	103·2	109·8	117·5
UK	92·6	55·1	73·5	79·1	87·8	86·3	78·8	96·0	95·1	100·3
Czechoslovakia	69·8	100·0	91·8	96·7	129·0	136·4	130·4	153·8	166·0	171·8
Finland	87·4	88·5	104·5	119·7	123·6	152·5	164·7	186·1	202·6	197·6
World	93·2	81·1	99·5	104·5	111·0	120·7	126·5	134·5	141·8	153·3

Source: League of Nations (1945, pp· 134–7)·

regain a plateau of prosperity which had been lost' (Loveday, 1931, p. 47).

The new standard was widely acclaimed by many contemporary observers as a panacea for international stability and recovery (Sayers, 1976a, p. 111). Speaking on the eve of the depression, O.M.W. Sprague, financial adviser to the US government and for several years also to the Bank of England, had this to say:

> The gold standard has emerged triumphantly from the welter of disorganised currencies of the World War period and gold has now become more universally than ever before the foundation of the structure of credit throughout the world. This return to the haven of familiar monetary practice is significant of the widespread conviction that the gold standard is an essential factor in the maintenance of a reasonable measure of international stability, for which there is no promising or practical substitute.
>
> (League of Nations, 1930, p. 53)

The short-term costs entailed in its restoration were considered worthwhile since much was expected from it. Referring to Britain's return to gold, Cassel (1936, p. 40) believed that the moderate deflation required was a price well worth paying since 'the relatively small sacrifices involved in that step were much more than counterbalanced by the restoration of international confidence and by the stimulus given to international trade through the replacement of the pound sterling in its old position as the principal currency of the world's trade'. Most countries faithfully believed that its restoration would solve the economic problems left outstanding from the war. Even some later writers conceded that its resurrection had some merit even though they were conscious of its shortcomings (Sayers, 1960, p. 324; Kunz, 1987, pp. 189–90; Hardach, 1995, p. 187; Brown, 1940, II, p. 801).

Generally, however, the gold exchange standard has been much maligned by more recent writers, and even the faith of contemporaries was somewhat shattered following its rapid disintegration during the depression. To some extent subsequent criticism has been based on misconceptions on what the new gold standard could or could not do within the context of the period.

First, we consider how the economic variables performed. As might be expected, nominal values in prices and exchange rates were remarkably stable compared with what had gone on previously. The average yearly depreciation of European currencies was a mere 0·2 per cent between 1927 and 1931, as against around 6 per cent in 1923–6 (excluding Germany), while exchange rate variability was minimal (Simmons, 1994, p. 109). World production rose steadily after 1924 in all regions, while in contrast to the early 1920s world trade rose more rapidly than output.

Table 1.4 European trade and currency fluctuations, 1922–7

	1922	*1923*	*1924*	*1925*	*1926*	*1927*
Trade[1]	100	105·5	123·8	129·5	130·2	145
Currency Fluctuations[2]	13·2	10·7	2·6	1·4	1·6	—

Notes: [1] Index of volume of Europe's foreign trade.
[2] Weighted index based on average monthly percentage variations in dollar value of European currencies.

Source: Strakosch (1937, p. 158).

The sustained expansion of the latter coincided with the marked improvement in currency stability after 1923, as shown by the figures for Europe's trade in Table 1.4 (see Woytinsky and Woytinsky, 1955, pp. 39–42; Svennilson, 1954, p. 292). It should be noted that there was also a strong gain in trade volume between 1921 and 1922 when currency instability was near its peak. But there were exceptional factors operating here, notably a sharp rebound in Anglo-Saxon trade following the postwar slump and also the artificial trade gains arising from currency depreciation in the hyperinflationary countries. On balance, therefore, this does not detract from the proposition that stable exchange rates were more conducive to sound trade growth. Moreover, as we have already noted, once countries had got over post-stabilisation adjustment they were in a better position to secure sound growth than had been the case in the disturbed conditions of the first half of the decade.

Thus the main thrust of the argument here is that, whatever the defects of the new standard, it was preferable to the chaotic conditions prevailing in the early 1920s. That it disintegrated in the early 1930s should not lead one to conclude that stability of exchanges was something to be ignored. This conclusion is reinforced by the experience of the 1930s.

If stable exchange rates were important for economic progress, why has the restored gold standard received such a bad press at the hands of later researchers? There are several possible reasons. First, too much was expected of the new standard. Contemporary observers fully anticipated that it would correct the postwar maladjustments, a view based on the misinterpretation of the working of the gold standard before 1914 and its operation in a different economic context postwar (Miller, 1934–6, p. 87). As Brown (1940, II, p. 801) succinctly put it: 'Before 1925 concentration upon the goal of a return to normal and upon the achievement of stable exchange rates, and after 1925 the splendours of a stable exchange standard blinded the eyes of bankers and of the world in general. The illusion that the economic maladjustments would be corrected by automatic forces was dominant in the world's financial thinking.' It was not that there was anything intrinsically wrong with a fixed exchange rate standard as such; rather, the problem lay in the manner in which it was restored, which meant that currency values were out of kilter from the start. No system, however good in principle, could be expected to work smoothly starting out from a position of disequilibrium.

Another reason why it fell into disrepute was that it was associated with unemployment, especially in countries which returned to parity. Again this is a misjudgment of the issue. All the unemployment of the 1920s cannot be laid at the door of the gold standard since there were structural problems arising out of the war which meant that unemployment would rise. In any case, stabilisation, at whatever value, was bound to involve a temporary setback to economic activity and a rise in unemployment. Some countries, especially the UK, suffered from an over-valued exchange rate following stabilisation, but many others gained from under-valued currencies.

But probably the major factor that conditioned views about the gold standard is the fact that it became associated with depression. That it disintegrated in the early 1930s after such a short life would seem to offer conclusive proof that it was inherently defective compared with its classical predecessor. In a sense it was, both in the nature of its restoration and in the manner in which it was operated. More pertinently, it has been seen as a significant contributor to depression in its own right (see Bernanke, 1995, for a review). The links forged by the fixed exchange rates of the gold standard ensured that the decline, once begun, would be worldwide, for, as Friedman and Schwartz (1963, p. 359) pointed out, no major contraction involving a substantial fall in prices could develop in any one country without those links enforcing its transmission and spreading to other countries. In turn, the pressures this imposed on countries eventually led to the disintegration of the gold standard itself. Additionally, the gold policies of the central banks may also have contributed to the turning point of the cycle. The sharp rise in gold reserve ratios from the autumn of 1929, indicative of a contractionary stance in central bank policies, had an important influence on the subsequent price decline. According to Sumner (1991, p. 379), 'shifts in central bank demand for monetary gold were of sufficient magnitude to have had a major impact on the world price level during the period from 1926–1932'. Whereas the world gold reserve ratio had increased at a rate of 2.53 per cent a year between December 1926 and October 1929, it rose by no less than 9·62 per cent in the following 12 months.

More recently, Johnson (1997, p. 186) has re-examined the wider question of world liquidity. He maintains that the price and profit deflation of the late 1920s and early 1930s were symptomatic of a worldwide liquidity shortage, caused by under-valuation of the price of gold, diminished gold production and national policies which encouraged gold hoarding and sterilisation. The French were the major culprits; their appetite for gold was insatiable following the *de jure* stabilisation of the franc, and the active policy of sterilising incoming gold further shrank the superstructure of world credit. Thus, although the degree of concentration of gold resources was little different from that before 1914, the postwar monetary system was faced with the intractable problems of diminished world liquidity and national policies which aggravated rather than relieved the situation.

Whether international collaborative effort by the major powers to take corrective macroeconomic action to combat depression would have retrieved the situation and saved the gold standard has become something of an academic debating point in recent years. Some see possibilities on this score (Foreman-Peck et al., 1996). But the arguments are tenuous and less than convincing. Sumner (1992, p. 315) reckons that policy coordination would have done no more, at best, than allowed the world to muddle through until the Second World War dealt the final blow to the system. There is also the question of whether the gold standard was worth saving in view of its inherent structural defaults and its contribution to depression. Johnson (1997, p. 182) concludes that it may have been too late by 1931 to save it: 'If the underlying liquidity problem could not be alleviated, it was better for the world economy that the gold standard fail.' Even contemporaries were doubtful about its viability in a disordered world. To quote Miller (1934–6, p. 86), 'The world was too disorganized, on both the economic and financial side, to provide the conditions essential for the satisfactory operation of the gold standard.'

The details of the chain of events leading to the disintegration of the gold standard need not concern us here. Suffice to say that cracks in the system began to appear in 1929–30, when several countries along the periphery abandoned the standard. But it was Britain's departure in September 1931 that effectively spelled the end of the system. 'England's abandonment of the gold standard,' wrote one contemporary, 'was ... a bomb loaded with enough dynamite utterly to shatter the international price and monetary structure' (Hansen, 1934–6, p. 66). Many other countries followed Britain's example and the process was all but completed when the USA broke the link with gold early in 1933. After a short period of free floating, managed currency systems became the order of the day.

Asymmetric currency management in the 1930s

The currency experience of the 1930s has been much maligned, partly no doubt because it became associated with the stagnation in trade, the welter of restrictions imposed on intercourse among nations, and the notably autarkic policies pursued by many countries. It is also a fact that currency markets were very unstable and uncertain in the years immediately following the general abandonment of gold, with exchange rate volatility akin to that of the early 1920s. Moreover, for a time, after the breakdown of the World Economic Conference (held in London) in the summer of 1933, it seemed that all hope of securing an orderly system of exchange rates had gone for good. Yet out of the wreckage in fact emerged a remarkably stable and resilient system based on regional currency and trading blocs.

The abandonment of gold was accompanied by a wave of exchange depreciations except in countries which chose to maintain official parities by means of exchange control (mainly those in central and eastern Europe, though many countries instituted temporary exchange control in the early 1930s). The extent of the currency depreciation varied considerably, but many devaluations fell within the range of 40–50 per cent by the mid-1930s. The move to the new values was accompanied initially by severe currency instability as exchange rates adjusted to the new conditions. Fluctuations were widest at the initial stage of depreciation of each currency, after which they tended to subside significantly (League of Nations, 1937a, p. 32). The most intense phase of currency depreciation occurred between the latter half of 1931 and the end of 1933; that is, when most countries broke the link with gold and allowed their currencies to decline.

But what is most remarkable, given the very unsettled conditions of the period, is the speed with which currencies stabilised once the main devaluations had taken place and the way in which traditional currency relationships were restored. By March 1934, *The Economist* (1934, pp. 685–6) was able to comment on the comparative stability of the major currencies of the world other than the dollar, and by the latter half of that year the volatility of currencies in general had become quite modest and it continued to decline in subsequent years. Comparative data on monthly and daily currency fluctuations in Tables 1.5 and 1.6 show the steady progress towards stabilisation. By the middle of the decade the daily or weekly fluctuations of the key currencies was almost back to the range of the old gold parity points, with significant movements occurring only at times of major policy changes, as for example the devaluation of the French franc in September 1936 following the final collapse of the gold bloc (Sayers, 1976b, pp. 475–83; League of Nations, 1936, pp. 267–8).

Table 1.5 Range of fluctuation of gold value of selected currencies, 1931–7
(percentage by which the highest monthly average exceeded the lowest during each half year period shown)

	1931 b	*1932 a*	*1932 b*	*1933 a*	*1933 b*	*1934 a*	*1934 b*	*1935 a*	*1935 b*	*1936 a*	*1936 b*	*1937 a*
USA	—	—	—	22·5	16·6	6·6	1·4	0·6	0·6	1·4	0·8	—
Mexico	63·3	46·1	16·2	33·6	17·8	6·7	1·2	1·1	0·7	1·4	0·7	—
Austria	18·5	5·5	1·9	9·9	1·9	1·6	0·8	1·8	0·5	0·3	1·5	0·1
Yugoslavia	—	—	24·3	1·2	1·3	2·3	0·6	0·6	0·2	0·1	0·8	0·2
Canada	20·6	5·6	5·3	19·4	8·5	5·9	1·3	1·8	0·7	1·1	0·7	0·2
China	14·6	9·7	10·9	6·6	7·0	11·5	5·4	17·3	30·8	1·3	3·2	0·4
Japan	13·6	18·8	33·1	3·9	12·2	7·0	4·4	3·8	1·8	2·2	3·9	0·4
UK	44·0	9·4	8·3	2·3	6·2	6·3	2·7	3·5	0·7	1·7	3·6	0·6
Portugal	36·8	6·9	6·9	3·4	1·8	6·8	3·0	3·5	0·4	1·3	3·4	0·4
New Zealand	44·0	9·3	8·3	9·1	6·0	6·3	2·9	3·5	0·7	1·8	3·5	0·6
Siam	—	34·0	6·9	2·3	6·1	6·3	2·6	3·5	1·3	1·7	3·6	0·6
Denmark	43·5	8·6	12·8	13·1	6·1	6·4	2·6	3·5	0·7	1·7	3·6	0·6
Sweden	43·3	6·2	4·6	6·1	6·1	6·4	2·5	3·5	0·7	1·7	3·6	0·6
Norway	44·3	8·5	5·4	3·1	6·3	6·2	2·5	3·4	0·6	1·7	3·6	0·6
Finland	49·1	14·8	8·0	4·0	5·8	6·8	2·5	3·4	0·6	1·5	3·5	0·6
South Africa	—	—	—	4·1	6·1	6·2	2·5	3·5	0·8	1·7	3·6	0·6
Greece	—	103·3	17·9	5·0	0·5	0·7	1·0	0·6	0·3	0·9	5·9	0·6
Australia	38·9	9·2	8·4	2·2	6·0	6·7	3·2	3·5	0·7	1·9	3·5	0·7
Peru	2·2	31·0	26·5	21·7	10·5	4·0	2·2	3·9	5·0	0·7	2·5	0·7
Estonia	—	—	—	6·3	4·6	6·5	2·5	3·4	0·7	2·2	3·5	0·8
Chile	—	—	—	15·7	6·9	8·2	6·9	1·5	6·6	4·5	0·8	—

Source: League of Nations (1937a, p. 32).

Thus, while the extent of currency depreciation in the 1930s (1932–9), averaging some 5·6 per year, was on par with that of the years 1923–6, exchange volatility in the later period was very much lower, about one-third that of the early 1920s (Simmons, 1994, p. 109). The speed with which the leading currencies stabilised, especially sterling, meant that exchange rates the world over were soon brought to heel. The great majority of important trading currencies moved into a stable relationship with sterling, the dollar and the franc. The major exceptions were the free rates in some of the South American republics and the fluctuations of the unofficial rates of countries maintaining nominal parities through exchange control (League of Nations, 1937b, pp. 15, 18).

While it would be misleading to imply that currency fluctuations were of minor importance in the 1930s, or that all exchange rates were in equilibrium after 1933, which in fact was far from being the case (Foreman-Peck, 1983, pp. 249–50), it is possible to argue that currency movements became far more orderly than many contemporary accounts would suggest, once the dust had settled from the wholesale abandonment of gold. Though many currencies were over-valued in terms of sterling at the end of 1931, by the autumn of 1936 exchange adjustments and price movements had ironed out much of the discrepancy and had brought many rates closer to their 1929 relationship with the pound sterling. The major exceptions were the under-valued rates of Japan and India and free rates of some of the South American Republics, while the official rates of Germany and most East European countries remained seriously over-valued (League of Nations, 1937a, pp. 37–9). Nor would it be correct to argue that competitive depreciations were a special feature of the period. In fact the majority of

Table 1.6 Yearly range of quotations of certain currencies in Switzerland, 1931–6
(Daily figures: maximum as percentage of minimum)

	1931	*1932*	*1933*	*1934*	*1935*	*1936**
USA	1.6	2.0	70.4	9.8	3.4	2.6
Sweden	51.3	19.1	17.2	13.1	6.5	3.3
UK	51.2	19.5	14.9	13.1	6.7	3.4
Norway	43.0	26.3	16.1	13.0	6.6	3.4
Denmark	53.4	26.3	28.0	12.8	7.0	3.4
Austria	21.8	18.2	14.8	2.8	5.1	3.8
Japan	42.7	84.8	24.4	17.0	6.5	4.4

Note: * nine months.

Source: League of Nations (1937a, p. 33).

devaluations were once-and-for-all events, most of which followed the leaders: Britain in 1931, the USA in 1933, and France in 1936. Hawtrey (1939, p. 240) thought the competitive depreciation view was ill-founded and, as Simmons (1994, p. 110) has noted more recently, none of the three major powers devalued simultaneously.

Given the inauspicious times, it may seem surprising that currency stability was restored with such ease, especially after the experience of the 1920s. But perhaps the latter served as a useful lesson since for most countries the experiment with free floating had been more than enough. As the League of Nations (1944, p. 122) noted in one of its later reports, 'one of the facts that stands out from this experience [currency instability of the early 1930s] is that monetary authorities in most countries had little or no desire for freely floating exchanges'. Most countries were in fact anxious to restore exchange stability as soon as possible, even via a return to the gold standard if possible, though this option was never really on the cards.

That order was brought to the exchanges can be ascribed to three major influences: the emergence of currency blocs or zones which permitted a degree of currency leadership under an asymmetrically managed system; the intervention by monetary authorities to dampen fluctuations in the exchanges; and thirdly, a slow but gradual improvement in the climate for international cooperation, once the shock of the failure of the London Conference had passed.

Trading blocs and currency zones

The distinctive feature of the commercial world in the 1930s was the emergence of several trade blocs and currency zones such that 'the pattern of multilateral settlements was submerged beneath a web of bilateral and regional commercial and monetary arrangements' (Eichengreen and Irwin, 1995, p. 8). The former included groupings centred on France, Belgium, the Netherlands, Italy and Portugal, with their respective colonies, the UK, British Commonwealth and colonies along with other sterling area countries, Japan with Korea, Formosa, Kwantung and Manchuria, and Germany with south-east Europe and, to a lesser extent, Latin America. Trade within the blocs tended to increase proportionately, though except in the case of the sterling area countries it is unlikely that there were any really significant gains in trade volume. The extent of the growing importance of trade within these groups can be seen from the data in Table 1.7

More or less simultaneously, and arising out of the currency turmoil of the early 1930s, a number of loosely drawn currency blocs or zones

Table 1.7 Great power trade blocs (as % of core country trade)

	Imports from bloc		*Exports to bloc*	
	1929	*1938*	*1929*	*1938*
UK: Empire	30	42	44	50
UK: Other sterling bloc	12	13	7	12
France: Empire	12	27	19	27
Italy: Colonies and Ethiopia	0.5	2	2	23
Japan: Korea, Formosa, Kwantung, Manchuria	20	41	24	55
Germany: Balkans	4.5	12	5	13
Germany: Latin America	12	16	8	11.5

Source: Hillman (1952, p. 486).

came into being; these included the sterling area which was more or less coterminous with the British/Commonwealth trade bloc; the gold bloc comprising west European countries which lasted until September 1936; the Reichsmark bloc mainly covering south-east Europe with Germany as the leader; and the dollar and yen zones. Most of these were very loosely organised; none had any formal organisation or executive power over currency activities. Nevertheless, there was undoubtedly a measure of informal leadership exercised by the dominant country which encouraged members to link their currencies or to track the currency of the leader. Einzig (1937, p. 309) reckoned that, because of these arrangements, 'there was *de facto* stability practically all over the civilised world by the end of the 1930s'. The manner in which the major currency blocs emerged and how they operated is considered below.

The sterling area

The largest of these systems was the sterling area, which came into being soon after Britain abandoned the gold standard. It was a very diffuse and informal grouping of countries which kept their currencies pegged to sterling, invoiced the bulk of their trade in sterling and held most, if not all, their official external reserves in sterling. The early members included the British Dominions and crown colonies (apart from Canada, Newfoundland and Hong Kong), Ireland, Portugal, Egypt and Iraq, to be joined later by the Scandinavian countries, Estonia, Latvia, Lithuania, Iran and Finland. Several other countries, including Argentina, Brazil, Bolivia, Greece, Japan, Siam, Yugoslavia and the Straits Settlements, also maintained a stable link with sterling for several years, though they were never regarded strictly as authentic members of the area since from time to time they practised exchange control and the use of multiple exchange rates (Cairncross and Eichengreen, 1983, pp. 23–4; de Vegh, 1939, pp. 8–10). By the mid-1930s, the area comprised more than one-fifth of the world's population and accounted for one-quarter of world exports, and members reaped the benefits of stable exchange rates by maintaining their local currencies at parity with sterling and holding the bulk of their monetary reserves in London (Kynaston, 1999, p. 403).

The emergence of the sterling area was a logical outcome of Britain's departure from gold. Many members of the group, especially the imperial countries, had strong commercial links with Britain and these were to become even stronger during the course of the decade. In the past they had relied heavily on Britain for people and capital, much of their trade had been financed through the City and they had held their reserves in the London money market. Thus they were bound together by 'interests and historical habits as much as by formal rules and obligations' (Llewellyn and Presley, 1995, p. 268). The system was extremely flexible since there were no formal constitution or terms of agreement, so that members could join or leave at will. The only exception to this generalisation was the monetary resolution adopted by the Ottawa Conference in the summer of 1932 which decreed that the general aim of monetary policy throughout the area should be that of ensuring the stability of sterling prices. The chief factor binding them together was the belief that it was in their best interests to maintain their currencies at a fixed rate with sterling (Scammell, 1961, p. 246). Compared with the alternatives available at the time, the sterling option seemed the most attractive (Bareau, 1945, pp. 131–6).

Despite its informality, the sterling area has been seen as much more than a holding operation in response to the crisis of the early 1930s. The French, and to a lesser extent the Americans, suspected that it was a new version of imperialism designed to bolster Britain's waning pre-eminence in international affairs, and specifically in international finance (Strange, 1971, pp. 50–52). There is some substance in this view, which Cain (1996, pp. 337–8) has forcibly emphasised. He argues that the main objective of British international economic policy (under the aegis of the Treasury and the Bank of England) was to safeguard the sterling area and to foster its extension in an effort to salvage as much as possible from the wreckage of 1931 and restore Britain's former international financial supremacy (cf. Williamson, 1992, p. 499). It is in this context that the Ottawa agreements for preferential trade among imperial countries and the monetary prescriptions laid down at the negotiations take on special significance, since it was essential for the survival of stable exchange rates that members followed consistent policies and maintained some form of monetary discipline.

A year later, on 24 July 1933, the British Empire Currency Declaration reaffirmed the Ottawa commitment to avoid undue fluctuations in the purchasing power of gold and to encourage non-imperial countries to join the sterling 'club' so as to widen the area over which exchange stability could be secured (Clavin, 1996, pp. 136–7). Several countries, notably Sweden and Denmark, were attracted by the prospect of exchange stability and promptly joined the scheme. Meanwhile, Montagu Norman, on behalf of the Bank of England, was busily trying to equip Commonwealth countries with the requisite local machinery and financial organisation to protect and strengthen the sterling system (Strange, 1971, p. 55). Cassel's view that the Bank of England never endorsed the sterling bloc programme seems somewhat at odds with Norman's imperial endeavours, though Norman, it is true, was initially lukewarm towards it (Cassel, 1936, p. 205). That the policy misfired in the case of Canada, whose divergent commercial interests led her to gravitate to the dollar zone, should not be construed as a failure of the overall strategy (cf. Cain, 1996, p. 338).

In essence, therefore, the sterling area was tantamount to a fixed exchange rate system similar to that of the gold exchange standard, the main difference being that it was sterling, not gold, that was the medium of account for settling imbalances among members. For the most part, exchange rates of the members remained remarkably stable and changes in sterling parities were something of a rarity despite the fact that they could be made at will. The success of the system owed much to the fact that sterling still retained much of its former status as an international currency in this period and, as in the 19th century, its stability in value and wide acceptability as a means of payment made it the most sought-after currency. Though it lost some 40 per cent of its former value relative to gold countries, most of the depreciation had taken place by the end of 1931. Thereafter, it retained a fairly stable value relative to other currencies which had followed it and so members of the sterling bloc were happy to keep a large part of their reserves in sterling (Scammell, 1961, p. 248). Drummond (1981, pp. 19–20, 253–4) notes that a large part of the trading world enjoyed reasonably stable exchange rates in the 1930s and this he attributes to the management of the sterling system, though it was probably less successful in restoring equilibrium between costs and prices (Cassel, 1936, p. 204). Only in the early 1930s and again late on in the decade was there really serious disorder in the foreign exchanges.

The gold bloc

The spate of devaluations and exchange restrictions of the early 1930s left those countries still on the gold standard in a somewhat exposed position. When it became apparent, pending the break-up of the World Economic Conference in July 1933, that an early resumption of the gold standard was out of the question, the governments of Belgium, France, Holland, Italy, Luxembourg, Poland and Switzerland issued a joint declaration on 3 July confirming 'their intention to maintain the free functioning of the gold standard in their respective countries at the existing gold parities and within the framework of existing monetary laws. They ask their central banks to keep in close touch to give the maximum efficacy to this declaration'. A few days later, the governors of the respective banks met at the Bank of France to review the practical measures required to give effect to this resolution and to protect their currencies from exchange speculation (Bank for International Settlements, 1934, p. 13).

It may seem anomalous that a small group of countries whose trading links and interests were both relatively weak and divergent should seek to maintain a gold regime in the face of its abandonment elsewhere. It is true that several of the countries in question (France, Belgium, Holland and Switzerland) were at the time in a relatively strong position, with gold reserves at their highest ever recorded (Yeager, 1976, p. 357). Questions of prestige and fear of inflation also played an important role since, apart from Holland and Switzerland, these countries had all suffered severely from inflationary pressures and currency depreciation in the first half of the 1920s. The Dutch government had the quaint notion that hanging on to gold would be good for recovery and stability and provide a measure of continuity for the time when the gold standard was eventually restored (de Vries, 1978, pp. 87–8). How else can one explain the relentless effort to adjust the economy to the situation? According to Einzig (1937, p. 69) the Dutch Prime Minister, Dr Colijn, 'regarded it as a matter of prestige to outbid any country in the civic virtues of deflation'. The French, for their part, were obsessed about the inflationary implications of devaluation which rekindled memories of the disastrous experience of the franc in the 1920s. Devaluation was also seen to be socially disruptive and there was little popular support for it. Moreover, France was initially in a very strong financial position and experienced a belated depression, though she did have a chronic budgetary problem. Hence there was little obvious pressure to resort to devaluation (Jackson, 1985, pp. 220–221; Mouré, 1991, p. 4; Schwarz, 1993, pp. 100–101).

Exchange rate stability within the gold bloc was purchased at a price.

Because the currencies of gold members became over-valued relative to those which had devalued, it was necessary to resort to domestic deflation to maintain international competitiveness. Throughout most of the first half of the 1930s, deflationary policies, together with defensive trade measures, were pursued relentlessly, though occasionally interspersed with reflationary policies, especially in France, with the result that recovery from depression was delayed (Hogg, 1987, pp. 208–9; Asselain and Plessis, 1995, pp. 202–11). But such draconian domestic measures were insufficient to offset the hefty over-valuation of their currencies or prevent periodic pressures on their exchange rates and external accounts. Within the gold bloc itself there was very little in the way of mutual assistance between members since each country was intent on husbanding its resources for the defence of its own currency. Thus what was hoped originally would develop into a monetary and economic union eventually became 'a small group of members who watched each other jealously, half hoping and half fearing that their fellow-members would be the first to devalue' (Einzig, 1937, p. 241).

In fact it was the smaller countries which were in the weakest position; their currencies were frequently subject to speculation as gold losses mounted. However, for most countries it was the intolerable internal compression required to compensate for over-valued currencies, rather than sheer inability to defend the old rates, that eventually forced them to abandon gold (Simmons, 1994, p. 253). By early 1935, the end was in sight for the gold bloc. Belgium, along with Luxembourg, was forced to devalue in March 1935; Italy withdrew from the gold bloc in the same year because of surreptitious devaluation of the lira and the introduction of exchange controls in the previous year; Poland ceased to be a member from early 1936 as a result of the introduction of exchange controls. These departures put even further pressures on the remaining members. The French situation was also exacerbated by the inflationary policies of Blum's Popular Front government in the summer of 1936 with the result that the franc became even more over-valued (Patat and Lutfalla, 1990, p. 82). The pressure was reflected in a flight of capital and a hefty discount on the pegged rate which eventually forced the French to give up the struggle on 26 September 1936. The franc was devalued by some 30 per cent, though even this still left it over-valued, so that it continued to come under pressure in later years. Within hours of the French announcement the remaining members of the gold bloc followed suit.

Though the gold bloc helped to maintain currency stability while it lasted, it turned out to be a costly exercise. It did little to promote intra-bloc trade or closer economic cooperation among its members. Its demise was followed by another period of currency uncertainty as the French franc adjusted to the new situation. Most of the countries involved performed poorly in the 1930s when set against their sterling area counterparts. The only worthwhile thing to emerge from the wreckage was the controversial Tripartite Agreement between France, America and Britain pertaining to cooperation on currency matters (see below).

Exchange control countries

Whereas many western countries removed the constraint of the 'golden fetters' by coming off gold and devaluing their currencies so as to allow more room for manoeuvre in domestic economic policy, this option was not followed by most countries in central and eastern Europe. They attempted to maintain their former parities by restrictive external policy rather that outright internal compression. Tariff levels were raised sharply between 1929 and 1931 and these were accompanied by extensive quantitative controls on imports and exchange control (Condliffe, 1941, p. 103; Pollard, 1981, p. 302). By the end of 1931, Austria, Germany, Bulgaria, Czechoslovakia, Hungary, Yugoslavia, Greece and Turkey had all imposed exchange control and Romania followed suit in May 1932. Only Poland resisted until the spring of 1936 by adhering to the gold bloc (League of Nations, 1933, pp. 222–3; 1937a, p. 11; 1942, p. 70).

Several factors explain this course of action. In virtually every case the imposition of exchange control originated as a result of exchange and balance of payments pressures arising from the crisis of the early 1930s (League of Nations, 1938a, p. 22; 1943, p. 10). Trade balances had been generally unfavourable before 1929 and they were considerably worsened by rapidly falling commodity export prices and unfavourable terms of trade thereafter. Rising protection in western countries, especially on agricultural products, did not help matters as far as many of Europe's primary producers were concerned. In addition, the sharp reversal of capital imports and the very limited international reserves held by these countries meant that import surpluses could no longer be financed and hence imports had to be reduced at all costs. Protection of domestic industry and agriculture also became an important concern in a world awash with goods. Initially, however, there were even more pressing motives for the introduction of exchange control and the defence of currencies. One was the desire to check capital outflows, especially in the financial panic of 1931. A second important consideration was the reluctance to relinquish former currency parities, grounded on the belief that depreciating currencies were bad for inflation; most of the countries in question had bitter memories of their disastrous experience in the previous decade. Currency depreciation also raised the burden of debt service costs, and in any case there was a belief that debt servicing should be maintained if at all possible in order to demonstrate financial soundness. Exchange control would facilitate the collection of foreign exchange for that purpose (League of Nations, 1943, pp. 9–11; 1944, pp. 162–7).

The initial results of trade restriction and exchange control were reasonably promising. Capital flows were staunched, trade balances generally improved and exchange rates remained fairly stable. In so far as exchange control was used as an instrument of commercial policy it did allow greater latitude in the use of macroeconomic policy for domestic purposes. However, in the longer term the costs probably outweighed the benefits. Exchange control tended to raise domestic prices and rendered exporting more difficult in so far as it maintained fictitious currency values. The currencies of bloc members were the most over-valued in the world. One estimate suggests that, in 1934, east European currencies were over-valued relative to the pound and the dollar by as much as 60 per cent (Nötel, 1986, p. 229; Foreman-Peck, 1983, pp. 249–50). Moreover, following the imposition of exchange control, the trade shares of these countries fell sharply and remained below the level of 1929 throughout the 1930s (League of Nations, 1938a, p. 30; Harris, 1936, pp. 101–2). In this respect they fared worse than the gold bloc countries. Most contemporary studies concluded that exchange control countries experienced a lower level of output and trade than countries with depreciated currencies (Heuser, 1939, p. 230; Harris, 1936, p. 103; Ellis, 1939; 1941, p. 152), a finding confirmed by more recent scholarship (Eichengreen, 1992a, p. 351; 1992b, p. 233).

Recognition of the perverse effects of maintaining official parities was manifest in the efforts made to relax or modify the control system. Most countries, apart from Poland, eventually introduced a measure of devaluation in a concealed form. This was done principally by the provision of export bonuses or currency premia, or through the use of multiple exchange rates, which meant that exporters received more domestic currency for their exports than they would have been entitled to under the official rates. The terms of the premia varied a great deal from country to country, ranging between 20 and 50 per cent. Such sub-species of currency created by means of multiple exchange rates were also used by a number of Latin American countries (Einzig, 1970, p. 257). It is not known what proportion of trade was transacted at the lower rates, but even with this relief the currencies still remained over-valued relative to those of free market economies (Lampe and Jackson, 1982, pp. 464–5; Royal Institute of International Affairs, 1936, pp. 85–9; League of Nations, 1938a, p. 5; 1944, p. 171).

By the end of the 1930s a substantial proportion of international trade (possibly as much as 30 per cent) was subject to exchange control in one form or another. Because exchange control required a high degree of state interference and control of economic activity, the countries which practised it tended to trade more among themselves and less with those countries having free exchange markets. However, the closer affinity among exchange control countries which developed in central and eastern Europe was predicated on two factors: the need for primary producers to find an outlet for their exports, and Nazi Germany's quest to secure access to the resources of its eastern hinterland without having to use scarce foreign exchange.

Clearing agreements became one of the principal instruments by which Germany sought to extend its control over the trade and payments of the region. Clearing agreements entailed the bilateral balancing of claims between exchange control countries, thereby minimising the need for free foreign exchange. Following the launch of Schacht's New Plan in 1934, by which foreign trade transactions were brought under centralised control and exchange control became a specific instrument of trade policy, Germany concluded a series of bilateral clearing agreements with both European and non-European countries (principally Latin American). By 1937, when some 12 per cent of world trade passed through clearings, more than 50 per cent of the trade of Germany, Hungary, the Balkans, Greece and Turkey was subject to clearing agreements (League of Nations, 1939, pp. 186–7; 1942, pp. 70–72; 1944, pp. 182–3).

There is continuing debate as to who gained from the whole exercise. Whether or not Germany exploited the region for her own long-term military purposes is part of another story. There is no doubt, however, that trade among the Reichsmark bloc members increased significantly, though most of this was due to the trading links with the centre country, since eastern Europe's share of world trade declined. As a result, Germany gained an increasing foothold in the trade of eastern Europe, especially in Hungary and the Balkans. Yet, despite the closer relations of the group, Germany still depended on the rest of Europe for some 40 per cent of her import requirements by the end of the decade (Griffiths, 1989, p. 27; League of Nations, 1939, p. 186; Hiden, 1977, p. 173; Kaiser, 1980, pp. 325–6).

Intervention in exchange markets

Free floating did not last long following the collapse of gold since many governments began to intervene in exchange markets to stabilise their currencies – hence the term 'managed floats'; countries were not averse to changes in their rates so long as these could be managed or negotiated so as to avoid widespread currency disorder.

The first of the more formal mechanisms, which became known as 'exchange stabilisation funds', was announced by Britain in the budget of April 1932. This was the Exchange Equalisation Account (EEA) which began operations in the June of that year. It was followed by similar institutions in many other countries including the USA (January, 1934), Belgium (March, 1935), Canada (July, 1935), the Netherlands and Switzerland (September, 1936), France (October, 1936), as well as in Argentina, Colombia, Czechoslovakia, Latvia, Mexico, Spain and Japan (League of Nations, 1937a, p. 57). These arrangements were essentially a more elaborate extension of classical central banking practice whereby specifically constituted funds held assets in gold and national currencies which they deployed in an attempt to insulate their domestic economies from excessive fluctuations in exchange rates caused by speculative activity and volatile capital movements (Condliffe, 1941, p. 237).

It is difficult to make broad generalisations about the nature and working of these funds since no two were alike in terms of assets held, their working practices or their underlying purposes, while for the most part their activities were kept highly secret. However, we do know that one of the chief aims of the funds was to try to smooth out fluctuations in exchange rates caused by erratic capital movements and the activities of speculators which, it was widely believed at the time, had caused so much disruption in the early 1930s. Active intervention in exchange markets, it was thought, would help to stabilise exchange rates for the benefit of recovery (League of Nations, 1944, p. 143; Bloomfield, 1944, pp. 69–87). Smoothing operations apart, a second important objective in some cases was that of establishing and defending what was thought to be an appropriate exchange rate in the light of the requirements of domestic economic policy. An additional factor, in the case of the British EEA at least, was the wish to offset the impact of short-term capital movements on the cash base of the domestic credit structure.

One of the main reasons for the creation of The British Fund was the authorities' belief that the pound, which had begun to rise from the low level of \$3·24 recorded in early December 1931, should be kept down so as to aid recovery, raise the price level and make cheap money effective. There was considerable debate as to the most appropriate target rate but eventually a value of \$3·40–\$3·50 was selected, adjusted to \$4·50–\$4·60 following the dollar devaluation in the spring of 1933 (Howson, 1975, pp. 83–6; 1980b, p. 54; Howson and Winch, 1977, pp. 104–5).

Howson (1976, pp. 249–51; 1980a, pp. 55–6) maintains that domestic objectives were of paramount importance in setting the exchange rate target in the 1930s. This was interpreted as being the lowest possible value for sterling which was consistent with the exchange rate priorities of Britain's main trading competitors. The formal repegging of the exchange rate was consistently ruled out on the ground that this would limit the authorities' room for manoeuvre on the domestic policy front, to the detriment of economic recovery. While this interpretation is no doubt consistent with the policy statements made at the time, it is somewhat at odds with the actual course of events. Though the EEA concentrated much of its interventionist operations on the sterling–dollar rate, it did find difficulty in preventing the pound from rising in the early years. But, in any case, its activities in this area may have been somewhat academic since, according to Drummond (1981, p. 256), the USA effectively took control of the sterling–dollar rate in 1933, which meant in practice that the British authorities were only free to prevent the pound falling below what the Americans deemed to be the most appropriate rate from their own domestic point of view (Pumphrey, 1942, pp. 808, 816). The USA was determined, it appears, to prevent the emergence of a really cheap pound.

Moreover, bilateral rates, even one as important as the sterling–dollar, give a somewhat one-sided view of a country's overall exchange rate position. In actual fact the pound's effective rate (measured against a basket of 28 currencies) appreciated continuously between 1932 and 1939, which hardly squares with the Treasury's stated intention of capping sterling (Redmond, 1980, pp. 88–9; 1988, p. 293). One reason for this seeming paradox may lie in the limited resources of the EEA in the face of large capital inflows, especially during the golden avalanche arising from the flight from the French franc in 1936–7, when the Account almost ran out of sterling reserves, so that it could do little more than dampen the upward pressure on the exchange rate.

Whether the EEA made for greater stability in exchange rates overall is a moot point. Howson (1980b, p. 56) reckons that the EEA's management of sterling made it a more stable currency than would otherwise have been the case. However, since the bulk of its operations were confined to the sterling–dollar market, one doubts whether it could have exerted much leverage on other rates. The relative stability of the sterling–dollar rate after the middle of 1933 suggests that the EEA had some success in this quarter, though it can be argued that US intervention and the more stable economic conditions and policies in the respective countries were more important to the outcome (Broadberry, 1987, p. 74; Whitaker and Hudgins, 1977, p. 1478). Nevertheless, Whitaker and Hudgins (1977, pp. 1483–4) do detect a modest contribution to the stabilisation of inter-month variations in the sterling–dollar rate and they suggest that the EEA may also have been successful in combating irrational speculation in the exchanges following disturbances such as the Belgian and French devaluations and Hitler's entry into the Rhineland during the period 1935–7.

In contrast to the virtually clean floating of currencies in the postwar years, currencies were extensively managed in the 1930s by new and more formal mechanisms. Howson (1980a, p. 59) describes the British float as being very dirty. Because of the secrecy shrouding the operation of the stabilisation funds, it is very difficult to determine just how effective they were. Though the scale and scope of their operations were constrained by their limited asset base, they probably made a modest contribution to the stabilisation of the exchanges, while their very presence may have helped to curb the volatility of markets. Bloomfield (1944, pp. 59, 85) believed they exerted a sobering influence on exchange markets by discouraging undue speculation and limiting the impact of short-term capital movements (cf. Bareau, 1938; Marjolin, 1938; Pumphrey, 1942). They may even have averted the danger of competitive depreciations, especially in the later 1930s when co-ordinated operations of the exchange stabilisation funds took place within the framework of the Tripartite Agreement.

Attempts at international monetary cooperation

The lack of adequate international monetary cooperation and economic leadership in the inter-war years, and more especially in the economic crisis of the early 1930s, is a much-debated issue. At the peak of the crisis, international economic management, both by bankers and by statesmen, was found to be wanting, hence the failure to save the gold standard (Sumner, 1992, p. 315). In a sense this could be considered a mixed blessing, if the view is taken that the gold standard had outlived its usefulness. In so far as the system was out of equilibrium from the start, and it became even more so once the dramatic fall in the general price level distorted the original structure of exchange rates even further, there is a strong argument in favour of its demise. For countries to have held on to it, as some unwisely did, would have entailed even greater distress and hardship for their domestic economies. As the Royal Institute of International Affairs (1933, p. 78) aptly remarked:

> The gold standard tends to be a fair-weather standard, especially helpful to trade and industry in time of prosperity. On the other hand, in abnormal periods it often serves to intensify depression rather than to relieve it. This must to some extent be the effect of any international standard, and is not a peculiarity of the gold standard.

A second point to bear in mind is that international cooperation did not evaporate completely in the early 1930s. The failure of inter-bank cooperation at the crucial point in the crisis of 1931, followed by the collapse of the London Conference two years later, may have seemed like the death knell of prospects on this score, but in fact it marked a nadir from which only improvement could ensue. Though the failure of the London Conference meant that collaboration at the political level was put into cold storage for the time being, central bankers continued to explore the possibilities of mutual cooperation in a modest way, and indeed they were instrumental in exerting some influence on governments with regard to currency and international monetary matters (Sayers, 1976b, pp. 458–9, 463–6). In fact the equilibrium attained by the principal trading currencies by the middle of the decade was in no small part due to monetary management and close cooperation between the national monetary authorities (League of Nations, 1937b, p. 270). In its sixth annual report, the Bank for International Settlements (see below) drew specific attention to this fact in the following words: 'The re-establishment of such a degree of order in the exchange situation has been possible only by very determined efforts and it is satisfactory to record that co-operation between the monetary authorities of the different countries has played a growing part in the execution of this policy' (Bank for International Settlements, 1936, p. 14). In fact, between 1935 and 1936, very little use was made of the discount rate in checking fluctuations in the exchanges, except in France, the Netherlands and Switzerland, and in many cases the discount rate remained unchanged (League of Nations, 1937b, p. 270).

International cooperation among the central banking community was given a welcome boost by the establishment of the Bank for International Settlements (BIS), located in Basle, a year before the eventful crisis of 1931. The main pretext for its establishment was for purposes of dealing with the reparations issue, and in particular the task of administering the Young loan to Germany under the revised reparations plan of 1929. Though personally he did not participate directly in its creation, Norman's conception, which he had long cherished, was a sort of bankers' club to provide a permanent channel of communication between central banks (Einzig, 1932, pp. 97–9). It was largely a private institution whose membership consisted of most of the main European central banks, the only non-European members being Japan and the USA (Schloss, 1958, p. 40; Simmons, 1993, p. 403).

Though one of the objectives of the BIS was to provide the means for inter-bank financial assistance, which were developed quite extensively later in the 1930s, it did not have the resources or the power to deal effectively with the crisis of the early 1930s (Schloss, 1958, pp. 136–9;

Dam, 1982, p. 70; Foreman-Peck, 1991, pp. 14–15). However, it very soon became an important forum for inter-bank cooperation and the exchange of views on currency and monetary matters. Following the collapse of the gold standard, the bank became a consistent advocate of currency stabilisation and a return to the gold standard and it frequently urged governments to make a move in that direction. 'That move means the return to an international monetary system based on gold, which remains the best available monetary mechanism, – and as a condition thereof, a stabilisation of the world's leading currencies' (Bank for International Settlements, 1935, p. 70). While the bank failed in its ultimate objective, the influential tone of its respected annual reports has perhaps been too little appreciated. Most governments were fully aware of the need to achieve some form of currency stability after the débâcle of the early 1930s, even though this might fall short of a full restoration of the gold standard. And though the London Conference foundered on that very issue, it did not spell the end of efforts to bring order to the exchange markets. The regional approach to stabilisation may have had its drawbacks, in that the exchange rates between the major currencies were more volatile than previously, but at least it provided a degree of stability of currencies within the different exchange zones. More significantly, by the middle of the decade there was a move to secure the alignment of some of the major currencies in the controversial and much-debated Tripartite Agreement of September 1936.

Though the untimely demise of the World Economic Conference put paid to any immediate formal stabilisation between the major currencies, neither the central bankers of Britain nor those of France abandoned the idea entirely, and a few years later the American government also became an enthusiastic supporter (Leith-Ross, 1968, p. 170). However, the factor which occasioned the negotiation of the Tripartite Agreement (TA) between the three countries was the need to provide some form of de facto stabilisation to facilitate the devaluation of the French franc and prevent an outbreak of disorderly exchange rate policies as a result of the French action (Einzig, 1937, p. 209). Thus by 25 September the governments of Britain, France and the USA had reached agreement on the terms of a declaration which was issued by the respective treasuries immediately prior to France's announcement of devaluation on the night of Friday/Saturday, 26/27 September (Sayers, 1976b, p. 480). The purport of the joint declaration was that the respective governments undertook to refrain from competitive devaluation and to do their best to defend their currencies around the then existing levels. Belgium, the Netherlands and Switzerland subsequently agreed to adhere to the terms of the agreement. The participants were enjoined to cooperate on a day-to-day basis to cooperate to this end so as 'to maintain the greatest possible equilibrium in the system of international exchanges and to avoid to the utmost extent the creation of any disturbance of that system [by their] monetary creation' (League of Nations, 1937a, p. 31; 1937b, p. 26). More specifically, the three governments gave an undertaking to use the appropriate available resources so as to avoid as far as possible any disturbance of the basis of international exchanges resulting from the proposed readjustment of the French franc, and to arrange consultation for that purpose (League of Nations, 1937a, p. 31; 1937b, p. 26; Einzig, 1937, pp. 222–3). Despite the grandiose pronouncements, it was a very loose and informal arrangement. There was no rigid commitment to maintain exchange rates at any specific level and each country reserved the right to change the international value of its currency at a moment's notice (the 24-hour rule). What this meant in practice was that the signatories would not be prepared to defend international currency stability at the expense of their domestic economies (Einzig, 1937, p. 223).

Much was expected of the new agreement and some contemporaries saw it as the beginning of a new era in international monetary relations. The League of Nations (1937b, p. 8) was very optimistic and saw it as the nucleus of a restored but more flexible international monetary standard. This view was somewhat wide of the mark, however, since it is doubtful whether the Tripartite Agreement can be seen as a real precursor of postwar monetary institutions (see Feinstein et al., 1995, p. 67). In fact, the Tripartite Agreement has in general had rather a bad press, no doubt because of its somewhat provisional and flimsy character, negotiated by governments who were not fully committed to international monetary cooperation at all costs.

On the other hand, it is easy to be critical of an agreement (or more correctly a statement of intent) drawn up at a very difficult time internationally, and when, for national reasons, there was still widespread aversion to any long-term commitment to fixed exchange rates. After all, as Clarke (1977, p. 57) points out, the Agreement did demonstrate a willingness to collaborate on exchange rate policy after several rather barren years. Moreover, it also marked the final usurpation of the position of the central banks in international exchange matters since the Agreement was negotiated by governments and not by bankers (Dam, 1982, p. 53).

It is difficult to discover any very positive impact of the Tripartite Agreement on the exchange rates of the participating countries. Clarke (1977, p. 57) noted that in the six months immediately following the Agreement the sterling–dollar rate was far more stable than it had been in 1934 and 1935. But further out the outlook was less promising. Drummond's careful analysis of the period 1936–9 led him to conclude that exchange rates were no more tranquil than they had been in 1931–6 (Drummond, 1979, pp. 1, 32). Both sterling and the franc were subject to bouts of weakness and strength during these years which to a large extent reflected the extent of intervention by the respective authorities to manage their exchange rates, rather than the benefits arising from international cooperation under the new arrangements. In practice there was relatively little systematic cooperation, there was no pooling of reserves and little in the way of mutual assistance among the members. In fact the degree of consultation and cooperation was little better than it had been prior to the Agreement, which had taken place intermittently between central banks and treasuries (Drummond, 1981, p. 249). The authorities tended to manage the exchanges in their own interests and did not feel unduly constrained to consult their partners about their intended actions. Moreover, in the immediate prewar period it seems to have been of little help in securing interallied cooperation on financial preparations for war, since the USA forced Britain to reduce its war chest reserves, which precipitated a sharp fall in the pound (Parker, 1983, pp. 261–76).

On a more positive note, it can be argued that, though the Agreement did not produce complete exchange stability, it was probably instrumental in preventing the devaluation of the franc from sparking off a wave of competitive devaluations and international monetary conflict (Oye, 1986, p. 197). It has also been noted that the Agreement helped to moderate the initial depreciation of the franc, while at the same time it served to strengthen the dollar as the anchor currency of the international monetary system (Clavin, 1996, p. 189; Cleveland, 1976, p. 56). Technical cooperation within the framework of the TA also helped to stave off disaster in the later slide of the French franc in mid-1937 and again in May 1938 (Sayers, 1976b, pp. 482–3). On the other hand, it is worth stressing again that, when the exchanges were relatively stable, as in the winter of 1936–7, this probably owed more to the domestic management of exchange rates than to any specific benefits flowing from the Agreement. At the time the French authorities were supporting a weak franc by using their gold reserves, while the British were buying gold in order to cap sterling (Drummond, 1979, p. 7). However, the suggestion that the TA was largely responsible for international recovery from depression because it permitted an expansion of the world's monetary base, appears somewhat far-fetched for reasons other than technical ones (Cleveland, 1976, p. 51). The fact is that considerable recovery had already taken place before the Agreement was negotiated, while defence needs were probably the key factor prolonging the recovery from 1937 onwards.

Economic recovery under alternative exchange rate regimes

How did different exchange rate regimes affect recovery from the depression? One fact is quite certain: widespread devaluation did not lead to a trade-induced recovery. By 1935, Europe 'had descended to a historical nadir in trade and commercial policy' (Friedman, 1974, p. 32). The value of European exports and imports were some two-thirds less than they had been at the peak of 1929, while trade volumes (constant prices) were some one-third lower. Almost every conceivable form of trade and payments restriction was being used apart from blockade. Not surprisingly, therefore, trade volumes failed to regain former levels even by the end of the decade, despite the fact that world output of primary products and manufactured goods had made modest progress since 1929.

On the surface, therefore, it would seem that the external side and commercial policy had little to contribute to recovery in the 1930s. It is true that the beginnings of recovery can be detected late in 1932 and that these coincided with the wave of devaluations and trade and payments restrictions following the financial crisis of the previous year. But it would be rash to draw positive conclusions from these two events. In any case, it was not until well into 1933 that recovery took firm hold on a wider front and even then the process was by no means rapid and universal. Several countries, notably France and Czechoslovakia, continued to experience further declines in economic activity, while in the USA the recovery was slow and patchy, partly owing to that country's late departure from gold (Temin and Wigmore, 1990). During the next two years the momentum gained increasing strength, with the result that by the middle of the decade many countries were recording at least modest gains in the level of activity above the previous cyclical peak of 1929. Recovery was temporarily interrupted in 1937–8, when several countries experienced a mild recession, but this was soon reversed as a result of defence requirements.

The data in Tables 1.8 and 1.9 compare the recovery experience of countries classified under different regimes. It should be pointed out that the classification of countries is sometimes somewhat arbitrary because of the overlapping of regimes and changes in regime structure through time. Greece is a prime example. It introduced exchange control in September 1931 and suspended convertibility in April 1932; this was followed by a large depreciation of the drachma (nearly 60 per cent by the end of that year). In June 1933, Greece joined the gold bloc and pegged its currency to the Swiss franc, but when the gold bloc finally disintegrated (September, 1936) she joined the sterling area and pegged the drachma to sterling (Lazaretou, 1996, pp. 664–7). The League of

Table 1.8 Fluctuations in GDP/GNP and exports, 1929–37/8

	Gross domestic product			*Export volume*		
	1929–1932/3	*1932/3–1937/8*	*1929–1937/8*	*1929–1932*	*1932–1937*	*1929–1937*
Exchange control						
Austria	–22.5	25.8	–2.5	–43.9	35.3	–24.1
Bulgaria	–7.1	63.3	51.8	—	—	—
Czechoslovakia	–12.9	13.1	–1.5	—	—	—
Germany	–23.5	63.7	25.2	–40.5	15.2	–31.5
Greece	36.7	25.4	71.4	—	—	—
Hungary	–3.7	18.0	13.6	—	—	—
Italy	–5.5[a]	21.7	15.0	–42.1	3.9	–39.8
Romania	–5.2	22.7	16.3	—	—	—
Spain	–5.3[a]	–9.4[b]	–14.2[c]	—	—	—
Yugoslavia	–9.4	24.5	12.7			
Gold bloc						
Belgium	–7.1	9.8	2.0	–31.4	51.4	3.8
France	–14.7	13.5	–3.1	–41.5	–2.3	–42.9
Netherlands	–7.6	14.2	5.5	–33.4	31.8	–12.2
Switzerland	–8.0	14.4	5.2	–50.1	39.4	–30.4
Poland	–20.7	40.8	14.9	—	—	—
Sterling bloc						
Australia	–5.8	27.5	20.1	31.8	1.1	33.2
Denmark	4.3	16.9	21.9	20.1	–10.6	7.3
Finland	–4.0	46.9	41.1	—	—	—
Ireland	–4.3	2.4	–2.0	—	—	—
Norway	–1.0[a]	32.5	31.2	2.6	36.1	39.6
Portugal	13.3	14.4	29.7	—	—	—
Sweden	–4.3	31.4	25.8	–37.0	60.8	1.3
UK	–5.1	24.7	18.4	–37.6	28.8	–19.7
Other countries						
Japan	–6.5[a]	47.0	37.4	1.3	145.7	149.1
USA	–29.6	39.7	–1.7	–48.6	54.5	–20.5
Canada	–29.5	41.5	–0.3	–32.0	53.7	4.4
USSR	20.5	40.7	69.6	—	—	—

Notes: [a] 1929–31; [b] 1931–40; [c] 1929–40. Italy was originally in the gold bloc but imposed exchange control in May 1934 and devalued in October 1936. Greece and Turkey, along with Bulgaria, Hungary, Romania and Yugoslavia, formed part of the Reichsmark bloc. Japan devalued early and the USA late.

Sources: Bairoch (1976, p. 295), Maddison (1991, pp. 316–18; 1995, pp. 148–50); Nunes *et al.* (1989, pp. 293–5); Spulber (1966, p. 58); Prados de la Escosura (1993), Hjerppe (1996, p. 93).

Table 1.9 Fluctuations in industrial/manufacturing production, 1929–37/8

	1929–1932	*1932–1937/8*	*1929–1937/8*
Exchange control			
Austria	–34.3	53.9	1.0
Bulgaria	8.9	25.6	36.9
Czechoslovakia	–39.8	60.0	–3.7
Germany	–40.8	122.2	31.6
Greece	0.9	60.0	61.5
Hungary	–19.8	64.2	31.7
Italy	–22.7	48.5	14.8
Romania	–18.2	63.4	33.6
Spain	–15.7	–19.7[a]	–32.3[b]
Yugoslavia	–17.1	63.8	35.7
Gold bloc			
Belgium	–27.1	42.3	3.7
France	–25.6	20.0	–10.7
Luxembourg	–32.0	40.2	–4.7
Netherlands	–9.8	35.1	22.0
Switzerland	–20.8	29.8	2.8
Poland	–38.6	99.6	22.5
Sterling bloc			
Australia	—	—	—
Denmark	–5.6	47.1	38.9
Finland	–15.0	89.4	60.9
Ireland	–9.0	54.0	40.3
Norway	–18.2[c]	58.7[d]	29.9
Portugal	33.0	9.8	46.0
Sweden	–10.8	72.4	53.8
UK	–11.4	52.9	35.4
Other countries			
Japan	–3.3[c]	100.0[d]	93.3
United States	–44.7	86.8	3.3
Canada	–32.3	68.3	14.0
World	–29.3	80.6	27.7

Notes: [a] 1933–40; [b] 1929–40; [c] 1929–31; [d] 1931–37.

Sources: OEEC (1960, p. 9), League of Nations (1936, Table 107), United Nations (1949, Table 36), Berend and Ranki (1974, pp. 298–300), Mitchell (1975, p. 357), Freris (1986, p. 90), David (1996), Lains and Reis (1991), Prados de la Escosura (1993), Hjerppe (1996, p. 128), Pryor (1973, p. 203).

Nations (1939, p. 186) also classed Greece as belonging to the German economic bloc by the later 1930s.

It can be seen that there was a great diversity of recovery experience among nations. Several countries made almost no headway at all from peak to peak of the cycle, 1929–37. These included Austria, Czechoslovakia, Spain, Belgium, France, the Netherlands, Switzerland, Ireland, Canada and the USA. Conversely, Bulgaria, Germany, Japan and most of the sterling bloc countries recorded substantial gains in output and industrial production. Three of the most successful countries were the USSR, Germany and Japan, but under regimes which imposed severe social costs on the population.

Generally speaking, the countries which left the gold standard and devalued their currencies fared better than those countries which clung to gold until the mid-1930s and were forced to deflate their economies to compensate for over-valued exchange rates. Leaving gold and devaluing removed constraints on both the domestic and external fronts. International competitiveness improved with benefits to the external account, prices firmed upwards and investment opportunities became more attractive (partly through import substitution), while there was more scope to relax the macroeconomic stance, that is monetary and fiscal policy. The advantages accruing to countries which jettisoned gold were fully recognised by contemporary economists (Gregory, 1936, pp. 218–22; Rist, 1936, pp. 223–43; Hawtrey, 1939, pp. 227–32, 243–4) and the League of Nations (1936, p. 56), and more recently several writers have written extensively on this issue (see, for example, Eichengreen, 1988; 1991; 1992a; 1992b; Eichengreen and Sachs, 1985; Cooper, 1992; Campa, 1990; Kitson and Michie, 1994; Bernanke, 1995). Countries which devalued early and by a large amount tended to experience the strongest recoveries: that is Denmark, Norway, Sweden, Finland, Great Britain and Greece (Haavisto and Jonung, 1995, pp. 264–5). It is particularly noteworthy that the last-mentioned country had the largest devaluation in Europe and the fastest rate of growth between 1929 and 1937 (Mazower, 1991a, pp. 225–6; 1991b, pp. 250–53). While much of this improvement could be attributed to import substitution through a combination of import restrictions, devaluation and exchange control, it should also be noted that a good part of it had already taken place before Greece suspended the gold standard in April 1932.

Overall, however, it would be true to say that countries with depreciated currencies performed much better than either gold bloc or exchange control countries. The former saw their industrial production rise on average by some 27 per cent between 1929 and 1936, whereas the gold bloc and exchange control countries experienced declines in industrial activity (Eichengreen, 1992b, p. 351). Some contemporary scholars (Harris, 1936, p. 103; Ellis, 1939; 1941, p. 152) concluded that exchange control countries tended to experience an inferior trade and income performance than either gold or paper currency countries, but recent research suggests that it was the gold bloc group that fared the worst.

The gold bloc group was in a very invidious position. Adherence to the former gold parity rates made it difficult to adopt any sort of reflationary action to promote recovery since, in order to maintain the old parities in the face of depreciation elsewhere, deflationary policies were unavoidable because of the continued pressure on the balance of payments and the exchange rate (Condliffe, 1941, p. 235). Adjustment was effected, albeit not always very successfully, by compressing the internal price level, and by using import controls, export subsidies and high interest rates, which in turn put pressure on state finances (League of Nations, 1936, p. 56). In the final analysis such policies proved intolerable because of the disastrous effects on domestic economies, quite apart from the fact that they proved largely ineffective in restoring equilibrium. Thus the gold bloc began to crumble in 1935 and broke up altogether in the following autumn, with France, the Netherlands and Switzerland the last to go as international pressure on their exchanges led to capital flight (League of Nations, 1937a, pp. 26–8). The gold bloc in fact paid a high price for its faithful attachment to gold. Industrial production declined on average by some 14 per cent between 1929 and 1936 and by the end of the decade output and production levels were little better than they had been in 1929 (Siegenthaler, 1976, p. 531; David, 1995; 1996; Griffiths, 1987; Eichengreen, 1992b, p. 351; Johnson, 1997).

There were, however, a number of notable exceptions to the general pattern, so that one has to be cautious about attributing too much importance to the influence of devaluation. The experience of the exchange control countries was far from uniform despite their weak trade performance. Austria and Czechoslovakia did very badly but Germany and several east European countries, especially Bulgaria, performed quite strongly despite their over-valued currencies. Of course much depended on the extent of the over-valuation and the use which was made of special rates for exporters and export subsidies, as well as the benefits arising from trade links with Germany. In the latter case, the economic strategy suppressed the normal working of the labour market and established a highly regulated regime to prevent short-circuiting of the economy, and by this means was able to achieve strong growth, though at a social cost unacceptable to liberal economies. One can also argue that the experience of Ireland, Canada and the United States do little to support the devaluation thesis. America, it is true, was a relatively late devaluer, but Canada and Ireland were not. The Canadian case is a little unusual, however, in that, although the gold standard was relinquished de facto early in 1929, the Canadian dollar did not depreciate until late in 1931; subsequently, its depreciation against the American dollar was only about half that of the pound sterling, but by late 1933 the traditional relationship between the three currencies was restored. Against competitive raw material-producing countries, the Canadian dollar tended to appreciate (Fishlow, 1985, p. 428). In other words, Canada did not benefit initially from her early departure from gold through reflation and currency depreciation (Bordo and Redish, 1990, pp. 358, 378).

On the other hand, the Baltic States did quite well even though Latvia and Lithuania were late devaluers (Royal Institute of International Affairs, 1938, pp. 187–8; Simutis, 1942, pp. 70–71). The British case is also worth reconsidering. Devaluation undoubtedly eased pressure on the external side in 1932 and allowed the authorities to loosen monetary policy, but the direct trade impact of devaluation was tempered by the fact that about one-half of Britain's trade was with countries whose currencies were linked with sterling (Kitson and Solomou, 1990, pp. 90–91) and also by the fact that the effective sterling exchange tended to strengthen during much of the 1930s. Thus the overall comparative advantage of devaluation in terms of export and import prices was quite modest. In fact, Kitson and Solomou (ibid., p. 63) see the tariff as being more important than devaluation in explaining manufacturing import substitution. The role of the tariff in the recovery process has been a source of debate for some years now and the arguments for and against are neatly summarised by Routh (1993, p. 272).

Finally, Spain and Portugal provide interesting case studies of substantial devaluations which had very little impact. Portugal had come through the depression quite strongly, with positive gains in output and industrial production. The gold standard was abandoned and the currency devalued at the end of 1931, but after 1932 the economy remained rather flat, and then subsequently felt the backwash of the Spanish Civil War. Thus industrial production charted an erratic course and actually fell slightly between 1932 and 1936, before rising sharply in 1937 and then falling back again (Nunes et al., 1989; Lains and Reis, 1991). Spain is a more exceptional case since she had by far the worst record in the 1930s, much of which could be attributed to the Civil War and its aftermath. It is sometimes argued that Spain avoided the worst effects of the depression because of her floating exchange rate (Temin, 1993, p. 92; Choudhri and Kochin, 1980, p. 569). This is not strictly correct. Though Spain initially fared better than many countries owing to her depreciating currency, the early 1930s still saw a considerable decline in industrial activity, even though good weather favoured agricultural output (Payne, 1968, p. 48; Lieberman, 1995, p. 18; Mitchell, 1975, p. 357). At the trough of 1933 industrial output was a fifth or more lower than in 1929, while trade volumes declined by one quarter (Ranki, 1985, p. 63; Prados de la Escosura, 1993). Spain in fact lost much of the advantage of her flexible exchange rate with the imposition of exchange control in May 1931 and the subsequent widespread devaluation elsewhere later in the year. The depression was of course prolonged with the Civil War and the emergence of the Franco regime which erected an extensive system of bureaucratic controls that led to a seizing up of the economy. Hence there was no recovery in the 1930s and it was not until the 1950s that the 1929 levels of economic activity were finally regained (Payne, 1968, p. 57; Lieberman, 1995, p. 18; Prados de la Escosura, 1993).

On a more general note, it is important to bear in mind that the benefits of devaluation were to some extent offset by the uncertainty created by the widespread exchange instability of the early 1930s, which merely served to complicate the economic situation. Fluctuating exchange rates, aggravated by speculative and non-economic capital movements, the prospects of competitive depreciation of currencies and restrictive measures of defence thrown up by this threat, together with renewed deflationary policy measures, banking crises and rigid exchange controls to protect weaker currencies, created a thoroughly unstable situation. These uncertainties were not only a serious impediment to early recovery, but they presented a constant threat of further deterioration. Contemporary accounts repeatedly stressed the gravity of the situation. The League of Nations in their world report for 1932–3 (League of Nations, 1933, pp. 15, 221) reckoned that exchange instability was the most destructive element resulting from the breakdown of the gold standard and it was seen as 'one of the principal causes of further economic deterioration in 1932 and figured prominently among the factors which limited and checked the revival of prices and productive activity in the third quarter of that year'.

It was not until 1933–4 that there was a slow approximation towards exchange rate stability as the majority of trading currencies gradually moved into a more stable relationship with sterling, the dollar and the franc (League of Nations, 1937b, pp. 15–16). Yet even by the spring of 1935 the Bank For International Settlements (1935, p. 5) was complaining that the world still suffered 'without relief from the unrest and uncertainties caused by moving currencies' and that 'no fundamental, durable recovery can be hoped for unless and until a general stabilisation at least of the leading currencies has been brought about'.

Although, as noted earlier, it is possible to exaggerate the currency turmoil of these years, there is no doubt that contemporary observers were very much concerned about the continued prospects of disorderly exchange markets. Secondly, while countries going off gold early secured temporary relief, the benefits reaped by the leaders soon evaporated as other countries followed suit. No doubt a coordinated programme of devaluation would have produced wider benefits than the sequential approach adopted at the time, but failing international action the second-best solution was better than none at all. Thirdly, trade expansion was certainly not the engine of recovery in the 1930s even for those countries which devalued early. One or two countries, notably Finland and Norway, did quite well on the export front through the complete cycle, but for the most part exports failed to regain their previous cyclical peaks. As Solomou (1996, p. 121) notes, 'the exchange rate regime did not have a significant effect on the cyclical recovery path of exports', since both gold bloc and sterling countries had weak export performances. Moreover, though early devaluers gained an initial competitive edge, this was later eroded through higher inflation rates in devaluing countries and the capitulation of the gold bloc after 1935. One reason for the desultory export performance was of course the restrictive policies adopted to protect external accounts despite some modest relaxation later in the decade. Protection, import quotas, exchange control and the drying-up of international investment all helped to depress economic intercourse, even though they may have helped domestic recovery through import substitution.

To an increasing extent also the trade of the major European countries gravitated towards 'economic blocs', within the orbit of the UK, France, Belgium, the Netherlands and Italy and their dependent territories, Japan with Korea, Formosa, Kwantung and Manchuria, and Germany with south-eastern Europe and, to a lesser extent, Latin America. One feature of the latter was the increasing importance of bilateral clearing agreements which had been almost unknown in 1929. By 1937, they accounted for about 12 per cent of world trade, though in the case of the Reichsmark bloc countries of Germany, Bulgaria, Greece, Turkey, Hungary, Romania and Yugoslavia the proportion of trade passing through clearing agreements exceeded 50 per cent (League of Nations, 1938a, pp. 172–3; 1939, pp. 186–9).

Though an increasing proportion of world trade took place within the trading blocs or zones, the overall effect was not especially beneficial except in the case of sterling area countries. In most of the other blocs the impact was adverse both for intra-bloc trade as well as for trade with the rest of the world (see Eichengreen and Irwin, 1995, pp. 21–2). This negative outcome was not simply a function of the existence of trading blocs *per se* but more the result of the network of restrictions on intercourse to prop up over-valued currencies.

Overall, therefore, currency changes of the 1930s did not generate trade-induced recovery. Those that devalued early secured an initial advantage but more important in the longer term was the fact that devaluation, along with defensive commercial measures, provided greater protection for the external account. This in turn allowed greater flexibility in domestic economic policy, especially in breaking the constraint on monetary policy (Kitson and Michie, 1994, p. 94). At the same time it helped to raise the general price level and encouraged import substitution, both of which were conducive to investment and economic recovery.

The inter-war years in retrospect

The international monetary system of the inter-war period cannot be written down as a success story. Exchange rate regimes came and went and none seemed capable of producing lasting stability. The free-floating system of the 1920s proved little short of disastrous, while the restored gold standard creaked at the seams. For contemporaries exchange stability was supposed to inspire confidence, yet few seemed to have much faith in the new gold standard. Once it disintegrated and instability emerged once again, there was a strong clamour for renewed stabilisation, even calls for the revival of the gold standard. But instead what emerged was a managed international monetary system, with regional patterns of exchange arrangements centred upon a recognised leader country or currency.

Contrary to popular conception, the latter system probably deserves more respect than it has hitherto been accorded. While it was not ideal, in the difficult and restrictive conditions of the time it was a miracle that orderly exchange rate behaviour emerged from the chaos of the early 1930s. After the initial disturbances following the general abandonment of gold, the exchanges were far less volatile than they had been in the first half of the 1920s. Moreover, the exchange regime of this period probably had more credibility than the restored gold standard of the later 1920s since few people had much confidence in its long-term sustainability. The managed system of the 1930s certainly provided more flexibility than the former gold standard, while it avoided the worst excesses of the free floating era after the war. Foreman-Peck's judgment seems basically sound: 'The managed float of the 1930s gave the international economy rather more stability than it had in the 1970s and almost as much as in the (later?) 1920s' (Foreman-Peck, 1983, p. 255).

The chief advantage of the regime of the 1930s is that it allowed countries much more room for manoeuvre in domestic policy once the restraint of fixed exchange rates had been removed. It is true that currency depreciation was not the only factor making for recovery but it certainly eased the process. What is perhaps most remarkable, given the general turmoil of the early 1930s, is the relative degree of stability in the exchanges for much of the decade and the speed with which realignment took place once the gold standard had been jettisoned. No doubt recovery and the more stable economic conditions after 1933 assisted the process, but important also were the role of the new currency zones or blocs, the more energetic management of currencies through official intervention and the groping towards a measure of international cooperation among the key currency countries. The system was by no means perfect and in the later 1930s there were renewed currency scares as the international political situation deteriorated. But in the difficult circumstances of the time, and against the background of the poor track record of the previous decade, the system was far from being an utter disaster.

We may draw several other conclusions from the currency experience of the 1930s. First, abandonment of metallic standards does not necessarily lead to monetary chaos, as Hawtrey noted in 1939 (Hawtrey, 1939, pp. 243–4). Secondly, asymmetric management can provide a workable alternative, at least for a time, to leadership under hegemonic rule, as in the case of classical gold or Bretton Woods. Thirdly, the 1930s cannot provide a specific guide to the merits or otherwise of either floating or fixed exchange rates since they were neither one thing nor the other. Exchange rates in this period were extensively managed, though often in a flexible manner, and free floating was the exception rather than the rule (Yeager, 1976, pp. 375–6).

Finally, we may ask, do exchange rate regimes really matter? The short answer is probably not that much. It is true that, in establishment circles, there has generally been a preference for fixed exchange rate regimes rather than floating ones, largely because the latter are perceived as being associated with unstable economic conditions. Periods of floating rates have witnessed the persistence of inflation, high volatility in price movements and greater unpredictability of inflation. The early 1920s is a good case in point. But such outcomes may simply be a function of the fact that fixed rate regimes cannot readily absorb shocks to the economic system, whereas the ease with which they can be accommodated by floating regimes – through monetary accommodation of international price shocks and exchange rate accommodation of relative price shocks – means that there are strong inducements to shift to floating regimes in times of economic turbulence. Hence the abandonment of fixed rates in the early 1930s and again in the early 1970s, and of course after 1918, all of which saw violent price disturbances (Alogoskoufis, 1992; Alogoskoufis and Smith, 1991; Lazaretou, 1991).

However, while floating regimes may facilitate the adjustment of nominal magnitudes at such times, it does not necessarily follow that floating rates lead to greater volatility in real economic variables. It is true that real variables performed better under the Bretton Woods system than under any regime of the inter-war years, while fixed regimes in general, as one might expect, have tended to record a better price performance. On the other hand, fixed rate systems have not always been good for growth. The classical gold standard (pre-1914) had a weak performance in this respect, and its volatility was quite high. The pure gold standard may have been fine for exchange rate and price stability (though in the latter case more in the long than the short term), but this was partly at the expense of growth and employment. This was one reason no doubt why many countries along the periphery were not prepared to commit themselves to such a rigid system (Nugent, 1973, p. 1130).

The transition to mixed system also throws up some interesting results. During the 1930s there was clearly a marked difference in economic performance between the managed floaters, exchange control countries and the gold bloc. The first group definitely benefited from early and substantial devaluation, even though after the initial float exchange rates were closer to fixed than floating ones. By contrast, for the post-1973 period there is little evidence to suggest that movements in real economic variables were systematically related to the type of exchange regime. From a sample of 49 countries, Baxter and Stockman (1989) found that the choice of exchange rate regime (pegged, floating or cooperative) had little significance in explaining differences in pre- and post-1973 behaviour of economic variables. A longer-term study for the UK by Mills and Wood (1983) came to a similar conclusion, namely that the exchange rate regime did not have a significant effect on the volatility of macroeconomic variables.

In other words, in a global context, the type of exchange rate regimes or international monetary system may not be that important in terms of the real economy. However, for individual countries or regions it could be of significance, depending on what happens to the real exchange rate. This underlines the significance of distinguishing between nominal and real exchange rates across different systems (Grilli and Kaminsky, 1991). The experience of the inter-war years demonstrates that what matters is how real (as opposed to nominal) magnitudes behaved. Generally speaking, under all three main regimes, floating, fixed and managed systems, countries with depreciated or under-valued currencies experienced superior economic performance.

Bibliography and References

Abelshauser, W. (1995), 'Between Myth and Reality: the Concept of Mitteleuropa', in M. Petricioli (ed.), *Une occasion manquée? 1922: la reconstruction de l'Europe,* Berne: Peter Lang.

Aldcroft, D.H. (1997), *Studies in the Interwar European Economy,* Aldershot: Ashgate.

Aldcroft, D.H. and M.J. Oliver (1998), *Exchange Rate Regimes in the Twentieth Century*, Cheltenham: Edward Elgar.

Alogoskoufis, G.S. (1992), 'Monetary accommodation, exchange rate regimes and inflation persistence', *Economic Journal*, 102.

Alogoskoufis, G.S. and R. Smith (1991), 'The Phillips curve, the persistence of inflation and the Lucas critique: evidence from exchange rate regimes', *American Economic Review*, 81.

Asselain, J.-C. and A. Plessis (1995), 'Exchange-rate policy and macroeconomic performance: a comparison of French and Italian experience between the wars', in C.H. Feinstein (ed.), *Banking, Currency, and Finance in Europe Between the Wars,* Oxford: Oxford University Press.

Bairoch, P. (1976), 'Europe's gross national product: 1800–1975', *Journal of European Economic History,* 5.

Bank for International Settlements (1934), *Fourth Annual Report, 1 April 1933–31 March 1934*, Basle: Bank for International Settlements.

Bank for International Settlements (1935), *Fifth Annual Report, 1 April 1934–31 March 1935,* Basle: Bank for International Settlements.

Bank for International Settlements (1936), *Sixth Annual Report, 1 April 1935–31 March 1936,* Basle: Bank for International Settlements.

Bareau, P. (1938), 'The Belgian, Dutch and Swiss exchange funds', *The Banker,* 45.

Bareau, P. (1945), 'The sterling area – its use and abuse', *The Banker,* 73.

Barkai, H. (1993), 'Productivity patterns, exchange rates, and the gold standard restoration debate of the 1920s', *History of Political Economy*, 25.

Basch, A. (1944), *The Danube Basin and the German Economic Sphere*, London: Kegan Paul, Trench, Trubner.

Baxter, M. and A.C. Stockman (1989), 'Business-cycles and exchange-rate regime', *Journal of Monetary Economics,* 23.

Berend, I.T. and G. Ranki (1974), *Economic Development in East Central Europe in the 19th and 20th Centuries,* New York: Columbia University Press.

Bernanke, B.S. (1995), 'The macreconomics of the great depression: a comparative approach', *Journal of Money, Credit and Banking*, 27.

Bloomfield, A.I. (1944), 'Operations of the American exchange stabilisation fund', *The Review of Economic Statistics*, 26.
Bonnell, A.T. (1940), *German Control Over International Economic Relations 1930–1940*, Urbana, IL: University of Illinois Press.
Bordo, M. and A. Redish (1990), 'Credible commitment and exchange rate stability: Canada's interwar experience', *Canadian Journal of Economics*, 23.
Broadberry, S.N. (1984), 'The North European depression of the 1920s', *Scandinavian Economic History Review*, 32.
Broadberry, S.N. (1987), 'Purchasing power parity and the pound–dollar rate in the 1930s', *Economica*, 54.
Brown, W.A. (1940), *The International Gold Standard Reinterpreted, 1914–1934*, two vols, New York: National Bureau of Economic Research.
Cain, P.J. (1996), 'Gentlemanly imperialism at work: the Bank of England, Canada and the sterling area, 1932–1936', *Economic History Review*, 49.
Cairncross, A. and B. Eichengreen (1983), *Sterling in Decline: the Devaluations of 1931, 1949 and 1967*, Oxford: Blackwell.
Campa, J.M. (1990), 'Exchange rates and economic recovery in the 1930s: an extension to Latin America', *Journal of Economic History*, 50.
Cassel, G. (1936), *The Downfall of the Gold Standard*, Oxford: Oxford University Press.
Choudhri, E.V. and L.A. Kochin (1980), 'The exchange rate and the international transmission of business cycle disturbances: some evidence from the great depression', *Journal of Money, Credit and Banking*, 12.
Clarke, S.V.O. (1977), *Exchange Rate Stabilization in the mid-1930s: Negotiating the Tripartite Agreement*, Princeton: Princeton University Press.
Clavin, P. (1991), 'The World Economic Conference 1933: the failure of British internationalism', *Journal of European Economic History*, 20.
Clavin, P. (1992), 'The fetishes of so-called international bankers: central bank cooperation for the world economic conference, 1932–3', *Contemporary European History*, 1.
Clavin, P. (1996), *The Failure of Economic Diplomacy: Britain, Germany, France and the United States, 1931–36*, Basingstoke: Macmillan.
Cleveland, H. van (1976), 'The international monetary system in the interwar period', in B.M. Rowland (ed.), *Balance of Power or Hegemony: the Interwar Monetary System*, New York: New York University Press.

Condliffe, J.B. (1941), *The Reconstruction of World Trade: A Survey of International Economic Relations,* London: Allen & Unwin.

Cooper, R.N. (1982), 'The gold standard: historical facts and future prospects', *Brookings Papers on Economic Activity 1.*

Cooper, R.N. (1992), 'Fettered to gold? Economic policy in the interwar period', *Journal of Economic Literature*, 30.

Dam, K.W. (1982), *The Rules of the Game*, Chicago: University of Chicago Press.

David, T. (1995), 'Un indice de la production industrielle de la Suisse durant l'entre-deux guerres', *Schweizerische Zeitschrift für Geschichte,* 45.

David, T. (1996), 'Indices de la production industrielle suisse', in H. Ritzmann (ed.), *Statistique Historique de la Suisse,* Zurich: Charonos.

de Vegh, I. (1939), *The Pound Sterling,* New York: Scudder, Stevens & Clark.

de Vries, J. (1978), *The Netherlands Economy in the Twentieth Century,* Assen: Van Gorcum.

Drummond, I. (1979), *London, Washington and the Management of the Franc, 1936–39,* Princeton: Princeton University Press.

Drummond, I. (1981), *The Floating Pound and the Sterling Area,* Cambridge: Cambridge University Press.

Eichengreen, B. (1986a), 'The Bank of France and the sterilization of gold, 1926–1932', *Explorations in Economic History*, 23.

Eichengreen, B. (1986b), 'Understanding 1921–1927: inflation and economic recovery in the 1920s', *Rivista di Storia Economica,* 3.

Eichengreen, B. (1988), 'Real exchange rate behaviour under alternative monetary regimes: interwar evidence', *European Economic Review*, 32.

Eichengreen, B. (1991), 'Relaxing the external constraint: Europe in the 1930s', in G.S. Alogoskoufis, L. Papademos and R. Portes (eds), *External Constraints on Macroeconomic Policy: the European Experience*, Cambridge: Cambridge University Press.

Eichengreen, B. (1992a), 'The origins and nature of the Great Slump revisited', *Economic History Review,* 45.

Eichengreen, B. (1992b), *Golden Fetters: the Gold Standard and the Great Depression, 1919–1939*, Oxford: Oxford University Press.

Eichengreen, B. and D.A. Irwin (1995), 'Trade blocs, currency blocs and the reorientation of world trade in the 1930s', *Journal of International Economics,* 38.

Eichengreen, B. and J. Sachs (1985), 'Exchange Rates and Economic Recovery in the 1930s', *Journal of Economic History*, 45.

Einzig, P. (1932), *Montagu Norman: a Study in Financial Statesmanship,* London: Kegan Paul, Trench, Trubner & Co.

Einzig, P. (1937), *World Finance 1935–1937,* London: Kegan Paul, Trench, Trubner.

Einzig, P. (1938), *Bloodless Invasion: German Economic Penetration into the Danubian States and the Balkans*, London: Duckworth.

Einzig, P. (1970), *The History of Foreign Exchange,* 2nd edn, London: Macmillan.

Ellis, H.S. (1939), 'Exchange control in Austria and Hungary', *Journal of Economics, 54.*

Ellis, H.S. (1941), *Exchange Control in Central Europe,* Cambridge, MA: Harvard University Press.

Feinstein, C.H., P. Temin and G. Toniolo (1995), 'International economic organisation: banking finance and trade in Europe between the wars', in C.H. Feinstein (ed.), *Banking, Currency, and Finance in Europe Between the Wars,* Oxford: Oxford University Press.

Fishlow, A. (1985), 'Lessons from the past: capital markets during the 19th century and the interwar period', *International Organization,* 39.

Foreman-Peck, J. (1983), *A History of the World Economy: International Economic Relations Since 1850*, Brighton: Wheatsheaf Books.

Foreman-Peck, J. (1991), 'The gold standard as a European monetary lesson', in J. Driffil and M. Beber (eds), *A Currency for Europe*, London: Lothian Foundation Press.

Foreman-Peck, J., A.G. Hallett and Y. Ma (1996), 'Optimum international policies for the world depression 1919–1933', *Economies et Sociétés*, 22.

Freris, A.F. (1986), *The Greek Economy in the Twentieth Century,* London: Croom Helm.

Friedman, M. and A.J. Schwartz (1963), *A Monetary History of the United States, 1867–1960,* Princeton: Princeton University Press.

Friedman, P. (1974), *Impact of Trade Destruction on National Incomes: a Study of Europe 1924–1938,* Gainesville: University Presses of Florida.

Friedman, P. (1976), 'The welfare costs of bilateralism: German–Hungarian trade 1933–38', *Explorations in Economic History*, 13.

Gregory, T.E. (1936), 'Memorandum on the experiences of the sterling area', in Carnegie Endowment/International Chamber of Commerce (eds), *The Improvement of Commercial Relations Between Nations and the Problems of Monetary Stabilization,* Paris: International Chamber of Commerce.

Griffiths, R.T. (1987), 'The policy makers', in R.T. Griffiths (ed.), *The Netherlands and the Gold Standard 1931–1936*, Amsterdam: NEHA.

Griffiths, R.T. (1989), 'The economic disintegration of Europe: trade and protection in the 1930s', European University Institute Colloquium Papers, 138/89.

Grilli, V. and G. Kaminsky (1991), 'Nominal exchange rate regimes and the real exchange rate: evidence from the United States and Great Britain, 1885–1986', *Journal of Monetary Economics*, 27.

Haavisto, T. and L. Jonung (1995), 'Off gold and back again: Finnish and Swedish monetary policies 1914–1925', in C.H. Feinstein (ed.), *Banking, Currency and Finance in Europe Between the Wars*, Oxford: Oxford University Press.

Hansen, A.H. (1934–6), 'The sterling area and the stabilization problem', *Proceedings of the Academy of Political Science*, 16.

Hardach, G. (1995), Endogenous versus exogenous causes of stabilisation and crisis in Germany, 1922–1932' , in M. Petricioli (ed.), *Une occasion manquée? 1922: la reconstruction de l'Europe*, Berne: Peter Lang.

Harris, S.E. (1936), *Exchange Depreciation: Its Theory and Its History 1931–35, with Some Consideration of Related Domestic Policies*, Cambridge, MA: Harvard University Press.

Hawtrey, R. (1939), *The Gold Standard in Theory and Practice*, 4th edn. London: Longmans Green.

Herschlag, Z.Y. (1968), *Turkey: the Challenge of Growth*, Leiden: E.J. Brill.

Heuser, H. (1939), *Control of International Trade*, London: Routledge.

Hiden, J. (1977), *Germany and Europe 1919–1939*, London: Longman.

Hillman, H.C. (1952), 'Comparative strength of the great powers', in A. Toynbee and F.T. Ashton-Gwatkin (eds), *Survey of International Affairs 1939–1946: the World in March 1939*, London: Oxford University Press.

Hjerppe, R. (1996), *Finland's Historical National Accounts 1860–1914: Calculation Methods and Statistical Tables*, Jyväskylä: Kari-Pekka Kivirauma.

Hogg, R.L. (1987), 'Belgium, France and Switzerland and the end of the gold standard', in R.T. Griffiths (ed.), *The Netherlands and the Gold Standard 1931–1936*, Amsterdam: NEHA.

Hoptner, J.B. (1962), *Yugoslavia in Crisis, 1934–1941*, New York: Columbia University Press.

Howson, S. (1975), *Domestic Monetary Management in Britain 1919–38*, Cambridge: Cambridge University Press.

Howson, S. (1976), 'The managed floating pound, 1932–39', *The Banker*, 126.

Howson, S. (1980a), 'The management of sterling, 1932–1939', *Journal of Economic History*, 40.

Howson, S. (1980b), *Sterling's Managed Float: the Operations of the Exchange Equalisation Account 1932–39*, Princeton: Princeton University Press.

Howson, S. and D. Winch (1977), *The Economic Advisory Council: a Study in Economic Advice During Depression and Recovery*, Cambridge: Cambridge University Press.

Jackson, J. (1985), *The Politics of Depression in France 1932–1936*, Cambridge: Cambridge University Press.

Johnson, H.C. (1997), *Gold, France and the Great Depression, 1919–1932*, New Haven: Yale University Press.

Jones, F.E. (1937), *Hitler's Drive to the East*, London: Gollancz.

Kaiser, D.E. (1980), *Economic Diplomacy and the Origins of the Second World War: Germany, Britain, France and Eastern Europe, 1930–1939*, Princeton: Princeton University Press.

Keynes, J.M. (1923), *A Tract on Monetary Reform*, London: Macmillan.

Keynes, J.M. (1971), *A Tract on Monetary Reform*, Vol. IV of *The Collected Writings of John Maynard Keynes*, London: Macmillan.

Keynes, J.M. (1977), *The Collected Writings of John Maynard Keynes*, Vol. XVII, *Activities 1920–1922: Treaty Revision and Reconstruction*, London: Macmillan.

Keynes, J.M. (1978), *The Collected Writings of John Maynard Keynes*, Vol. XVIII, *Activities 1922–1932: The End of Reparations*, London: Macmillan.

Kitson, M. and J. Michie (1994), 'Depression and recovery: lessons from the interwar period', in J. Michie and J. Grieve Smith (eds), *Unemployment in Europe*, London: Academic Press.

Kitson, M. and S. Solomou (1990), *Protectionism and Economic Revival: the British Interwar Economy*, Cambridge: Cambridge University Press.

Kunz, D. (1987), *The Battle for Britain's Gold Standard in 1931*, London: Croom Helm.

Kynaston, D. (1999) *The City of London: Vol. III Illusions of Gold 1914–1945*, London: Chatto & Windus.

Lains, P. and J. Reis (1991), 'Portuguese economic growth, 1833–1985: some doubts', *Journal of European Economic History*, 20.

Lampe, J.R. and M.R. Jackson (1982), *Balkan Economic History 1550–1950*, Bloomington: Indiana University Press.

Laursen, K. and J. Pedersen (1964), *The German Inflation, 1918–1923*, Amsterdam: North-Holland.

Lazaretou, S. (1991), 'Inflation and real exchange rate behaviour under alternative nominal exchange rate regimes: an historical overview of the Greek experience, 1877–1936', unpublished paper, University of Macedonia.

Lazaretou, S. (1996), 'Macroeconomic policies and nominal exchange rate regimes: Greece in the interwar period', *Journal of European Economic History*, 25.

League of Nations (1920), *Currencies after the War: A Survey of Conditions in Various Countries*, Geneva: League of Nations.

League of Nations (1925), *Memorandum on Currency and Central Banks, 1913–1924*, Geneva: League of Nations.

League of Nations (1930), *First Interim Report of the Gold Delegation of the Financial Committee*, Geneva: League of Nations.

League of Nations (1933), *World Economic Survey 1932–33*, Geneva: League of Nations.

League of Nations (1936), *Money and Banking 1935/36,* Geneva: League of Nations.

League of Nations (1937a), *Money and Banking 1936/37,* Geneva: League of Nations.

League of Nations (1937b), *World Economic Survey 1936/37,* Geneva: League of Nations.

League of Nations (1938a), *Report on Exchange Control,* Geneva: League of Nations.

League of Nations (1938b), *World Economic Survey 1937/38,* Geneva: League of Nations.

League of Nations (1939), *World Economic Survey 1938/39,* Geneva: League of Nations.

League of Nations (1942), *Commercial Policy in the Interwar Period,* Geneva: League of Nations.

League of Nations (1943), *Europe's Overseas Needs 1919–1920 and How They Were Met,* Geneva: League of Nations.

League of Nations (1944), *International Currency Experience: Lessons of the Interwar Period,* Geneva: League of Nations.

League of Nations (1945), *Industrialisation and Foreign Trade,* Geneva: League of Nations.

League of Nations (1946), *The Course and Control of Inflation: a Review of Monetary Experience in Europe After the First World War,* Geneva: League of Nations.

Leith-Ross, F.W. (1968), *Money Talks: Fifty Years of International Finance*, London: Hutchinson.

Lieberman, S. (1995), *Growth and Crisis in the Spanish Economy: 1940–93,* London: Routledge.

Llewellyn, D.T. and J.R. Presley (1995), 'The role of hegemonic arrangements in the evolution of the international monetary system', in J. Reis (ed.), *International Monetary Systems in Historical Perspective*, Basingstoke: Macmillan.

Loveday, A. (1931), *Britain and World Trade,* London: Longmans, Green.

Maddison, A. (1982), *Phases of Capitalist Development*, Oxford: Oxford University Press.

Maddison, A. (1991), *Dynamic Forces in the World Economy*, Oxford: Oxford University Press.

Maddison, A. (1995), *Monitoring the World Economy 1820–1992*, Paris: OECD.

Marjolin, R. (1938), 'The French exchange fund', *The Banker*, 48.

Mazower, M. (1991a) 'Banking and economic development in interwar Greece', in H. James, H. Lindgren and A. Teichova (eds), *The Role of Banks in the Interwar Economy*, Cambridge: Cambridge University Press.

Mazower, M. (1991b), *Greece and the Interwar Economic Crisis*, Oxford: Oxford University Press.

Miller, A.C. (1934–6), 'Whence and whither in the gold standard?', *Proceedings of the Academy of Political Science*, 16.

Mills, T.C. and G.E. Wood (1983), 'Does the exchange rate regime affect the economy?', *Federal Reserve Bank of St. Louis Review*, 75.

Mitchell, B.R. (1975), *European Historical Statistics 1750–1970*, London: Macmillan.

Moggridge, D.E. (1992), *Maynard Keynes; an Economist's Biography*, London: Routledge.

Momtchiloff, N. (1944), *Ten Years of Controlled Trade in South-eastern Europe*, Cambridge: Cambridge University Press.

Mouré, K. (1991), *Managing the Franc Poincaré: Economic Understanding and Political Constraint in French Monetary Policy, 1928–1936*, Cambridge: Cambridge University Press.

Munk, F. (1940), *The Economics of Force*, New York: George W. Stewart.

Neal, L. (1979), 'The economics and finance of bilateral clearing agreements: Germany, 1934–8', *Economic History Review*, 32.

Nötel, R. (1986), 'International credit and finance', in M.C. Kaser and E.A. Radice (eds), *The Economic History of Eastern Europe 1919–1975*. Vol. II, *Interwar Policy, the War and Reconstruction*, Oxford: Oxford University Press.

Nugent, J.B. (1973), 'Exchange-rate movements and economic development in the late nineteenth century', *Journal of Political Economy*, 81.

Nunes, A.B., E. Mata and N. Valério (1989), 'Portuguese economic growth 1833–1985', *Journal of European Economic History*, 18.

OEEC (1960), *Industrial Statistics 1900–1959*, Paris: OEEC.

Oye, K.A. (1986), 'The sterling–dollar–franc triangle: monetary diplomacy 1929–1937', in K.A. Oye (ed.), *Cooperation Under Anarchy*, Princeton: Princeton University Press.

Parker, R.A.C. (1983), 'The pound sterling, the American Treasury and British preparation for war, 1938–1939', *English Historical Review*, 98.

Patat, J.-P. and M. Lutfalla (1990), *A Monetary History of France in the Twentieth Century*, Basingstoke: Macmillan.

Payne, S.G. (1968), *Franco's Spain,* London: Routledge & Kegan Paul.

Pentzopoulos, D. (1962), *The Balkan Exchange of Minorities and its Impact on Greece*, Paris: Mouton.

Pollard, S. (1981), *Peaceful Conquest: the Industrialisation of Europe 1760–1970,* Oxford: Oxford University Press.

Prados de la Escosura, L. (1993), *Spain's Gross Domestic Product, 1850–1990,* Madrid: Ministerio de Economía y Hacienda.

Pryor, Z.P. (1973), 'Czechoslovak economic development in the interwar period', in V.S. Mamatey and R. Luza (eds.), *A History of the Czechoslovak Republic 1918–1948,* Princeton: Princeton University Press.

Pumphrey, L.M. (1942), 'The exchange equalization account of Great Britain, 1932–1939: exchange operations', *American Economic Review*, 32.

Ranki, G. (1985), 'Problems of southern European economic development (1918–38)', in G. Arrighi (ed.), *Semiperipheral Development: the Politics of Southern Europe in the Twentieth Century,* Beverly Hills: Sage Publications.

Redmond, J. (1980), 'An indicator of the effective exchange rate of the pound in the nineteen-thirties', *Economic History Review*, 33.

Redmond, J. (1988), 'Effective exchange rates in the nineteen-thirties: the European gold bloc and North America', *Journal of European Economic History,* 17.

Rist, C. (1936), 'Memorandum on the depression experience of gold bloc countries', in Carnegie Endowment/International Chamber of Commerce (eds), *The Improvement of Commercial Relations Between Nations and the Problems of Monetary Stabilization*, Paris: International Chamber of Commerce.

Rothschild, J. (1974), *East Central Europe Between the Two World Wars,* Seattle: University of Washington Press.

Routh, T. (1993), *British Protection and the International Economy: Overseas Commercial Policy in the 1930s,* Cambridge: Cambridge University Press.

Royal Institute of International Affairs (1933), *Monetary Policy and the Depression*, London: Oxford University Press.

Royal Institute of International Affairs (1936), *The Balkan States: a Review of the Economic and Financial Development of Albania, Bulgaria, Greece, Roumania and Yugoslavia Since 1919*, London: Oxford University Press.

Royal Institute of International Affairs (1938), *The Baltic States: a Survey of the Political and Economic Structure and the Foreign Relations of Estonia, Latvia, and Lithuania,* Oxford, Oxford University Press.

Royal Institute of International Affairs (1939), *South Eastern Europe: a Political and Economic Survey*, London: Oxford University Press.

Sayers, R.S. (1960), 'The return to gold, 1925', in L.S. Pressnell (ed.), *Studies in the Industrial Revolution*, London: Athlone Press.

Sayers, R.S. (1976a), *The Bank of England 1891–1944*, Vol. I, Cambridge: Cambridge University Press.

Sayers, R.S. (1976b), *The Bank of England 1891–1944,* Vol. II, Cambridge: Cambridge University Press.

Scammell, W.M. (1961), *International Monetary Policy,* 2nd edn, London: Macmillan.

Schloss, H.H. (1958), *The Bank for International Settlements: an Experiment in Central Bank Cooperation*, Amsterdam: North Holland Publishing Company.

Schwarz, L.D. (1993), 'Searching for recovery: unbalanced budgets, deflation and rearmament in France during the 1930s', in W.R. Garside (ed.), *Capitalism in Crisis: International Responses to the Great Depression,* London: Pinter Publishers.

Siegenthaler, H. (1976), 'Switzerland 1920–1970', in C. Cipolla (ed.), *The Fontana Economic History of Europe: Contemporary Economies,* Part Two, London: Collins.

Simmons, B.A. (1993), 'Why innovate? Founding the Bank for International Settlements', *World Politics*, 45.

Simmons, B.A. (1994), *Who Adjusts? Domestic Sources of Foreign Economic Policy During the Interwar Years*, Princeton: Princeton University Press.

Simutis, A. (1942), *The Economic Reconstruction of Lithuania after 1918*, New York: Columbia University Press.

Solomou, S. (1996), *Themes in Macroeconomic History: the UK Economy, 1919–1939*, Cambridge: Cambridge University Press.

Spulber, N. (1966), *The State and Economic Development in Eastern Europe*, New York: Random House.

Strakosch, H. (1937), 'The money tangle of the postwar period', in A.D. Gayer (ed.), *The Lessons of Monetary Experience: Essays in Honor of Irving Fisher*, New York: Rinehart & Company.

Strange, S. (1971), *Sterling and British Policy*, London: Oxford University Press.

Sumner, S. (1991), 'The equilibrium approach to discretionary monetary policy under an international gold standard, 1926–1932', *The Manchester School, 59.*

Sumner, S. (1992), 'The role of the international gold standard in commodity price deflation: evidence from the 1929 stock market crash', *Explorations in Economic History*, 29.

Sumner, S. (1997), 'News, financial markets, and the collapse of the gold standard: 1931–1932', *Research in Economic History*, 17.

Svennilson, I. (1954), *Growth and Stagnation in the European Economy*, Geneva: United Nations.

Temin, P. (1993), 'Transmission of the great depression', *Journal of Economic Perspectives*, 7.

Temin, P. and B. Wigmore (1990), 'The end of one big deflation', *Explorations in Economic History*, 27.

United Nations (1949), *Statistical Yearbook 1948*, New York: United Nations.

van der Wee, H. and K. Tavernier (1975), *La Banque Nationale de Belgique: l'histoire monétaire entre les deux guerres mondiales*, Brussels: Banque Nationale de Belgique.

Whitaker, J.K. and W. Hudgins (1977), 'The floating pound sterling of the nineteen-thirties: an econometric study', *Southern Economic Journal*, 43.

Williamson, P. (1992), *National Crisis and National Government: British Politics, the Economy and Empire 1926–1932*, Cambridge: Cambridge University Press.

Woytinsky, W.S. and E.S. Woytinsky (1955), *World Commerce and Governments*, New York: Twentieth Century Fund.

Yeager, L.B. (1976), *International Monetary Relations: Theory, History and Policy*, New York: Harper & Row.

CHAPTER TWO

Exchange rates crises and US financial markets during the 1930s

Scott Sumner

Introduction

The USA experienced periods of sharply declining output during 1929–32, and again during 1937–38. In both cases, prices also fell sharply, suggesting that a shortfall in aggregate demand was a likely cause of these contractions. Similarly, an expansion in output after March 1933 was associated with sharply rising prices, again pointing to aggregate demand as a likely causal factor. This chapter analyses the role that exchange rate crises played in the fluctuations of US aggregate demand during 1931–8. To do this, it will look at the response of US financial markets to these exchange rate crises.

The question of causality is one of the most troublesome issues faced by macroeconomic historians. One problem is that it is difficult to distinguish between endogenous and exogenous economic shocks. And even if exogeneity can be demonstrated, the existence of variable lags can make it difficult to connect movements in output with previous macroeconomic shocks. Because financial markets respond almost immediately to economic news, the movements in these markets can provide information about causality that is unavailable from traditional time-series analyses of macroeconomic aggregates.

The next section briefly examines the relationship between the international gold standard, aggregate demand and the price level during the 1930s. The third section summarises and expands on a previous study of the 1931–2 period. The fourth section looks at Roosevelt's 1933 policy of dollar depreciation. The fifth section examines how the 'gold panic' of early 1937 and the 'dollar panic' of late 1937 contributed to a sharp recession in 1937–8. The final section includes some observations on the problems inherent in modelling these episodes, and draws a few tentative conclusions.

Models of the inter-war gold standard

Many economic historians have argued that monetary factors played an important role in determining aggregate demand during the 1930s. Bernanke (1995) used the following identity to analyse the impact of the international gold standard on monetary policy during the depression:

$$M1 = (M1/Base)^{*}(Base/Reserves)^{*}(Reserves/Gold)^{*}(PGold)^{*}(QGold). \tag{2.1}$$

where the term (*M1/Base*) is simply the (world) money multiplier and *QGold* is the physical quantity of gold. We can simplify this expression by combining several of the ratios:

$$M1 = [(M1/Base)/(Gold/Base)]^{*}(PGold)^{*}(QGold). \tag{2.2}$$

The ratio of the monetary gold stock (in dollar terms) to the monetary base is sometimes referred to as the 'gold reserve ratio', and is determined by the monetary authorities. The price of gold (*PGold*) is, of course, fixed under a gold standard. Because the physical quantity of gold increased during the early 1930s, the sharp fall in M1 was primarily due to a large increase in the gold reserve ratio and a large decline in the money multiplier.

A similar identity allows us to focus on the world price level:

$$P = [QGold^{*}PGold]/[(Base/P)^{*}(Gold/Base)]. \tag{2.3}$$

A higher price level can result from either an increase in the price of gold, an increase in the physical quantity of gold, a decreased real demand for base money (that is, decreased currency hoarding) or a decreased gold reserve ratio (that is, a contractionary monetary policy). Like the equation of exchange, equations (2.1)–(2.3) are simple identities which are only useful if we can identify factors influencing the key parameters.

There are several ways in which an exchange rate crisis could effect the variables in equation (2.3). Sumner (1997) showed that changes in the world monetary gold stock seem highly correlated with exchange rate crises. Although the long-run growth of the monetary gold stock is closely related to the output of gold mines, during the 1930s short-run fluctuations seemed determined by waves of private gold hoarding and dishoarding. Table 2.1 shows the (negative) relationship between various exchange rate crises and the growth rate of the world (physical) monetary gold stock during the 1930s.[1]

Although many countries devalued their currencies during the 1930s, no country revalued its currency in terms of gold. Thus, during most exchange rate crises, speculators in a currency could anticipate either a devaluation or no change in the value of the currency. Given the extremely low opportunity cost of holding gold during this period (that is, the low nominal interest rate), exchange rate crises often led to dramatic increases in gold hoarding.

Table 2.1 Annualized changes in the world (physical) monetary gold stock and related crises, 1929–39

Time period	*DLG*	*Event*
Dec. 1929–June 1931	6·0 per cent	
June 1931–Oct. 1931	–3·4 per cent	UK/German crises
Oct. 1931–Apr. 1932	6·7 per cent	
Apr. 1932–June 1932	–8·7 per cent	Run on the dollar
June 1932–Jan. 1933	8·4 per cent	
Jan. 1933–Feb. 1933	–18·8 per cent	Run on the dollar
Feb. 1933–Apr. 1933	11·8 per cent	
Apr. 1933–Jan. 1934	–0·1 per cent	Dollar devaluation
Jan. 1934–Mar. 1935	7·6 per cent	
Mar. 1935–May 1935	–15·8 per cent	Belgian crisis
May 1935–Mar. 1936	5·3 per cent	
Mar. 1936–Sep. 1936	0·4 per cent	French crisis
Sep. 1936–June 1937	11·3 per cent	
June 1937–Mar. 1938	0·0 per cent	US devaluation fears
Mar. 1938–Dec. 1939	9·8 per cent	

Note: DLG is the (annualized) first difference of the log of the world monetary gold stock.

An exchange rate crisis can also affect the gold reserve ratio. Under the inter-war gold standard many central banks held reserves in the form of foreign exchange, rather than gold. After Britain left the gold standard in September 1931, fear of further devaluations led many central banks, particularly within the gold bloc, to replace their foreign currency reserves with gold. This led to a 5·8 per cent increase in the world's gold reserve ratio between August 1931 and December 1932.

Wigmore (1987) and Wicker (1996) discussed the possibility that exchange rate crises may have contributed to some of the banking panics of the early 1930s. If these crises led to expectations of either bank failures and/or a moratorium on convertibility, then they may have also generated currency hoarding. As with changes in the monetary gold stock and the gold reserve ratio, changes in currency hoarding triggered by exchange rate crises tended to contract aggregate demand and the world price level.

The final variable in equation (2.3), the price of gold, affected aggregate demand only when a country suspended convertibility of its currency. We see below (pp. 82–87) that, during 1933, changes in the dollar price of gold had a strong (positive) impact on aggregate demand in the USA. At the same time, there is some evidence that the US policy of dollar depreciation reduced aggregate demand in Europe. And the transmission mechanism for its European impact seemed to be gold hoarding, rather than the more traditional 'terms of trade' effect (that is, deviations from purchasing power parity).

The preceding analysis suggests that increases in the monetary gold stock should increase aggregate demand and that increases in the gold ratio and/or banking panics should decrease aggregate demand. Unfortunately, monthly data for aggregate demand are unavailable for the 1930s. If aggregate demand shocks had a major impact on output during the 1930s, however, the preceding variables should also be correlated with short-run changes in output. Equation (1) in Table 2.2 shows the results of estimating a CORC regression of the first difference of the log of US industrial production (DLIP) on the first difference of the log of the world monetary gold stock (DLG), the log of deposits of failed US banks (LDFB), and the weighted average of the first difference of the log of the gold ratio for seven important industrial countries (DLR), during the period from January 1927 to April 1933. The weights used to construct DLR reflect each country's share of the world monetary gold stock. This variable represents a crude proxy for world monetary policy.[2] The signs on the coefficients of each of the independent variables are consistent with the preceding analysis, although the coefficient on the gold reserve ratio is not significant at the 5 per cent level. (The data are from various issues of the *Federal Reserve Bulletin*.)

A crude proxy for nominal output growth can be generated by adding DLIP to the first difference of the log of the cost of living (as estimated by the National Industrial Conference Board). Equation (2) shows the results of a CORC regression using this proxy for nominal output growth (DLY) as a dependent variable. The qualitative results are similar to those in equation (1).

An expectation of higher future levels of aggregate demand should tend to increase current aggregate demand. If actual devaluations resulted in increased aggregate demand and increased price levels, then, on theoretical grounds, one might expect fear of devaluation also to increase aggregate demand and prices. Thus, despite all of the previous reasons to suppose that exchange rate crises are deflationary, it is also

Table 2.2 The relationship between US industrial production, the gold ratio, the world monetary gold stock and the deposits of failed US banks, January 1927–April 1933, monthly

	Dependent variables	
	(1)	*(2)*
Coefficients on independent variables	*DLIP*	*DLY*
DLR_{-1}	−0·242 (−1·50)	−1·668 (−1·01)
DLG_{-1}	1·927 (3·60)	1·714 (2·92)
LDFB	−0·0084 (−3·78)	−0·0101 (−4·17)
$DLIP_{-1}$	0·4104 (3·60)	
DLY_{-1}		0·379 (3·41)
Adj R^2	0·408	0·435
Durban–Watson	1·57	1·63

Notes: T-statistics are in parentheses. The Cochrane–Orcutt procedure was used to correct for serial correlation. DLR_{-1}, DLG_{-1}, $DLIP_{-1}$, and DLY_{-1} are the first lags of each variable. Because DLG and DLR use end of month figures, the actual lag is only about 15 days. The regressions included a constant term (not shown).

possible that they may be inflationary. Before exploring this issue more fully, it may be useful to examine the historical record regarding the impact of exchange rate crises on financial markets. The following three sections examine empirical evidence that has important implications for the theoretical puzzle at the centre of this chapter.

The dollar panics of 1931, 1932 and 1933

The 'Great Contraction' in the USA lasted from roughly August 1929 to March 1933. Only the latter half of this period, however, experienced significant exchange rate crises. Sumner (1991) showed that the world's central banks (particularly in the USA, France and Britain) adopted a highly contractionary policy after October 1929. This policy led to a dramatic 9·6 per cent increase in the world's gold reserve ratio between October 1929 and October 1930, which sharply reduced the world price level. After October 1930, banking instability led to an increase in currency hoarding which led to even more deflation. Only in July 1931, however, did an exchange rate crisis begin to have a discernible impact on the world's monetary gold stock, and on the US financial markets.

After rising sharply during June 1931 on hopes engendered by Hoover's debt moratorium proposal, the Dow Jones Industrial Average (DOW) declined by 10·4 per cent during July. Virtually all of this decline occurred during the nine days preceding Germany's 15 July suspension of the convertibility of the mark. July also saw the first significant monthly decline in the world monetary gold stock since the Depression began.[3]

The DOW levelled off during August, and then declined by a stunning 36·7 per cent during September 1931. Although it would be natural to attribute this decline to the developing crisis in Britain, evidence from the forward exchange rate market suggests that expectations of a British devaluation probably remained fairly low until 18 September. Thus only the 8·6 per cent decline in the DOW between 17 and 19 September seems directly attributable to the devaluation.[4] The efficient market theory suggests that financial markets respond almost immediately to important news events. What then could explain the 29·4 per cent plunge in the DOW between 23 September and 5 October 1931?

On 24 September 1931, the DOW plunged 7·3 per cent and on the following day the *New York Times* (*NYT*) headline stated that 'Sales Of Gold Upset Money Market Here; Stock Prices Break'. This was only the first of a series of runs on the dollar during the 1930s. Among many members of the 'gold bloc', the British devaluation led to fears that the USA would follow suit, and as a result large quantities of gold began to flow from the USA to Europe. By themselves, gold flows provide no evidence as to the stance of *world* monetary policy. These flows might have reflected either easy money in the USA or tight money in Europe. What is indicative of a contractionary worldwide monetary policy is the increase in the world gold reserve ratio which followed the British devaluation.[5]

There are at least two other mechanisms by which the British devaluation could have had a deflationary impact on the USA. October 1931 saw the sharpest decrease in the world monetary gold stock seen since the beginning of the Depression. Not only were gold bloc central banks hoarding gold, but private gold hoarding was also increasing rapidly. In addition, if the British devaluation did contribute to the US banking crisis, it may have also triggered an increase in currency hoarding which could have further reduced aggregate demand. Only with the discount rate increases of 8 and 15 October did the run on the dollar end. And, despite the fact that these discount rate increases are now viewed as huge mistakes, the response of the stock market was, if anything, slightly positive.[6]

Between 10 and 13 February 1932, the DOW rose by an astounding 17·8 per cent, the largest increase ever recorded over two consecutive trading days. This was attributed to Hoover's proposal (later embodied in the Glass–Steagall Act) for a change in Federal Reserve regulations which would greatly augment their holdings of 'free gold', and thus presumably reduce devaluation fears. This action led the Fed to embark on an ambitious programme of open market purchases at the rate of roughly $100 million per week during April, May and June 1932.

Despite, *or perhaps because of*, the Fed's open market purchases, US stock and commodity markets plunged sharply during the spring of 1932. The DOW fell from 88·78 on 8 March to its Depression low of 41·22 on 8 July 1932. The growth of the world monetary gold stock slowed dramatically in April 1932, and then the stock declined by $167 million in May and June. As with the decline in October 1931, this decline was associated with a run on the dollar. Contemporaneous accounts attributed the run to devaluation fears engendered by both expansionary fiscal policy proposals and the Fed's open market purchases. These same fears led the major gold bloc central banks to increase their gold reserve ratios again, and once again large quantities of gold began to flow from the USA to Europe.

If devaluation fears were driving down US stock prices, changes in the world monetary gold stock should have been positively correlated with changes in US stock prices during the early 1930s. The Cowles Index provides a fairly comprehensive monthly US stock market index from 1871. In Table 2.3, the first difference of the log of real stock prices (DLRCI)[7] is regressed on changes in the world monetary gold stock (DLG).

Note that US stock prices do seem to be positively correlated with changes in the world monetary gold stock, but only during periods dominated by devaluation crises (such as June 1931 to April 1933).

Bernanke (1995) suggests that the tendency for economic recovery to follow devaluation is one of the key stylised facts of the Great Depression. And both the British devaluation of 1931 and the American devaluation of 1933 triggered major increases in their respective stock indices. Much less clear, however, is the impact of expansionary monetary and fiscal policies that led to expectations of devaluation. The financial markets often welcomed expansionary policies, but not if they

Table 2.3 The relationship between variations in the real value of the Cowles index of stock prices (DLRCI) and the world monetary gold stock (DLG), January 1927–April 1933, selected periods, monthly

Dependent variable: DLRCI

	Sample periods		
	(1)	*(2)*	*(3)*
Coefficients on independent variables	*1/27–4/33*	*1/27–6/31*	*6/31–4/33*
DLG	5·921 (3·25)	1·338 (0·55)	7·772 (2·51)
Adj R^2	0·115	0·000	0·201
Durban–Watson	1·56	1·26	1·81

Notes: T-statistics are in parentheses; the regressions included a constant term (not shown).

provoked a crisis of confidence which neutralised their expansionary effect:

> The financial community is in general strongly opposed to the scheme [to print 'greenbacks' in order to pay a large bonus to war veterans], but it is a curiously sympathetic opposition in many quarters. The professed object of proponents of the plan, which is to bring about an advance in the price level, is viewed widely as commendable, but the method by which it is sought to achieve this end is felt to be unsound. It would result, in the opinion of most bankers, in great disturbance to confidence here and abroad and would, despite this sacrifice, *fail of achieving its purpose.*
>
> (*NYT*, 12/4/32, p. 27, emphasis added)

> Wall Street as a whole is strongly in sympathy with the idea behind the Goldsborough bill, which imposes a mandate upon the Treasury and the Federal Reserve System to lower the purchasing power of the dollar, but is opposed ever more strongly to the bill on practical grounds.
>
> (*NYT*, 3/5/32, p. 29)

The following quotation anticipates the central puzzle which motivates this chapter:

> The contrast presented by these fears of inflation and the unremitting fall in the prices of stocks and commodities is one of the curious aspects of the current situation. Obviously if there was any genuine belief in the likelihood of inflation, the attempt of capital to escape depreciation by conversion into some tangible form of wealth

> would be reflected at once in a demand for commodities and common stocks.
>
> (*NYT*, 14/5/32, p. 23)

During July 1932 the Fed began to cut back sharply on its policy of open market purchases. Ironically, in the period from 8 July to 7 September the DOW increased from 41·81 to 79·93, one of the largest percentage increases ever observed in a two-month period. As with the October 1931 discount rate increases, the Fed's switch to a much more contractionary policy in July 1932 has been widely criticized by economic historians. And yet, just as with the discount rate increases of 1931, this switch was followed by a major bull market.

Contemporaneous press coverage suggested that the ending of the 1932 dollar crisis was one of the key factors behind this bull market. A 29 July *NYT* story (p. 1) suggested that one reason for the bull market was a 'spectacular rise of the dollar in terms of foreign currencies which reflected the further reinforcement of the gold position of the United States'. Another story (p. 23) noted the 'discovery that the United States is securely anchored to the gold standard'. Not surprisingly, the world monetary gold stock rose sharply between July and September as the private sector began dishoarding gold. Along with sharply rising stock and commodity prices, industrial production rose by 12·5 per cent between July and November 1932.

Between 4 and 10 October 1932, the DOW plunged by 19·6 per cent. This decline appears to have been triggered by a gaffe made in a Hoover campaign speech on 4 October. By suggesting that his adroit leadership had saved the USA from being forced off the gold standard in early 1932, Hoover merely reinforced the precarious nature of the US position and created further doubts about the future.

On 9 October the *NYT* (p. 1) noted: 'No Danger To Dollar From Foreign Raids Seen Now In Capital', 'Hoover Blamed In Paris' and 'Papers Lay Decline To His Speech – The Dollar Takes Sharp Drop, Along With Sterling'. They also cited some of the reaction in Europe:

> What evils can result from an election! ... Now President Hoover, to recover votes which seemed on the point of escaping, is willing to sacrifice the dollar. For the dollar again has become feeble and delicate ... following the declarations of President Hoover, who in order to get business started again, has indicated the possibility of inflation.
>
> (*La Liberté*)

'Everyone is saying that if the dollar is vulnerable, so must be most European moneys' (*Agence Economique et Financière*); 'The President, seeking to restore confidence, seems somehow to accomplish the opposite result' (*Paris Midi*).

The *NYT* also suggested (p. F1) that the decline in the dollar and the stock market was widely believed to be due to the president's comments and that 'Business men are reported now to be apprehensive of the effects of a falling stock market on trade.'

As 1933 began, congressional proposals for 'currency tinkering' brought a renewed attack on the dollar. The *Times* noted that 'A European raid upon the dollar, reminiscent of last Spring, hit the foreign exchange market yesterday as news of Senator Borah's plan to introduce legislation to devalue the American monetary unit reached Paris and other foreign markets' (*NYT*, 5/1/33, p. 29).

Although the dollar would not come under severe pressure until late February, the unwillingness of President-elect Roosevelt to issue a blanket endorsement of the gold standard resulted in persistent inflation rumours throughout early 1933. The conservative financial press was critical of Roosevelt's non-committal attitude towards the gold standard, and pointedly contrasted Roosevelt's vague promises of a 'sound currency' with President-elect Cleveland's forthright endorsement of the gold standard during the pre-inauguration periods of 1885 and 1893. They also argued that this uncertainty was hurting the economy:

> Yet it will not have been forgotten that, on numerous older similar occasions, doubt and mistrust prevailed with exceedingly bad effect on financial sentiment, until the President-elect took matters into his own hands and publicly avowed his purposes ... It is probable enough that the present spirit of hesitancy, not only on financial markets but in general trade, is more or less influenced by the lack of such reassurance.
>
> (*NYT*, 23/1/33, p. 19)

During the winter of 1932–3, conditions in the farm belt deteriorated rapidly. A 13 February *Times* headline (p. 1) cited 'DANGER OF REVOLT' and 'INFLATION DEMANDS GROW':

> A few months ago there was in the minds of the people who wrote these letters [to Congressmen] only a sad bewilderment at the financial swamp in which they were sinking, appeals for help and angry protests. But now the predominant emotion in them is fear – fear of greater economic and business chaos, fear of revolution.

On 14 February, the imminent failure of several large Detroit banks led the governor of Michigan to declare a statewide banking holiday, and stock and commodity prices declined in response. The real surprise, however, was that the financial markets did not respond even more dramatically to the 1933 financial crisis. True, the DOW did fall by nearly 17 per cent between 11 February and the low point on 27 February. But stocks never even approached their July 1932 lows, despite the fact that the 1933 crisis was by far the most severe financial crisis faced by the USA during the Great Depression. And stocks actually rose steadily after 27 February, even though the crisis intensified dramatically during early March. Commodity prices declined only modestly during late February.

There are two reasons why the financial markets held up fairly well during the 1933 financial crisis. First, the inauguration of a new president was only a few days away. And second, during this period the federal government was perceived by the markets as having a much greater ability to influence real asset prices than is the case today. This second point may seem counter-intuitive, given the fact that the role of the federal government in the economy at that time was much smaller than it is today. But the markets had soared on expansionary proposals such as Glass–Steagall, and the investors had every reason to believe that Roosevelt would try something similar.

The 15 February *NYT* also reported that 'HEAVY EARMARKING OF GOLD CONTINUES' and suggested: 'To a large extent the movement is believed to be tied with Europe's reaction to the renewed outbreak of banking trouble here and to the recent discussions of inflationary proposals in Washington' (p. 29). The causality probably ran both ways, with banking troubles leading to fears of devaluation, and fears of devaluation leading to currency hoarding, and thereby triggering more banking holidays. On 27 February, the *NYT* noted:

> The unsettlement of last week's stock market, the recurrent weakness in the bond market, and the indication that hoarding of currency had increased resulted partly from the not very skillfully handled Michigan episode, but they equally reflected the mental influence of the mischievous talk of experimenting with the currency.
>
> (*NYT*, p. 23)

During early March 1933, Treasury bond prices fell sharply as the crisis intensified and devaluation fears increased, and yet these same devaluation fears led to higher stock and commodity prices as the market looked forward to possible 'currency tinkering' by the incoming administration.[8] The more severe the crisis became, the greater became the expectation of dramatic policy changes in the near future: 'The market and those who follow it appear to be building their hopes on the possibility of a sweeping psychological change after the Presidential inauguration' (*NYT*, 3/3/33, p. 25). By the close of the Hoover administration, virtually the entire banking system was shut down and gold was pouring out of the country at an unprecedented rate. Yet the only significant macroeconomic consequence of this crisis would be a modest dip in industrial production during March 1933.

Despite all of the preceding shocks, the forward markets showed little evidence that an immediate, and large, devaluation was expected after the new administration took office. On 3 March 1933, the three-month forward dollar sold at only a 1·2 per cent discount against the pound. Yet, by 3 June, the spot pound had appreciated by nearly 15 per cent. Perhaps the large gold outflows during the first few days of March would have reflected a belief that Roosevelt would move to further restrict gold outflows and/or domestic hoarding. Essentially, the markets were betting that Roosevelt would take some type of effective policy action to allow for a more expansionary monetary policy. In the short run, the markets were correct, as Roosevelt made no immediate moves to devalue the dollar, but did restrict gold outflows as well as domestic hoarding.

Roosevelt's dollar depreciation programme

The year 1933 saw two of the most dramatic macroeconomic policy experiments ever undertaken by the US government. From April 1933 to February 1934, the Roosevelt administration took control of monetary policy away from the Federal Reserve, and pursued an avowedly inflationary policy directly out of the White House. On 19 July 1933, President Roosevelt issued an executive order that almost immediately raised the aggregate wage level by approximately 20 per cent. Both of these experiments are unique in post-Civil War US history, and both had an immense impact on the performance of the US economy. Because these policies tended to neutralise each other, however, their individual impacts have been underestimated by researchers focusing on each policy in isolation.

Despite the fact that the forward discount on the dollar was even greater in March than in February, world monetary gold stocks rebounded by 1·7 per cent during March, an indication that Roosevelt's anti-hoarding policies were having some effect. Because markets were now confident that Roosevelt's policies would prevent gold (and currency) hoarding from having an adverse impact on the money supply, stock market investors appeared to take a more benign view of the risk of devaluation. The DOW rose by 14·3 per cent on the day the New York Stock Exchange (NYSE) reopened after a two-week hiatus associated with the bank holiday.

Throughout March and early April 1933, there was some recovery in output and wholesale prices. Yet the DOW was at almost exactly the same level on 18 April (the day before the dollar was allowed to float) as it had been after the markets reopened on 15 March. Roosevelt's decision on 19 April 1933, to abandon temporarily the gold standard

Table 2.4 The relationship between the Dow Jones industrial average and the dollar price of French francs, 17 April 1933–1 February 1934, daily

Independent variable: DLFF					
Dependent variables	*Coefficient*	*T-statistic*	*D–W*	R_2	*n*
DLDOW	0·563	(5·21)	2·10	0·103	229
$DLDOW_{-1}$	0·534	(4·92)	2·07	0·093	228

Note: $DLDOW_{-1}$ is first lag of DLDOW.

ushered in one of the most remarkable years in the history of US financial markets. It would be difficult to find any other period where movements in all of the markets were so dominated by the whims of a single individual. Between 18 and 20 April, the DOW rose by 14·3 per cent. By 18 July, the DOW was up over 55 per cent from its level three months earlier. Even more than by its size, this bull market is distinguished by the close relationship between stock prices and the international value of the dollar. Table 2.4 shows the relationship between changes in the (log of the) dollar price of French francs (DLFF) and the first difference of the (log of the) DOW during the period of dollar depreciation.[9]

Table 2.5 shows that the devaluation of the dollar also appears to have had a significant effect on commodity prices. A regression of the first

Table 2.5 The relationship between commodity prices and the dollar price of French francs, 17 April 1933–1 February 1934, daily

Dependent variable: DLMCI		
Independent variable	*Coefficient*	*T-statistic*
DLFF	0.362	(7.12)
Adj. R^2 = 0.179, n = 229, Durbin–Watson Statistic = 1.74		
Dependent variable: $DLMCI_{-1}$		
Independent variable	*Coefficient*	*T-statistic*
DLFF	0.218	(4.02)
Adj. R^2 = 0.063, n = 228, Durbin-Watson Statistic = 1.67		

difference of the log of the Moody's Commodity Index (DLMCI) against the first difference of the log of the dollar price of French francs (DLFF) suggests that dollar depreciation raised commodity prices. Since available foreign exchange data are based on noon prices, one lag of DLMCI was also regressed on DLFF and again the coefficient was both positive and significant.

It is interesting to contrast the stock market's enthusiastic response to the Fed's decision (on the evening of 25 May) to reduce the discount rate with the previous non-reaction to the discount rate increases of 8 and 15 October 1931. With the Fed now able to adopt expansionary policies without fear of a run on the US gold stocks, markets reverted to their usual posture of welcoming lower discount rates.

Although on several occasions Roosevelt stated an intention to raise prices back to the level reached in 1925, financial markets initially seemed reluctant to accept these statements as official administration policy. This perception began to change in late June and early July as Roosevelt continued to resist currency stabilisation proposals. A key turning point occurred on 3 July, when FDR stunned the delegates at the World Monetary and Economic Conference (WMC) by stating his adamant opposition to any currency stabilisation agreement. Furthermore, Roosevelt suggested that he was serious about a 'commodity dollar':

> So, too, old fetishes of so-called international bankers are being replaced by efforts to plan national currencies with the objective of giving those currencies a continuing purchasing power which does not greatly vary in terms of the commodities and need of modern civilization.
>
> Let me be frank in saying that the United States seeks the kind of dollar which a generation hence will have the same purchasing power and debt-paying power as the dollar value *we hope to obtain in the near future.*
>
> (*NYT*, 4/7/33, p. 1, italics added)

This was a clear indication that Roosevelt's policy of devaluation represented far more than simply a negotiating tool to be used to gain concessions at the WMC.[10] In retrospect, this statement can be seen as an intimation of the dollar buying programme adopted in the autumn of 1933. Again, stocks and foreign exchange rose strongly on the report.

Roosevelt's hand was undoubtedly strengthened by the fact that production was rising at the most rapid rate in US history. In the four-month period from March to July 1933, industrial production recovered over one-half of the decline incurred during the previous 44 months. And this vigorous recovery was not being generated by a 'beggar-thy-neighbour' exchange rate policy. The 8 October 1933 *NYT* (p. 20) reported that exports only increased by 3 per cent in the first five months after devaluation, whereas imports soared by 20 per cent, suggesting that rising domestic aggregate demand, not improved terms of trade, was the key to industrial recovery.

In retrospect, it is surprising that the stock market did not show even greater strength during this period. The economy seemed to be repeating the cyclical pattern of 1920–22: output recovered rapidly once prices stopped declining. One factor that may have restrained the rise in stock prices during this period was concern over the possible effects of New Deal legislation, particularly the National Industrial Recovery Act (NIRA).

By mid-July 1933, it was becoming increasingly obvious that FDR saw a need to increase wages sharply to match the price rises engendered by his policy of dollar depreciation. Stocks plummeted by 20·3 per cent in the three days following the announcement of the 'Blue Eagle' programme on 19 July 1933, the third-greatest crash[11] in modern stock market history. The most important aspect of this programme was a provision that sharply raised hourly wages and reduced hours worked for millions of workers. Within two months, both real and nominal wages had risen by almost 20 per cent. After peaking in July, the economy plunged into renewed depression and output declined by nearly 20 per cent by year end.

By 21 October the DOW had reached its lowest point since May, and the administration finally decided to act. On the following day, Roosevelt authorised the Reconstruction Finance Corporation (RFC) to buy gold in order to depreciate the dollar in the hopes that it would lead to a continued rise in commodity prices. Each day Roosevelt met the secretary of the Treasury to determine a new (and usually higher) price of gold. This policy completely bypassed the Fed. On 23 October, the dollar fell by 2·7 per cent and the DOW soared by 5·2 per cent. Roosevelt continued to insist on his policy of restoring commodity prices to their 1925 level, and that a recovery of commodity prices must precede gold (that is, dollar) stabilisation.

From late October to the first half of November, the gold buying programme continued to depress the value of the dollar. During this period gold hoarding increased dramatically and there was increasing opposition to dollar depreciation among Europeans as well as among conservatives in the USA. As wholesale prices measured in gold continued to decline, fears increased that the US gold buying programme might force other countries off the gold standard. And although the dollar could be depreciated either through open market purchases or through gold purchases, the latter was obviously more likely to have a deflationary impact on gold bloc nations.

By mid-November, the dollar had reached its lowest point of the year and as more and more pressure was placed on the administration there were renewed expectations of dollar stabilisation. Key administration advisors such as O.M.W. Sprague (of the Treasury Department) and James Warburg resigned in protest at the gold policy. On 15 November, secretary of the Treasury (and sound money advocate) William Wooden also resigned in protest and on that very same day the price of gold hit its highest value of the year. A 3·6 per cent drop in the DOW on 27 November was attributed to the growing opposition to dollar depreciation. At about the same time the forward discount on the dollar reached its maximum point and weekly output indices showed the economy reaching a trough. The RFC gold price then remained relatively stable throughout December 1933.

The gold buying programme has received relatively little attention from economic historians and is still poorly understood. Friedman and Schwartz ([1963] 1971, p. 465) state that 'For a time, the large scale RFC purchases abroad made the announced price of newly-mined gold the effective market price.' There are several problems with this assertion. The announced price was generally either higher or lower than the market price, even during the initial stages of the programme. In fact, given the somewhat predictable rate at which the announced price changed, strict equality with the market price would appear to be inconsistent with market efficiency. In addition, during late October and early November, when the programme was at its most active, the level of RFC purchases was relatively small (totalling less than $50 million in a gold market exceeding $15 billion). This makes it exceedingly unlikely that the gold purchases were materially affecting the market price of gold.

Perhaps the most puzzling question raised by the gold buying programme is why Roosevelt adopted this circuitous technique for depreciating the dollar. He had the legal authority to devalue the dollar by up to 50 per cent. The most likely explanation is that Roosevelt did not have a firm conviction as to what gold price and/or exchange rate would be required to achieve his macroeconomic objectives (including commodity price reflation). The gold buying programme affected the exchange rate, not through the direct effect of the gold purchases, but through the indirect effect of altering expectations regarding the future value of the dollar. Thus the London gold market responded, not so much to the incremental increases in the RFC gold price, as to the changing perceptions of Roosevelt's policy intentions. Changing the RFC price of gold was just one technique for altering market expectations, but allowed Roosevelt to experiment with the link between gold and commodity prices without committing himself to a formal devaluation.

The economy did begin to improve in December 1933. During the final two months before the price of gold was fixed, the dollar depreciated slightly and the forward discount on the dollar fell gradually. The only significant movement occurred in mid-January 1934, when the dollar fell and the DOW soared by 4·5 per cent on news that the administration had decided to reduce the par value of the dollar by between 40 and 50 per cent, and then stabilise its value.

With a growing expectation of dollar stabilisation, gold-denominated wholesale price indices stopped declining. In February 1934, the world monetary gold stock began rising rapidly, and in the USA the money supply, the price level and output also began recovering. Industrial production, however, would not regain its July 1933 peak until August 1935, three months after the NIRA was declared unconstitutional by the Supreme Court.

Gold panics and dollar panics, 1934–8

Although 1933 is often viewed as the date when the USA permanently left the gold standard, in some respects, after 1934, the USA was even more firmly tied to the gold standard than it had been prior to 1933. Three criteria are often cited as indicators of adherence to a gold standard: maintenance of a fixed price of gold, free convertibility of the currency into gold, and adherence to the rules of the game, that is a relatively stable gold reserve ratio. Prior to 1933, the USA did conform to the first two criteria, but did not even come close to adhering to the rules of the game. After 1934, the dollar was no longer freely convertible into gold, but its market price was still fixed, and Friedman and Schwartz ([1963] 1971) showed that changes in the monetary base were closely correlated to changes in the monetary gold stock.

It was not apparent at the time, but the dollar price of gold would remain unchanged for the next 34 years. Although the 52·7 per cent devaluation between 1933 and 1934 was large enough to lead to rapid inflation, wholesale prices rose by only about 20 per cent during the period of depreciation, and another 5 per cent between February 1934 and August 1940, when the Second World War inflation began in earnest. The dollar remained undervalued, and over the next three years, as gold bloc currencies were facing speculative attacks of overvaluation, the dollar would face the opposite problem. The devaluation of the dollar also contributed to a substantial acceleration of gold production, which greatly increased world monetary gold stocks during the mid-to-late 1930s.

Although prices rose only modestly between 1934 and 1940, there were some interesting fluctuations during this period. Wholesale prices rose during 1934, but all of the increase was in the agricultural commodities, presumably reflecting the impact of the 'Dust Bowl'. A much more widespread inflation developed in mid-1936 as prices first increased by about 10 per cent from mid-1936 to mid-1937, and then fell back by nearly 10 per cent over the subsequent 12 months. In this section it will be argued that much of the 1936–8 price level fluctuations can be attributed to changes in private gold hoarding triggered by exchange rate crises.

On 6 March 1936 the *NYT* (p. 29) reported a sharp fall in the pound and noted that 'The pound's fall is disastrous for Belgium.' Five days later, it was reported (p. 25) that the pound had been 'disturbing' Wall Street and that 'Gold hoarding once more is being indulged in on a large scale.' By 16 March the *NYT* was suggesting that 'prospects of devaluation of the gold-bloc currencies' were dominating Wall Street. A 19 March headline (p. 38) emphasised the deflationary impact of this crisis: 'GRAIN PRICES CUT BY HEAVY SELLING ... FOREIGN CRISIS A FACTOR'.

In retrospect, these events marked the beginning of an 18-month crisis which would culminate in the demise of the gold bloc. World monetary gold stocks declined significantly during the spring of 1935, and again during the spring of 1936. Yet, surprisingly, this crisis did not seem to have a significant impact on prices and production in the USA.

In an article entitled 'Inflation or Deflation', the 20 March *NYT* (p. 31) noted:

> There is a considerable difference of opinion in financial circles whether a breakdown of the gold bloc would be seriously deflationary in its effects upon this country. It is conceded that the dollar likely would rise sharply and that, if prices and business here have received any stimulation from the fall of the dollar in foreign exchange, a rise might, presumably, reverse that condition. On the other hand there are those who believe that the abandonment of gold by the gold bloc would lead to all-around inflation, since it would involve a world-wide appreciation in the money value of gold stocks and there are still others who hold that it might lead to general stabilization of currencies – a move which is almost universally considered conducive to recovery.

There are actually at least five possible ways in which the gold bloc crisis could affect the US price level: (a) deflation in the USA, resulting from European currency devaluations, (b) an international currency war leading to inflation in the USA, (c) all-around currency stabilisation leading to economic recovery in the USA, (d) the crisis could lead to gold hoarding which would be deflationary, and (e) actual devaluation could lead to gold dishoarding which would be inflationary. Only the third and the fifth hypotheses appear to have been borne out in practice. There are several possible reasons for the relative stability of US prices during this extended crisis. Perhaps the most important was the asymmetry of the responses of central banks to these gold flows. During 1935–6 the gold bloc central banks did not allow the gold outflows to reduce their currency stocks significantly, yet the USA *did* allow its equally large gold inflows to expand dramatically its monetary base. This asymmetric response may have helped offset the deflationary effects of the private gold hoarding.

There is another important difference between the currency crises of the mid-1930s and the currency crises of the early 1930s. The deflationary impact of the German and British crises was not ended with decisions regarding devaluation. Rather, resolution of these crises simply triggered a loss of confidence in other currencies. In 1935, the situation was much different. The French franc was the last major currency that had not been adjusted to reflect the deflationary environment of the 1930s. It was widely believed that a decision to devalue the franc would quickly be copied by the smaller gold bloc currencies such as the Dutch guilder and the Swiss franc. The reason why the Belgian devaluation of March 1935 was important was that it triggered expectations of further devaluations and led to a massive gold outflow from the gold bloc. But if investors correctly foresaw the benign consequences of the final collapse of the gold bloc, it is easier to understand why this final crisis of the international gold standard had a much milder impact on the world price level than did the earlier German, British and US crises.

Despite heavy gold hoarding during April and May, markets were already looking ahead to the restoration of currency stability:

> Recent estimates have placed the total of gold being hoarded in the world at about $2,000,000,000 and half of that is thought to be lying in the vaults of banks in London for the account of hoarders all over the world. When the hard struggle back to worldwide currency stability is achieved, the release of this store of hoarded gold will be an important contribution to the monetary stocks of central banks and governments.
>
> (*NYT*, 4/5/35, p. 19)

Ten days later the *NYT* reported (p. 1) that the World Bank head went so far as to argue that 'such a general return to gold would serve to raise instead of lower prices'.

During July 1936, the Fed announced plans to increase bank reserve requirements sharply, and the stock market rise on the following morning was widely viewed as a response to that event. It should be noted that, despite this step, as well as subsequent moves such as gold sterilisation, the USA was just entering a major inflation which would push wholesale prices up by 9·3 per cent between June 1936 and April

1937. The markets might well have agreed with the Fed's view that these steps were necessary to maintain steady, but controlled, expansion in the economy. This does not necessarily mean that the Fed's actions did not contribute to the 1937–8 depression, but it does indicate that these steps were not as obviously foolish as is suggested in many modern accounts. (And it is clear from the 1933 dollar depreciation episode that the market's approval of Fed restraint was not due to a 'conservative' point of view on monetary policy issues.)

The final crisis of the gold bloc occurred in late September, 1936, and it is interesting to contrast this crisis with the British devaluation of 1931. Whereas the British devaluation helped create an international monetary crisis, the gold bloc crisis helped to restore stability to the international monetary system, at least for a brief period of time. The subsequent performance of the world price level suggests that the impact of foreign devaluations on the US terms of trade was much less important than its impact on the international gold market. Both the British and the gold bloc devaluations turned the terms of trade against the USA. But the British devaluation of 1931 led to a huge increase in gold hoarding which reduced commodity and stock prices in the USA. In contrast, the gold bloc devaluations led to massive gold *dishoarding*, which raised commodity and stock prices in the USA.

On several occasions during late September 1936 the *NYT* suggested that the French crisis was modestly depressing stock prices in the USA. But it also suggested that the devaluation of the franc had already been heavily discounted and was not expected to have a major impact on stock prices, particularly if it led to world currency stabilisation. On 26 September, it reported the 'Tripartite Agreement' for currency stabilisation between the USA, Britain and France, and on the following day suggested (p. F1) that the agreement had helped boost the US stock market.

In the short run, the Tripartite Agreement was successful in restoring some measure of stability, but unsettled conditions in Europe prevented any major outflow of funds from the USA: 'Fear that heavy repatriation of foreign funds lodged in this country would immediately follow devaluation of the erstwhile gold-bloc currencies was dispelled last week, and the stock market closed the week with a vigorous advance' (*NYT*, 4/10/36, p. F1). Three days later, the *NYT* (p. 41) suggested that 'speculative interest in the stock market has risen to the highest level witnessed since last February' and 'Wall Street continues to believe that the spark that touched off the recent rise in stocks was the devaluation in foreign currencies'. In addition, commodity prices, which had been gradually rising for several years, began increasing rapidly in October. The massive dishoarding of gold touched off by the Tripartite Agreement raised the world's monetary gold stock by almost 3 per cent in just the month of December. Although some dishoarding was anticipated, comments in the financial press suggest both that the actual dishoarding was much greater than anticipated and that the willingness of European powers to absorb those hoards was much less than anticipated:

> It was widely believed that if the gold bloc nations devalued, the flow of gold here would cease and even turn about in the other direction ... When the gold bloc did capitulate last September, however, nothing of the sort occurred. Gold continued to come here as before. It no longer came directly from the Bank of France and other central banks but it came from all the gold mines of the world and from private hoards.
>
> (*NYT*, 13/6/37, p. E3)

Even though the 'international gold standard' was now reduced to the USA and Belgium, the international gold *market* was playing an increasingly important role in the world economy. Although nominally operating under a floating rate regime, the important sterling bloc maintained a relatively stable exchange rate with the dollar, and thus with gold. Thus the inflation of 1936–7 was a worldwide phenomenon.

By mid-December it was clear that the August increase in reserve requirements had failed to slow commodity price speculation: 'Since the devaluation of the French franc late in September, speculative interest in commodities has been increasing steadily' (*NYT*, 16/12/36, p. 41). The second step in the Fed's anti-inflation programme was announced on 20 December 1936. This plan called for the sterilisation of all gold imports into the USA and, as with the previous increase in reserve requirements, it was received relatively calmly by the financial markets. Three days later the *NYT* (p. 29) argued that this step would provide the Fed with the flexibility to control excess bank reserves without pushing reserve requirements above their maximum (legally) allowable levels.

At first, these policies lacked credibility, and commodity prices continued to accelerate. On 30 January 1937, the Fed announced that the third and final step of its anti-inflation programme would involve two additional increases in bank reserve requirements. These increases, set to occur on 1 March and 1 May, would bring the required reserve ratio up to its legal maximum. As with the first increase, this announcement was viewed as being significant by the financial press, but failed to have a perceptible influence on stock prices. By early 1937, inflation was an even greater concern than had been the case in July of 1936.

During mid-March it was reported that the Russians had begun dumping large quantities of gold on the London market and at about this time a 'gold panic' developed in the major world markets. The world monetary gold stock was now rising so rapidly that the perception began to develop that only a revaluation of the dollar could prevent rapid inflation. The view that we were headed for 'another 1929' (*NYT*, 3/4/37, p. 6) led the administration to begin to move towards a much more aggressive anti-inflation policy. On 19 March the *NYT* reported (p. 35) that statements of concern by administration officials regarding the inflation problem led to an increase in Treasury bond prices and a sharp fall in stock prices. This policy shift led to a very unusual crisis in the gold market – a worldwide fear of *revaluation*.

Throughout recorded history, there are relatively few examples of formal revaluations of currencies in terms of gold. Yet just such a rumour developed vis-à-vis the dollar during the spring of 1937. On 8 April both stocks and commodities fell sharply and the next day the *NYT* cited rumours of a cut in the gold price as a market influence. The *NYT* (p. 33) suggested: 'Unneeded gold continues to flow to this country and, at best, the recent procedure of "sterilizing" ... has been a makeshift to get around a situation fraught with grave financial and economic consequences.'

Two days later, the rumour had become headline news: 'ROOSEVELT DENIES PLAN TO CUT GOLD, BUT FRANC PLUNGES' (10/4/37, p. 1) and the *NYT* noted that such a move would 'be deflationary, checking prices and tending to lessen the influx of foreign money to this country, a tendency over which the President has expressed concern'. In the USA, the 'stock market got off to a bad start but rallied on the President's statement' (ibid., p. 23). And the rumour had an impact on markets worldwide:

> Dispatches reaching London tonight from all the financial centers of the British Empire indicate how complete was the unsettlement of the exchange, commodity and security markets as a result of rumors that the United States Government intended substantially to reduce its buying price of gold ... Frenzied scenes were enacted in Throgmorton Street tonight, when operators, taking courage from the President's denial, rushed in to buy gold and copper shares and United States securities. For an hour the street was impassable to traffic.
>
> (Ibid., pp. 1, 7)

Despite rapidly rising prices, there was never any belief that the Roosevelt administration actually preferred to reduce the price of gold, but it was felt that the huge gold flows into the USA would ultimately force such an action:

> The rapidly growing production of gold in Russia which the U.S. has to absorb, it is held here, is especially pushing Washington toward revaluation.

> The effect of these considerations upon speculators and the large European corporations which have their reserves now in gold bars is, bankers here explain, to encourage them to put their gold on the market. It is reported that there still are large quantities of this hoarded gold left. Dehoarding of this gold, in addition to the new gold that is coming from the mines ... only adds to the pressure on Washington to cease buying at so high a price, thus increasing the danger of a sudden upset in the general price structure. One odd result is that the bankers who a year ago were denouncing the hoarders of gold for not bringing it out are now praying that they won't dehoard.
>
> (*NYT*, 13/4/37, p. 37)

Two additional factors which reduced the credibility of government denials were the recent abandonment of the silver purchase programme and the desire to balance the budget:

> Before the United States abandoned its policy of buying foreign silver, it was besieged with tenders of the metal from all points of the compass; so long as this country is the only nation to buy gold continuously and freely at $35 an ounce, it will not want for offerings, through London, from South Africa and India, and now from Soviet Russia. In the meanwhile, the Treasury must finance the Federal deficits and carry the added burden of paying for this unneeded gold.
>
> (*NYT*, 18/4/37, p. F1)

During the months of April, May and June, the already rapid growth in the world monetary gold stock accelerated further as dishoarding was spurred by fears of an imminent decrease in the price of gold. A sharp drop in stocks and commodities on 26 April was attributed to 'persistent rumors regarding the lowering of the price of gold' (*NYT*, 27/4/37, p. 31). In a letter to Congress made public late on 27 April, Roosevelt issued another statement about inflation, and on 29 April the *NYT* (p. 1) reported that the previous day's market 'was weak from the start on the overnight news of President Roosevelt's warning against the "present hazard of undue advance in prices, with a resulting rise in the cost of living"'.

Even though the 1937 'gold panic' was the mirror image of the devaluation scares of 1931–3, its effect on the US price level was actually in the same direction as those earlier crises. Although the flood of dehoarded gold would be expected to raise the US price level, the rumours of an *imminent* revaluation of the dollar exerted an even more powerful deflationary impact on the price level. The strongest evidence for this interpretation comes from the commodity markets and gold mining stocks; both plummeted sharply on news relating to the gold panic. The US wholesale price index fell only slightly between April and June 1937, but the rapid inflation of 1936–7 had come to an end.

Ironically, the panicky reaction of markets to these rumours may have prevented the very problem which so worried stock and commodity speculators. Stocks rose modestly in early May, and on 6 May the *NYT* (p. 37) argued that the impact of the rumours had 'served to remind the world that it has a vital interest at stake in the maintenance of the existing value of gold' and that, as a result, the British and the Dutch governments were now buying gold to assist the USA in that endeavour.

The revaluation rumours would not die easily, however, and after stocks dropped sharply during the week of 10–15 May, the *NYT* (16/5/37, p. F1) reported: 'The plans announced last week by the Swedish Government for monetary measures to check a possible inflation, including, if necessary, an upward revaluation of the currency, attracted interest in Wall Street banking circles as a portent of the changing trend in world monetary affairs.' During the following week, stocks regained almost all of the previous week's losses and the *NYT* (24/5/37, p. 29) reported that, in London:

> The suggestion that the Swedish krona should be revalued in terms of sterling caused a flutter here similar to that occasioned by the United States gold scare, although less severe.
>
> Although not seriously crediting this report, financial London nevertheless was glad to have an official denial by the Swedish Finance Minister of any such intention.

Stocks broke again on 1 June and the next day's *NYT* (p. 33) reported that a BIS report recommending gold revaluation was worrying London financiers and that, despite the fact of 'GOLD CUT DENIED AGAIN BY TREASURY', 'Europe [was] in Rush to Sell Dehoarded Gold' (p. 1). Two days later the *NYT* reported a record daily volume in the London gold market ($16 million) and, the following day, another record ($20 million), clear signs that dishoarding was accelerating. It reported (5/6/37, p. 23) that the British view was that 'stock and commodity markets have been disturbed by these exceptional gold sales, since they have been regarded as indicating the possibility of deflationary currency developments'.

On 4 June, stocks rallied on Roosevelt's reassuring statement that there was no change in government policy, but the *NYT* (5/6/37, p. 23) noted that these denials did not solve the problem of credibility:

> But the persistence of this fear about gold, in the face of denials by the highest authorities, reflects the public's loss of faith, all over the world, in the word of governments where money is concerned. Devaluation and its concomitant, abrogation of gold clauses, was a breach of faith on the part of the devaluing governments, however much it may have been demanded by the circumstances. Moreover, devaluation was preceded everywhere by solemn assurances that it would not occur. People became inured to disregarding official

> pledges on the currency because they saw that the force of economic events was nullifying such pledges. Similarly now it appears to many as though the current gold situation, involving governments in the costly purchase of huge unwanted stocks of the metal, is too difficult to continue unchanged for very long, regardless of what governments say.

A few weeks after this article was written, the 'gold problem' vanished for good. First, the gold inflows ceased for one year. Then, when the gold flows resumed, they were fully absorbed by huge increases in excess reserves beginning in 1938. In essence, banks relieved the US Treasury of the burden of buying all the world's surplus gold.

It makes no sense to view the high prices of mid-1937 as the inevitable effect of the devaluation of 1934, even if, ex post, it is possible to trace a chain of causation between those two events. These high prices did not exist at any other time in the 1934–40 period, and financial markets did not anticipate them in the summer of 1936. If markets are efficient then new information should have been arriving as the commodity prices were rising. And the most rapid increases occurred during the winter of 1936–7. Einzig argues:

> Even though the 'alarming' figures for 1936 [gold stocks] became available in January 1937, it was not until three months later that their sinister significance was discovered. From April onwards it became fashionable to present gold statistics in the gloomiest possible light. The one-sided presentation of the facts and figures of past production would in itself have caused but little harm, but when they were used as the basis for forecasting future gold supplies, the prophets indulged in extreme exaggeration.
>
> (1937, p. 28)

Einzig seems only half-right. It seems quite likely that the 'sinister significance' of rapidly growing gold stocks was influencing commodity prices in early 1937; rapid inflation is exactly what one would expect from the growing perception that gold supplies would increase rapidly over time. The intelligentsia generally picks up on a problem some time *after* market participants become aware of it. Thus, in April 1937, the markets begin reacting to signs of the way the political establishment would respond to rising prices in the commodity markets.

The gold panic continued throughout most of June, but during mid-June the French franc came under increasing pressure, and it was this occurrence that most likely ended the panic. The 1 July *NYT* (p. 41) noted that 'devaluation of the franc hardly implies deflation of world prices' and on 19 July (p. 23) it suggested that French currency problems had ended speculation about a cut in the price of gold and led to a resumption of hoarding. Although the world monetary gold stock declined in July, the prices of commodities began rising as fears of a revaluation of the dollar subsided.

There was an alternative theory as to the cause of the inflation; the armaments buildup associated with the European political tensions. But this theory doesn't really explain why prices rose so rapidly after the Tripartite Agreement, why prices suddenly stopped rising with rumours of revaluation, or why they fell sharply during the fall of 1937.

Between August 1937 and March 1938, the DOW fell almost by half, losing all of the ground gained during the 1935–7 bull market. It will be useful to segment this bear market into three parts. Between mid-August and mid-September, the price of US stocks fell by about 10 per cent, while commodity prices were essentially unchanged. Then, between mid-September and late November, stocks, commodities and industrial production all declined precipitously. During the winter of 1937–8, each series continued to fall, but more erratically and at a much slower pace.

Numerous reports suggested that hopes for autumn business were predicated on business's ability to pass higher costs on to the consumer:

> Continued indecision of the stock market reflects above all else the mixed views with respect to the seasonal Autumn pick-up in industry and trade. In the main, the outlook is viewed with a fair show of optimism. But the point at issue has to do with the effects of *higher price levels made necessary by higher wages* and attendant higher costs of raw materials.
>
> (*NYT*, 1/9/37, p. 23, italics added)

Even without the 1937–8 deflation, the wage shock related to unionisation drives resulting from the Wagner Act would have slowed business considerably during late 1937. The big surprise of late 1937, however, had to do with prices. Rather than continuing to rise, the price level in early September was about to begin a sharp plunge which, by the spring of 1938, would return the wages and prices index to the level of early 1936.

The 1937–8 deflation was at least partially caused by a reversal of the factors that pushed prices higher in late 1936 and early 1937. Whereas the previous inflation was spurred by dishoarding triggered by the Tripartite Agreement, the renewed deflation was aggravated by hoarding triggered by currency instability in France and devaluation fears in the USA. Because of the renewal in gold hoarding, there was no increase in the world monetary gold stock from mid-1937 to mid-1938, and this helped turn fears of 'runaway inflation' associated with a 'superabundance' of gold into renewed fears of deflation.

By 1 October, the *NYT* (p. 31) was reporting a complete turnabout in the world gold market:

> The recent acute weakness of the franc with its accompanying unsettlement of confidence in other currencies has completely altered the popular sentiment toward gold. Fears for the price of that metal, which existed last Spring and which caused extensive dishoarding in Europe, have been driven out by the renewed fears for the future of currencies, and gold is once more in active demand in London for purposes of private hoarding.

The following day the *NYT* (p. 25) suggested that 'Apprehension over another French "financial crisis" probably contributed to the mild sell-off in share prices in the morning' and that it led to even more gold hoarding in London.

It would be several more weeks before the *NYT* would mention concerns over the possibility of dollar devaluation. The conservative press was reluctant even to print these rumours, but there were already some hints in early October. An 8 October *NYT* article (p. 35) entitled 'The About-Face on Gold' discussed the renewed formation of the 'Committee for the Nation' which advocated raising the price of gold 'in order to combat the "steady fall of commodity and security prices"'. Clearly, there was great uncertainty about monetary policy, but it was not until 30 October that the *NYT* (p. 25) finally conceded that revaluation fears had been replaced by devaluation rumours, and that these rumours had been floating around Wall Street 'for weeks'. It was also reported that the French franc was now rising on rumours that gold would soon flow back to France.

From 29 October to 8 November there were almost continuous declines in stock and commodity prices as well as an increasing run on the dollar. The 2 November *NYT* (p. 39) reported 'Rumors of Gold Price Rise Depress Dollar; Metal Quoted at 9-Cent Premium in London' and naturally there were expectations of a gold outflow. On 5 November the *NYT* (p. 33) reported that 'The movement of foreign funds away from New York continues to be hastened by the willingness of European money centers to entertain the rumors that "further devaluation of the dollar is inevitable". The current action of the stock market, however, hardly lends any comfort to this topic.' As we have already seen, the market reaction seems to imply that the bearish influence provided by the gold outflow more than offset the bullish influence which would be provided if market participants had thought devaluation was likely in the near future. The *NYT* also indicated that the problem of gold hoarding was not just confined to private individuals:

> According to bankers here in touch with European markets, the scare abroad over a second devaluation of the dollar is not confined to irresponsible or ignorant elements but is shared by a good many

> important banks, particularly on the Continent, which have been buying gold to protect themselves.
>
> (Ibid.)

On 6 November the *NYT* (p. 21) reported that the gold outflow did not mean confidence in European currencies, but rather fear of a US devaluation, and then suggested that the 'gold price must be raised again if a serious deflation of prices is to be avoided'. By 7 November the *NYT* (p. F8) noted that 'Curiously enough, the current dollar scare seems to be confined almost entirely to Europe. In contrast to the fears there that the dollar will be further "inflated", the markets here give rein to the deepest fears of deflation.' Of course, had the French franc still been linked to gold, instead of rapidly depreciating in terms of gold, deflationary fears would have existed there as well. Although the *NYT* did attribute the continuing decline in stock prices to the gold outflow, it often seemed confused as to how devaluation rumours could cause a *deflation* of prices.

A front page story in the 8 November *NYT* ('FLOW OF GOLD NOW AWAY FROM U.S.A.; CREDIT BASE FIRM') might help us to understand why US observers were so confused by the situation. It said that Treasury officials 'find comfort in the fact that the United States can lose up to about $1,270,000,000, the amount of its "sterilized" gold, without experiencing the type of reaction *which sometimes has followed such a flight of capital*' (p. 1, italics added). But just as the sterilisation in early 1937 had not prevented the current inflation of commodity prices, so the export of sterilised gold would not prevent a deflation of prices. In early 1937, there was fear that a much higher world gold stock would eventually force a more inflationary policy, now the market expectation of the future world monetary gold stock was falling dramatically, as was the expectation of future price levels. At least the *NYT* (ibid.) recognised the fact that a 'serious slump ... on some occasions in the past, has followed a sudden outward movement of foreign capital'.

At this time the Europeans were becoming very pessimistic about US economic prospects. The French saw FDR following the failed high wage policies of the Blum government. As capital fled to London, the price of gilts rose by 1½ to 3½ points. On 9 November the *NYT* reported (p. 33) that 'DOLLAR DESERTION GAINS MOMENTUM' and that the French government had chosen to import gold rather than let the franc appreciate.

After the markets closed on 8 November, Secretary Morgenthau announced (ibid.) the export of more than $10 million in gold to France, and also indicated that the USA would 'let gold go willingly'. Finally on 9 and 10 November, the stock market, the commodity markets and the dollar all rallied strongly and the *NYT* noted that:

> Europe seems to have worked up enough excitement over the rumors of a further dollar devaluation to have raised some doubts about our attitude toward gold exports. The fact that the Treasury did not merely release the gold *but advertised the fact that it had done so* must have helped to discredit the rumors.
>
> (10/11/37, p. 39, italics added)

Devaluation rumours continued to recur throughout the first half of 1938. In late May, political problems associated with the Czech situation were blamed for stock and commodity prices declines, and the European political situation was blamed for an increase in gold hoarding in London. These falling commodity prices were blamed, in early June, for a new round of devaluation rumours, and modest stock price increases in early June were attributed to these rumours. The devaluation was rumoured to be likely to occur immediately after congressional adjournment, which occurred on 16 June. A stock market decline on 13 June was attributed to a denial of the rumour by Morgenthau, but administration denials were not regarded as sufficiently categorical, and uncertainty continued.

On about 20 June, two dramatic changes occurred which pushed stocks sharply higher over the following several weeks. First, on Sunday, 19 June, Wall Street began to receive reports that suggested business was beginning to recover from the recession. In addition, the dollar crisis came to a definitive conclusion. There had been no devaluation after the 16 June congressional adjournment, and on 20 June Morgenthau issued a much more forceful denial of rumours that the dollar might be devalued. The 21 June *NYT* noted that the rumours had been 'spiked with emphasis' and reported:

> Investors and traders in the security and commodity markets looked hopefully yesterday toward the probable effect of the government's spending-and-lending program on the ailing business situation and prices were strong all around. More official denials that dollar devaluation is a near-term prospect failed to lessen enthusiasm in the markets. On the contrary, the denials *aided* market sentiment.
>
> (*NYT*, p. 29, italics added)

There is a striking similarity between the 1938 summer rally in stocks and commodities and the August 1932 bull markets that were associated with the realisation that the dollar was again firmly tied to gold. On 22 June, the *NYT* reported (p. 35) that 'Dollar Continues Recovery on Assurances By Morgenthau Against Devaluation Move' and stocks and commodities continued to show gains. They also suggested that 'Foreign participation here coincided with the diminution of the hoarding demand for gold in London ... In other words, with the dollar devaluation topic laid on the shelf temporarily, at least, floating funds are drifting into equity investments.' The end of the last dollar crisis contributed to an extraordinary weekly gain of 15·3 per cent in the DOW. Over the next several years the US price level stabilised and the economy gradually recovered from the Depression.

Concluding remarks

In all of the preceding evidence there is really only one irrefutable fact: the devaluation of the dollar had a profoundly positive effect on US stock and commodity prices. Given this fact, it is hard to see how an increased expectation of dollar devaluation during the 1930s could have been anything but bullish for the stock market. Yet there is also strong circumstantial evidence that three of the most important runs on the dollar, in 1931, 1932 and late 1937, greatly depressed stock and commodity prices.

On theoretical grounds, the impact of an exchange rate crisis is ambiguous. The expectation of a change in the price of gold is expansionary, the resulting increase in the demand for gold is deflationary. The question of which effect is stronger may depend on a number of factors. These include the probability of devaluation, the likely date of devaluation and the elasticity of demand for gold with respect to expected changes in the price of gold. This elasticity will in turn depend on factors such as the nominal interest rate as well as on discretionary decisions by foreign central banks.

Exchange rate crises probably did not trigger the Great Depression, but they almost certainly did play a role in depressing aggregate demand during 1931–2 and again during 1937–8. There is a need for better theoretical models of the impact of exchange rate crises on the international price level.

Notes

1. Sumner also showed that the growth rate of the world monetary gold stock was negatively correlated with the (absolute value of the) forward discount on the US dollar or the French franc. These forward discounts are presumably a good proxy for the public's fear of devaluation.
2. These include the USA (1927–33), Britain (1927–31), France (1928–33), Germany (1927–31), Belgium (1927–33), Holland (1927–33) and Switzerland (1927–33). These countries possessed 70·1 per cent of the world monetary gold stock on 31 December 1929 and 76·8 per cent on 31 December 1933.
3. The gold stock declined by \$51·7 million, or about 0·4 per cent.

4. See Sumner (1997). The three-month forward discount on the pound (against the dollar) rose from less than ½ cent during the first half of 1931, to just over 2 cents in early August, and then stabilised at that level until right before the devaluation. Yet the actual spot exchange rate had declined by over 100 cents by the autumn of 1931. Thus the forward markets provide no evidence that a substantial devaluation was considered likely during the two months preceding the actual devaluation. Although the suspension of convertibility occurred on 20 September, word that the government was considering devaluation appeared to have leaked out several days earlier. The price of British government bonds (5½ per cent coupon), which had traded in the 104¾–105⅝ range throughout the first 17 days of September, fell to 101¼ on 18 September and then plunged to 93 on 19 September. Thus data from the British bond market complement the forward market evidence that a devaluation was not considered likely until the last moment.
5. See Sumner (1991).
6. The first discount rate increase (from 1·5 to 2·5 per cent) was announced at 3:30 pm on 8 October, and the DOW decreased by just over 1 per cent on the following day. A week later, the DOW actually increased by 3·8 per cent after an additional one percentage point increase in the discount rate.
7. Real stock prices were generated by deflating the Cowles Index by the National Industrial Conference Board's Cost of Living Index.
8. See Temin and Wigmore (1990) for a good discussion of this episode.
9. The first lag of the DOW is included to reflect the fact that the exchange rate is from European markets, which close long before the New York Stock Exchange.
10. Roosevelt's policy was very similar to Irving Fisher's famous 'Compensated Dollar Plan'. Prof. George Warren was regarded as the most forceful advocate of this plan within the 'Brain Trust'.
11. The only greater declines over any three-day period occurred during October 1929 and October 1987.

Bibliography

Bernanke, Ben S. (1995), 'The Macroeconomics of the Great Depression: A Comparative Approach', *Journal of Money, Credit and Banking*, 27.

Eichengreen, Barry (1992), *Golden Fetters: The Gold Standard and the Great Depression, 1919–1939*. New York: Oxford University Press.

Einzig, P. (1937), *Will Gold Depreciate?*, London: Macmillan.

Friedman, M. and A. Schwartz ([1963], 1971), *A Monetary History of the United States, 1867–1960*, Princeton: Princeton University Press.

Hawtrey, R.G. (1947), *The Gold Standard in Theory and Practice*, London: Longmans, Green.

Johnson, H. Clark (1997), *Gold, France, and the Great Depression*, New Haven: Yale University Press.

Silver, Stephen and Scott Sumner (1995), 'Nominal and Real Wage Cyclicality During the Interwar Period', *Southern Economic Journal*, 62.

Sumner, Scott (1991), 'The Equilibrium Approach to Discretionary Monetary Policy under an International Gold Standard: 1926–1932', *The Manchester School of Economic and Social Studies*, 59.

Sumner, Scott (1997), 'News, Financial Markets, and the Collapse of the Gold Standard: 1931–1932', *Research in Economic History*, 17.

Temin, Peter and Barrie Wigmore (1990), 'The End of One Big Deflation', *Explorations in Economic History*, 27.

Wicker, Elmus (1996), *The Banking Panics of the Great Depression*, Cambridge: Cambridge University Press.

Wigmore, Barrie (1987), 'Was the Bank Holiday of 1933 Caused by a Run on the Dollar?', *Journal of Economic History*, 47.

CHAPTER THREE

The political economy of money supply, exchange rate and inflation targets since Bretton Woods

Michael J. Oliver

Introduction

Following the breakdown of the Bretton Woods system in the early 1970s and the move to widespread floating, one of the biggest challenges facing economic policymakers was how to control inflation in a world without any internationally agreed monetary rules. The problem of inflation became increasingly pressing as changes in the pattern of world payments, increased global capital mobility and OPEC 1 combined to inflict nominal and real shocks on the international economic community.

The move to a floating exchange rate regime was accompanied by a recognition that the expansionist and activist policies of the 1950s and 1960s could no longer guarantee full employment, high rates of economic growth and price stability. As stagflation and the breakdown of the Phillips curve became widespread, Keynesian demand management policies were rejected in favour of new techniques which could control inflation. Since 1973, these techniques have broadly fallen into three groups, which can be identified and briefly summarised as follows.

Monetary targets

It was argued by the monetarists that there was a stable relationship between one or more monetary aggregates and the general level of prices. Monetary policy was directed at a particular rate of growth in the monetary aggregate (the intermediate target) compatible with low inflation. There was a gradual move towards monetary targets in many of the industrialised countries and, by the end of the 1970s, six of the G7 members had adopted targets. However, by the end of the 1980s, there had been a rapid downgrading of rigid monetary rules so that, by the early 1990s, monetary targets had been dropped by many countries in favour of exchange rate targets and inflation targets.

Exchange rate targets

The prospect of widespread floating rates led a core group of European countries to form a European Common Margins Agreement (the 'snake') which was designed to narrow the margin of fluctuation of EC member currencies below those set by the 1971 Smithsonian agreement. The Exchange Rate Mechanism (ERM) of the European Monetary System (EMS) was formed in 1979 and developed into a Deutschmark (DM) block during the 1980s where the DM was the key currency and member countries were required to follow the monetary policy of the Bundesbank. The intermediate target for members was to maintain an announced exchange rate against the DM, while the final objective was low inflation.

Inflation targets

Whereas monetary targets and exchange rate targets are weapons of control, an inflation target is a target and nothing else. Inflation targets have been a recent innovation, introduced when other techniques of monetary control have failed, for instance in the UK, Finland and Sweden in the wake of leaving the ERM, or in Canada following the failure of monetary targeting.

It must be noted that, while each of these regimes uses an explicit nominal anchor to achieve price stability, some countries have eschewed such a nominal anchor and instead rely on an implicit nominal anchor. The USA is perhaps the best example, where the Federal Reserve has adopted a strategy which involves forward-looking behaviour to monitor carefully signs of future inflation and conducts periodic pre-emptive strikes by raising interest rates if there appears to be a threat of inflation. While the pre-emptive strategy is a feature of inflation-targeting regimes, the USA does not have an official nominal anchor and its monetary policy regime is not as transparent as that of other countries which are under a regime of inflation targets. During the 1990s, the Federal Reserve was criticised for creating unnecessary volatility in financial markets because of this approach to policymaking and, arguably, the Federal Reserve is more prone to time-inconsistency problems than many other central banks.

This chapter does not intend to dwell on regimes which have used an implicit nominal anchor to achieve price stability and instead focuses on the first three techniques discussed above. In what follows, we first examine the theory underlying each technique, before turning to evaluate how these techniques have been implemented. While this chapter will draw on a number of country case studies, it will pay special attention to the UK, which has used all three techniques in the last 25 years as well as having an implicit nominal anchor between 1986 and 1990.

Theoretical considerations

The collapse of the Bretton Woods regime gave countries the freedom to employ their own devices to control inflation, although the abandonment of the fixed exchange rate coupled to the supply-side shocks of the early 1970s did lead to several problems for a number of OECD members.

Just before the collapse of the Bretton Woods regime, monetary policy was fairly expansionary in many industrial countries in response to the rising unemployment of the early 1970s. Thereafter it slowed significantly in Germany, Japan and the USA. Far from abusing its freedom from the external constraint, Germany used its monetary and fiscal policies to aim at a lower domestic inflation rate. Germany's success in achieving a current account surplus in 1974 placed further upward pressure on the Deutschmark (which made the external constraint more binding in those countries which were pegged to the Deutschmark).

Germany was one of the few countries which accepted quite rapidly that a nominal anchor was required to promote price stability and would act as a constraint on discretionary policy. In turn, the nominal anchor would help to reduce time-inconsistency problems and achieve long-run price stability. The shift towards rules-based approaches by many other countries (the apogee of which included the adoption of monetarism during the 1970s) was the result of a combination of factors. The work of Friedman and Schwartz seemed to show that there was a stable, lagged relationship in the USA between changes in the rate of growth of broad money and changes in nominal income, and that monetary policy mistakes had been made in the past; interest in monetary rules grew as inflation burgeoned following the first oil shock; and the discrediting of the long-run Phillips curve analysis which convinced policymakers that there were no benefits to allowing inflation to ratchet upwards. While strict monetary targets were eventually downgraded, the rules-based approach offered by monetary policy was continued in the form of exchange rate and inflation targets.

Before the practical implications of these policies are discussed, the underlying theory characterising each approach needs to be examined. We start by considering the Fleming (1962) and Mundell (1963) models which neatly married Keynesian demand management to economic policy during the Bretton Woods period.

The Fleming–Mundell model argued that, with a fixed exchange rate, any monetary expansion would cause interest rates in an economy to fall, followed by an increase in income and a deterioration in the capital and current accounts. As the central bank would seek to maintain the exchange rate by purchasing domestic currency (in accordance with Bretton Woods requirements), the foreign exchange reserves would be reduced and there would be a concomitant reduction in the supply of money. This process, known as sterilisation, can only work in the short run.

Sterilised intervention can be effected either through a compensating open market sale of domestic securities (an operation logically equivalent to offsetting reduction in the rate of domestic credit expansion) or by direct sales (or absence of purchases) by the authorities of the excess foreign exchange itself or by a combination of both methods. For a given inflation rate, the choice of one or the other method of sterilisation will result in a different combination of paths for domestic interest rates (which will be higher than otherwise in the case of offsetting open market sales of domestic securities) and for the exchange rate (which will be higher – that is, a more appreciated domestic currency – than otherwise in the case of offsetting sales or absence of purchases of foreign exchange). However, sterilised intervention may not be very effective in relieving pressure on the exchange rate beyond the short term and there will come a time when no amount of domestic credit expansion can compensate for the loss in the central bank's reserves. In practice, the currency markets will intervene before the reserves are exhausted and will sell all the currency they can at the existing exchange rate. Ultimately, an expansive monetary policy will be ineffective as the purchase of domestic bonds by the central bank will be offset by a loss of reserves, leaving the money supply, interest rates, income and the balance of payments unchanged.

However, if monetary expansion occurred under purely floating rates it would not be offset through the central bank's intervention (as there would be no exchange rate target). Instead, the interest rate in an economy would fall below international levels, there would be an outflow of capital and the exchange rate would depreciate. Following the depreciation, the demand for an economy's exports would increase and domestic income and employment would rise. The boost to demand would push the interest rate back to near its original level, with the effect of reducing the capital account deficit to a level where the current account surplus created by the depreciation in the currency is sufficient to cover it.

A variant on the Fleming–Mundell analysis is Mundell's (1960) 'Holy Trinity', more formally known as the 'assignment problem'. The Holy Trinity holds that policymakers can choose only two out of three policy options at any one time: free capital flows, a fixed exchange rate and monetary policy autonomy. Thus, if a country wishes to keep its exchange rate fixed in the context of international capital mobility, national monetary policy must be used to maintain exchange rate parity as in the above example, and cannot be directed towards other internal goals. Quite simply, in the Bretton Woods era the monetary authorities had a 'limited policy dilemma'. Concomitantly, in the absence of sufficient domestic institutional mechanisms to pre-commit the monetary authorities to low inflation, fixed exchange rate regimes offered a way to affect expectations of wage-setters and keep inflation down.

Although the scope for discretionary monetary management was limited under the Bretton Woods system until the late 1960s, it would be a gross simplification to describe it as absent. As is well known, the USA, which was the anchor of the Bretton Woods system, did not see the exchange rate as a constraint on monetary policy, particularly after the mid-1960s. Even for the other members of the system, there was considerable freedom for an independent monetary policy as long as the constraints of exchange controls and limited capital mobility persisted. One of the practical problems with the fixed exchange rate was that it was difficult to identify whether a deficit was either structural or merely short-term in nature on the current and capital accounts of the balance of payments. The Fleming–Mundell model tended to ignore the interaction between the current and capital accounts and, as such, it was essentially short-run in outlook.

As Andrew Crockett (1994, p. 173) has explained, most central banks operated monetary policy through the discretionary adjustment of interest rates in response to the perceived changes in aggregate demand conditions, for three reasons: first, because monetary policy was believed to be subservient in aggregate demand policy and the objective of macroeconomic policy was seen as the maintenance of full employment. Secondly, there was no empirical evidence which suggested a stable relationship between money and income. The final reason was the importance attached to funding the government's borrowing requirement as cheaply as possible, particularly important in the UK context.

The monetary approach to the balance of payments, developed from the late 1950s, concurred with the Keynesian conclusion about the impact of monetary policy in the open economy but showed that an excessive increase in the money supply would lead to a depreciation in the exchange rate and leave an economy with a higher price level (Johnson, 1972; Polak, 1957). The crucial difference between the monetarist and the Fleming–Mundell models is that the former argued that a monetary expansion affects prices rather than output in the long run. This argument attracted considerable interest when inflation rose in the six-year period after the 1967 devaluation in the UK, much as the monetarist model had predicted.

Indeed, monetarists had long stated that exchange rates should be allowed to float because the only appropriate policy target is the money supply. Where a totally flexible exchange rate prevails, the emergence of unanticipated capital flows would not influence the money supply as the external accounts would always balance. In these circumstances, what happens is that money and domestic credit expansion will coincide, and it can be argued that such coincidence renders money equivalent to domestic credit as a policy instrument. This is why the IMF favours domestic credit expansion (DCE) as a monetary aggregate: it chooses DCE rather than the growth of broad money as an intermediate target because a balance of payments deficit reduces the latter. At its simplest, a government can raise funds to finance excessive public expenditure by selling its foreign exchange reserves. The IMF obviously does not want this to happen. More generally, if the domestic supply of money in a country exceeds the domestic demand for money, some of the excess will tend to flow out of the country.

In a fully liberalised system with full convertibility on the current and capital accounts, the central bank *cannot* set an independent domestic monetary policy (whether on interest rates or the money supply) and an exchange rate target over a long period. Where market imperfections or administrative controls exist, the central bank will *temporarily* be able to set both domestic monetary policy and an exchange rate target. This is achieved through either sterilised intervention or the introduction of controls on foreigners' purchase of domestic financial assets, both of which are only effective in the short term.

Monetary targets do have an advantage over exchange rate targets in that they allow a central bank to adjust its monetary policy to domestic conditions but they are also similar because they both send almost immediate signals to the markets about the stance of monetary policy and the intentions of policymakers. Exchange rate targets are more transparent to the general public and financial markets and involve setting the exchange rate against a low inflation anchor country. More recently, some countries have adopted a crawling peg in which their currencies are allowed to depreciate at a steady rate so that their inflation can be higher than that of the anchor currency. Over time this will result in a convergence of tradable prices and price inflation to foreign levels, but it will not necessarily result in the convergence of overall domestic prices and price inflation.

Exchange rate targets have a long history, but as the international economy has moved away from the strict rules of the gold standard to the discretionary management of inconvertible paper money, there has been a greater emphasis placed on control of inflation through domestic means; that is, monetary targets and inflation targets.

Concentrating on monetary aggregates can only work if there is a strong and reliable relationship between nominal income or inflation and the target aggregates and if the central bank can effectively control the monetary aggregates. Monetary targets were adopted during the course of the 1970s when there were a number of constraints on domestic finance and velocity of circulation was predictable. However, as a number of countries underwent a process of financial liberalisation during the course of the 1980s, velocity became difficult to predict. Financial liberalisation can result in a permanent increase in broad money, so that the velocity of money declines. This would mean that an increase in broad money growth during the process of financial liberalisation may not be a guide to future inflation, and policy might be tightened unnecessarily. Conversely, when the demand for broad money declines and velocity increases, money growth will be more inflationary, and policy might be loosened unnecessarily.

Owing to the unpredictable nature of velocity and the difficulties associated with hitting the broad money targets precisely, the monetary authorities were forced to redefine the components of broad money aggregates while simultaneously introducing narrow monetary targets. The outcome was a loss of credibility in the authorities' monetary strategy, and intermediate monetary targets were abandoned in favour of intermediate exchange rate targets and, increasingly, final targets for future inflation.

Inflation targeting has a similar advantage to monetary targeting and contrasts to exchange rate targets in that it enables monetary policy to focus on domestic considerations and to respond to shocks in the domestic economy. The authorities also use all available information to determine the optimum setting for monetary policy, and velocity shocks are irrelevant because the strategy does not rely on a stable money–inflation relationship. Like exchange rate targeting, inflation targeting is also highly transparent (clear, simple and understandable) and central banks have even begun to produce regular inflation reports to improve the channels of communication between the general public, financial markets and the politicians.

However, every central bank has imperfect control over inflation and there are three reasons generally given as to why inflation control is imperfect. First, the lags between monetary policy actions and the effect on inflation are long and variable. Second, inflation is affected by things other than monetary policy such as fiscal policy and supply-side shocks, including changes in inflation expectations. These shocks invariably occur after the change in monetary policy but before the effect on inflation. Finally, economists are uncertain about the workings of the economy, including the transmission mechanism, and about the nature of the shocks affecting the economy.

Owing to the lags between changes in monetary policy and their impact on inflation, monetary policy is designed to be forward-looking. The procedure to determine what degree of monetary stringency is needed to achieve the inflation target is as follows. First, the authorities will prepare a forecast of inflation, for example, for one to two years, assuming an unchanged monetary policy. Second, they will estimate how future inflation is likely to be affected by changes in the current setting of interest rates. Third, they will set monetary policy conditions so that inflation projections meet the inflation target. If the inflation projection is above the target, monetary policy is tightened; if it is below, then it is loosened. So suppose a country has a target range for inflation, currently 0–4 per cent per year. In order to maximise the probability of inflation staying within this range, the authorities aim for a midpoint, 2 per cent per year.

Some critics have claimed that inflation targeting is heavily reliant on forecasting, and have argued that this is the fundamental weakness of the technique, as forecasts are unstable. Yet even monetary targets are based on the assumption about the relationship between current monetary growth and future inflation, and current interest rates and future monetary growth. Moreover, just as a monetary aggregate is the intermediate target in a strategy designed to control the growth of the money supply, so the inflation projection is the intermediate target in an inflation targeting regime. The authorities will adjust monetary policy conditions so that the corresponding inflation projection (the intermediate target variable) is on target at an appropriate horizon. By regarding the inflation projection as an intermediate target and adjusting monetary policy accordingly, this partly solves the problem of imperfect control of inflation.

The experience with money supply targets

The debate about whether to adopt monetary targets was protracted in several countries during the 1970s. For instance, in the USA, money targets could be traced back to the open-market directive of the 'proviso clause' in 1966 and then the 1970 provision for interim revisions of target money-market conditions when particular monetary aggregates departed from a specific range. In the British case, more attention was devoted to monetary aggregates following the 1971 reforms known as

Competition and Credit Control, although the Bank of England was quick to point out that the aggregates should be regarded 'as guide lines for overall policy rather than as targets' (Bank of England 1971, p. 44). In 1970, the council of the German Bundesbank was divided on the issue of whether or not to adopt monetarism, and it was largely through the strenuous efforts of its vice-president, Otmar Emminger, that monetarism was adopted in Germany. Indeed, as Johnson (1998, pp. 82–4) has detailed, in 1973 Emminger managed to push through a crucial vote to abandon the defence of fixed exchange rates and to adopt floating rates and money targets when two of his key opponents were in hospital and a third was on a skiing trip.

With the removal of the fixed exchange rate, the authorities in the UK, Germany and Switzerland acknowledged that they needed to provide some form of monetary discipline and, over a very short period of time, the behaviour of the money stock became the focus of central bank attention. The governor of the Bank of England in the annual Mais lecture of 1978 acknowledged that domestic monetary policy could provide the stability previously associated with fixed exchange rates. The adoption of a so-called 'aggregate strategy', as Price (1977) and Thunberg (1977) have shown, was generally attributed to the deficiency of interest rates as a monetary indicator under conditions of rapid inflation. However, in some countries, by the late 1970s, there did seem to be a certain amount of inconsistency in statements on monetary control: the British chancellor in 1979 told the House of Commons that monetary expansion would not accommodate inflation, and then went on to explain that the money supply growth rate would be reduced in direct response to declines in the rate of inflation. As Laidler (1974) has pointed out, official thinking in some American quarters implied that direct controls would permit deceleration of the high monetary growth rates without the short-run adjustment costs normally associated with deflation.

Perhaps some of this inconsistency arose because the authorities were unsure why they had introduced monetary targets. On the one hand, monetarists advocate a target for the money supply as an intermediate target for controlling nominal GDP. However, there is another reason why monetary targets can be adopted, and that is because such targets can be used for political purposes, in particular to influence expectations in financial markets in an attempt to stop them from behaving in an undesirable way (Pepper and Oliver, 1999a).

There are two ways of trying to ensure stable monetary growth. The North American and Swiss schools of monetarism argue that the stock of money in the economy (the money stock) should be regulated by the central bank controlling the *supply* of money; that is, the monetary base should be controlled. In contrast, the Bank of England has always argued that, if the money stock is be controlled, this should be achieved by operating on people's *demand* for money and that this should be done by altering interest rates. In the UK, the monetarists agreed that the money supply needed to be controlled, but there was a clear division between those who believed in demand-side control of the money stock and those who advocated supply-side control of the monetary base.

The floating of the pound in 1972 had implications for the conduct of British economic policy in general and for monetary policy in particular. The monetarists argued that an excessive increase in the money supply would lead to a depreciation in the exchange rate and leave the UK economy with a higher price level (Johnson, 1972). Yet the authorities showed little interest in controlling the money supply, as they had increased the lending power of the banking system in the spring of 1971. Coupled to the freeing of the pound, two big constraints on monetary policy had been abolished within a very short time and these were reinforced by the relaxation of controls on commercial rents and property development. The combination of falling interest rates in 1971–2 with an expanding bank and property market, led to a boom in house and property prices and an emerging current account deficit. Notwithstanding the imposition of quantitative restrictions on the banking system via the Supplementary Special Deposit Scheme (the 'corset') in December 1973, the rise in world commodity prices in the same year and the quadrupling of oil prices in 1973–4 added to the upward trend in inflation in the UK. Although inflation had reached its peak by 1975, the authorities were concerned by three developments: the growth of the public sector borrowing requirement (PSBR), the fall of sterling on the foreign exchanges, and the high rate of inflation. By December 1976, the IMF had agreed to help overcome the UK's worsening financial difficulties on condition that monetary targets were reintroduced and adhered to (Oliver, 1997; Pepper and Oliver, 1999a).

Soon after becoming prime minister, Margaret Thatcher commissioned an inquiry into monetary base control, and the conclusion was that the UK should not adopt this procedure. While the decision was reviewed on several occasions during the 1980s, monetary base control was not introduced in the UK, mainly as a result of the hostility of the Bank of England (Pepper and Oliver, 1999b).

The experiences of the UK in the 1980s can be divided into three phases (Oliver, 1997). During phase one (1979–83), the government's monetarist economic experiment faced two difficulties. First, the chosen monetary aggregate (£M3) consistently overshot its target band. This gave the impression that monetary policy was loose when in fact it was very tight, and merely encouraged a continuation of tight policies.

Secondly, the domestic economy underwent a period of rapid contraction which was exacerbated by the tight monetary regime. A debate opened in policymaking circles as to whether the government should adopt a different monetary target or abandon monetarism altogether.

In phase two (1983–6), the government began to get bogged down with the sterling issue and money technicalities. Those economic advisers who had been supporting the government began to argue for membership of the Exchange Rate Mechanism (ERM) as a means of stabilising currency fluctuations and controlling inflation. There were also widespread arguments beginning to appear in the monetarist camp over which money aggregates to aim at. The chancellor, Nigel Lawson, was left with the problem of having to choose between conflicting advice from the experts. From 1985, the money targets were suspended and policy become more pragmatic.

In phase three (1986–90), the government returned to crude demand management with macroeconomic policies set for a traditional 'stop–go' cycle. Conflicts in policy and personality became widespread, including the disagreements between the prime minister, her economic adviser, Alan Walters and Chancellor Lawson over whether the UK should join the ERM. It was during the course of phase three (between March 1987 and May 1988) that Chancellor Lawson came up against his greatest problems with the exchange rate versus the money supply dichotomy as he pursued an exercise in currency shadowing, undertaken to show the prime minister how well the economy could perform if it had the stability of the ERM.

In his *Tract on Monetary Reform*, first published in 1923, Keynes argued that the exchange rate

> cannot be stable unless both internal and external price levels remain stable. If, therefore, the external price level lies outside our control, we must submit either to our own internal price level or to our exchange being pulled about by external influences. *If the external price level is unstable we cannot keep both our own price level and our exchanges stable. And we are compelled to choose.*
>
> (Keynes, 1923, pp. 125–6; italics added)

The authorities had faced such a dilemma in 1977. As the exchange rate strengthened over the first half of the year, so the Bank of England intervened in the foreign exchange market to check the appreciation of sterling. The result was faster growth in the money supply than officials had planned (16 per cent outturn against a target range of 9–13 per cent in the 1977–8 financial year), which breached the strict requirements of the IMF programme. The choice between holding sterling at a competitive level and following the monetary targets was a difficult one and, while the authorities responded to the call from the monetarists and stopped the intervention for fear of higher inflation, some accounts of this episode have suggested the policy predicament was intense within the government.

From the writings of Keynes and the experiences of 1977, it had been made clear to the authorities that some form of money supply targeting was essential under a floating exchange rate and that any attempt to pursue exchange rate targets under a floating rate would result in unstable monetary growth and possibly higher inflation. Unfortunately, this lesson was forgotten 10 years later. As the pound appreciated between the Louvre Accord in February 1987 and the budget in March, Lawson cut interest rates by one percentage point, in two stages. The exchange markets believed that it was the intention of the chancellor to keep the sterling/Deutschmark rate below DM3·00 and, to prevent the rate from rising above DM3, the monetary authorities sold sterling and bought convertible currencies, but were later forced to cut interest rates to prevent the exchange rate from rising. The massive interventions by the Bank of England in the foreign exchange markets ultimately grew to such a level that Treasury and bank officials were becoming worried about sustaining them. For example, during the first four days of March 1988, more than $4 billion was spent on keeping sterling down, causing consternation within the Number 10 Policy Unit, with officials urging the chancellor to abandon targeting.

The problem with this policy was that, until the first quarter of 1988, the intervention was not sterilised, which failed to neutralise the monetary consequences. While interest rates were raised by one percentage point to 10 per cent in August 1987, this was done under the auspices of the 1987 Louvre agreement and not because of a fear of domestic overheating. From a political perspective it might have seemed wise to loosen monetary policy in the wake of Black Monday on 17 October 1987, but this was not justified economically. While the Federal Reserve tightened monetary policy in 1987, the shadowing exercise being pursued by the chancellor effectively ruled out higher interest rates. In short, excessive monetary growth was ignored and inflation then rose, more or less precisely in accordance with monetarist theory.

The US experiment with monetarism between October 1979 and May 1982 also had some similarities with the British experience, yet, in contrast to the Bank of England, the Federal Reserve attempted to control bank reserves, albeit in a peculiar way. The outcome was a huge rise in interest rates followed by huge fluctuations in interest rate movements. According to Poole (1982), the Fed's mechanism bore no resemblance to the textbook model of monetary base control and it was qualitatively very similar to the old interest rate mechanism. In short, there is some doubt about whether the Fed was seriously trying to control the base: the experiment may have been merely a political exercise which enabled the Fed to raise interest rates by more than would otherwise have been acceptable. The Fed may have been giving priority to the politics of money supply targets rather than control of the money supply in its own right (Pepper and Oliver, 1999b).

Equally, in Switzerland and Germany, the regimes have been very far removed from a Friedman-type monetary targeting rule. As Issing (1996, p. 120) notes, 'one of the secrets of success of the German policy of money-growth targeting was that ... it often did not feel bound by monetarist orthodoxy as far as its more technical details are concerned'. For instance, when Germany set its first monetary targets, it announced a medium-term inflation goal of 4 per cent, which was above what it considered to be the appropriate long-run goal for inflation, stating that the former was the 'unavoidable rate of price increase'. It took nine years before the medium-term inflation goal (then renamed as the 'normative rate of price increases') was considered to be consistent with price stability, which was perhaps the most gradual 'gradualist approach' to reducing inflation in the industrial world.

While the money supply target has been missed 50 per cent of the time since 1979, Germany's monetary targeting regime has resulted in low inflation (von Hagen, 1995). Yet, as Clarida and Gertler (1997) have argued, the Bundesbank has reacted asymmetrically to target misses, raising interest rates in response to overshooting of the money growth target and choosing not to lower interest rates in response to undershooting. Indeed, the Bundesbank was criticised for its particularly tight monetary stance in the mid-1990s – when German inflation had fallen below the 2 per cent normative goal – which led to an increase in unemployment in Germany and those countries tied to the Deutschmark.

Switzerland has had similar problems to the UK with its experience of monetary targets, but the National Bank pursued targets longer and more successfully than their British counterpart. Following the 40 per cent trade-weighted appreciation of the Swiss franc between 1977 and 1978, the authorities suspended monetary targets and moved to an exchange rate target until the spring of 1979, whereupon it reintroduced an unannounced monetary target. From 1980, the Swiss National Bank switched to monetary base control. Between 1989 and 1992, the authorities failed to maintain price stability, despite having reduced inflation. This was a result of two factors. First, the strength of the Swiss franc caused the authorities to allow the monetary base to grow at a faster rate. Secondly, a new inter-bank payment system was introduced, and a wide-ranging revision of the commercial banks' liquidity requirements in 1988. These factors contributed to an excessive loosening of monetary policy and a rise in inflation to above 5 per cent. Although inflation was subsequently controlled, the Swiss National Bank abandoned the one-year targets for money base growth and announced a new medium-term framework for money base growth.

Other European governments have been far from ideologically purist when they followed a more pragmatic approach to monetarism after the break-up of the Bretton Woods agreement. In the aftermath of the first oil crisis, monetary targets were seen as only one of numerous tools to achieve national economic goals. Moreover, European governments viewed the fixing of their exchange rate in the European Monetary System (EMS) as a way to reinforce the attempt to reduce inflation. This more pragmatic monetarism was promoted by experts in international organisations such as the OECD, in policy reports written for the European Community and in economic policy circles inside the national governments. The decision to pursue fixed exchange rates in the EMS was clear early on in the EMS debate, as the various OPTICA reports made clear in the mid-1970s.

An exchange rate discipline in Europe

Exchange rate targeting has several advantages and has been successfully adopted by many industrial countries as a more robust nominal anchor than monetary targets. The results of exchange rate targets are frequently impressive: for instance, when the UK pegged itself to the German mark between 1990 and 1992, inflation fell from 10 per cent to 3 per cent, respectively. When France first pegged the franc to the mark in 1987, inflation stood at 3 per cent, which was two percentage points above the German inflation rate. By 1992, its inflation rate was 2 per cent and below that in Germany.

Exchange rate targeting has also reduced inflation quickly in emerging market countries: Argentina's successful experience with a currency board is one such example. Inflation was reduced from an annual rate of over one thousand per cent in 1989 to under 5 per cent by the end of 1994. This was accompanied by economic growth averaging almost 8 per cent annually between 1991 and 1994. *Per contra*, although an exchange rate target might bring inflation down relatively quickly, many central banks in such economies do not have an established reputation for sound money. Consequently, a successful speculative attack can lead to a sharp depreciation of a currency which can result in resurgence of inflation. For instance, inflation in Mexico stood at an annual average of over 100 per cent prior to the adoption of exchange rate targets in 1988, but was in single digits by 1994; however, a foreign exchange crisis in 1994 led to a return to double digit inflation (50 per cent) by 1995.

The remainder of this section focuses on the experiences of Europe under exchange rate targets since the end of Bretton Woods, specifically the first proposals for monetary union, the evolution of the 'snake', the problems of the 1980s and the currency crises of the early 1990s.

According to Giavazzi and Giovannini (1989, p. 1):

> Europeans dislike exchange rate fluctuations for three reasons. First, they all live in relatively open countries. Second, many of them hold the floating rates of the 1920s and 1930s responsible for the ensuing collapse of national economies and of the international trading and monetary systems. Third, postwar European institutions – particularly the common agricultural market – depend for their survival on exchange rate stability.

Consequently, the unstable dollar and the disorderly revaluation of European currencies by the end of the 1960s prompted fears within Continental Europe that there would be a return to floating exchange rates. Anxious to avoid a widespread return to floating rates, the European Commission submitted a report in March 1970 (Commission of the European Communities, 1970) which proposed a three-stage approach to economic and monetary union (EMU), beginning in 1971 and ending in 1981. In the last stages, the report proposed that the margins of fluctuation of member countries' currencies should be eliminated, and that there should be an irrevocable fixing of parities. This was followed by the Werner Report, which examined in detail how EMU could be achieved in stages by 1980. The report did not recommend a single European currency or a European Central Bank but it did call for the centralisation of members' macroeconomic policies, politically responsible to the European Parliament. Ultimately, monetary union would entail 'the total and irreversible fixing of parity rates and the complete liberation of movements of capital' (Werner et al., 1970, chs 3, 10).

The Werner Plan was never implemented, for several reasons. First, while the exchange rate stability of the first half of the 1960s was achieved when domestic policy targets did not have to be sacrificed, in the 1970s European countries were desperate to hold on to their independence in setting macroeconomic policy in the wake of international disturbances. Second, the Community was also widened in 1973, when the original six members were joined by Denmark, Ireland and the UK. This enlargement further complicated integration efforts. Finally, but by no means least, the initial implementation stages of the Werner Plan would have coincided with the break-up of Bretton Woods.

The attempts to salvage the Bretton Woods system through the Smithsonian Agreement in December 1971 allowed member currencies to fluctuate by plus or minus 2·25 per cent, creating a band of 4·5 per cent around the dollar. Intra-European exchange rates were able to fluctuate by as much as plus or minus 4·5 per cent, or a 9 per cent variation. There was widespread agreement among EC officials and agricultural representatives that this potential 9 per cent variation was too wide to work alongside the CAP pricing system, as it would require large and continual adjustments to monetary compensation amounts payable to producers. This need for increased exchange rate stability was reinforced by the belief among economists and business leaders that growing intra-European trade flows would be disrupted by the potentially wide variance in European exchange rates.

Consequently, in March 1972, the six members of the EC and the three prospective members agreed to limit exchange rate fluctuations among the European currencies to plus or minus 1·123 per cent relative to one another. This became known as the 'snake in the tunnel' (or, more formally, the European Common Margins Agreement). The snake was the European currencies fluctuating within a narrow range of plus or minus 2·25 per cent (the snake), against the wider world of 4·5 per cent (the tunnel). While the European currencies would continue to fluctuate against the US dollar and other non-European currencies within the wider band, their intra-European fluctuations would be decreased.

The evolution of the snake in the 1970s did not bequeath Europe with solid foundations for European monetary union. Not only did the snake lose its tunnel when the European currencies accepted a joint float with the dollar in March 1973, but the snake soon mutated into little more than a Deutschmark zone (Tsoukalis, 1997, pp. 141–2). Concomitantly, there were frequent and large exchange rate adjustments and several countries showed schizophrenic tendencies by entering and then leaving the system.

It was perhaps unrealistic for the members of the snake to have expected anything less than disaster. Loose fiscal and monetary policies in several European countries in the mid-1970s were generating budget deficits and inflation. National governments ignored the prescriptions of the Werner Report for the harmonisation of fiscal and monetary policies for domestic reasons and were able to do this because the authorities in Brussels did not have the jurisdiction to press for the necessary adjustments (Gros and Thygesen, 1992). The weakness of the US dollar also had a destabilising influence on the exchange rates between European currencies: as financial assets were moving out of the US dollar and into strong European currencies, the divergence between weak and strong European currencies was accentuated, requiring enormous interventions and realignments to keep the European currencies within the snake margins. The result of divergences in members' monetary policies and economic performance between 1973 and 1979 can be clearly illustrated in the average annual rate of inflation, which was 11 per cent in France but only 4·7 per cent in Germany over this period. The revival of interest in EMU during the succeeding four years can be explained by two factors.

First was the initiative taken by the Dutch on assuming presidency of the EC in July 1976. To counter the violent movements in the lira and sterling which had occurred in the first half of the year, the Dutch government suggested that EC countries should move towards the adoption of so-called 'target zones' for their exchange rates. The idea was that countries would declare a zone within which they were aiming to contain their trade-weighted exchange rate and, if the rate moved outside the declared zone, there would be consultation at the EC level. While this proposal was rejected by Germany, the Council of Ministers encouraged the Commission, the Committee of Governors and the Monetary Committee to extend their consultation on exchange rate matters.

Secondly, the political climate was beginning to change, which slowly added momentum to the process. The centre right coalition in France was re-elected following the national parliamentary election in March 1978. This allowed President Valéry Giscard d'Estaing to continue with the Plan Barre which was designed to stabilise the French economy. Germany was encouraged by this development and, with this coupled to the growing conflicts with the USA, Chancellor Schmidt sought to establish a firmer and wider alliance within the EC. Chancellor Schmidt also recognised that political developments in Italy, where the Communist Party was brought into the government's parliamentary majority, called for a wider, more stable European political and economic framework. Schmidt later recalled, 'I had always regarded the EMS not only as a mere instrument to harmonise the economic policies of the EC member countries, but also as part of a broader strategy for political self-determination in Europe' (Fratianni and von Hagen, 1992, pp. 17–18).

Consequently, Germany became keener to link the Deutschmark to as many of the individually floating major EC currencies as possible, thereby insulating the German economy from the effects of a renewed dollar depreciation. While the UK favoured a more global approach, the dollar's instability and the political inclination of France and Germany concentrated discussions on a regional solution to exchange rate instability. Both France and Germany were more realistic than the British in making the assumption that the prospect of a reformed international monetary system was remote, although the British president of the European Commission, Roy Jenkins, was the catalyst for the relaunching of monetary integration. Thus the relaunching of monetary union in the late 1970s combined political and economic factors. On a political level,

Germany felt unease after the Bonn Summit in July 1978 that the USA had abdicated its role of western leadership and something had to be done to fill the vacuum. On the macroeconomic level, Germany and France in particular wanted exchange rate stability to be backed by an increased convergence between national economies, with greater emphasis placed on control of inflation.

The EMS was intended by the Commission and the main participants to lead on to a full Exchange Rate Mechanism (ERM) from which would emerge a European Monetary Fund (or European Central Bank). The European Monetary Fund would ultimately replace the European Monetary Cooperation Fund and manage the combined foreign exchange rate reserves of the members, to intervene in currency markets and to create ECU (European currency unit) reserves to serve as European Special Drawing Rights (SDRs). When domestic policies threatened currency pegs, strong-currency countries would expand and weak-currency countries would contract. Those that agreed to be part of the ERM would be required to have their currencies held within 2¼ per cent bands (those countries in a weak financial position were allowed to operate wider 6 per cent bands for a transitional period). Capital controls were permitted to allow governments to negotiate realignments while providing them with a degree of policy autonomy. While eight of the nine EC countries participated in the EMS from the beginning, only Britain decided not to join the ERM. For the majority of the EC, the time was now ripe to proceed to the next level of EMU.

In contrast to the UK and the USA who let their exchange rates float in the early 1980s, the EMS countries could not use 'shock therapy'. Shock therapy has the advantage of establishing the anti-inflation reputation of the authorities, thereby leading to a quicker reduction of inflationary expectations. In the EMS arrangement, gradualism has the disadvantage that the authorities gain an anti-inflation reputation slowly, with the result that inflationary expectations decline only slowly. Concomitantly, this forces the authorities to apply deflationary policies longer than if they had used shock therapy.

The persistence of inflation differentials across EMS countries during the first half of the 1980s meant that there was a need for exchange rate realignments. There were 11 EMS realignments from the inception of the EMS to January 1987 and a twelfth on 8 January 1990, when the Italian lira's wide band was replaced by the narrow EMS band. Over half the realignments for the entire period were clustered around the first five years of the EMS. With the second oil shock, which raised inflation, coupled to the deteriorating current accounts, stagnating output and rising unemployment in European countries, it was perhaps surprising that the ERM did manage to survive the first five years. Although the realignments were frequent, they were not always large enough to offset inflationary differentials with Germany.

Despite the poor outlook for economic growth in the recessionary conditions of the early 1980s, western Europe subsequently experienced nearly a decade of unbroken growth, weak at first in 1982–3, but averaging around 2·5 per cent (of GDP) a year over 1984–7 and then rising to 3 per cent or more in the latter years of the 1980s. Unemployment remained stubbornly high, however, and there was a growing belief that, unless the flexibility and efficiency of the labour market was improved, 'Eurosclerosis' would inevitably slow down the growth momentum. This fear, coupled to the reduced number of realignments in the EMS after 1983 and falling inflation rates, edged several European governments towards a renewed drive for European integration.

This drive culminated in the 1986 Single European Act which sought to create an integrated market, free of obstacles to the unimpeded movement of commodities, capital and labour by the end of 1992. Proponents of the Act argued that eliminating currency conversion costs was the only way of removing hidden barriers to internal economic flows, while abolishing the opportunity for countries to manipulate their exchange rates would prevent protectionist opposition to the liberalisation of trade. Consequently, the Act contained a reference to the October 1972 statement by heads of state and government approving the objective of economic and monetary union; this was followed by the setting up of the Delors Committee to examine how a single currency could be achieved within 10 years.

Unlike the Werner Report, the Delors Report (Committee for the Study of Economic and Monetary Union, 1989) recommended that capital controls should be abolished at the start of the transition to monetary union and that a centralised institution, the European Central Bank, should be responsible for executing the common monetary policy and for issuing a single European currency. As for fiscal policy, the report did not propose transferring control of national budgets to the EC, but recommended rules imposing ceilings on budget deficits and excluding governments' access to direct central bank credit and other forms of money financing.

Concurrently with the moves towards EMU, the ERM had also evolved from the mid-1980s. After the general realignment of parities in July 1985, and the devaluation of the French franc in 1986, 1987 marked the end of the 'old EMS' with a new realignment. The authorities argued that this realignment was necessary because of the declining dollar and self-fulfilling speculative expectations. What followed was a revision of EMS arrangements to strengthen intervention and to encourage policy coordination, with the resulting Basle–Nyborg Agreement in September 1987 allowing for the support of intermarginal intervention through Very Short-Term Financing (VSTF) and lengthening VSTF from one to three and a half months. This agreement provided for small realignments more frequently, but apart from the 1990 realignment of the lira, this option was discarded by policymakers (Eichengreen and Wyplosz, 1993). Consequently, by the start of the 1990s, the evolution of the EMS was about to take another turn which few saw at the time.

With hindsight, it is now clear that the apogee of the ERM was reached in the final years of the 1980s. Not only had the major participants achieved a substantial reduction in exchange rate variability over the 1980s, but the credibility of the mechanism steadily increased throughout its first 10 years (Giavazzi and Giovannini, 1989). By 1 July 1990, most members of the EMS had removed exchange and capital controls. Ironically, it was the removal of capital controls as part of the requirement of fulfilling the Single European Act which fatally undermined the viability of the 'old' EMS.

As is well known, the EMS was a mixture of pegged and adjustable exchange rate regimes. Periods of exchange rate stability provided many of the benefits of fixed exchange rates and the realignments readdressed serious competitiveness problems. The periods of exchange rate stability with the occasional realignment were only possible, however, because capital controls protected central banks' reserves against speculative attacks driven by anticipations of realignment (Eichengreen, 1993). In the first 10 years of the EMS's existence, the authorities did at least retain limited policy autonomy. Yet the 'new' ERM was described by some economists as 'half-baked' (Walters, 1988) and Padoa-Schioppa (1988) pointed out that there was now an 'inconsistent quartet' of policy objectives: free trade, capital mobility, fixed (managed) exchange rates and independent monetary policies. Thus Spain, the UK and Portugal all joined the ERM just when the system was about to become more volatile but appeared more stable. While the strategy of no realignments and no controls did seem to work for a while, the Jeremiahs' predictions eventually unfolded during the early 1990s.

A major problem with exchange rate targeting is that there is a loss of independent monetary policy. While there might be a considerable advantage in 'tying one's hands' to those of an anchor currency, an exchange rate target does mean that shocks to the anchor country are directly transmitted to the targeting country because changes in interest rates in the anchor country lead to a corresponding change in interest rates in the targeting country. This problem was cruelly demonstrated when German short-term and long-term interest rates began to rise in the wake of reunification in 1990 and were transmitted directly to the other countries in the ERM who were pegged to the mark and who also had to raise interest rates.

This then led to a practical demonstration of another major weakness of exchange rate targets discussed earlier in the case of Mexico, namely speculative attacks on currencies (Obstfeld, 1996). As member countries struggled to maintain their parities within the ERM, speculators began to question how long such a commitment could last in the wake of rising unemployment. In short, it was only a matter of time before the British pound, French franc, Swedish krona, Italian lira and the Spanish peseta would be devalued against the mark, and selling these currencies enabled speculators to make high profits with little risk. By September 1992, only France was able to sustain her commitment to the fixed exchange rate, while the aforementioned members decided to suspend their ERM membership.

With the advantage of five years of hindsight, the perverse outcome of the collapse of the ERM in 1992 was that it made monetary unification inevitable. In the 'old EMS', capital controls guarded central banks' reserves from speculators, but, once these had been abolished in the 'new EMS', the system collapsed. To resolve this problem, there were two solutions. One was to return to floating exchange rates. Arguably, with floating rates countries can still integrate their economies while retaining monetary autonomy (as with Canada, Mexico and the USA in the North American Free Trade Area). However, in Europe the calls for greater exchange rate stability arose because of the problems associated with floating rates and the Common Agricultural Policy (CAP), coupled to the *sentiment* that fixed rates are preferable to floating rates. The second solution was to fix irrevocably exchange rates between existing national currencies. Yet in this instance there will always be the possibility that exchange rates will change in the future under dire circumstances (the 'escape clause') and, because such circumstances are often unobservable, nominal exchange rates may end up being destabilised (Obstfeld, 1992). In short, an irrevocably fixed exchange rate system has less credibility than a system in which the countries share a common currency.

Inflation targets

From the early 1990s, several countries began to announce quantitative inflation targets. The first country to introduce inflation targets was New Zealand in March 1990, and other countries which have introduced them include Canada (February 1991), Australia (about April 1993), Israel (1992), Sweden (January 1993) and the United Kingdom (October

1992). Finland took up inflation targets temporarily, but then returned to a fixed exchange rate when it joined the European single currency. While it is too soon to provide a detailed assessment of the experience with inflation targets within each country, several points can be raised.

First, in many cases, inflation targets have been introduced when other monetary policy techniques have failed. In the case of New Zealand and Canada, disappointment with monetary targeting led to the switch: the Governor of the Bank of Canada, Gerald Bouey, conceding that 'we didn't abandon monetary targets, they abandoned us' (quoted in Allen, 1999, p. 6). For the UK, Sweden and Finland, inflation targets were seen as a way of providing a new nominal anchor, having been forced off fixed exchange rates.

Second, the horizon of the inflation target varies in each country. For example, in Canada and New Zealand, 18 months was allowed for the achievement of the initial target; thereafter, targets were set at 18-month and 12-month intervals, respectively. In the UK, the first target was set as early-to-mid-1997, and following the Bank of England Act (1998), the inflation target was set at 2·5 per cent at all times. Similar time horizons are found in other countries, although Australia is different because the time horizon for the inflation target is the length of the business cycle.

Third, the move to inflation targets has also coincided with a decision by many authorities to promote openness and transparency, which is an effective means of improving credibility. For instance, in the UK the Bank of England publishes a quarterly *Inflation Report*, outlining the Monetary Policy Committee's (MPC) analysis of recent economic developments and a forecast of inflation and output growth over the coming two years. The minutes of the monthly MPC meetings are published within six weeks of each meeting, and the members of the MPC are regularly questioned by the Treasury Select Committee. MPC members make frequent speeches about monetary policy in all parts of the country and these are published on the web pages of the Bank of England and the Treasury. Moreover, if the rate of inflation does stray from the target by more than plus or minus 1 per cent, the governor of the bank has to write an open letter to the chancellor explaining how the discrepancy arose, how long it is expected to last and how the MPC will correct it. As Vickers (1998, p. 370) has acknowledged, however, there is some information relevant for policymaking which is 'simply incapable' of being made public, so that the optimal monetary policy can never be absolutely transparent.

Fourth, all of the countries pursuing inflation targets have chosen to set targets above zero, ranging from 1·5 per cent in the case of New Zealand to 8·5 per cent in Israel. Arguably, targeting inflation above zero diminishes the possibility of negative effects on real economic activity

Table 3.1 Average inflation performance in inflation-targeting countries

	Decade preceding inflation target		*Period following inflation target*	
	Average rate of inflation	*Variance*	*Average rate of inflation*	*Variance*
Australia	6·2	8·41	2·7	1·71
Canada	5·8	7·90	2·0	2·51
Finland	5·2	3·37	1·1	0·51
Sweden	6·6	6·65	2·3	2·29
New Zealand	11·6	25·70	2·5	2·70
UK	5·2	2·21	2·8	0·09
Average	6·8	9·0	2·2	1·60

Source: Adapted from King (1997, p. 436).

and some recent evidence has suggested that this does not lead to instability in inflation expectations or a decline in the central bank's credibility (Laubach and Posen, 1997).

Finally, it is important to ask how successful inflation targets have been. The oldest regime is not 10 years old at the time of writing, so any evaluation must be preliminary and requires several business cycles before a reliable appraisal can be made. However, as Table 3.1 shows, inflation has been more than halved in comparison with the preceding decade and, as Table 3.2 indicates, the reduction in inflation has not come at the expense of either average output growth or greater variability in output.

As King (1997) notes, however, the UK has benefited considerably from a large appreciation of sterling since 1996 and falls in world commodity prices. Consequently, the imported component of UK inflation has been negative but overall inflation has not fallen below target. In other words, domestically generated inflation must have been significantly above target, and leaves the possibility that, without greater control of domestically generated inflation, overall inflation might escalate in the absence of the favourable external effects.

While Friedman and Kuttner (1993) have criticised inflation targeting because it imposes a rigid monetary rule on policymakers and stymies any form of discretion even in the event of unforeseen circumstances, this is not necessarily the case. Central banks do take into account a variety of information when setting the targets, and modify the targets according

Table 3.2 Average GDP growth in inflation-targeting countries

	Decade preceding inflation target		*Period following inflation target*	
	Average rate of GDP growth	*Variance*	*Average rate of GDP growth*	*Variance*
Australia	3·2	10·18	4·2	0·96
Canada	2·8	9·99	1·9	3·09
Finland	1·4	17·33	3·2	6·49
Sweden	1·6	4·73	1·9	5·09
New Zealand	1·8	6·95	2·4	7·78
UK	2·4	5·76	3·0	1·04
Average	2·2	9·2	2·8	4·1

Source: Adapted from King (1997, p. 436).

to economic circumstances. Yet, given the forward-looking nature of this strategy, it is not correct to conclude that the inflation targets are either subject to time-inconsistent problems or are rigid rules.

Conclusions

Since the break-up of the Bretton Woods fixed exchange rate system, broadly speaking the industrial countries have chosen to set targets for either the money supply, exchange rate or inflation to limit the increases in prices.

The problem with the money supply targets for many countries was that, when wide monetary aggregates were chosen, the targets were more visible but their controllability was lower. Ultimately, monetary targets became discredited. Even controlling high-powered money (the monetary base) has not been problem-free, as the case of Switzerland has shown.

The use of an exchange rate target eliminates the trade-off between controllability and visibility which exists with an inflation target or a money supply target. The exchange rate target is fully controllable (provided that there are sufficient foreign exchange reserves) and highly visible. However, an exchange rate anchor creates other trade-offs, for example in the area of the balance of payments, and there is a loss of independent monetary policy.

While inflation targets are at present in vogue with several monetary authorities, not all countries need to have this framework for the successful conduct of monetary policy (exceptions include Germany and the USA). In countries where the credibility of monetary policy is in question, and the reputation of the central bank poor, inflation targeting has controlled the growth of inflation. In the long run, however, the single most important element in any anti-inflation strategy is the degree of commitment of the central bank to achieve low inflation. The jury is still out on whether inflation targets can deliver low inflation over longer time periods, and whether central banks are prepared to persevere with this technique.

References

Allen, W.A. (1999), *Inflation Targeting: The British Experience*, London: Bank of England.

Bank of England (1971), 'Monetary Management in the United Kingdom', *Bank of England Quarterly Bulletin*, 11.

Clarida, R. and M. Gertler (1997), 'How the Bundesbank Conducts Monetary Policy', in Christina D. Romer and David H. Romer (eds), *Reducing Inflation: Motivation and Strategy*, Chicago, IL: University of Chicago Press.

Commission of the European Communities (1970), 'A Plan for the Phased Establishment of an Economic and Monetary Union', *Bulletin of the European Communities* (supplement), 3.

Commission of the European Communities (1989), *Report on Economic and Monetary Union in the European Community*, Luxembourg: Office for Official Publications of the European Communities.

Crockett, A. (1994), 'Rules versus Discretion in Monetary Policy', in J. Onno de Beaufort Wijnholds, Sylvester C.W. Eijffinger and Lex H. Hoogduin (eds), *A Framework for Monetary Stability*, Dordrecht: Kluwer Academic Publishers.

Eichengreen, B. (1993), 'European Monetary Unification', *Journal of Economic Literature*, 31.

Eichengreen, Barry J. and C. Wyplosz (1993), *The Unstable EMS*, London: Centre for Economic Policy Research.

Fleming, J.M. (1962), 'Domestic Financial Policies Under Fixed and Floating Exchange Rates', *IMF Staff Papers*, 9.

Fratianni, Michele, Jürgen von Hagen and Christopher Waller (1992), *From EMS to EMU*, London: Centre for Economic Research.

Friedman, B.M. and K.N. Kuttner (1993), 'Another Look at the Evidence on Money–Income Causality', *Journal of Econometrics*, 57.

Giavazzi, F. and A. Giovannini, A. (1989), *Limiting Exchange Rate Flexibility: the European Monetary System*, Cambridge, MA: MIT Press.

Gros, Daniel and Niels Thygesen (1992), *European Monetary Integration: from the European Monetary System to the Monetary Union*, Harlow: Longman.

Issing, O. (1996), 'Is Monetary Targeting in Germany Still Adequate?', in Horst Sibert (ed.), *Monetary Policy in an Integrated World Economy*, Tübingen: Mohr.

Johnson, H. (1972), 'The Monetary Approach to Balance of Payments Theory', *Further Essays in Monetary Economics*, London: Allen and Unwin.

Johnson, P.A. (1998), *The Government of Money: Monetarism in Germany and the United States*. Ithaca, NY: Cornell University Press.

Keynes, J.M. (1923), *A Tract on Monetary Reform*, reprinted in *The Collected Writings of John Maynard Keynes, Vol. IV*, Basingstoke: Macmillan.

King, M. (1997), 'The Inflation Target Five Years On', *Bank of England Quarterly Bulletin*, 37.

Laidler, D.E.W. (1974), 'Two Issues in the Economic Report of the President, 1973: The Control of Inflation and the Future of the International Monetary System', *American Economic Review*, 64.

Laubach, T. and A.S. Posen (1997), 'Some Comparative Evidence on the Effectiveness of Inflation Targeting', working paper, 97–14, Federal Reserve Bank of New York.

Mundell, R. (1960), 'The Monetary Dynamics of International Adjustment under Fixed and Flexible Exchange Rates', *Quarterly Journal of Economics*, 74.

Mundell, R.A. (1963), 'Capital Mobility and Stabilisation Policy Under Fixed and Flexible Exchange Rates', *Canadian Journal of Economics and Political Science*, 29.

Obstfeld, M. (1992), 'Destabilising Effects of Exchange Rate Escape Clauses', NBER Working Paper, no. 3606, Cambridge, MA: National Bureau of Economic Research.

Obstfeld, M. (1996), 'Models of Currency Crises with Self-Fulfilling Features', *European Economic Review*, 40.

Oliver, M.J. (1997), *Whatever Happened To 'Monetarism?*, Aldershot: Ashgate Publishing.

Padoa-Schioppa, T. (1988), 'The European Monetary System: A Long-Term View', in F. Giavazzi, S. Micossi and M. Miller (eds), *The European Monetary System*, Cambridge: Cambridge University Press.

Pepper, G.T and M.J. Oliver (1999a), 'Monetary Targets: An Unfinished Experiment', *Economic Affairs*, 19.

Pepper, G.T. and M.J. Oliver (1999b), *Monetarism Under Thatcher – Unfinished Business*, London: IEA.

Polak, J. (1957), 'Monetary Analysis of Income Formation and Payments Problems', *IMF Staff Papers*, 6.

Poole, W. (1982), 'Federal Reserve Operating Procedures: A Survey and Evaluation of the Historical Record Since October 1979', *Journal of Money, Credit and Banking*, 14.

Price, L.D.D. (1977), 'Monetary Objectives and Instruments in the United Kingdom', *Cahiers Economiques et Monétaires*, 6.

Thunberg, R. (1977), 'Monetary Objectives and Instruments in the United States', *Cahiers Economiques et Monétaires*, 6.

Tsoukalis, Loukas (1997), *The New European Economy Revisited*, 3rd edn, Oxford: Oxford University Press.

Vickers, J. (1998), 'Inflation Targeting in Practice: the UK Experience', *Bank of England Quarterly Bulletin*, 38.

von Hagen, J. (1995), 'Inflation and Monetary Targeting in Germany', in Leonardo Leiderman and Lars E.O. Svensson (eds), *Inflation Targets*, London: CEPR.

Walters, A.A. (1988), 'Money on a Roller-Coaster', *The Independent*, 14 July.

Werner, P., H. Ansiaux, G. Brouwers, B. Clappier, U. Mosca, J.B. Schöllhorn and G. Stammati (1970), *Report to the Council and the Commission on the Realisation by Stages of Economic and Monetary Union in the Community*, Supplement to Bulletin II-1970 of the European Communities, Brussels: European Community.

CHAPTER FOUR

European monetary union: does recent economic history in the UK suggest that exchange rates pose significant trade barriers?

Allan Webster

Introduction

This chapter is concerned with using the evidence of recent economic history in the UK to establish whether membership of the European monetary union would be likely to produce significant benefits. The focus of the chapter is microeconomic. That is, it starts from a position that the literature concerning the potential macroeconomic benefits suggests that membership of the monetary union would yield at least highly debatable benefits and, more likely, would involve economic costs. The literature concerning microeconomic benefits, which arise from the removal of barriers to trade created by exchange rates, provides a less ambiguous case for supposing that potential gains exist from membership of the monetary union. The critical question, therefore, is whether these microeconomic benefits are likely to be sufficient to offset macroeconomic costs (if there are any) or, at least, to nullify doubts arising from the risk that macroeconomic costs might arise.

The object of this chapter is to use evidence from the recent history of the UK to establish how important the microeconomic costs of exchange rates have been. This provides a basis for making a broad assessment of the likely gains to be secured from abolishing exchange rates between the UK and the relevant European countries.

The approach of the chapter is in five stages. In the next section a brief review of the main macroeconomic issues is provided. This is intended neither to be a comprehensive treatment of the macroeconomics of monetary union nor even necessarily to provide a balanced treatment of the issues. It serves only to demonstrate that it is possible to make a case that the microeconomic issues are of particular importance. In the third section a brief summary of the literature concerning the nature of the microeconomic costs – transactions costs and risk – of exchange rates is provided with a summary of available quantitative evidence on their magnitude.

The fourth section summarises the relevant aspects of the theory of trade policy. This provides a basis for understanding how any trade barriers arising from the microeconomic costs of exchange rates would adversely affect the UK economy. That is, the microeconomic case for monetary union is that exchange rates create trade barriers and, because trade barriers have adverse effects, these barriers could gainfully be removed. In the fifth section simulations of key measures of trade policy are provided for the UK in 1989 and 1990. These provide an indication of the extent to which trade barriers caused by exchange rates have been historically significant for the UK. Finally, in the sixth section, the analysis is concluded and the implications for monetary union are outlined.

Macroeconomic issues

The object of this section is to demonstrate that it is possible to adopt a point of view in which the macroeconomic gains from monetary union are debatable or negative and, therefore, the existence of microeconomic benefits is critical for the issue of membership. This section does not attempt to provide either a comprehensive or a balanced view of the macroeconomic issues. Readers desiring a good general summary of these issues are referred to Crawford (1996).

Probably the most common macroeconomic justification for monetary union has been the control of inflation. If we presume that purchasing power parity holds between European economies over the long run, this would imply that

$$p_d = p_f + e, \tag{4.1}$$

where p_d is the (percentage) domestic rate of inflation, p_f the rate of inflation in the foreign country and e the percentage change in the exchange rate.

Note that, if e is eliminated by virtue of monetary union, purchasing power parity predicts that rates of inflation will be equalised between the two countries over the long run. If the domestic country initially has a higher rate of inflation than the partner country this would normally mean that it would achieve a lower rate of inflation as a result of monetary integration. However, it would also mean that, under normal conditions, the partner country would also face a resulting higher rate of inflation. For monetary union to offer lower inflation for high inflation countries it is, therefore, necessary that low inflation countries be prepared to accept an increase in their own inflation rates. The existence of convergence criteria for European monetary union which impose not only inflation but also monetary and fiscal criteria suggests the contrary. That is, the convergence criteria at least reduce and, possibly, eliminate any potential gain by exporting inflation to partner countries.

An alternative argument is that creation of a monetary union removes monetary policy from national political control and, hence, prevents inflationary surges associated with the political cycle. This is certainly an argument for an independent central bank but it is not necessary to form a monetary union in order to have an independent central bank.

Whether or not monetary union is likely to lead to gains in the control of inflation is immaterial if membership is anyway unlikely to impose significant transitional costs. The standard theory in this respect is that of the optimum currency area as put forward by Mundell (1961). According to this approach two or more countries represent an optimum currency area if there is a high degree of labour mobility between them. That is, if labour can move freely between contracting and expanding regions, transitional costs will be small. However, given the number of different languages, cultures and practices within the European Union it is difficult to imagine that labour could be even approximately perfectly mobile between member states.

Even without perfect labour mobility the European Union could still represent an optimum currency area if one of two main alternative conditions were satisfied, namely that free movement of goods substitute for free movement of factors, or wages are flexible downwards. Whether or not either of these alternatives is satisfied for the European Union in the short run is debatable, although a better case could be made for the long run. That is, the possibility that monetary union would impose significant macroeconomic costs in a transitional period cannot be discounted.

To summarise, in this section it has been argued that the proposed macroeconomic gains of monetary union in the form of reduced inflation can be subject to doubt. At the same time it could also be argued that there is a possibility of significant transitional costs. Clearly, this is not the only possible point of view and is not necessarily even the view of the author. The point is that the proposed macroeconomic benefits of monetary union can be subjected to significant doubts. For the argument for monetary union to be wholly convincing there must be further reasons – potential microeconomic gains – to suppose that potential gains exist overall.

Microeconomic gains

The case that there are potential microeconomic gains from monetary union rests upon the argument that exchange rates create barriers to international trade. Specifically, they are argued to create trade barriers in two ways, through the transactions costs associated with foreign exchange transactions, and exchange rate risk. The transactions costs are, in principle, simple. Banks charge for the service of converting one money into another either through commission charges or, more normally, by buying and selling at rates which allow them a margin above or below the market exchange rate. In practice, it is not easy to measure these transactions costs because the bank's commission or margin is often proportionately less for large transactions than for small ones.

Crawford (1996) outlines three types of exchange rate risk: transactions risk, translation risk and competitiveness risk. Transactions risk is the risk arising from changes in the exchange rate which would affect the domestic currency value of future transactions to which the firm is committed. Firms can avoid this risk either by hedging or by the use of forward markets. However, there are two possible problems with this. Firstly, as Crawford (ibid.) argues, forward transactions are often expensive or difficult to obtain for small amounts of currency. This would suggest that it may only be possible for larger firms to offset this risk.

Secondly, even if forward markets are used to offset this risk, they will only do so at an appropriate premium. As is discussed further in the fifth section of this chapter, forward premia or discounts on exchange rates have been shown to comprise two elements: the difference between the expected future exchange rate and the current rate plus a risk premium. For the purposes of this chapter, this risk premium will be taken as the appropriate cost to firms of exchange rate risk. Firms can offset transactions risk by engaging in forward transactions. In this case they must pay the appropriate risk premium. If, however, they choose not to undertake forward transactions, or are unable to do so, these firms will face risk. In this case the appropriate way to assign a cost to this risk would be to take the market price of risk associated with the currency concerned. Thus, whether or not firms actually use forward markets to offset transactions risk, the appropriate cost of this is the risk premium determined by these forward markets.

Translation risk concerns the firm's accounts and arises from the impact of exchange rate changes on the domestic currency value of net assets and earnings. This may include some transactions risk, for example, on the domestic currency value of future earnings. However, as Crawford (ibid.) notes, under normal circumstances companies can ignore the risk of any impact on their balance sheet under current accounting regulations and translation risk can be largely ignored.

Competitiveness risk concerns the impact of exchange rate changes on the costs of the firm. As Crawford (ibid.) points out, competitiveness risk arises, not from changes in bilateral nominal exchange rates, but from changes in multilateral real exchange rates. The real exchange rate (RE) is normally defined as

$$RE = (P^* s)/P, \quad (4.2)$$

where P^* is the price level of foreign output, s the nominal exchange rate and P the price level of domestic output.

It is immediately clear that this risk could only be partially addressed by European monetary union. Monetary integration would remove short-run variations in nominal exchange rates but not necessarily in national price levels. European monetary integration would also only remove the risk of changes in nominal exchange rates for member currencies; the exclusion of a number of important world currencies would mean that it could not provide a comprehensive stabilisation of multilateral rates.

A case could even be made that nominal exchange rates provide some stabilisation of the real exchange rate. Indeed, a number of economists have recommended flexible nominal exchange rates as a means of preventing the gradual erosion of competitiveness through inflationary pressures. Suppose, for example, that goods prices adjust more slowly than exchange rates and that purchasing power parity (see equation (4.1)) holds in the medium to long term. Suppose also that there is a shock which increases domestic inflation such that the purchasing power parity condition no longer holds in the short run. Without nominal exchange rates, domestic and foreign inflation rates must adjust to restore purchasing power parity and the initial real exchange rate. With nominal exchange rates this adjustment can be made by an exchange rate depreciation which, since exchange rates are assumed to adjust more quickly than goods prices, would restore purchasing power parity and the initial real exchange rate more quickly.

In conclusion, the view taken by this chapter is that translation risk is no longer of particular relevance and that the case for including competitiveness risk as a cost which European monetary integration would eliminate or substantially reduce is sufficiently debatable for it to be excluded. This means that the existence of nominal exchange rates is presumed to create two types of cost: direct transactions cost and the cost of transactions risk, whether or not firms use forward markets to offset this risk.

The theory of trade policy

This section reviews the key findings of the theory of trade policy which are relevant to the discussion of trade barriers as posed by exchange rates. This is intended to provide the basis for assessing the potential benefits from eliminating exchange rates between European countries and, hence, the barriers to trade that they create.

Exchange rates impose costs in the form of exchange rate risk and transactions costs which are borne by imports but not by domestic supply. In this respect they have a protective effect similar to an import tariff. However, exchange rates also create essentially the same set of costs for exporters and, therefore, also have an effect similar to an export tax. The remainder of this section traces the economic implications of these effects in terms of the standard theory of trade policy.

Nominal and true rates of protection

In the theory of trade policy the first concept of relevance is the nominal rate of protection (NRP). This is defined as

$$NRP_j = [(P_{jd} - P_{jw})/\ P_{jw}].100, \tag{4.3}$$

where P_{jd} is the domestic price of good *j* and P_{jw} the 'world' price of good *j*. Thus import competing producers can charge a higher price than that for imports in the domestic market because imports must bear the costs of exchange rates. Consequently, the nominal rate of protection is positive. Assuming that the UK faces given European prices (that is, it is a price taker in European markets) this means that UK producers can charge higher prices in domestic markets than they would otherwise be able to ($P_{jd} > P_{iw}$). Note, however, that if the UK faces given prices in European markets, exporters would have to absorb the costs of exchange rates by charging prices which are lower than prevailing European prices by the amount of these costs per unit ($P_{jx} < P_{jw}$), where P_{jx} is the domestic price for export markets. In this case the nominal rate of protection would be negative.

The theory of trade policy predicts that the existence of a positive nominal rate of protection will have four main effects in a partial equilibrium context (that is, in the terms of the domestic market for a single good):

1. a transfer of economic welfare from consumers to producers because consumers must pay higher prices than they otherwise would;

2. a transfer from consumers, who ultimately bear the exchange rate costs, to the financial sector;
3. a net loss of economic welfare arising from the substitution of higher cost domestic production for lower cost imports; and
4. a net loss of economic welfare arising from restricted consumption choices.

Readers desiring a more detailed discussion of these points are referred to a specialist text on the subject such as that by Greenaway (1983). For the reasons listed above, the first conclusion of the theory of trade policy is that trade barriers should, on balance, be as low as possible.

Trade barriers can also affect relative prices and, hence, production decisions. They are likely to do so in a number of ways. Firstly, they affect relative prices between broad aggregates of goods. Thus the trade barriers created by exchange rates, as discussed earlier, raise the price in domestic markets of importable goods and lower the price of exportable goods. This means that the price of importables relative to exportables is raised by the existence of exchange rates and, consequently, production incentives are distorted in favour of importables and against exportables.

For an import tariff, which raises only the domestic price of imports and does not affect export prices, this effect is known as an export tax effect. Note, however, that trade barriers created by exchange rates, unlike an import tariff, also directly lower the price of exportables. In this sense they can be argued to have a double export tax effect.

Non-tradable goods and services are not directly affected by trade barriers by definition. However, the rise in the price of importables leads to an initial increase in their price relative to non-tradables. This provides incentives for producers to switch from non-tradables to importables and for consumers to switch from importables to non-tradables. Under normal conditions the resulting reduction in the supply and increase in the demand for non-tradables would result in a secondary increase in the price of non-tradables. Import barriers, therefore, also imply that the price of non-tradables will be distorted relative to exportables. The increase in price of importables relative to non-tradables is, after Clements and Sjaastad (1984), known as the true rate of protection. The true rate of protection will normally be less than the nominal rate because of the secondary increase in the price of non-tradables.

The case of trade barriers arising from exchange rates is again different because they lower export prices as well as raising domestic prices of imported competing goods. Specifically, the price of exportables would initially lower the price of exportables relative to non-tradables. This would provide incentives for producers to switch from exportables to non-tradables and for consumers to switch from non-tradables to exportables. The effects on the market for non-tradables are, therefore, the reverse of those arising from the price-raising effect of importables. Under normal conditions this would mean that the secondary increase in the price of non-tradables arising from the increase in the price of importables is offset or dampened by the secondary effects of the reduction in export prices. For this reason, secondary effects on non-tradable prices are likely to represent lesser distortions in the case of exchange rate barriers and, consequently, are not examined further in this chapter.

Trade barriers also create an anti-export bias in a different sense. Leaving aside the effects on relative prices between broad aggregates of goods, they also create a difference between the price of the same good on different markets. An import tariff, by raising the price on the domestic market, makes the home market more attractive to domestic producers relative to export markets. With the trade barriers created by exchange rates this effect is re-enforced by the reduction in export prices. These effects are covered in more detail below.

Finally, import protection normally creates arbitrary distortions in production incentives between one good and another. This is because import tariffs are rarely uniform. If, for example, one importable good receives a nominal rate of protection of 50 per cent and another 10 per cent, this would imply a distortion which raises the price of the former relative to the latter by about 36 per cent (150/110). For this reason, texts concerning trade policy reform such as that by Thomas et al. (1991) usually advocate trade barriers not only which are on balance low (to minimise adverse effects on consumers, economic welfare and exports) but also which are as uniform as possible across different goods.

Effective rates of protection and investment disincentives

Corden (1970) pointed out that producers are more concerned by the value added per unit of a good than its price. Where any producer whose own price is raised by trade barriers uses imported inputs or import competing inputs they will be paying higher prices for their inputs where these are also subject to trade barriers. What matters to producers is the extent to which the margin between their prices and their input costs, the value added, is affected by trade barriers on both outputs and inputs.

To measure these effects Corden (ibid.) developed the concept of the effective rate of protection. The effective rate of protection (ERP) is defined as

$$ERP = [(VA_d - VA_w) / VA_w].100, \qquad (4.4)$$

where VA_d is the value added at domestic prices and VA_w the value added at 'world' or undistorted prices. The effective rate of protection is, in effect, the percentage increase or decrease in value added per unit resulting from trade barriers on both inputs and outputs. It is determined not only by the degree of nominal protection of both inputs and outputs but also by the cost structure of firms. Where the value added per unit is, for example, small in relation to the product price, a quite small increase in prices can lead to a disproportionately large increase in value added.

There are two properties of effective rates of protection that are of relevance to exchange rate barriers. Firstly, effective rates of protection can be negative where costs are raised sufficiently to more than offset any increase in output prices. In the case of exchange rate barriers this would create anti-export bias. This is particularly likely to happen when they are calculated for export markets.

The costs of producing for both the domestic and export markets will be equally affected by any increase in input costs arising from exchange rate barriers since producers pay the same price for inputs irrespective of the final destination of their outputs. However, prices for domestic markets are raised by these barriers while export prices are lowered. This means that effective rates of protection (a) will normally be negative for export markets and (b) must be lower for export markets than for domestic markets even where they are also negative for domestic markets, a phenomenon known as anti-export bias. Anti-export bias (AXB) is defined as

$$AXB = \{(1 + ERP_x)/(1 + ERP_d)\}.100, \qquad (4.5)$$

where ERP_x is the effective rate of protection of a good in export markets and ERP_d the effective rate of protection of the same good in the domestic market. The greater this measure, the lower the degree of anti-export bias.

The second property of effective rates of protection is that they can vary substantially between one product and another in the domestic market even where trade barriers have a uniform effect on output prices. This arises because effective rates of protection will vary between one product and another as a consequence of differences in the share of value added in the final product price. Thus, even if exchange rate barriers affect all prices equally, the effect on the incentives to produce one good rather than another can be substantially distorted.

Effective rates of protection are probably not the best measure to identify potential distortions to investment. They are based upon value added, whereas investors are more concerned with the returns to their capital. Corden (1966) proposed a modification to the effective protection framework known as the effective rate of protection of capital (EPK). This, in effect, treats labour as an input such that the effective rate of protection is redefined as

$$EPK = [(R_d - R_w)/R_w].100, \tag{4.6}$$

where R_d is the returns to capital per unit and R_w the returns to capital at 'world' or undistorted prices. The effective protection of capital is, therefore, a simple modification of the effective protection approach which provides a more appropriate measure of the distortion effects on the profit incentives for investment.

Measures of the trade barrier effects of exchange rates

This section addresses the issue of whether the trade barrier effects of exchange rates have historically been sufficiently important to provide a key justification for European monetary union. Firstly, the findings of previous studies which have estimated the strength of these effects are briefly summarised. Secondly, estimates of exchange rate risk from the literature on international finance are summarised and crude estimates of transactions costs presented. Based on these estimates, simulations for the UK in 1989 and 1990 of effective rates of protection are presented as, subsequently, are simulations of the effective protection of capital in 1990.

Previous studies

Many studies in the area of monetary integration, such as Ungerer et al. (1986) have focused upon the use of the European Exchange Rate Mechanism to reduce real and nominal exchange rate volatility. These are of little interest for the purposes of this chapter, which is more concerned with the way such volatility affects international trade and investment. Other studies have sought to find evidence of effects of exchange rate volatility upon trade and investment. An example of such a study is Cushman (1986). This study linked the volatility of exchange rates to effects upon trade.

Studies of these types, while clearly of interest and relevance to the issue of monetary integration, do not directly model trade barriers in the way that the theory of trade policy would suggest. They provide a direct link between exchange rate volatility and observed values of exports and imports. One problem with this approach for identifying the role of exchange rates in creating trade barriers is that the intermediate stages are of importance. For example, as was argued in the previous section of this chapter, the theory of trade policy is as concerned with distortions arising from trade barriers in the incentives to produce one good rather than another for the domestic market as it is concerned with distortions which would reduce exports and imports. The object of this chapter is to provide a focus on these distortions in policy incentives rather than to try to measure the final impact on export and import volumes.

There are very few studies which actually have sought to quantify the precise effects of exchange rates as trade barriers. An important exception to this was the paper by the European Commission (1990), which provided estimates of the potential savings in foreign currency transactions costs as being between ECU 13·1 billion and ECU 19·2 billion in total, equivalent to about 0·4 per cent of total European Union GDP. To this was added a multiplier to account for indirect gains arising from increased trade and competition, suggesting an overall potential gain of between 0·5 per cent and 1 per cent of total European Union GDP. Crawford (1996) has used these estimates to suggest that the results would be comparable to a tariff reduction of 1·2 per cent.

From the viewpoint of this study, the estimate of a tariff equivalence of 1·2 per cent is clearly relevant. However, the original study by the European Commission still does not deal directly with possible distortions to production and investment incentives as outlined in the previous section of this chapter. Moreover, for very similar reasons, the author would be reluctant to accept the validity of the European Commission's estimates of the potential gains in the form of increased trade, competition and investment without the distortions that would be removed by monetary integration having been more clearly identified. For this reason the approach of this chapter is to examine how exchange rates, acting as trade barriers, may have affected production and investment incentives rather than to provide estimates of the effects on overall economic welfare.

Estimates of exchange rate risk and transactions costs

There is an extensive literature which deals with risk premia in foreign exchange markets. It has generally been concerned with the efficiency of foreign exchange markets and the finding that the forward exchange rate is a biased predictor of the future spot exchange rate. Specifically, papers such as that by Madsen (1996) have found that this forward bias of the exchange rate is attributable to a risk premium. That is, agents in the foreign exchange market are found to be risk-averse rather than risk-neutral and, in consequence, forward exchange rates comprise both an unbiased predictor of the future spot rate and a risk premium. Specifically, Madsen estimated the risk premium at about 2·5 per cent for the Deutschmark and 4 per cent for the US dollar on a yearly basis. He did not, however, provide estimates for sterling.

Similarly, Kho (1996) produces estimates of time-varying risk premia for foreign currency markets based upon the capital asset pricing model. In this case, he produces estimates of risk premia for sterling, the Deutschmark, the Japanese yen and the Swiss franc based on futures contracts traded on the Chicago Mercantile Exchange between January 1980 and December 1991. Kho produced two separate estimates of the average weekly risk premium on sterling – 0·093 per cent and 0·088 per cent. Lauterbach and Smoller (1996) produced estimates of exchange rate futures premia based on Eurodollar futures contracts traded on the Chicago Mercantile Exchange between January 1983 and December 1989. Gencay (1995) tested the significance of a risk premium associated with sterling and with the Deutschmark, finding strong support for the existence of such premia.

Concerning the transactions cost of foreign currency transactions, no estimates were readily available, other than from the European Commission (1990), so these were directly estimated. These were very simply calculated. For a sample of different sterling exchange rates over a period, the percentage difference between the spot exchange rate and tourist rates ('bank sells' and 'bank buys') were calculated. Data for these calculations were taken from the *Guardian* newspaper for a series of random dates in 1989 and 1990, totalling a sample of 65 observations. Exchange rates included were between sterling and the French franc, Deutschmark, Italian lira, Spanish peseta and Netherlands guilder. The average margin between the spot exchange rate and either the tourist 'bank sells' or 'bank buys' rate was estimated at approximately 3 per cent.

This average is very much a maximum for the likely transactions costs involved in foreign currency transactions. Tourist rates generally only apply to the smallest transactions and banks will generally impose smaller charges for even relatively modest transactions. For the purposes of analysis it was, therefore, treated as an upper limit to the transactions costs of exchanging currencies.

Simulations of effective rates of protection and anti-export bias

Any attempt to estimate the trade barrier effects of the hypothetical situation of UK membership of a European monetary union which did not exist in any form before 1999 is fraught with difficulties. Concerning exchange rate risk, estimates of risk premia have generally shown that these are time-varying. The precise cost of risk, therefore, depends upon the length of time for which firms are exposed to this risk. For example, it would depend upon the specific length of time between an exporter contracting to supply a foreign market and the date of receipt of payment. This would obviously vary, not only by industry, firm and destination of the goods, but also between one transaction and another.

Risk premia on forward foreign currency transactions can also vary between one nominal exchange rate and another. The most appropriate risk premium would be for the sterling–euro exchange rate, but this rate did not exist historically. As a second-best, the sterling-ECU rate would arguably be appropriate but, given that the ECU was more a unit of account than a currency in the normal sense, it is not immediately apparent whether futures markets would yield the most suitable information. Given these problems, Kho's (1996) estimates of the risk premium on future transactions in the sterling–US dollar rate were selected as a proxy for the exchange rate risk associated with sterling relative to the euro.

Transactions costs of foreign currency exchange are also difficult to estimate with a satisfactory degree of precision. As already discussed, these have been estimated as about 3 per cent for small transactions. However, firms engaging in larger transactions will normally face much lower costs. These not only vary according to the firm but can also vary according to the type of transaction conducted by the firm. For example, business travel transactions will typically be small and likely to incur proportionately high transactions costs while contract settlements are more normally large and would incur proportionately smaller costs.

Given these problems, this chapter makes no attempt to produce figures which are described as estimates. Instead simulations are produced according to the following assumptions for exchange rate risk:

1. exchange rate risk of 0·09 per cent per week (based on Kho's estimates of the sterling–US dollar risk premia) between sterling and currencies to be replaced by the euro;
2. a typical period of five weeks' exposure to exchange rate risk for foreign currency transactions; and
3. all foreign currency transactions were between sterling and currencies to be replaced by the euro and would become (currency) risk-free under monetary integration.

This implies a total cost attributed for exchange rate risk of 0·45 per cent. The first two assumptions are intended to be realistic, while the third is clearly not. Since a significant share of the UK's foreign transactions are with non-European countries, monetary integration would reduce and not eliminate exchange rate risk. To this was added 3 per cent for foreign currency transactions costs. As this is a maximum, the combined figure of 3·45 per cent represents a deliberate overstatement of the likely costs of exchange rates between European countries. Note that this compares with Crawford's (1996) estimate of an effect equivalent to a tariff of 1·2 per cent.

To allow for a variety of different assumptions concerning these costs, a limited sensitivity analysis was conducted. Simulations were also conducted for costs double those of the core scenario and for cost one-half of the core scenario.

Recalling that the theory of trade policy (see the fourth section) suggests that the distortions caused by trade barriers are least damaging where these barriers are (a) low and (b) uniform, we can immediately see that the barriers to trade posed by exchange rates are indeed likely to be low in terms of nominal protection. Crawford's estimate of 1·2 per cent is low not only compared to import tariffs in many countries, including the EU's external tariff, but also compared to other policy interventions likely to act as trade barriers (an issue that is dealt with later in this chapter). Moreover, these trade barriers are uniform across industries, although perhaps not according to size of firm. This uniformity makes them much less likely to create serious distortions than some other policy interventions.

The theory of trade policy also predicts that trade barriers can be substantially magnified in terms of their effects on value added (effective rates of protection) and on the relative incentives to supply domestic rather than export markets (anti-export bias). These require specific calculations. Accordingly, Table 4.1 reports simulations of effective rates of protection (for both domestic and export markets) and of anti-export bias for the UK in 1989. Table 4.2 reports comparable simulations for the UK in 1990. Both sets of simulations (found at the end of this chapter) made use of the UK input–output table for the year concerned. Since there was some change in the classification of the UK input–output tables between 1989 and 1990, some sectoral categories are not the same in both years.

The results for both 1989 and 1990 provide very little evidence for the magnification of trade barriers in terms of their effect on value added. Based on the core scenario of nominal barriers of 3·45 per cent, which is deliberately overstated, this is only slightly magnified to a sample average in the domestic market of 4·4 per cent for 1989 and a sample average of 4·5 per cent for 1990 in terms of the impact on value added. In consequence, there is little to suggest any widespread major distortion in producer incentives. Dispersion of rates also matters because this implies shifts in relative incentives. For both 1989 and 1990, sample standard deviations are small for the core scenario: 1·6 per cent and 0·8 per cent, respectively. This suggests that the trade barriers created by exchange rates do little to distort producer incentives to produce one type of good rather than another.

As would be expected, average effective rates and their dispersion are proportionately lower for both 1989 and 1990 for the more realistic scenario of one-half of the core values of nominal trade barriers (scenario 3) and proportionately higher for the pessimistic scenario of double the values for the core scenario (scenario 2).

A stronger case for exchange rates causing distortions in incentives can be made in the case of anti-export bias. For 1989, the measure of anti-export bias produced an average of 90·4 per cent for the core scenario and 91·2 per cent for 1990. The anti-export bias effect is stronger because firms, whether they supply export or domestic markets, must incur exchange rate costs and correspondingly higher prices of import competing goods in buying their inputs. For domestic markets these costs are typically more than offset by the protective effect of exchange rate costs. For export markets, their is no protective effect and firms must also absorb exchange rate costs on their sales. Despite the effect of exchange rates being stronger in the case of anti-export bias, it remains arguable whether this constitutes a strong effect in an absolute sense or relative to trade barriers resulting from other policies.

Simulations of effective protection of capital

The case that exchange rates create microeconomic costs does not rely solely upon barriers to trade, it also relies upon an argument that the same barriers also create impediments to investment. As discussed in the fourth section, the most appropriate way to measure the effect of these barriers on investment incentives is through their impact on the profitability of different industries. The effective protection of capital provides such a measure. As with trade barriers, the impact on profitability should, on average, be as low as possible, since this would minimise any deterrent to investment. Dispersion should also be low, since substantial variations across industries in the effect on profits would provide arbitrary incentives to invest in one industry at the expense of another. Finally, for the same reasons as for effective rates of protection exchange rate barriers will differentially affect investment to supply the domestic market and investment to supply export markets. That is, anti-export bias continues to apply.

To assess the impact of exchange rate barriers on investment incentives, Table 4.3 reports simulations of the effective protection of capital for a sample of UK industries in 1990. The UK input–output table for 1990 was used for the analysis and the same set of assumptions as outlined above (pp. 142–3) was employed. Note, however, that no simulations are provided for 1989. This is because the UK input–output table for 1989, unlike that for 1990, does not provide any decomposition of value added. Returns to capital could not, therefore, be separately identified.

The results of Table 4.3 suggest that the impact of exchange rate barriers is likely to have a stronger effect on profits and, hence, investment than value added. In itself this is an unremarkable finding: profit margins account for a smaller share of the final product price than value added, and any policies affecting both prices and costs will be magnified more in their effect on profits than for value added.

The results do, however, highlight an important limitation of the effective protection analysis. As reported above, the average effective rate of protection for the domestic market under the core scenario was 4·5 per cent. When measured solely in terms of the returns to capital rather than value added, this becomes 21·4 per cent. That is, the impact of exchange rates on value added, according to the base scenario, can reasonably be argued to have been marginal but cannot be argued to be marginal in terms of the impact upon returns to capital. Even for the more realistic scenario 3, the simulations suggest that exchange rate barriers lower returns to capital, on average, by about 9 per cent. This makes a much stronger case that exchange rates have a significant and adverse impact and, given that future returns to capital are of key importance to investment decisions, arguably a more pertinent case.

Moreover, the dispersion of rates is also significantly higher for effective protection of capital than for value added. Under the core scenario (scenario 1) the sample standard deviation was 12·2 per cent and, under scenario 3, 4·8 per cent. While the dispersion of rates remains small relative to mean values, these are still probably sufficiently large in absolute terms for us to suspect that exchange rates may have created arbitrary incentives to invest in one industry rather than another.

In terms of their impact on the returns to capital, the impact of exchange rate barriers cannot be so readily dismissed as in the case for value added. Nonetheless, the question still needs to be asked whether they represent significant barriers compared to the many different policy influences which can also be argued to create barriers to trade and investment. To provide a basic assessment of this issue, further simulations of the effective protection of capital were conducted on a small number of alternative policy influences.

Firstly, most European countries retain important differences in key policies which affect labour costs. These would include differences in employment legislation, national insurance contributions or equivalent, income taxes and hours of work. To provide a basis for assessing the potential impact of these differences, the effect on the returns to capital of labour costs being reduced by 1 per cent was simulated.

Secondly, many European countries maintain substantially different policies towards road transport, which would affect the costs of road transport to user industries. These would include road taxes, toll charges and fuel taxes. To capture these effects, a reduction in road transport costs of 20 per cent was simulated. An important further set of influences which are likely to act as trade and investment barriers are the expenditure taxes paid and subsidies received by industry, which can vary significantly between one European country and another. To capture these effects, the impact of the abolition of both expenditure taxes upon and subsidies to business were simulated. Finally, since European countries have different policies towards utilities and the financial sector, a reduction of 5 per cent in utility costs and 5 per cent in financial costs was simulated.

These simulations are based on entirely arbitrary assumptions. No evidence is offered to suggest that they are even approximately true, with the exception of expenditure taxes and subsidies, for which the UK input–output table provided data. The point of the exercise is to identify the extent to which hypothetical nominal differences between countries are magnified or not in terms of their effects on profits. Table 4.4 reports the results of these simulations. Readers should note that, because of the nature of the calculations, alternative hypotheses can readily be constructed by simply multiplying the output by the same number as the initial assumption. Thus, for example, to find the impact of a 10 per cent effect on labour costs, the values of the simulation for a 1 per cent change need only be multiplied by 10.

As shown in Table 4.3, exchange rate costs of about 3·45 per cent have an impact of 21·4 per cent on profits, a significant degree of magnification. For utility costs, financial costs and road transport costs, the simulations indicate a dampening of the effect on the returns to capital. That is, for each of these elements, they are sufficiently small in the total costs of firms for policy differences between European countries to have a disproportionately small effect on the returns to capital. In these cases, unless policy differences lead to particularly large cost differences between member states, it is unlikely that they will pose more significant trade and investment barriers than exchange rates.

Of the areas of potential policy differences considered, only labour costs exhibited a magnification effect. On average, the evidence of the simulations is that a reduction of 1 per cent in labour costs would increase returns to capital by about 3 per cent. While the extent of the magnification effect is less than for exchange rate barriers (about seven times) it is still possible or even likely that differences in labour policies could represent a more significant barrier than exchange rates. If, for example, differences in national policies mean that labour costs are more than 3 per cent lower in the UK than they would be under partner country policies then these differences would be likely to represent a greater influence on profits than for the most realistic of the exchange rate scenarios used (scenario 3). While this chapter can offer no evidence on the magnitude of differences in labour costs arising from national policy differences, it is certainly conceivable that variations of more than 3 per cent exist.

Concerning expenditure taxes on business, the results are not, strictly speaking, simulations but measures of the extent to which returns to capital would be affected by the hypothetical removal of these policies. The results, on average, are not strictly comparable to the exchange rate results since no differences in national policies are necessarily hypothesised. That is, the simulations examine complete abolition of both expenditure taxes on business and subsidies. The most important feature of the results is the very high degree of dispersion of rates (34·8 per cent).

A high dispersion of these effects indicates that the policies involved are highly distortionary, providing producers with arbitrary but strong incentives to direct resources to subsidised industries and away from those which are, on balance, taxed. The reason for this dispersion should be readily apparent from reference to Table 4.4. A number of sectors reveal a negative sign with respect to the elimination of expenditure taxes and subsidies, indicating that they received a greater value of subsidies than they paid in expenditure taxes. All of these sectors are agricultural or agriculturally related. This suggests that, for the UK in 1990, the effects of the Common Agricultural Policy had a substantially stronger distortionary effect on producer incentives than exchange rate barriers. To the extent that the objectives of the European Union are to reduce trade barriers, the economic logic of giving monetary union priority over further reform of the Common Agricultural Policy is highly questionable. The political logic is, of course, an entirely different matter.

Conclusions

The role of exchange rates as barriers to trade and investment can be argued to be an important component of the case for monetary union. Theoretically, there can be little doubt that the existence of exchange rates can create barriers through the transactions costs associated with foreign currency transactions and through the risk attached to foreign currency transactions. The key question is whether any gains from the removal of these barriers are likely to be of sufficient magnitude to offset fears that macroeconomic costs of UK membership of the European monetary union might exceed benefits.

Previous work has estimated links between exchange rate volatility and trade flows. The European Commission has also published estimates of the potential effects on economic welfare of (a) the removal of exchange rate transactions costs and (b) the indirect effects of removing these costs on competition and economic efficiency. These studies to some extent miss a key point. An important part of the theory of trade policy is not only that trade barriers affect consumer welfare but also that they affect economic efficiency by arbitrarily altering the relative incentives to produce one good rather than another. In order to form a view as to whether economic efficiency is likely to be affected, it is first necessary to establish how exchange rates affect these producer incentives. As producer incentives are determined more by value added and by returns to capital than directly by prices, this does require analysis beyond the mere identification of the barriers themselves.

To perform this analysis, recent historical data for the UK for 1989 and 1990 were used to provide simulations of effective rates of protection and anti-export bias resulting from exchange rate barriers. The core scenario deliberately assumed higher barriers than are likely. Despite this exchange rate barriers were found to have only a limited effect on value added in simulations for both 1989 and 1990. The very low degree of dispersion of these effects across different industries also suggested that significant distortions to economic efficiency would be unlikely to result from the elimination of exchange rate barriers.

There is probably a strong case to argue that it is the effect on the returns to capital rather than on value added which really influences producer decisions, particularly where investment is concerned. To assess these effects, further simulations were run for the UK in 1990, this time for the effects upon the returns to capital. The impact of exchange rate barriers on the returns to capital must necessarily be greater than on value added (which includes the returns to labour and indirect taxation as well as the returns to capital). The simulations suggested a markedly stronger effect on average upon the returns to capital than upon value added. In this sense, a case could be made that the removal of exchange rate barriers could significantly affect economic efficiency. However, it must be noted that distortions to economic efficiency also depend on the dispersion of these effects as well as their average levels. Dispersion of these effects remains low relative to average values, suggesting that profit incentives to supply one good rather than another might not be significantly distorted by exchange rate barriers.

Finally, if we see the removal of barriers to trade and investment as being the goal to which monetary integration is striving, it is highly relevant to ask whether it is the best means of achieving this goal. To this end, a wide range of different policies which have not been fully harmonised between European Union countries could represent trade barriers. To check on these, simulations were also run for a small sample of hypothetical policy differences for the UK in 1990. Policies affecting utility costs, financial costs and road transport costs were found to be unlikely to have significant influences on producer incentives for user industries unless very substantial differences in the effects of national policies exist.

Differences in policies affecting labour costs are more likely to affect profits than the other simulated policy differences, but profits were found to be less sensitive to differences in labour costs than to exchange rate barriers. This is not to say that exchange rates are a more important source of trade barriers than differences in national policies affecting labour costs. The simulations presented here suggest that it would only take a policy-induced difference in labour costs in excess of about 3 per cent for these to represent a more serious barrier than exchange rates. Although no evidence is presented, there remains a clear possibility that significant differences in national policies have led to larger differences than this in labour costs between European countries.

Differences in expenditure taxes on business and, in particular, subsidies are, according to the simulations presented, also likely to generate substantially greater distortion to relative economic incentives than exchange rate barriers. The simulations, unsurprisingly, suggest that the Common Agricultural Policy is a main cause. In conclusion, the results of this analysis suggest that, if the removal of internal barriers to trade and investment is the key objective for the European Union, further policy harmonisation and further reform of agricultural policy are more likely to bear fruit than monetary union.

Acknowledgment

The author gratefully acknowledges the assistance of Maxwell Stamp PLC with the earlier development of the effective protection of capital technique.

References

Clements, K.W. and L.A. Sjaastad (1984), *How Protection Taxes Exporters*, Thames Essay no. 39, London: Trade Policy Research Centre.

Corden, W.M. (1966), 'The Structure of a Tariff System and the Effective Protection Rate', *Journal of Political Economy*, 74, 200–216.

Corden, W.M. (1970), *The Theory of Protection*, Oxford: Clarendon Press.

Crawford, M. (1996), *One Money for Europe?: The Economics and Politics of EMU*, London: Macmillan.

Cushman, D. (1986), 'Has Exchange Rate Risk Depressed International Trade?: the Impact of Third Country Exchange Risk', *Journal of International Money and Finance*, 5.

European Commission (1990), 'One Market, One Money', *European Economy*, 44.

Gencay, R. (1995), 'Tests of the Risk Premium on Foreign Currency Futures Implied by the Intertemporal Asset Pricing Theory', *Applied Financial Economics*, 5, 85–94.

Greenaway, D. (1983), *International Trade Policy: From Tariffs to the New Protectionism*, London: Macmillan.

Kho, B.-C. (1996), 'Time Varying Risk Premia, Volatility and Technical Trading Rule Profits: Evidence from Foreign Currency Futures Markets', *Journal of Financial Economics*, 41, 249–90.

Lauterbach, B. and M.M. Smoller (1996), 'Risk Premia in Eurodollar Futures Prices', *Applied Financial Economics*, 6, 49–57.

Madsen, E.S. (1996), 'Inefficiency of Foreign Exchange Markets and Expectations: Survey Evidence', *Applied Economics*, 28, 397–403.

Mundell, R.A. (1961), 'A Theory of Optimum Currency Areas', *American Economic Review*, 51, 509–17.

Thomas, V., J. Nash and Associates (1991), *Best Practices in Trade Policy Reform,* Oxford: Oxford University Press.

Ungerer, H., O. Evans, T. Mayer and P. Young (1986), 'The European Monetary System: Recent Developments', IMF occasional paper no. 48, Washington, DC.

Table 4.1 Simulations of trade policy equivalents for 1989

Sectors (input–output classification), excluding non-tradables	*Scenario 1: cost of risk = 0·45% cost of transactions = 3%*			*Scenario 2: costs double those for Scenario 1*			*Scenario 3: costs one-half of those for Scenario 1*		
	ERP domestic (%)	*ERP export (%)*	*Anti-export bias (%)*	*ERP domestic (%)*	*ERP export (%)*	*Anti-export bias (%)*	*ERP domestic (%)*	*ERP export (%)*	*Anti-export bias (%)*
Agriculture	5·0	−3·1	92·3	10·1	−6·2	85·2	2·5	−1·5	96·1
Forestry & fishing	5·1	−5·8	89·6	10·5	−11·7	79·9	2·5	−2·9	94·7
Coal extraction etc	2·9	−1·9	95·3	5·8	−3·8	90·9	1·5	−1·0	97·6
Extraction of oil & gas	3·6	−1·4	95·1	7·3	−2·8	90·6	1·8	−0·7	97·5
Mineral oil processing	17·8	−15·6	71·7	41·2	−36·2	45·2	8·3	−7·3	85·6
Electricity etc	4·0	−3·3	93·0	8·1	−6·6	86·4	2·0	−1·6	96·4
Extraction of metal ores etc	4·0	−3·0	93·3	8·0	−6·1	87·0	2·0	−1·5	96·6
Iron and steel	4·0	−7·5	88·9	8·1	−15·1	78·6	2·0	−3·7	94·4
Aluminium etc	4·3	−13·0	83·4	8·7	−26·3	67·8	2·1	−6·5	91·5
Other non-ferrous metals	4·1	−12·3	84·3	8·3	−24·7	69·5	2·0	−6·1	92·0
Extraction of stone etc	4·1	−1·7	94·5	8·2	−3·3	89·3	2·0	−0·8	97·2
Cement etc	3·7	−3·8	92·8	7·5	−7·5	86·0	1·9	−1·9	96·3
Concrete etc	4·1	−4·5	91·7	8·2	−9·1	84·0	2·0	−2·3	95·8
Glass	4·3	−3·2	92·8	8·7	−6·4	86·1	2·1	−1·6	96·4
Refractory and ceramic goods	4·1	−2·4	93·8	8·2	−4·9	88·0	2·0	−1·2	96·8
Inorganic chemicals	4·3	−5·4	90·7	8·7	−10·8	82·1	2·1	−2·7	95·3
Organic chemicals	4·2	−5·7	90·5	8·5	−11·4	81·7	2·1	−2·8	95·2
Fertilisers	4·7	−6·3	89·4	9·5	−12·8	79·6	2·3	−3·2	94·6
Synthetic resins etc	4·8	−8·2	87·6	9·8	−16·5	76·0	2·4	−4·1	93·7
Paints, dyes etc	4·4	−5·3	90·7	9·0	−10·6	82·0	2·2	−2·6	95·3
Special chemicals	4·0	−3·8	92·4	8·1	−7·7	85·3	2·0	−1·9	96·1
Pharmaceuticals	4·1	−2·1	94·0	8·3	−4·2	88·4	2·1	−1·0	97·0

Table 4.1 *continued*

Sectors (input–output classification), excluding non-tradables	*Scenario 1: cost of risk = 0·45% cost of transactions = 3%*			*Scenario 2: costs double those for Scenario 1*			*Scenario 3: costs one-half of those for Scenario 1*		
	ERP domestic (%)	*ERP export (%)*	*Anti-export bias (%)*	*ERP domestic (%)*	*ERP export (%)*	*Anti-export bias (%)*	*ERP domestic (%)*	*ERP export (%)*	*Anti-export bias (%)*
Soap and toiletries	5·0	–5·7	89·8	10·2	–11·6	80·2	2·5	–2·8	94·8
Chemical products	4·1	–5·1	91·1	8·4	–10·4	82·7	2·1	–2·6	95·5
Man-made fibres	4·0	–4·2	92·1	8·1	–8·4	84·7	2·0	–2·1	96·0
Metal castings etc	4·0	–3·8	92·5	8·1	–7·7	85·4	2·0	–1·9	96·2
Metal doors, windows etc	4·2	–4·5	91·7	8·5	–9·0	83·9	2·1	–2·2	95·8
Metal packaging products	4·2	–7·1	89·2	8·4	–14·2	79·1	2·1	–3·5	94·5
Metal goods	4·2	–3·9	92·2	8·5	–7·9	84·9	2·1	–1·9	96·0
Industrial plant and steelwork	4·2	–5·0	91·1	8·5	–10·1	82·8	2·1	–2·5	95·5
Agricultural machinery etc	5·5	–11·1	84·3	11·1	–22·6	69·7	2·7	–5·5	92·0
Machine tools	4·3	–4·4	91·6	8·6	–9·0	83·8	2·1	–2·2	95·7
Engineering small tools	4·0	–2·2	94·0	8·1	–4·3	88·5	2·0	–1·1	97·0
Textile etc machinery	4·5	–4·5	91·4	9·0	–9·2	83·3	2·2	–2·3	95·6
Processing machinery etc	4·1	–2·4	93·8	8·3	–4·8	87·9	2·1	–1·2	96·8
Mining etc machinery	4·1	–5·4	90·9	8·2	–10·8	82·5	2·0	–2·7	95·4
Mech power transmission equipment	4·0	–2·8	93·4	8·1	–5·7	87·3	2·0	–1·4	96·7
Other machinery etc	4·1	–3·7	92·5	8·3	–7·5	85·4	2·0	–1·9	96·2
Ordnance etc	4·0	–6·0	90·3	8·1	–12·2	81·2	2·0	–3·0	95·1
Office machinery, computers etc	4·2	–5·5	90·7	8·5	–11·1	82·0	2·1	–2·7	95·3
Insulated wires and cables	4·0	–5·7	90·7	8·0	–11·4	82·0	2·0	–2·8	95·3
Basic electrical equipment	4·0	–3·9	92·4	8·1	–7·8	85·3	2·0	–1·9	96·1
Industrial electrical equipment	4·2	–3·8	92·3	8·5	–7·6	85·1	2·1	–1·9	96·1
Telecommunications etc equipment	4·2	–3·5	92·6	8·4	–7·1	85·7	2·1	–1·8	96·2

Table 4.1 *continued*

Sectors (input–output classification), excluding non-tradables	*Scenario 1: cost of risk = 0·45% cost of transactions = 3%*			*Scenario 2: costs double those for Scenario 1*			*Scenario 3: costs one-half of those for Scenario 1*		
	ERP domestic (%)	*ERP export (%)*	*Anti-export bias (%)*	*ERP domestic (%)*	*ERP export (%)*	*Anti-export bias (%)*	*ERP domestic (%)*	*ERP export (%)*	*Anti-export bias (%)*
Electronic components	4·3	–4·3	91·8	8·6	–8·6	84·1	2·1	–2·1	95·8
Electronic consumers goods etc	4·3	–7·0	89·1	8·7	–14·1	79·0	2·1	–3·5	94·5
Domestic electric appliances	4·5	–5·4	90·5	9·2	–10·9	81·6	2·3	–2·7	95·2
Electric lighting equipment	4·1	–3·9	92·4	8·2	–7·8	85·2	2·0	–1·9	96·1
Motor vehicles and parts	4·1	–6·6	89·7	8·2	–13·3	80·1	2·0	–3·3	94·8
Shipbuilding and repairing	4·4	–5·6	90·4	9·0	–11·3	81·4	2·2	–2·8	95·1
Aerospace etc	4·0	–4·3	92·0	7·9	–8·7	84·6	2·0	–2·2	96·0
Other vehicles	4·0	–4·8	91·5	8·1	–9·6	83·6	2·0	–2·4	95·7
Instrument engineering	4·3	–3·5	92·5	8·8	–7·1	85·4	2·2	–1·8	96·2
Oils and fats	5·0	–37·8	59·2	10·2	–76·7	21·1	2·5	–18·8	79·3
Slaughtering & meat processing	4·1	–11·3	85·3	8·4	–22·5	71·5	2·0	–5·6	92·5
Milk and milk products	3·6	–12·5	84·5	7·2	–25·0	70·0	1·8	–6·3	92·1
Fruit, veg and fish processing	4·4	–8·8	87·4	9·4	–17·3	75·6	2·2	–4·4	93·6
Grain milling and starch	3·9	–11·8	84·9	8·2	–23·5	70·7	2·0	–5·9	92·3
Sugar	3·3	–6·7	90·3	6·5	–13·5	81·2	1·6	–3·4	95·1
Confectionery	4·4	–5·6	90·4	8·8	–11·4	81·5	2·2	–2·8	95·1
Miscellaneous foods	4·3	–5·8	90·3	8·8	–11·6	81·2	2·1	–2·9	95·1
Alcoholic drink	8·9	–4·8	87·4	18·8	–10·1	75·7	4·3	–2·3	93·6
Soft drink	4·8	–7·8	88·0	9·7	–15·8	76·8	2·4	–3·9	93·9
Woollens and worsted	4·0	–7·0	89·4	8·1	–14·1	79·5	2·0	–3·5	94·6
Cotton etc spinning & weaving	4·1	–6·0	90·4	8·2	–12·0	81·3	2·0	–3·0	95·1
Hosiery and other knitted goods	4·0	–4·0	92·2	8·1	–8·1	85·0	2·0	–2·0	96·0

Table 4.1 *continued*

Sectors (input–output classification), excluding non-tradables	*Scenario 1: cost of risk = 0·45% cost of transactions = 3%*			*Scenario 2: costs double those for Scenario 1*			*Scenario 3: costs one-half of those for Scenario 1*		
	ERP domestic (%)	*ERP export (%)*	*Anti-export bias (%)*	*ERP domestic (%)*	*ERP export (%)*	*Anti-export bias (%)*	*ERP domestic (%)*	*ERP export (%)*	*Anti-export bias (%)*
Carpets etc	4·2	–5·6	90·6	8·4	–11·3	81·9	2·1	–2·8	95·2
Jute etc	4·1	–4·5	91·7	8·2	–9·1	84·0	2·0	–2·3	95·8
Leather and leather goods	4·1	–8·9	87·5	8·3	–17·8	75·8	2·1	–4·4	93·7
Footwear	3·9	–3·4	92·9	7·9	–6·8	86·3	2·0	–1·7	96·4
Clothing and furs	4·0	–3·7	92·6	8·0	–7·4	85·7	2·0	–1·8	96·2
Household and other textiles	4·4	–6·2	89·8	9·0	–12·5	80·3	2·2	–3·1	94·8
Timber and wood products	4·3	–6·0	90·2	8·7	–12·0	80·9	2·1	–3·0	95·0
Wood furniture	4·2	–4·8	91·3	8·4	–9·8	83·3	2·1	–2·4	95·6
Pulp, paper and board	4·3	–8·3	87·9	8·6	–16·7	76·7	2·1	–4·1	93·9
Paper and board products	4·2	–5·4	90·7	8·5	–10·9	82·1	2·1	–2·7	95·3
Printing and publishing	4·2	–3·1	93·1	8·4	–6·2	86·5	2·1	–1·5	96·5
Rubber products	4·1	–3·3	92·9	8·2	–6·7	86·2	2·0	–1·7	96·4
Processing of plastic	4·2	–5·0	91·2	8·4	–10·1	82·9	2·1	–2·5	95·5
Other manufacturing	4·2	–4·6	91·6	8·4	–9·3	83·7	2·1	–2·3	95·7
Construction	4·4	–4·2	91·7	8·9	–8·6	83·9	2·2	–2·1	95·8
Distribution etc	5·4	–1·7	93·3	11·0	–3·5	87·0	2·7	–0·9	96·6
Hotels, catering etc	4·4	–2·6	93·4	9·1	–4·9	87·1	2·2	–1·3	96·6
Railways	3·3	–2·6	94·4	6·5	–5·1	89·1	1·6	–1·3	97·1
Road transport etc	3·8	–1·8	94·7	7·6	–3·6	89·7	1·9	–0·9	97·3
Sea transport	5·2	–14·5	81·3	10·6	–29·5	63·7	2·6	–7·2	90·5
Air transport	3·8	–6·2	90·4	7·7	–12·4	81·3	1·9	–3·1	95·1
Transport services	3·8	–1·4	95·0	7·6	–2·9	90·3	1·9	–0·7	97·4

Table 4.1 *concluded*

Sectors (input–output classification), excluding non-tradables	*Scenario 1: cost of risk = 0·45% cost of transactions = 3%*			*Scenario 2: costs double those for Scenario 1*			*Scenario 3: costs one-half of those for Scenario 1*		
	ERP domestic (%)	*ERP export (%)*	*Anti-export bias (%)*	*ERP domestic (%)*	*ERP export (%)*	*Anti-export bias (%)*	*ERP domestic (%)*	*ERP export (%)*	*Anti-export bias (%)*
Postal services	3·6	–0·3	96·2	7·1	–0·7	92·7	1·8	–0·2	98·1
Other services	4·2	–0·6	95·3	8·6	–1·3	91·0	2·1	–0·3	97·6
Sample mean	4·4	–5·6	90·4	9·0	–11·4	81·5	2·2	–2·8	95·1
Sample standard deviation	1·6	4·5	4·8	3·7	9·3	9·3	0·7	2·2	2·4
Minimum	2·9	–37·8	59·2	5·8	–76·7	21·1	1·5	–18·8	79·3
Maximum	17·8	–0·3	96·2	41·2	–0·7	92·7	8·3	–0·2	98·1

Table 4.2 Simulations of trade policy equivalents for 1990

Sectors (input–output classification), excluding non-tradables	*Scenario 1: cost of risk = 0·45% cost of transactions = 3%*			*Scenario 2: costs double those for Scenario 1*			*Scenario 3: costs one-half of those for Scenario 1*		
	ERP domestic (%)	*ERP export (%)*	*Anti-export bias (%)*	*ERP domestic (%)*	*ERP export (%)*	*Anti-export bias (%)*	*ERP domestic (%)*	*ERP export (%)*	*Anti-export bias (%)*
Agriculture and horticulture	4·7	–4·1	91·6	9·6	–8·2	83·7	2·4	–2·0	95·7
Forestry	4·2	–1·6	94·4	8·4	–3·3	89·2	2·1	–0·8	97·2
Fishing	3·8	–1·8	94·7	7·9	–3·3	89·7	1·7	–1·0	97·3
Coal extraction and manufacture of solid fuels	4·4	–2·0	93·9	9·0	–3·8	88·2	2·1	–1·0	96·9
Extraction of mineral oil & natural gas	3·7	–1·7	94·8	7·4	–3·3	90·0	1·8	–0·8	97·4
Coke ovens, mineral oil processing and nuclear fuel production	4·0	–8·0	88·4	8·0	–16·2	77·6	2·0	–4·0	94·1
Extraction of metalliferous ores & minerals	1·7	–7·1	91·4	6·9	–10·9	83·4	–0·9	–5·2	95·6
Iron and steel, and steel products	5·0	–4·9	90·6	10·2	–10·0	81·7	2·5	–2·4	95·2
Aluminium and aluminium alloys	4·5	–5·3	90·6	9·9	–10·0	81·8	1·9	–3·0	95·2
Other non-ferrous metals (including precious metals)	4·6	–4·9	90·9	9·8	–9·6	82·3	2·1	–2·6	95·3
Extraction of stone, clay, sand & gravel	1·9	–4·5	93·7	6·9	–6·2	87·7	–0·5	–3·7	96·8
Cement, lime and plaster	4·2	–3·7	92·4	9·7	–6·4	85·3	1·6	–2·3	96·1
Concrete, stone, asbestos and abrasive products	6·5	–2·9	91·2	13·4	–6·0	82·9	3·2	–1·4	95·5
Glass	4·6	–2·6	93·2	9·6	–4·9	86·8	2·1	–1·4	96·5
Refractory and ceramic goods	4·4	–2·0	93·9	9·1	–3·8	88·2	2·0	–1·1	96·9
Inorganic chemicals	4·5	–5·3	90·7	9·8	–10·0	81·9	1·9	–3·0	95·2
Organic chemicals	5.1	–5.5	90.0	10.4	–11.0	80.6	2.4	–2.8	94.9
Fertilisers	4·6	–7·4	88·5	11·1	–13·7	77·7	1·5	–4·4	94·2

Table 4.2 *continued*

Sectors (input–output classification), excluding non-tradables	*Scenario 1: cost of risk = 0·45% cost of transactions = 3%*			*Scenario 2: costs double those for Scenario 1*			*Scenario 3: costs one-half of those for Scenario 1*		
	ERP *domestic (%)*	ERP *export (%)*	*Anti-export bias (%)*	ERP *domestic (%)*	ERP *export (%)*	*Anti-export bias (%)*	ERP *domestic (%)*	ERP *export (%)*	*Anti-export bias (%)*
Synthetic resins and plastic materials, synthetic rubber	4·8	–6·0	89·7	9·9	–12·0	80·1	2·2	–3·1	94·8
Paints, dyes, pigments, printing ink	4·8	–5·0	90·7	9·9	–9·9	82·0	2·2	–2·6	95·3
Specialised chemicals for industry and agriculture	4·5	–4·1	91·8	9·3	–8·1	84·1	2·2	–2·1	95·8
Pharmaceutical products	4·2	–2·1	94·0	8·4	–4·2	88·4	2·1	–1·0	96·9
Soap and toilet preparations	5·3	–6·3	89·0	11·0	–12·6	78·7	2·5	–3·2	94·4
Chemical products	4·5	–5·1	90·9	9·0	–10·2	82·3	2·2	–2·5	95·4
Man-made fibres	3·9	–4·0	92·4	8·4	–7·5	85·3	1·7	–2·2	96·1
Metal castings, forgings, fastenings, springs, etc	4·6	–2·6	93·1	9·2	–5·4	86·7	2·4	–1·2	96·5
Metal doors, windows, etc	4·8	–4·3	91·3	9·7	–8·7	83·2	2·4	–2·1	95·6
Packaging products of metal	4·4	–6·2	89·8	9·4	–12·2	80·3	2·0	–3·3	94·8
Metal goods	4·5	–3·3	92·6	9·1	–6·6	85·6	2·2	–1·6	96·2
Industrial plant and steelwork	4·3	–4·4	91·7	8·8	–8·7	83·9	2·0	–2·3	95·8
Agricultural machinery and tractors	5·4	–8·4	86·9	11·8	–16·5	74·7	2·3	–4·5	93·3
Metal-working machine tools	4·0	–4·9	91·4	8·6	–9·5	83·3	1·8	–2·7	95·6
Engineer's small tools	3·5	–2·6	94·2	7·7	–4·5	88·7	1·4	–1·6	97·0
Textile machinery, machinery for working other materials	4·4	–4·3	91·7	9·1	–8·5	83·9	2·1	–2·2	95·8
Process machinery and contractors	3·7	–2·5	94·0	7·7	–4·8	88·3	1·7	–1·4	96·9

Table 4.2 *continued*

Sectors (input–output classification), excluding non-tradables	*Scenario 1: cost of risk = 0·45% cost of transactions = 3%*			*Scenario 2: costs double those for Scenario 1*			*Scenario 3: costs one-half of those for Scenario 1*		
	ERP domestic (%)	*ERP export (%)*	*Anti-export bias (%)*	*ERP domestic (%)*	*ERP export (%)*	*Anti-export bias (%)*	*ERP domestic (%)*	*ERP export (%)*	*Anti-export bias (%)*
Mining, construction and mechanical handling equipment	4·4	–5·3	90·8	8·9	–10·6	82·1	2·1	–2·7	95·3
Mechanical power transmission equipment	3·9	–3·2	93·2	8·1	–6·1	86·8	1·8	–1·8	96·5
Other machinery and mechanical equipment	4·3	–3·6	92·5	8·7	–7·2	85·4	2·1	–1·8	96·2
Ordnance, small arms & ammunition	4·3	–5·4	90·7	8·9	–10·6	82·0	2·0	–2·8	95·3
Office machinery and computer equipment	4·9	–6·1	89·6	10·0	–12·2	79·8	2·4	–3·0	94·7
Insulated wires and cables	4·8	–5·3	90·4	10·1	–10·3	81·5	2·2	–2·8	95·1
Basic electrical equipment	4·3	–3·5	92·5	8·7	–7·1	85·5	2·1	–1·8	96·2
Electrical equipment for industry, batteries, etc	4·7	–3·6	92·1	9·4	–7·3	84·7	2·4	–1·7	96·0
Telecommunications etc equipment, electronic capital goods	4·6	–3·4	92·4	9·4	–6·8	85·2	2·3	–1·7	96·1
Electronic components and sub-assemblies	4·7	–3·4	92·3	9·5	–6·9	85·0	2·3	–1·7	96·1
Electronic consumer goods, records and tapes	6·9	–11·7	82·6	14·9	–23·9	66·3	3·2	–6·0	91·1
Domestic electric appliances	4·7	–5·2	90·6	9·7	–10·4	81·7	2·2	–2·7	95·2
Electric lighting equipment, etc	4·2	–3·3	92·8	8·7	–6·5	86·0	2·0	–1·7	96·3
Motor vehicles and parts	4·5	–7·3	88·7	9·2	–14·7	78·1	2·2	–3·7	94·2

Table 4.2 *continued*

Sectors (input–output classification), excluding non-tradables	*Scenario 1: cost of risk = 0·45% cost of transactions = 3%*			*Scenario 2: costs double those for Scenario 1*			*Scenario 3: costs one-half of those for Scenario 1*		
	ERP domestic (%)	*ERP export (%)*	*Anti-export bias (%)*	*ERP domestic (%)*	*ERP export (%)*	*Anti-export bias (%)*	*ERP domestic (%)*	*ERP export (%)*	*Anti-export bias (%)*
Shipbuilding and repairing	4·3	–2·9	93·1	8·5	–6·0	86·7	2·2	–1·4	96·5
Aerospace equipment manufacturing and repairing	3·8	–3·5	92·9	7·7	–7·0	86·3	1·9	–1·8	96·4
Other vehicles	4·4	–4·6	91·4	8·8	–9·3	83·4	2·2	–2·3	95·6
Instrument engineering	4·4	–3·3	92·6	9·0	–6·5	85·7	2·1	–1·7	96·3
Slaughtering and meat processing	5·1	–10·9	84·8	10·4	–22·1	70·6	2·5	–5·4	92·3
Milk and milk products	5·3	–14·1	81·5	11·0	–28·7	64·3	2·6	–7·0	90·6
Fruit, vegetables and fish processing	5·7	–7·1	87·9	11·4	–14·6	76·6	2·9	–3·4	93·9
Grain milling and starch	4·6	–10·6	85·5	10·0	–20·9	71·9	2·0	–5·6	92·6
Bread, biscuits and flour confectionery	4·4	–3·7	92·3	8·9	–7·4	85·0	2·2	–1·8	96·1
Sugar	4·3	–8·6	87·6	9·4	–16·9	76·0	1·8	–4·6	93·7
Confectionery	4·9	–5·3	90·3	10·2	–10·5	81·2	2·3	–2·8	95·1
Animal feeding stuffs	6·1	–14·0	81·1	12·6	–28·6	63·4	2·9	–7·0	90·4
Miscellaneous foods	5·0	–5·4	90·1	10·4	–10·8	80·8	2·4	–2·7	95·0
Alcoholic drink	4·7	–3·6	92·1	9·6	–7·2	84·7	2·4	–1·8	96·0
Soft drinks	5·3	–7·1	88·2	10·9	–14·5	77·2	2·6	–3·5	94·0
Tobacco	4·3	–3·0	93·0	8·9	–6·0	86·4	2·1	–1·6	96·4
Woollen and worsted	4·5	–5·7	90·2	9·1	–11·5	81·1	2·2	–2·8	95·0
Cotton etc spinning and weaving	4·0	–5·6	90·7	8·6	–10·8	82·1	1·8	–3·0	95·3
Hosiery and other knitted goods	4·0	–3·8	92·5	8·4	–7·4	85·4	1·9	–2·0	96·2
Carpets and other textile floor-coverings	4·4	–5·0	90·9	9·2	–10·0	82·5	2·1	–2·6	95·4

Table 4.2 *continued*

	Scenario 1: cost of risk = 0·45% cost of transactions = 3%			*Scenario 2: costs double those for Scenario 1*			*Scenario 3: costs one-half of those for Scenario 1*		
Sectors (input–output classification), excluding non-tradables	*ERP domestic (%)*	*ERP export (%)*	*Anti-export bias (%)*	*ERP domestic (%)*	*ERP export (%)*	*Anti-export bias (%)*	*ERP domestic (%)*	*ERP export (%)*	*Anti-export bias (%)*
Jute etc yarns and fabrics, and miscellaneous textiles	3·9	–4·7	91·8	8·5	–8·8	84·1	1·6	–2·6	95·8
Leather and leather goods	3·0	–8·2	89·1	7·6	–15·0	79·0	0·7	–4·9	94·5
Footwear	4·1	–3·7	92·6	8·4	–7·2	85·6	1·9	–1·9	96·2
Clothing and furs	4·1	–3·4	92·8	8·4	–6·7	86·1	2·0	–1·7	96·3
Household and other made-up textiles	4·7	–5·2	90·5	9·6	–10·5	81·7	2·3	–2·6	95·2
Timber processing and wood products (not furniture)	4·8	–5·7	89·9	9·9	–11·5	80·5	2·3	–2·9	94·9
Wooden furniture, shop and office fittings	4·5	–4·9	91·0	9·2	–9·7	82·7	2·1	–2·5	95·4
Pulp, paper and board	4·7	–4·1	91·6	9·8	–8·1	83·7	2·3	–2·1	95·7
Paper and board products	4·6	–5·3	90·5	9·5	–10·6	81·7	2·2	–2·8	95·2
Printing and publishing	4·4	–2·9	93·0	8·9	–5·9	86·5	2·2	–1·5	96·4
Rubber products	4·4	–3·0	92·9	9·0	–5·9	86·3	2·2	–1·5	96·4
Processing of plastics	4·9	–4·4	91·1	10·0	–9·0	82·7	2·5	–2·2	95·5
Jewellery and coins	4·0	–5·2	91·1	9·0	–9·7	82·9	1·5	–3·0	95·5
Sports goods and toys	3·1	–6·6	90·6	8·2	–11·5	81·8	0·7	–4·2	95·2
Other goods	3·7	–3·5	93·1	8·1	–6·4	86·6	1·5	–2·1	96·5
Hotels, catering, public houses, etc	4·5	–1·6	94·2	9·1	–3·2	88·8	2·2	–0·8	97·1
Railways	5·5	–1·7	93·1	11·3	–3·4	86·7	2·7	–0·9	96·5
Sea transport	6·5	–11·1	83·5	13·4	–22·9	68·0	3·2	–5·5	91·6
Air transport	5·6	–2·6	92·3	11·4	–5·3	85·0	2·8	–1·3	96·1

Table 4.2 *concluded*

	Scenario 1: cost of risk = 0·45% cost of transactions = 3%			*Scenario 2: costs double those for Scenario 1*			*Scenario 3: costs one-half of those for Scenario 1*		
Sectors (input–output classification), excluding non-tradables	*ERP domestic (%)*	*ERP export (%)*	*Anti-export bias (%)*	*ERP domestic (%)*	*ERP export (%)*	*Anti-export bias (%)*	*ERP domestic (%)*	*ERP export (%)*	*Anti-export bias (%)*
Transport services	4·3	–1·6	94·3	8·7	–3·2	89·0	2·1	–0·8	97·1
Telecommunications	4·1	–1·0	95·1	8·3	–2·0	90·5	2·1	–0·5	97·5
Auxiliary financial services	4·4	–1·0	94·8	8·9	–2·1	89·9	2·2	–0·5	97·4
Other professional services	5·0	–0·9	94·3	10·1	–1·9	89·1	2·5	–0·5	97·1
Other business services	5·0	–2·3	93·1	10·1	–4·6	86·6	2·5	–1·1	96·5
Research and development	3·9	–0·6	95·7	7·8	–1·1	91·7	1·9	–0·3	97·8
Sample average	4·5	–4·7	91·2	9·4	–9·3	82·9	2·1	–2·5	95·5
Sample standard deviation	0·8	2·6	2·8	1·3	5·3	5·4	0·6	1·4	1·4
Minimum	1·7	–14·1	81·1	6·9	–28·7	63·4	–0·9	–7·0	90·4
Maximum	6·9	–0·6	95·7	14·9	–1·1	91·7	3·2	–0·3	97·8

Table 4.3 Simulations of effective protection of capital for 1990

Sectors (input–output classification), excluding non-tradables	*Scenario 1: cost of risk = 0·45% cost of transactions = 3%*			*Scenario 2: costs double those for Scenario 1*			*Scenario 3: costs one-half of those for Scenario 1*		
	ERP domestic (%)	*ERP export (%)*	*Anti-export bias (%)*	*ERP domestic (%)*	*ERP export (%)*	*Anti-export bias (%)*	*ERP domestic (%)*	*ERP export (%)*	*Anti-export bias (%)*
Agriculture and horticulture	7·2	–6·2	87·5	15·0	–12·8	75·9	3·5	–3·0	93·7
Forestry	9·0	–4·0	88·0	19·1	–8·5	76·8	4·4	–2·0	93·9
Fishing	5·1	–2·4	92·9	10·7	–4·4	86·3	2·3	–1·4	96·4
Extraction of mineral oil and natural gas	4·2	–1·9	94·2	8·4	–3·8	88·7	2·1	–0·9	97·0
Coke ovens, mineral oil processing and nuclear fuel production	6·2	–12·7	82·2	12·9	–26·0	65·5	3·0	–6·3	90·9
Iron and steel, and steel products	22·3	–28·2	58·7	54·3	–69·1	20·0	10·3	–12·9	79·0
Aluminium and aluminium alloys	23·4	–46·3	43·5	68·8	–115·9	–9·4	8·2	–22·9	71·3
Other non-ferrous metals (including precious metals)	44·3	–86·0	9·7	168·7	–300·9	–74·8	16·1	–37·2	54·1
Cement, lime and plaster	8·5	–7·5	85·3	20·6	–13·8	71·5	3·1	–4·6	92·5
Concrete, stone, asbestos and abrasive products	20·6	–9·3	75·2	49·5	–22·3	52·0	9·5	–4·3	87·4
Glass	23·9	–13·5	69·8	63·1	–32·1	41·6	10·0	–6·9	84·7
Refractory and ceramic goods	24·3	–11·2	71·5	63·6	–26·8	44·8	10·3	–5·7	85·5
Inorganic chemicals	15·3	–18·2	71·0	38·5	–39·3	43·8	6·0	–9·6	85·2
Organic chemicals	15·2	–16·4	72·6	34·9	–36·7	46·9	7·0	–7·9	86·0
Fertilisers	15·7	–25·4	64·5	44·4	–54·9	31·2	4·8	–14·1	81·9
Synthetic resins and plastic materials, synthetic rubber	14·0	–17·8	72·1	32·3	–39·2	46·0	6·3	–8·8	85·8
Paints, dyes, pigments, printing ink	19·1	–20·4	66·8	47·0	–47·4	35·7	8·3	–10·0	83·1

Table 4.3 *continued*

	Scenario 1: cost of risk = 0·45% cost of transactions = 3%			*Scenario 2: costs double those for Scenario 1*			*Scenario 3: costs one-half of those for Scenario 1*		
Sectors (input–output classification), excluding non-tradables	*ERP domestic (%)*	*ERP export (%)*	*Anti-export bias (%)*	*ERP domestic (%)*	*ERP export (%)*	*Anti-export bias (%)*	*ERP domestic (%)*	*ERP export (%)*	*Anti-export bias (%)*
Specialised chemicals for industry and agriculture	9·3	−8·4	83·8	20·1	−17·6	68·6	4·4	−4·3	91·7
Pharmaceutical products	7·7	−3·8	89·3	16·1	−8·0	79·2	3·8	−1·9	94·5
Soap and toilet preparations	11·6	−13·8	77·2	25·9	−29·6	55·9	5·3	−6·9	88·4
Chemical products	14·1	−16·0	73·6	31·5	−35·6	49·0	6·7	−7·6	86·6
Man-made fibres	7·9	−8·1	85·1	17·9	−16·1	71·2	3·4	−4·5	92·4
Metal castings, forgings, fastenings, springs, etc	31·2	−19·7	61·2	83·2	−54·4	24·9	14·2	−8·4	80·3
Metal doors, windows, etc	30·9	−27·9	55·1	84·1	−75·9	13·1	13·6	−12·3	77·2
Packaging products of metal	14·4	−20·7	69·3	34·7	−45·4	40·5	6·1	−10·5	84·4
Metal goods	28·1	−20·7	61·9	74·4	−54·3	26·2	12·4	−9·4	80·6
Industrial plant and steelwork	22·2	−23·0	63·0	56·2	−55·6	28·4	9·6	−11·0	81·2
Agricultural machinery and tractors	49·1	−77·8	14·9	215·4	−304·0	−64·7	16·7	−33·8	56·7
Engineer's small tools	27·3	−20·5	62·5	83·2	−49·9	27·3	9·8	−11·2	80·9
Process machinery and contractors	9·7	−6·7	85·1	21·5	−13·5	71·2	4·4	−3·5	92·4
Mining, construction and mechanical handling equipment	32·4	−39·4	45·8	92·3	−109·4	−4·9	13·8	−17·6	72·4
Mechanical power transmission equipment	35·6	−29·5	52·0	112·7	−85·1	7·0	13·9	−13·9	75·6
Other machinery and mechanical equipment	22·4	−18·6	66·5	54·7	−45·5	35·2	10·2	−8·5	83·0

Table 4.3 *continued*

Sectors (input–output classification), excluding non-tradables	*Scenario 1: cost of risk = 0·45% cost of transactions = 3%*			*Scenario 2: costs double those for Scenario 1*			*Scenario 3: costs one-half of those for Scenario 1*		
	ERP domestic (%)	*ERP export (%)*	*Anti-export bias (%)*	*ERP domestic (%)*	*ERP export (%)*	*Anti-export bias (%)*	*ERP domestic (%)*	*ERP export (%)*	*Anti-export bias (%)*
Ordnance, small arms and ammunition	33·4	–42·1	43·4	99·9	–119·1	–9·6	13·6	–19·1	71·2
Office machinery and computer equipment	10·2	–12·6	79·3	22·0	–26·8	60·0	4·8	–6·2	89·5
Insulated wires and cables	26·7	–29·6	55·6	73·2	–75·6	14·1	11·0	–14·0	77·4
Basic electrical equipment	40·6	–33·4	47·3	129·0	–104·5	–1·9	16·9	–14·4	73·2
Electrical equipment for industry, batteries, etc	46·9	–35·7	43·8	156·9	–122·7	–8·8	19·9	–14·4	71·4
Telecommunication etc equipment, electronic capital goods	39·4	–29·1	50·9	121·8	–89·0	4·9	16·7	–12·5	75·0
Electronic components and sub-assemblies	35·2	–25·7	54·9	101·7	–74·3	12·8	15·3	–11·1	77·1
Electronic consumer goods, records and tapes	28·8	–48·8	39·8	81·1	–130·0	–16·6	11·8	–22·4	69·4
Domestic electric appliances	52·0	–57·5	28·0	206·5	–220·8	–39·4	20·1	–23·9	63·4
Electric lighting equipment, etc	12·2	–9·6	80·5	27·4	–20·6	62·3	5·6	–4·8	90·1
Motor vehicle and parts	29·7	–47·8	40·3	80·3	–128·1	–15·6	13·0	–21·3	69·6
Aerospace equipment manufacturing and repairing	11·2	–10·5	80·5	24·5	–22·5	62·3	5·3	–5·1	90·1
Instrument engineering	38·1	–28·4	51·9	118·1	–85·0	6·9	15·8	–12·6	75·5
Slaughtering and meat processing	13·4	–28·5	63·0	29·7	–63·1	28·4	6·4	–13·6	81·2
Milk and milk products	8·4	–22·3	71·7	17·9	–46·7	45·2	4·0	–10·9	85·6

Table 4.3 *continued*

Sectors (input–output classification), excluding non-tradables	*Scenario 1: cost of risk = 0·45% cost of transactions = 3%*			*Scenario 2: costs double those for Scenario 1*			*Scenario 3: costs one-half of those for Scenario 1*		
	ERP domestic (%)	*ERP export (%)*	*Anti-export bias (%)*	*ERP domestic (%)*	*ERP export (%)*	*Anti-export bias (%)*	*ERP domestic (%)*	*ERP export (%)*	*Anti-export bias (%)*
Fruit, vegetables and fish processing	15·1	–18·8	70·5	33·4	–42·7	43·0	7·3	–8·7	85·0
Grain milling and starch	8·9	–20·7	72·8	20·4	–43·1	47·3	3·7	–10·6	86·2
Bread, biscuits and flour confectionery	21·6	–18·1	67·4	52·4	–43·8	36·9	9·9	–8·3	83·4
Sugar	5·7	–11·4	83·8	12·6	–22·7	68·7	2·4	–6·0	91·8
Confectionery	14·3	–15·6	73·8	33·3	–34·3	49·3	6·4	–7·8	86·7
Animal feeding stuffs	10·0	–23·2	69·8	21·8	–49·4	41·6	4·7	–11·4	84·6
Miscellaneous foods	11·7	–12·5	78·4	25·8	–26·9	58·1	5·5	–6·1	89·0
Alcoholic drink	10·7	–8·1	83·1	22·9	–17·3	67·3	5·2	–3·9	91·4
Soft drinks	11·6	–15·4	75·8	25·1	–33·4	53·3	5·6	–7·4	87·7
Tobacco	6·2	–4·3	90·1	12·9	–8·7	80·9	3·0	–2·2	95·0
Woollen and worsted	42·2	–53·5	32·7	134·9	–171·2	–30·3	17·8	–22·5	65·8
Cotton etc spinning and weaving	27·0	–37·4	49·3	76·6	–96·7	1·9	10·7	–17·9	74·2
Hosiery and other knitted goods	21·8	–20·6	65·2	55·6	–49·3	32·6	9·3	–10·0	82·3
Carpets and other textile floorcoverings	15·3	–17·4	71·6	35·7	–38·8	45·1	6·8	–8·6	85·6
Jute etc yarns and fabrics, and miscellaneous textiles	24·1	–29·3	57·0	68·0	–72·0	16·7	9·1	–14·8	78·1
Leather and leather goods	15·0	–41·4	50·9	47·0	–92·6	5·0	3·2	–22·6	75·0
Clothing and furs	22·4	–18·2	66·8	55·3	–44·5	35·8	10·1	–8·5	83·1
Household and other made-up textiles	29·6	–32·4	52·1	79·3	–86·8	7·4	13·1	–14·4	75·7

Table 4.3 *continued*

Sectors (input–output classification), excluding non-tradables	*Scenario 1: cost of risk = 0·45% cost of transactions = 3%*			*Scenario 2: costs double those for Scenario 1*			*Scenario 3: costs one-half of those for Scenario 1*		
	ERP domestic (%)	*ERP export (%)*	*Anti-export bias (%)*	*ERP domestic (%)*	*ERP export (%)*	*Anti-export bias (%)*	*ERP domestic (%)*	*ERP export (%)*	*Anti-export bias (%)*
Timber processing and wood products (not furniture)	37·9	–45·4	39·6	117·5	–136·6	–16·8	15·6	–19·9	69·3
Wooden furniture, shop and office fittings	49·5	–54·0	30·8	187·4	–197·8	–34·0	19·4	–22·6	64·8
Pulp, paper and board	15·9	–19·2	69·7	37·1	–43·3	41·3	7·2	–9·3	84·6
Paper and board products	30·4	–35·5	49·5	86·0	–95·9	2·2	12·7	–16·2	74·3
Printing and publishing	16·9	–11·2	75·9	39·0	–25·8	53·4	7·9	–5·3	87·7
Rubber products	20·2	–13·5	72·0	48·7	–32·0	45·7	9·1	–6·4	85·7
Processing of plastics	22·0	–19·7	65·8	53·7	–48·1	33·8	10·1	–9·1	82·6
Jewellery and coins	18·7	–29·7	59·2	52·4	–67·9	21·0	6·4	–15·7	79·3
Other goods	13·5	–13·0	76·7	33·2	–26·9	54·9	5·3	–7·2	88·1
Hotels, catering, public houses, etc	20·5	–7·2	77·0	49·3	–17·2	55·5	9·5	–3·3	88·3
Air transport	19·2	–9·4	76·0	45·4	–22·3	53·5	8·9	–4·4	87·8
Transport services	9·7	–3·6	87·9	20·6	–7·7	76·5	4·7	–1·8	93·8
Telecommunications	7·9	–1·9	90·9	16·5	–3·9	82·4	3·9	–0·9	95·4
Auxiliary financial services	47·4	–10·9	60·5	163·0	–38·3	23·5	19·7	–4·4	79·9
Other professional services	29·6	–7·8	71·2	79·1	–20·8	44·2	13·2	–3·4	85·3
Other business services	32·7	–14·8	64·2	91·0	–41·2	30·8	14·3	–6·5	81·8
Research and development	13·5	–2·1	86·2	30·2	–4·6	73·3	6·4	–1·1	93·0

Table 4.3 *concluded*

	Scenario 1: cost of risk = 0·45% cost of transactions = 3%			*Scenario 2: costs double those for Scenario 1*			*Scenario 3: costs one-half of those for Scenario 1*		
Sectors (input–output classification), excluding non-tradables	*ERP domestic (%)*	*ERP export (%)*	*Anti-export bias (%)*	*ERP domestic (%)*	*ERP export (%)*	*Anti-export bias (%)*	*ERP domestic (%)*	*ERP export (%)*	*Anti-export bias (%)*
Sample mean	21·4	–22·2	65·6	60·6	–60·1	33·5	9·1	–10·4	82·5
Sample standard deviation	12·2	16·4	17·6	46·6	57·9	34·1	4·8	7·1	9·0
Minimum	4·2	–86·0	9·7	8·4	–304·0	–74·8	2·1	–37·2	54·1
Maximum	52·0	–1·9	94·2	215·4	–3·8	88·7	20·1	–0·9	97·0

Table 4.4 Effective protection of capital simulations for alternative policy barriers to trade

Sectors	*Labour costs less 1% (per cent)*	*Road transport costs less 20% (per cent)*	*No expenditure taxes or subsidies (per cent)*	*Utility costs less 5% (per cent)*	*Financial costs less 5% (per cent)*
Agriculture and horticulture	0·6	0·4	−8·5	0·3	0·5
Forestry	1·8	1·2	−269·0	0·2	0·0
Fishing	0·3	0·0	1·6	0·0	0·3
Min oil ex and natural gas extraction	0·1	0·1	0·2	0·0	0·2
Min oil processing – coke ovens and nuclear fuel production	0·3	0·3	19·1	0·1	0·3
Iron and steel, and steel products	2·4	5·2	18·6	2·0	1·1
Aluminium and aluminium alloys	2·8	10·9	16·1	2·6	1·4
Other non-ferrous metals (including precious metals)	4·7	4·1	30·8	2·3	2·5
Cement, lime and plaster	0·8	7·5	9·6	1·3	0·3
Concrete, stone, asbestos and abrasive products	1·7	32·5	14·9	0·7	0·9
Glass	3·3	8·3	18·8	1·9	1·5
Refractory and ceramic goods	3·7	10·4	11·4	1·5	1·3
Inorganic chemicals	1·8	4·7	25·1	1·8	1·2
Organic chemicals	1·3	3·0	33·3	1·8	1·0
Fertilisers	1·6	10·4	34·8	3·9	1·4
Synthetic resins and plastic materials, synthetic rubber	1·3	1·9	30·8	1·1	1·1
Paints, dyes, pigments, printing ink	2·4	4·5	15·8	0·8	1·5
Specialised chemicals for industry and agriculture	0·9	1·3	7·4	0·6	0·6
Pharmaceutical products	0·8	0·0	0·8	0·1	0·7
Soap and toilet preparations	1·1	2·3	0·5	0·3	1·7

Table 4.4 *continued*

Sectors	*Labour costs less 1% (per cent)*	*Road transport costs less 20% (per cent)*	*No expenditure taxes or subsidies (per cent)*	*Utility costs less 5% (per cent)*	*Financial costs less 5% (per cent)*
Chemical products	1·8	1·3	12·8	0·4	0·9
Man-made fibres	0·9	0·3	5·3	0·6	0·5
Metal castings, forgings, fastenings, springs, etc	4.3	3.2	15.2	1.7	1.5
Metal doors, windows, etc	4.2	2.4	13.0	0.4	1.8
Packaging products of metal	1.9	3.4	9.2	0.6	0.9
Metal goods	4.1	3.0	11.6	0.6	1.8
Industrial plant and steelwork	3.4	1.8	12.2	0.4	1.3
Agricultural machinery and tractors	5.5	6.7	21.1	16.7	1.8
Engineer's small tools	5.5	1.4	14.7	0.7	1.5
Process machinery and contractors	1.4	0.2	5.8	0.1	0.4
Mining, construction and mechanical handling equipment	4.9	1.9	13.4	0.6	1.8
Mechanical power transmission equipment	6.2	1.7	17.1	0.9	1.6
Other machinery and mechanical equipment	3.4	1.3	8.6	0.5	1.3
Ordnance, small arms and ammunition	5.1	0.8	19.4	0.8	1.7
Office machinery and computer equipment	0.9	0.3	4.7	0.1	0.8
Insulated wires and cables	3.5	2.6	16.0	0.6	1.5
Basic electrical equipment	6.2	1.9	16.4	0.7	2.2
Electrical equipment for industry, batteries, etc	6.3	2.0	16.4	0.9	2.4
Telecommunication etc equipment, electronic capital goods	5.6	0.8	11.6	0.3	2.2
Electronic components and sub-assemblies	5.0	0.6	8.9	0.8	2.2

Table 4.4 *continued*

Sectors	*Labour costs less 1% (per cent)*	*Road transport costs less 20% (per cent)*	*No expenditure taxes or subsidies (per cent)*	*Utility costs less 5% (per cent)*	*Financial costs less 5% (per cent)*
Electronic consumer goods, records and tapes	2.4	3.6	9.4	0.4	3.1
Domestic electric appliances	6.8	5.3	18.4	0.7	3.6
Electric lighting equipment, etc	1.7	0.9	5.6	0.2	0.7
Motor vehicle and parts	4.4	3.6	8.2	0.6	1.7
Aerospace equipment manufacturing and repairing	1.7	0.0	5.8	0.1	0.5
Instrument engineering	5.7	0.8	9.6	0.5	2.5
Slaughtering and meat processing	1.8	3.6	–48.7	0.6	1.4
Milk and milk products	0.9	1.0	–58.0	0.5	1.0
Fruit, vegetables and fish processing	1.7	4.8	–33.6	0.8	1.4
Grain milling and starch	0.8	6.6	7.6	0.7	0.8
Bread, biscuits and flour confectionery	3.2	1.9	9.2	0.7	1.5
Sugar	0.5	2.8	–21.0	0.3	0.5
Confectionery	1.7	6.3	4.9	0.5	1.8
Animal feeding stuffs	1.0	4.3	–55.0	0.5	1.5
Miscellaneous foods	1.2	2.5	4.0	0.3	1.7
Alcoholic drink	0.8	1.0	22.7	0.5	1.2
Soft drinks	1.0	3.0	7.8	0.3	1.1
Tobacco	0.4	0.0	0.4	0.0	1.2
Woollen and worsted	6.0	2.7	15.7	1.5	2.9
Cotton etc spinning and weaving	4.4	2.3	17.9	1.3	2.0
Hosiery and other knitted goods	3.6	2.0	11.1	0.6	1.4
Carpets and other textile floorcoverings	2.1	2.8	8.9	0.5	1.3
Jute etc yarns and fabrics, and miscellaneous textiles	4.2	3.0	15.4	1.1	1.8

Table 4.4 *concluded*

Sectors	*Labour costs less 1% (per cent)*	*Road transport costs less 20% (per cent)*	*No expenditure taxes or subsidies (per cent)*	*Utility costs less 5% (per cent)*	*Financial costs less 5% (per cent)*
Leather and leather goods	3.5	0.8	12.2	0.6	2.2
Clothing and furs	3.6	1.6	9.5	0.2	1.4
Household and other made-up textiles	4.1	3.3	12.2	0.5	2.1
Timber processing and wood products (not furniture)	4.9	8.3	23.7	0.8	3.3
Wooden furniture, shop and office fittings	6.9	6.3	22.3	0.6	3.9
Pulp, paper and board	1.7	7.6	10.7	2.2	1.3
Paper and board products	4.3	10.6	17.7	0.9	2.7
Printing and publishing	2.4	1.7	5.5	0.2	1.5
Rubber products	2.9	2.4	10.9	0.7	1.6
Processing of plastics	2.8	4.1	10.4	0.7	1.9
Jewellery and coins	2.8	0.2	25.1	0.4	1.8
Other goods	2.3	1.4	5.5	0.2	1.1
Hotels, catering, public houses, etc	2.8	1.9	19.6	0.6	1.5
Air transport	1.8	0.6	20.5	0.5	2.7
Transport services	1.1	1.4	8.0	0.1	0.6
Telecommunications	0.8	0.4	5.7	0.2	0.3
Auxiliary financial services	5.8	0.6	53.3	0.3	5.4
Other professional services	3.8	2.6	5.7	0.2	3.8
Other business services	4.3	1.5	6.7	0.5	4.5
Research and development	2.2	0.2	1.2	0.4	0.1
Sample average	2.9	3.2	6.2	0.9	1.6
Sample standard deviation	1.8	4.2	34.8	1.9	1.0
Minimum	0.1	0.0	–269.0	0.0	0.0
Maximum	6.9	32.5	53.3	16.7	5.4

CHAPTER FIVE

The cart before the horse? Australian exchange rate policy and economic reform in the 1980s

Kieron Toner

Introduction

The aim of this chapter is to demonstrate that exchange rate liberalisation in itself is not necessarily a wise or beneficial thing, especially when combined with reforms in other areas of economic policy. The chapter will take a macroeconomic focus, and will concentrate primarily on the economic reform programme in Australia under the administrations of Bob Hawke and Paul Keating (1983–96). The reform processes between 1983 and 1996 had what could be termed a classical flavour, in that they were heavily influenced by the notions of free markets, free trade and deregulation. Hawke and Keating believed that the policies of the governments that had gone before them had allowed Australia to stagnate in the domestic economy, and had failed to embrace fully the realities of the modern global economic order. Australian trade policy from the 1940s through to the 1960s was based on the notion of 'populate or perish' and this idea, coupled with the Australian notion that it was a developing nation, led governments to attempt to develop an industrial structure, and maintain full employment, by following a policy of import substitution based on high trade protection. Although this policy contributed to what has been termed the 'long boom' from the 1940s to the 1970s, it failed to boost either import-competing industries or exporting industries, and Australia became at best a marginal player in the global economy.

Classical economic theory, stemming from Adam Smith and others, suggests that the free market and free factor flows will ensure that the market clears and that resources are used efficiently. In the case of exchange rate policy this implies that a free-floating exchange rate is the optimal arrangement. It is small wonder, then, that global organisations such as the International Monetary Fund (IMF) frequently advocate exchange rate reform as an integral part of any reform package.

Likewise, classical trade theories suggest that pure free trade is always the best policy for any country to pursue. Despite the growth of regional trading agreements, and the rise of what could be termed oligopolistic competition between nations, there are those who still cling to this view.

The purpose of this chapter is to explore the reality of using a classical foundation for economic reform in a modern world setting, using Australia in the 1980s as an example. Some, such as Villanueva and Mirakor (1990), suggest that macroeconomic stabilisation should always come before market liberalisation. In Australia, this was not the case, as exchange rate liberalisation and the abolition of capital controls were achieved within the first year of the Hawke government in 1983.

Although an appropriate exchange rate regime is important, it is vital that it be supported by an appropriate macroeconomic environment, and this is particularly the case when an economy is undergoing structural evolution. By examining the process of Australian economic reform in the 1980s there is evidence that the freely floating Australian dollar was actually undermining some other areas which Hawke and Keating were seeking to modernise, and jeopardising the outcomes they hoped to achieve. From this, it may thus become possible to question both the principle and the practice of reform packages imposed on many less developed nations by global organisations such as the IMF, which follow, almost without exception, the 'classical strategy'.

The paper is divided as follows. The first section provides an outline of both the rationale for Australian economic reform and the mechanisms for achieving it. Clearly, Hawke and Keating attempted to reform a number of areas, often simultaneously, and so this section should not be taken to be comprehensive in its coverage. For more comprehensive coverage of these areas, see Hawke (1994) and Edwards (1996).

The second section examines the success or otherwise of the Hawke/Keating reform process, particularly the problem of the sequencing of the reforms and the effects of a classical strategy in a modern world setting. The section concentrates on trade policy, industrial policy and financial deregulation, and sets these against the backdrop of the free-floating exchange rate.

The third section provides a brief outline of the reform process in the Republic of Ireland since the late 1950s, and in the light of this suggests that the classical strategy pursued by the Australians in the 1980s may not have been the best course of action. By drawing together evidence from both Australia and the Irish Republic it is possible to suggest that Villanueva and Mirakor have made a valid point as regards the sequencing of economic reform, in particular the exchange rate, and that this issue was visibly demonstrated by the behaviour of the Australian dollar during the 1980s. These issues also raise problems for international organisations such as the IMF, who frequently advocate classical strategies and free-floating exchange rates as fundamental parts of reform packages in the less developed world.

Australia: the theory and practice of economic reform

Bob Hawke, the former prime minister of Australia, writes in his memoirs:

> It was untenable to promote the cause of free trade abroad and yet be deaf to it at home. From the outset my government committed itself to lowering tariffs and other barriers to free trade. It was equally ridiculous to talk of modernisation, globalisation and openness when Australia lay closed at its borders, the arteries of its financial life suffering a sclerosis of regulation and bureaucratic red tape. The world was kicking at Australia's door; to stand there with our hands pressed against it was folly.
>
> (Hawke, 1994, p. 234)

Hawke was referring to the early 1980s, a time when continued Australian prosperity seemed to be under threat. Hawke and his federal treasurer, Paul Keating, saw the need for the reform of the Australian economy, and the integration of Australia into the wider global economy, if it was to meet the challenges of the late 20th century and beyond.

When Bob Hawke and the Australian Labor Party came to power in March 1983, the Australian economy was suffering from high unemployment, inflation and two years of low growth (see Figures 5.1, 5.2 and 5.3), and had been performing relatively poorly for a number of years. Even throughout the long boom Australia had been under-performing relative to trends in the global economy. The World Bank in 1993 suggested that, in terms of GDP per capita, Australia had fallen to 18th in the world (World Bank, 1993), and this was a far cry from the beginning of the 20th century, when it was suggested that Australian per capita income was the highest in the world (Maddison, 1977).

Various explanations have been advanced for this slow but consistent slide down the world prosperity league. Perhaps the three most important, particularly in the views of Bob Hawke and his successor as prime minister, Paul Keating, were Australia's relatively high levels of protectionism, its post-colonial trade patterns and its overly regulated domestic economy.

However, the first area that Hawke and Keating sought to reform was the exchange rate regime. From early December 1983, the Australian dollar was allowed to float freely: before this time the federal government in Canberra employed the crawling peg system of exchange

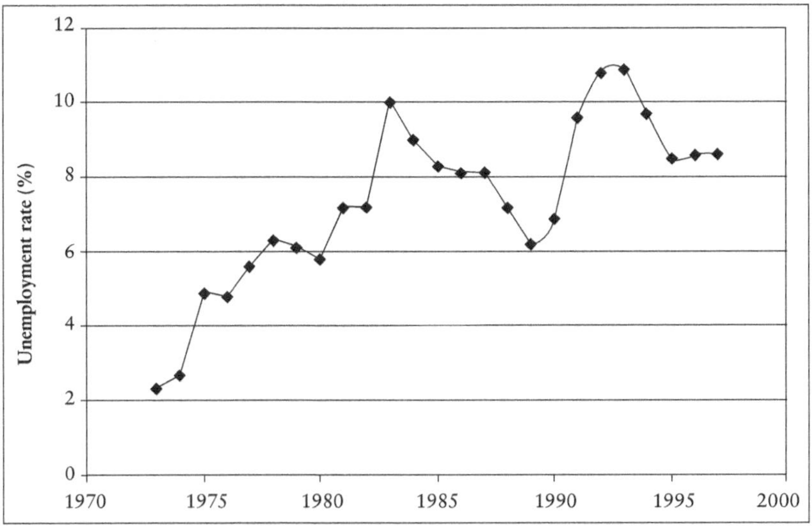

Source: US Government Bureau of Labor Statistics.

Figure 5.1 Australian unemployment rates, 1973–97

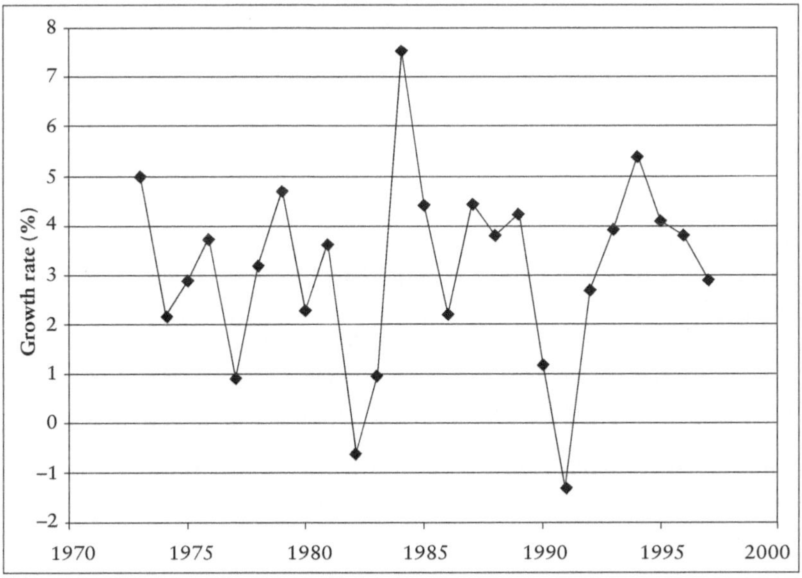

Source: IMF, *International Financial Statistics Yearbook* (1998).

Figure 5.2 Australian GDP growth rates, 1973–97

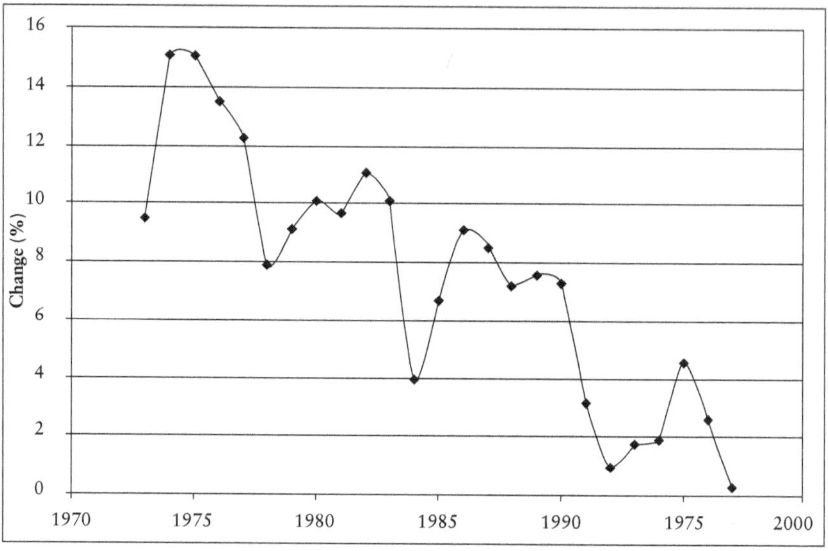

Source: IMF, *International Financial Statistics Yearbook* (1998).

Figure 5.3 Australian consumer price inflation, 1973–97

rate management. Under this system the Reserve Bank had to buy and sell dollars to keep the value of the dollar at the required level, and these dollars taken into or out of the banking system caused instability in the money supply. Because of the recession of the early 1980s, and the feeling that the policies of the Fraser government were making Australia uncompetitive, one of the first acts of the new Hawke administration was to devalue the dollar.

In the early 1980s, Australia was suffering from high and persistent inflation, and the speculators thus believed that the Australian government really favoured a stronger dollar in the longer term to tackle this problem. Following the devaluation of March 1983, and the weakening of the American dollar following lower US interest rates, buying Australian dollars therefore appeared to be a profitable strategy for international speculators. Thus, during 1983, the government was forced to revalue the dollar to the extent that, over a few months, the 10 per cent devaluation of earlier that year had been reversed. Keating sums up this period as follows:

> A big run of money against the currency makes an impression on you. Effectively I had done the devaluation ... in the first week of the government in March 1983 so I had a daily and weekly interest in watching the rate in the weeks and months thereafter. Once you take

> an exchange rate management system, which defined itself by small discrete movements, and then subject it under pressure to a large adjustment, effectively the market has your form; you have exposed your hand.
>
> Speculators make money from central banks by shifting the rate in small then relatively larger amounts. After a while they are playing you like a trout on a line ... Even before the speculative runs against us later in 1983 ... I thought the crawling peg system had seen its best, and even its best was not good enough in terms of competitiveness ... The idea of buying foreign exchange each day, adding it to the money supply and then chasing it out with a long-run cost to the Budget was so absurd that one felt a bunny running such a system.
>
> (Edwards, 1996, p. 543)

Paul Keating clearly felt that the crawling peg exchange rate regime was inappropriate to Australian needs. His reasons for believing this appear to be twofold, the first simply being that trying to maintain a crawling peg exchange rate regime was becoming a game between the government and the speculators. In 1983, the speculators appear to have outguessed the Australian government and won the game. The capital flows into Australia were making it increasingly difficult and costly to maintain the crawling peg exchange rate regime.

Keating's second reason concerns the effect on the money supply of buying and selling currencies to fix the exchange rate. Although Australia did not dabble with full-scale monetarism in the early 1980s, this period saw a growing acceptance of the role of money in determining price levels. Under the crawling peg the Reserve Bank was forced to match each dollar that flowed into Australia by creating domestic currency, and this was adding to the money supply and creating inflationary pressure. Keating was attempting to keep some control over monetary growth, and the crawling peg system was making this task much more difficult. Floating the dollar thus seemed to be inevitable, given the circumstances of late 1983. As Keating says, 'If someone wanted to speculate they would have to find someone else, some other private interest to tango with; anyone but us' (Edwards, 1996, p. 544).

In principle the exchange controls that Australia employed to support its crawling peg policy should have limited the large inflows of funds, but in practice they proved to be ineffective against the surges of capital moving towards Australia. Trade in Australian dollars during the middle of 1983 was significant, as, to use Keating's phrase, speculators felt that they 'had the form' of the new government. Owing to the fixed exchange rate system, this caused a volatility in the Australian measured money supply, and made the meeting of the government's monetary targets much more difficult.

There was thus a deep debate within both the government and the Reserve Bank of Australia about the merits of allowing the dollar to float. Some, such as John Stone, the treasury secretary, argued that, while the crawling peg system had its limitations, it had helped to insulate Australia from significant currency volatility, and floating the dollar would mean that Australia, as a relatively small economy, would be 'thrown around like a cork in the ocean'. Also, given Australia's recent inflationary problems, Stone and others feared a continued appreciation of the dollar, riding on the coat-tails of higher interest rates, which would further worsen Australian competitiveness.

In October 1983, in response to another run against the currency, it was agreed to allow the forward rate to float so as to enable the currency markets to gain experience in setting the forward rate, and also to permit the government to gain a better understanding of the market for the occasion when the inevitable floating of the spot rate occurred. This was deemed to be a success and so, in December of that year, the government allowed the Australian dollar to float freely on the foreign exchange markets.

During 1984, despite interest rates remaining high, the Australian economy was recovering; unemployment and inflation were both being contained, and economic growth was speeding up. Australian business was slowly coming to terms with the increased volatility of the floating dollar but, even so, the Australian government regarded the float as a success. With what appeared to be the unfolding of a benign economic scenario, Hawke called a general election for 1 December 1984, which the government won, albeit with a reduced majority.

In early 1985, although the Australian economy was still in an upturn, the Australian dollar began to depreciate as the FOREX markets became concerned by a variety of political and economic problems in Australia. These included, but were not limited to, a public sector dispute which delayed the depositing of cheques into the government coffers and an announcement that monetary targets would be dropped in favour of a checklist on interest rate decisions. This last problem was forced on the government by its financial market/banking reforms which were distorting the various measures of money supply.

From the end of January to the end of February 1985, the dollar declined by nearly 14 per cent against a trade-weighted basket of currencies, and by almost 16 per cent against a weakening US dollar. Although depreciation was the outcome which Keating had hoped to achieve from the float in 1983, there was concern that such a sharp and sustained depreciation would result in higher inflation in Australia, which when fed through to wages and the prices of imported raw materials would offset any competitive gains brought about by the dollar's fall. It was therefore agreed that interest rates needed to rise to support the dollar, and so from February 1985 to early 1986 they were increased from 12 per cent to 17 per cent, and threatened the economic recovery.

The boom and bust of the 1980s and early 1990s was caused almost entirely by the Australian government's attempts to use its monetary policy to tackle, not only the persistent inflation, but also the current account deficit. At the time, Keating hoped that domestic demand could be gently slowed by manipulating interest rates, but he now believes that the effect of interest rate increases is unpredictable and exponential: '[We were nudging up interest rates] quarter after quarter and then suddenly – bang! ... I'll tell you what, this is all bullshit about the science of monetary policy ... you have to be able to feel what is happening' (Edwards, 1996, p. 320).

Commencing in March 1988, Keating authorised a series of interest rate rises which were the primary cause of the deepest Australian recession in half a century. Keating claimed that the recession was 'the recession that Australia had to have', and ironically it was this deep recession that finally cured the country of the inflation that had plagued it for many years. Unfortunately, the free-floating dollar tended to follow the path of the interest rates used to tackle the country's domestic economic problems.

Exchange rate liberalisation lies at the heart of the Hawke/Keating reforms, but the 'classical strategy' also involved tariff reform, trade pattern reform and financial deregulation. The historical precedent for liberalisation of the Australian economy comes from the last years of the 19th century, when the Australian economy was one of the most open in the world, and when Australia was estimated to have one of the highest GDPs per capita. At this time its tariff rate on manufactured goods averaged around 6 per cent, compared with the USA (73 per cent), Europe (20 per cent), and Japan (10 per cent). Exports and imports at this time made up around 60 per cent of GDP. However, after federation, Australia's protection increased, as governments followed a policy of 'protection all around' to protect Australian workers, farmers and industry from the whims of the global economy. Fears about national security in Asia led successive Australian governments to view increased protectionism as vital in order to support the larger populations seen as necessary for the nation's longer-term survival. Even while the rest of the world under GATT (now the World Trade Organisation – WTO) was moving towards freer trade, Australia remained outside because GATT (the General Agreement on Tariffs and Trade) did not cover the agricultural produce which formed the bulk of Australia's exports. So, by the early 1970s, Australia was one of the most protected economies in the world, with average tariff levels on manufactures at 23 per cent.

The high levels of protectionism allowed what little industry Australia had to become lethargic and inefficient, and thus internationally uncompetitive. So, in spite of the rapid growth of global trade in manufactures which occurred in the postwar period, Australia was unable to participate strongly. Australian exports were geared to the primary sector, where trade was growing much more slowly (partly because of greater agricultural self-sufficiency in a number of countries, and partly because of continued protectionism in this sector) and this led to a decline in Australia's terms of trade. Australia, specialising in the export of primary products, saw its export earnings fall, and these same earnings became more unpredictable owing to the fluctuations in commodity prices on the global market.

In the early 1970s, there was growing recognition of these problems; for example, in 1973, the Labor government of Gough Whitlam cut tariffs by an average of 25 per cent across the board. However, this reduction came at the same time as the first oil price shock and the resulting global economic slowdown of the 1970s. The Fraser government of 1975 to 1983 resisted further cuts in tariff levels and even increased trade protection in some areas. It was not until Hawke/Keating that tariff cuts were once again on the political and economic agenda. In line with classical trade theories, the Hawke administration attempted to boost the competitiveness of Australian industry by making reductions in overall tariff protection. Protection for manufacturing was reduced from 21 per cent in 1983 to 15 per cent in 1991. (These figures are heavily weighted by the significantly above-average protection for the textile, clothing and footwear, and cars and autoparts sectors.)

In addition to tariff reform, the Hawke governments introduced various measures aimed at specific sectors of the economy which were designed to enhance industrial production and also to boost exports in these key sectors. Perhaps the most significant of these was the 'Button Plan', the main planks of which aimed to rationalise the Australian car industry and create economies of scale by reducing both the number of manufacturers and the range of models they manufactured. This was accompanied by measures that allowed manufacturers to offset the value of exports against the requirement for local content. (For an overview of the Button Plan, see Waterson, 1988.)

The second explanation for Australian economic decline is that it has historically perceived itself, and perhaps more importantly been perceived by others, as a European enclave in an Asian region (Trood, 1997). This influenced its trading patterns to the extent that much less trade than might be expected was with its immediate neighbours in Asia and the Pacific rim (see Figure 5.4). Australia, worried about aggression from its neighbours, particularly Indonesia, and concerned about the

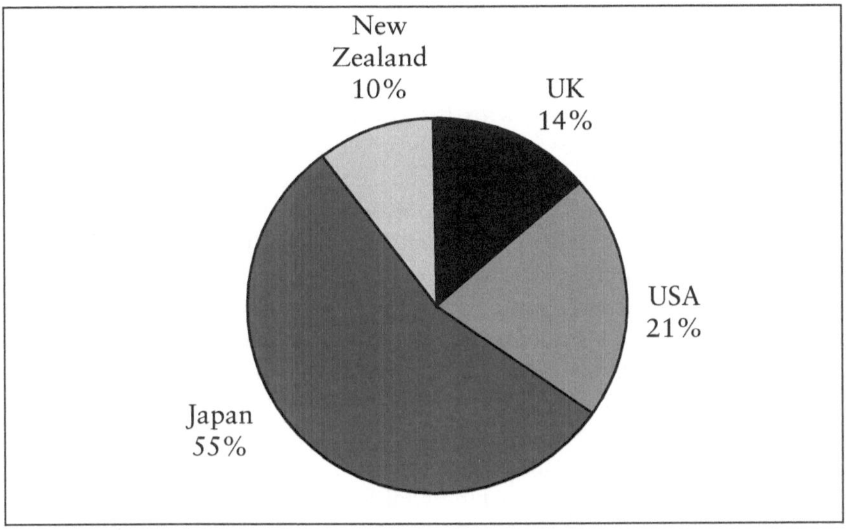

Note: These countries were chosen to represent trading partners in Asia, North America and Europe. Percentage shares include these nations only.

Source: Calculated from IMF, *Direction of Trade Statistics Yearbook* (1979).

Figure 5.4 Australian exports to selected countries, 1973

erosion of its predominantly European society, came to regard its Asian neighbours as security and cultural threats and not as viable trading partners.

Australian trade patterns were then what Paul Krugman would term 'supernatural', in that trade was not as strongly influenced by geographical proximity as would be expected. The problem with such trade patterns is that of geographical isolation: some of Australia's main trading partners were often thousands of miles away, and the significant transport costs which arose from the transport of primary products made Australian products uncompetitive in their export markets. This problem was compounded by the fact that Australian industry was alleged to be lazy and sluggish, protected as it was by some of the highest trade barriers in the world.

Under the Hawke and Keating administrations Australia began to refocus its cultural outlook, and with it its trading flows. The development of ASEAN (Association of South East Asian Nations) and APEC (Asia Pacific Economic Cooperation) has, firstly, increased the strength of the Asian region, both economically and politically, and secondly, has caused barriers to trade in Asia to fall, and this has opened up new markets for Australian businesses. This, together with the involvement of the USA in the APEC grouping, has placed Australia within easy reach of some of the world's fastest growing and most significant economies. Ties with Britain and Europe have weakened as Australia has become more multicultural in both demographic composition and outlook, and this has led to changes in the direction and composition of Australia's trade flows.

The third explanation for Australian stagnation concerns the regulation and structure of its economy. In keeping with the 'classical strategy', the Hawke/Keating domestic economic policies were very much supply-side in orientation, involving as they did reductions in public spending, privatisation and deregulation.

A major plank of this domestic policy was the deregulation of the financial services sector, particularly banking, so as to increase transparency and competition. In 1979, Sir Keith Campbell's Committee of Inquiry into the Australian Financial System was established and this reported its findings to the Fraser government in 1981. According to this report, Australian banks were crippled by overregulation in a number of areas. These included the amount they could borrow or lend, the interest rates they could pay or charge, and the types of securities they could buy or debts they could issue. Furthermore, foreign banking institutions were denied licences to establish themselves in Australia. The Campbell committee proposed a deregulation of this sector, in line with the trends in other industrialised nations, and warned that, without this, Australia risked becoming a closed backwater in an increasingly globalised financial marketplace. The government of Malcolm Fraser was highly sceptical about financial deregulation (although, paradoxically, the Liberal/National Party coalition government of which he was the head claimed to be the party of the free market) and so reform in this area was limited in scope. Fraser's treasurer, John Howard (the current Australian prime minister), had removed government limits on bank lending, and partially removed the interest rate ceiling on bank deposits.

It was not until 1985 that significant steps in line with Campbell's recommendations were taken, by opening up the Australian banking system to foreign banks. According to Hawke, in the new global arena Australia could not afford to show itself abroad as being nervous about foreign bank competition. The domestic banking system at that time was dominated by 'the big four', and Hawke felt that, by keeping foreign banks out, this was merely encouraging these banks to remain inefficient and unresponsive. Thus, in February 1985, Paul Keating announced that 16 foreign banks would receive licences to operate, and that this would more than double the number of banks in the system. By the 1990s, the Australian banking system was more efficient, more responsive and better managed than it had been in the early 1980s, and much trade which would have gone elsewhere now remained in Australia.

Australia: the triumph of the classical strategy?

It is clear that Australia is, to some extent, culturally, politically and economically a product of its colonial past, and that history has cast a long shadow over its modern development. It is also clear that, prior to 1983, economic and foreign policies had to some extent accommodated the legacies of the past instead of tackling them. Arguably, the Hawke and Keating governments were the first to attempt to break from the past by committing their administrations to reform in a number of areas, the aim being to increase Australian competitiveness and thus growth. However, some suggest that, despite the rhetoric, the policies of the Australian government during the 1980s did not in fact tackle the economy's structural problems, and in some areas created new problems. They argue that the policies of these Labor governments led to overvalued and volatile exchange rates, supported by high interest rates, to curb inflation, and a continuation of the boom and bust policies of the past. This, combined with the deregulation of both the financial services sector and the floating of the dollar, has served to exacerbate Australia's balance of payments problems in both the long and short term, and has

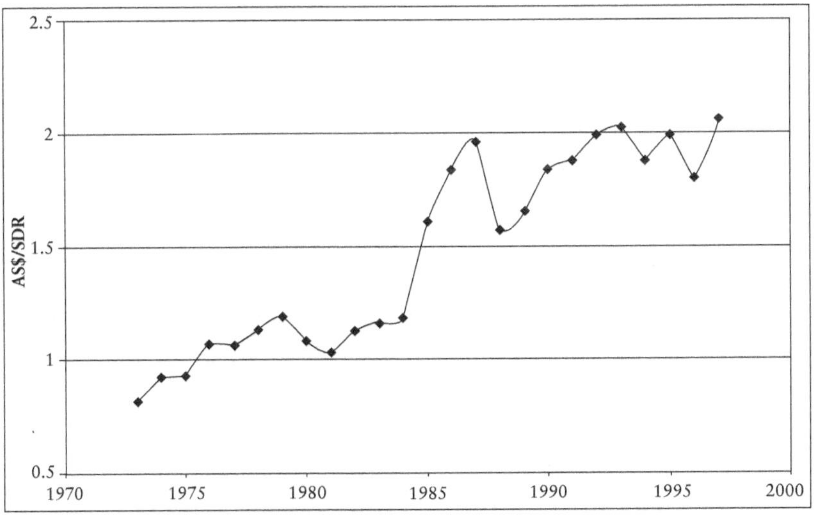

Source: IMF, *International Financial Statistics Yearbook* (1998).

Figure 5.5 Australian dollar/SDR exchange rate, 1973–97

added to the volatility of the Australian dollar on the FOREX markets. (See Figure 5.5.)

An unstable and overvalued dollar was just what John Stone, the Australian treasury secretary during the early 1980s, feared. He claimed that floating the dollar would mean that Australia, as a relatively small economy, would be 'thrown around like a cork in the ocean'. The volatility of the dollar and the speculative inflows and outflows suggest that his fears may have some grounding.

The main impact of the free-floating dollar is in its effects on Australia's international competitiveness and industrial development. From 1984 onwards, the dollar began a sharp appreciation on the FOREX markets, and this occurred at the same time as Hawke and Keating were attempting to open the Australian economy to the outside world through enmeshment with Asia and the reduction of Australia's protectionist cocoon. Thus Australia was attacked on two sides simultaneously, and this illustrates the weakness of the classical strategy. Economic theory suggests that freer trade is beneficial because it forces previously protected domestic industries to compete, and encourages economies of scale. However, the real-world experience may differ from the theory. Classical trade theories imply that, when nations move towards freer trade then the larger market size which results allows business units to expand their production to meet the increased demand. In doing this they begin to enjoy benefits of larger-scale operation, which lowers average costs and improves the firm's competitive position.

The invisible hand of the market is an attractive idea, but the fact that *theoretically* market access is enhanced does not mean that the same is true in practice. In the real world, markets are not perfect and will not necessarily ensure that nations with a weak or fragmented industrial base (like Australia) will diversify and move into the larger markets. Classical trade theories ignore the fact that, to gain fully from the expanded market, nations and their business units must have prepared themselves for the change in arena. If they have not, they may be overwhelmed by competition from better-financed rivals who already enjoy economies of scale, for example the developed nations of southeast Asia. The problem is that strategic trade policies which may serve to prepare firms for free trade are not always possible for smaller nations such as Australia. Consequently, competition may be, not a beneficial force, but a destructive one which wrecks fragile industrial bases and prohibits the development of scale economies. The problems of moving to freer trade were compounded by the volatile and stronger dollar, as any competitive gains brought about by free trade were at best reduced, and at worst offset by the stronger currency.

The combination of free-floating exchange rates and the liberalisation

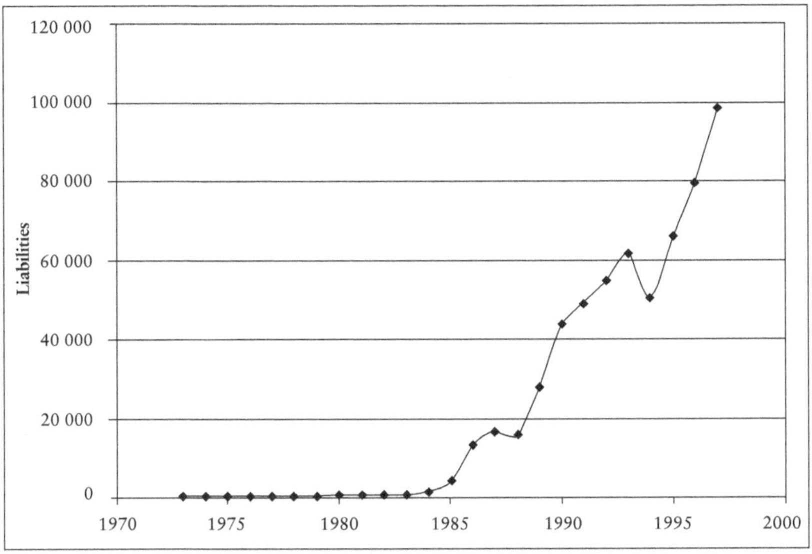

Source: IMF, *International Financial Statistics Yearbook* (1998).

Figure 5.6 Growth of Australian deposit money banks' foreign liabilities (AS$millions) (1973–97)

of the financial services sector has hindered Australian industrial development. Financial deregulation allowed Australian citizens and corporations to borrow much more than they were able to before, and to borrow from sources outside Australia. From 1983, the amount of foreign debt held by banks, for example, increased significantly. (See Figure 5.6.)

This debt expansion in the 1980s contributed to both the length and depth of the recession of the early 1990s, as companies and individuals had become more financially vulnerable. This deep recession added to Australian unemployment levels and caused an estimated loss of output to the value of AS$50 billion. Evidence from Australia, the UK and other nations indicates that sharp downturns in economic activity hit manufacturing and other industry hardest and, in the case of Australia, with an already fragile industrial base coping with the reduction in its protective crutch and an evolving trading arena, the damage was significant. In addition to this, as Australian nationals and corporations were now free to invest funds abroad, the temptation to reap higher yields from, for example, investments in the Asian Tiger economies than were available in Australia meant that investment that would have otherwise remained in Australia now went abroad.

The Australian experience also demonstrates that external debts and free-floating currencies are not always a beneficial combination. This is particularly the case when the domestic currency is prone to volatility or depreciation, as this varies the amount of the foreign debt repayable in the domestic currency. After the float, Australia had just such a currency.

There are lessons for Latin America and Africa here. As is well known, these are regions with large levels of external debt, much of it denominated in other currencies, such as the US dollar. It is interesting to note that exchange rate liberalisation is widely seen as vital to economic well-being, particularly by the IMF in its dealings with Africa. While floating exchange rates can act to adjust automatically balance of payments disequilibriums, without an appropriate economic structure to underpin it a floating exchange rate can cause more problems than it solves.

Financial deregulation also caused increased interest in the financial markets, and increased investment in financial assets, a large proportion of which are traded on the secondary markets and so provide no new industrial investment. Figure 5.7 shows the effect of this increased interest as the value of Australian shares increased dramatically after 1983. In addition these surplus funds invested in the paper economy may otherwise have been more usefully invested in the real economy.

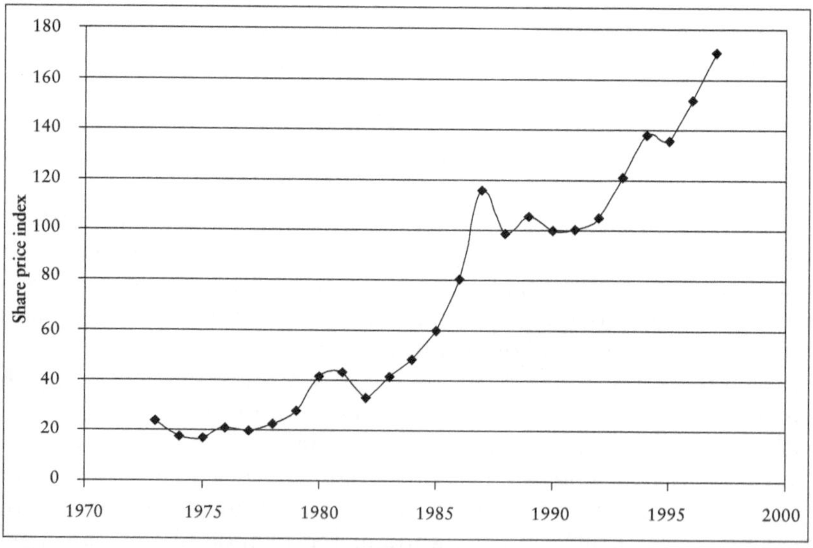

Source: IMF, *International Financial Statistics Yearbook* (1998).

Figure 5.7 Australian share price index, 1973–97

In addition to failing to develop fully a domestic industrial base of its own, Australia has failed to attract significant or useful multinational corporate activity. Halevi and Kriesler (1993) use evidence from the 1960s onwards and suggest that the limited multinational corporate activity in Australia has taken a different form than in other countries in that it has tended to be passive and small-scale, content merely to serve the protected domestic market. In states such as Japan and South Korea, such activities have aimed to create economies of scale so as to allow the development of an industrial export base. For Australia, the opportunity was there, in a period of tariff protection and fixed exchange rates, and when Australia was more economically advanced than its Asian neighbours, to develop and export specialist manufactured goods, but such opportunities were never developed, as the governments of the day continued their support of the declining primary sector and commonwealth trade routes. The Hawke/Keating reforms appear to have made such industrial development even less likely, as exchange rate liberalisation and tariff reduction have opened up a structurally weak Australia to the world, while its close economic links with the Pacific rim means that multinational corporation (MNC) investment is more likely to find its way to the tiger economies than to Australia.

Hawke and Keating aimed to shift Australia away from its over-reliance on the declining primary sector. However, it can be argued that

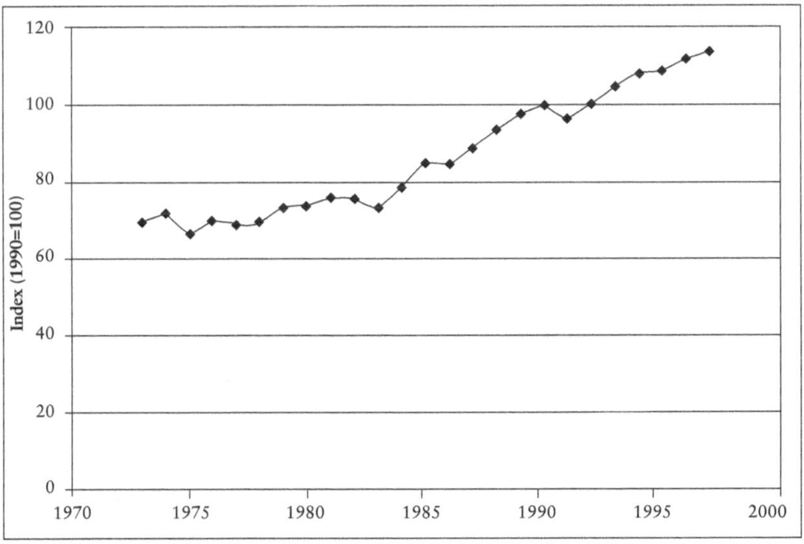

Source: IMF, *International Financial Statistics Yearbook* (1998).

Figure 5.8 Australian industrial production, 1973–97

truly significant Australian manufacturing development has actually been hindered by some planks of the classical strategy. Certainly, although the Hawke/Keating reforms succeeded in increasing Australian industrial production faster than its trend between 1973 and 1983 (see Figure 5.8), this is hardly surprising given the unfortunate global economic conditions prevailing during this period. The fact is that manufacturing, in terms both of its share of GDP and of its share of employment, has declined since 1960, and fallen behind the OECD averages (see Table 5.1).

Table 5.1 Manufacturing, share of GDP and employment, selected countries and groups

	Share of GDP (%)			*Share of employment (%)*		
	1960	*1974*	*1990*	*1960*	*1974*	*1990*
Australia	29	25	15	31	25	17
Japan	35	34	29	21	27	24
United States	28	23	18	26	24	18
European Union	33	30	23	29	30	23
All OECD	29	27	22	26	27	21

Source: Anderson (1995), using OECD historical statistics, 1960–1990.

In addition, the Hawke/Keating reforms meant that production is biased towards certain sectors such as the car industry, where specific programmes were enacted, but even this may have a downside. The Button Plan, for example, has produced significant gains for the Australian motor industry, in terms of both production and exports, but its benefits to the Australian economy in the aggregate are questionable, and there are two reasons for this. The first is that the Australian motor industry is based primarily on the urban areas of the country, and so gains are not necessarily felt in rural areas. Secondly, and perhaps more importantly, the increased volume of exports in both cars and car parts has aided the appreciation in the value of the Australian dollar on the world markets, and added to its volatility. This has had an unfavourable impact on Australian industry in general by reducing its global competitiveness, and by making primary product prices more unpredictable.

Halevi and Kriesler (1993) suggest that, given the structure of the Australian economy, any movements in the exchange rate will have a detrimental effect on industrial development and the balance of trade. They suggest that, as a large proportion of Australian exports are primary products (see Table 5.2), they are relatively price-inelastic, whereas much of what Australia imports takes the form of intermediate or final goods, the demand for which is more price-elastic. As Australian industry is still much smaller in scale than its industrial rivals, there are limited import competing domestic industries. Thus a weakening of the value of the Australian dollar raises the costs of imported capital goods and, given the limited numbers of import competing industries, the effect of this is likely to be inflationary. An appreciation of the Australian dollar, on the other hand, would increase the demand for imported consumer goods while making Australian industry less competitive in its export markets. Given the volatility of the dollar in the 1980s, the negative effects on Australian industrial development might be quite profound.

Table 5.2 Composition of Australian exports (% share)

	Unprocessed primary	*Processed primary*	*Simply transformed manufactures*	*Elaborately transformed manufactures*	*Gold*
1985	59.3	21.6	8.1	8.9	2.1
1986	57.4	21.6	8.3	9.8	3.0
1987	52.8	21.3	9.9	11.2	4.8
1988	49.5	20.7	11.6	11.5	6.7
1989	47.8	22.7	12.0	11.6	5.9
1990	45.4	23.5	11.0	12.9	7.2
1991	44.6	23.3	10.6	14.4	7.1
1992	43.1	22.7	10.3	15.7	8.2
1993	40.8	23.5	10.1	17.6	8.0
1994	38.9	23.4	10.8	19.1	7.8
1995	35.6	21.7	11.1	24.2	7.5

Source: Ravenhill (1997), citing Trade Analysis Branch, Dept. of Foreign Affairs.

In general, the tools of the reform process itself appear, with a few exceptions, to have been ineffective or countered by other planks of the wider reform package, in particular the floating exchange rate and financial market liberalisation. These problems are of course compounded by the volatility of Australian interest rates and the real economy throughout the 1980s and early 1990s. Although Hawke and Keating largely succeeded in arresting the decline in Australia's terms of trade, they did not succeed in reversing it. (See Figure 5.9.)

Perhaps less easy to criticise are the moves to refocus geographically Australian trade patterns, and lock into the growth of the Asian region.

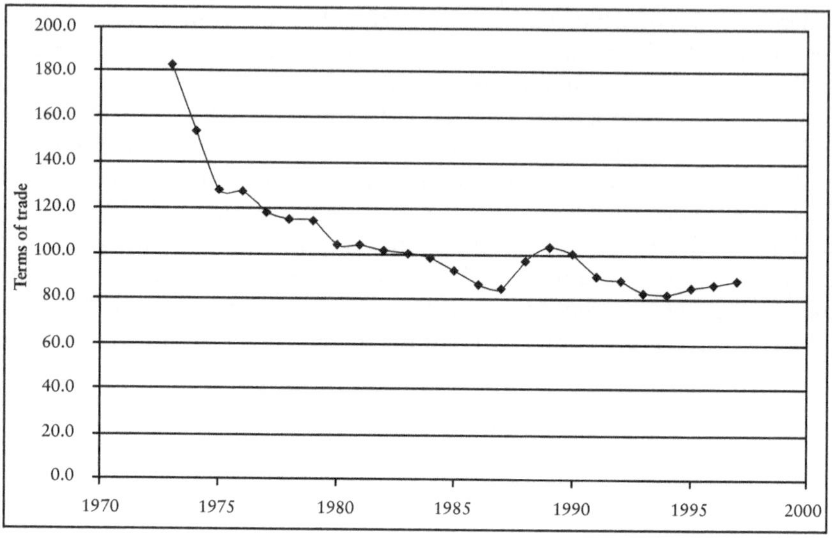

Source: IMF, *International Financial Statistics Yearbook* (1998).

Figure 5.9 Australian terms of trade, 1973–97

Again, however, there may be problems. Countries such as Australia, which primarily export raw materials and other factor inputs, and have trade flows spread throughout Asia, Europe and North America, may have little to gain from membership of just one region. Arguably, this problem is compounded by the nature of the regional groupings of which Australia is a member. For example, the APEC, although created through the efforts of Bob Hawke, may not be the most effective way of ensuring freer trade and closer links with Asia.

Hawke's original proposal for APEC was to attempt to create an Asia/Pacific equivalent of the Paris-based Organization for Economic Cooperation and Development (OECD) and, given that the primary thrust of his administration's foreign/economic policies was enmeshment with this region, this is not surprising. The OECD is an organisation that provides governments with an arena in which to discuss and develop their economic and social policies. Members compare their experiences and seek solutions to common problems and work to coordinate their domestic and international policies. For Australia, attempting to break from decades of mutual suspicion with its Asian neighbours, such a 'softly softly' approach to integration was perhaps the best course to take.

However, within a few years the North Americans (Canada and the

United States) and the Australasians began pushing for a more ambitious programme for APEC in the form of trade liberalisation. It was not until the APEC summit at Bogor in 1994 that it was agreed to take steps towards this goal. The targets set were free trade by 2010 for the industrialised APEC members, and 2020 for the less developed members.

It soon became clear, however, that there were serious disagreements between members regarding the interpretation of their agreements and obligations, and that the nature of APEC was compounding this problem. For example, although the Bogor meeting committed APEC to free trade by 2020 at the latest, it failed to define what the term 'free trade' actually meant. Some members' interpretation was zero tariffs, completely free trade, while others believed they had committed themselves merely to substantially lower tariffs. In addition to this, some members stressed that the commitments they had made at Bogor were simply a statement of intent, and not a binding guarantee of firm action. By the time of the next APEC summit meeting, at Osaka in 1995, the organisation was showing signs of internal strain, and to avoid a split in the group it was agreed to proceed with flexibility in implementing APEC's free trade agenda.

The events of 1994 and 1995 reveal much about the nature of APEC and perhaps about its future success. The emergence of self-interpretation of obligations, rather than a centrally and clearly defined interpretation, suggests that APEC could quickly become simply another talking shop organisation. This problem is compounded by APEC's lack of carrots and sticks for liberalising trade. Open regionalism offers reductions in trade barriers on a non-discriminatory basis, and the benefits of this are open to all countries, even those who are not APEC members. There is then, it seems, little reason for APEC to exist as a force for regional trade liberalisation: any benefits its members may glean in the form of lower trade barriers are shared with every country that trades with them. The World Trade Organization (WTO) has been following these principles since 1947.

In addition, there are the problems of 'free-riders', who take but never give, and those who appear to fail to fulfil their commitments. APEC, by its very nature, has little in the way of sanctions to punish or coerce those nations suspected of failing to fulfil their commitments, but, with the principle of self-interpretation of those commitments, no member of APEC can ever be accused of behaving dishonourably.

Evidence from the early 1990s suggests that, in terms of trade with Asia, the Hawke/Keating reforms have not significantly improved Australia's competitive position. While overall trade with Asia had increased, this increase had not been as great as might have been expected. For example, in 1985, 42·8 per cent of Australian trade was with Asia, but by 1990 it had only risen to 43·8 per cent and in 1995 to 48·3 per cent. In 1990, 52·5 per cent of Australian exports went to Asia, and 35·1 per cent of Australian imports came from Asia. In 1995, these figures were 60·5 per cent and 37·0 per cent, respectively. The growth in trade, however, masks the reality that, while the volume of Australian exports to Asia has increased, Australia's actual share of the APEC markets has fallen. Between 1989 and 1994, the share of trade had fallen from 3·1 per cent to 2·8 per cent. Two lessons can be drawn from this.

The first is that the efforts of Hawke/Keating to integrate Australia into the Asian region met with limited success, at least in economic terms, as its exports are still a minor part of overall Asian trade. Hughes (1991) questioned the merit of placing so much diplomatic emphasis on APEC, believing that the gains were not worth the heavy investment in terms of time and back-scratching which the Australian government had made. She believed that membership of APEC would have at best a marginal role in rectifying Australian structural problems. She suggested that the efforts expended on APEC would have been more effectively employed in domestic reforms, particularly in the labour market, which she argues was too inflexible and tightly regulated. The Hawke governments failed to embark on any significant labour market reforms, and Hughes believes that this has kept Australian unemployment higher than it would have otherwise been.

The second lesson, related to the first, is that, despite making the development of APEC a major priority, membership has failed to increase significantly the competitiveness of the Australian economy. Freer trade along classical lines has so far failed to encourage the development of scale economies and greater competitiveness in many areas, and it seems that the strengthening of the Australian dollar during the 1980s has contributed to this problem. It is also strange that the high interest rates and a stronger currency failed to impose much in the way of significant downward pressure on Australian domestic inflation. It is possible that the financial market deregulation has made it easier for commercial banks to create credit and so boost broad measures of money, a problem which Margaret Thatcher encountered in the UK during the early 1980s.

Perhaps Australia is a victim of the fact that, because APEC is non-discriminatory, its use as a tool of strategic trade policy is limited. The APEC agenda of non-discrimination, while laudable in concept, is naïve in a real-world context as it demonstrates that the fallacies of the classical trade theories are alive in the modern world. Two such fallacies are that all nations benefit from free trade, and that free trade is always the best policy, no matter what other nations do. Sometimes it is in the interests of countries which enjoy a dominant position in a market or sector to restrict total output, or exports, of that commodity to inflate the world price.

Secondly, a passive policy of free trade whatever other nations do is not a rational policy. Traditional free trade theory implies that the idea that a country should depart from free trade because other countries do is similar to suggestions that, because other countries have rocky coasts, we should block up our own harbours. However, the notion that free trade is always the best response is clearly nonsense, as it ignores important strategic considerations. To continue the shipping analogy, it is irrational to continue to allow the ships of other nations to use our harbours, if they persistently refuse to allow our ships access to theirs (Krugman, 1987b).

Only in recent years have ideas such as this come to be questioned, and two main factors have combined to highlight the inadequacy of traditional trade theories in their explanations of world trade patterns. First is the changing nature of the global trading system, which has moved away from being simply an exchange of goods or services as envisaged by classical economic theory. Instead, much trade has come to reflect transient political alliances, random and fluid advantages resulting from economies of scale, or a sudden breakthrough in technological advances. The second factor which highlights the weaknesses of traditional trade theory are the changes in economic theory itself, particularly those which have questioned the notion of the perfect market. Theoretical developments like the notion of interdependence in oligopolistic markets have reduced the rationale for the belief in the existence of perfect markets and passive trade policies.

The rethinking of trade theory (Krugman, 1987b), implies that a more activist, or strategic trade policy, could benefit a country relative to free trade, by using the power of individual trading nations (if economically powerful) or discriminatory trading blocs to gain a larger share of the world trade cake, perhaps at the expense of its competitor countries or blocs in the global marketplace. In the traditional analysis of trade it is suggested that there is no real point in a nation moving its productive capacity into an area of economic activity which appears to offer a high return, as in the long run in a perfect free trade market these abnormal profits will be competed away as many others will be similarly attracted. The new view of trade suggests, however, that important trading sectors are those where the abnormal profits may not easily be competed away. If, for example, these areas of activity require large-scale production processes or involve complex technologies, new entry into an industry may appear to be unprofitable to those outside, even if those firms or nations already operating within are enjoying high levels of return. If this is indeed the case, it makes sense for national governments to attempt to employ their trade policies to give their domestic producers a foothold in these markets so as to secure for their nation a greater share of this abnormal profit.

Membership of a discriminatory bloc such as NAFTA or the EU, for example, gives better access to large-scale production capacities, and this and the use of subsidies to firms operating in the profitable sectors or tempted to move into them, or some form of protectionism may serve to secure a nation's access to these profitable markets and thus raise its national income. This gain is not, however, a 'WIN–WIN' situation, as it would be under free trade, but more a beggar-thy-neighbour trade policy, where any gains are realised at the expense of others. The size and significance of a NAFTA-style bloc may mean that other nations/blocs think twice before engaging in retaliatory trade policies. In looser blocs such as APEC, some of this market power is lost.

Activist trade policies are, then, one possible way in which national governments can attempt to secure a larger share of global trade. If this is the case, however, it is likely that other national governments will be simultaneously attempting to secure a larger share for their own domestic industries, and so trade policy should be employed so as to counter the actions of foreign governments.

These new ideas suggest an alternative to the notion that free trade is appropriate and desirable whatever other nations do. Instead, trade is a potentially aggressive activity where gains for one party may be derived at the expense of other parties, and the policies of one country are by definition shaped by the actions and reactions of its trading partners. In the case of APEC, however, the strong influence of the classical trade theories may mean that, although the traditional gains from trade are realised by the member states, they fail to harness their combined economic power to force concessions from their trading rivals. As the world continues to drift towards regionalism, APEC may begin to be left behind. Australia may find that, having nailed its colours to the APEC mast, it suffers by opening its adolescent industrial sector to competition from its arguably more industrialised Asian neighbours.

It is still perhaps too early to fully evaluate the Hawke/Keating reforms, although Australia would seem to be better off after the reforms than it was before. However, the sequence of that reform process, perhaps most importantly the timing of the dollar float, can be questioned. It is also possible that Australia could have been much better off had it followed a more unorthodox 'non-classical' reform strategy. For example, economic growth rates under Hawke/Keating were only marginally better than the growth rates of the 1970s, and biased upwards by the strong growth in 1984. Certainly, it seems to have been a mistake to have floated the dollar so early. There are two principal reasons for suggesting this. The first is that the structural fundamentals of the Australian economy which would be required to support a free-floating exchange rate regime were not in place in the early 1980s. The second reason is that certain elements of the reform process, and in particular the exchange rate regime, appear to have undermined other areas, or created other unforeseen problems.

The question, then, is 'what makes an exchange rate policy appropriate?' Perhaps the answer is to be found in the circumstances and evolution of the domestic economy: in other words, where it is now, and where it is going. Clearly, Australia under Hawke and then Keating was undergoing significant evolution: it was rethinking its cultural ties, and its foreign policies, trade policies and economic policies were all becoming more global in focus, particularly with regard to the Asian region. It was freeing its domestic economy through deregulation and privatisation. In the sort of economy which Australia was moving towards becoming, a crawling peg exchange rate system and fairly rigid exchange controls appeared to be an anachronism. The motives for floating the dollar in late 1983 were understandable in the circumstances of the time, but floating the dollar before the economy was structurally reformed was like putting the cart before the horse. Inflation and unemployment were still problematic, industry was still small-scale and fragmented when compared with industrial rivals, and Australia was uncompetitive in its export markets, particularly in the secondary sector.

Basic economic theory, and common sense, suggest that, from the point of view of international trade competitiveness, what is needed is an exchange rate which is stable over time, and not over- or under-valued. Under Hawke and Keating, Australia did not have such a currency and the reason is that the Australian economy in the 1980s was not suited to such a free-float regime. There are two primary reasons for this. The first is that the interest rate was being used as a tool of monetary policy to tackle inflation. Thus the dollar became stronger but more volatile on the back of higher and volatile interest rates, and this had an impact on competitiveness and external debt servicing.

Australia was not the last to make this mistake. In the early 1990s, the Major government in the UK was attempting to pursue an exchange rate policy involving an over-valued sterling, influenced by high interest rates, to combat domestic inflationary pressure, and succeeded in causing and prolonging a recession. Throughout the period from 1983 onwards, Australia was varying interest rates (see Figure 5.10) to try to manipulate its domestic demand, with predictable effects on the exchange rate and the real economy.

The second reason is that, during the 1980s, Australian governments were simply trying to juggle too many balls. The reforms in trade policy,

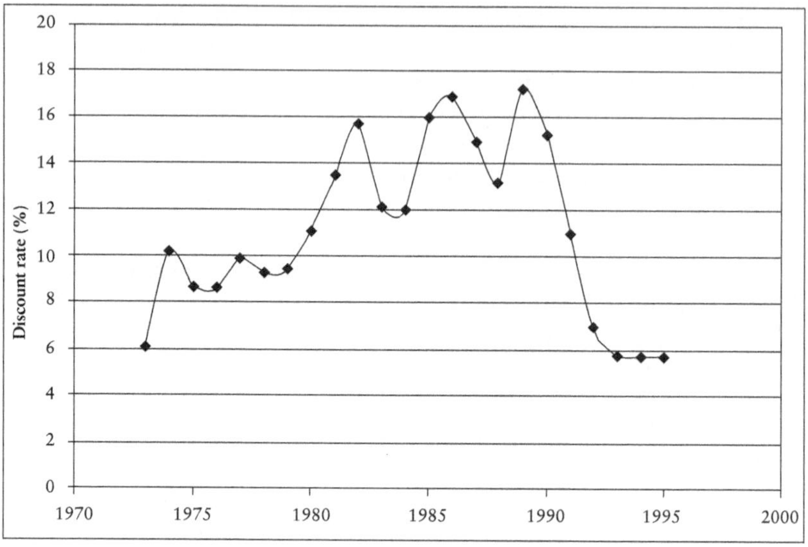

Source: IMF, *International Financial Statistics Yearbook* (1998).

Figure 5.10 Australian discount rate (1973–95)

foreign economic policy and domestic deregulation might have been more successful without the additional distractions and problems caused by the volatility of the dollar. It could be suggested that Hawke and Keating concentrated too heavily on grand gestures in terms of macroeconomic reform, and largely failed to use microeconomic policies to remedy Australia's inherent structural problems, a view probably shared by Hughes. It seems clear that some areas of their macroeconomic reforms were contradictory and undermined by the exchange rate regime.

There may, then, be a chicken and egg situation as regards economic reform and exchange rates. All too often, indeed almost universally, 'structural' reform and exchange rate reform go hand in hand, and this is the case in Australia, Latin America and also in Russia. It may well be better to maintain some degree of fixed or banded exchange rate system, or at least some limits on speculative inflows as in Chile, until the fundamentals of the economy can better withstand the external shocks associated with floating rates.

There are perhaps lessons for the IMF in this. In recent years, the IMF has suffered from a shortage of liquidity, and so does not have the capital to do an effective job. It is also increasingly perceived as a tool of western, particularly American, economic interests. It is therefore no surprise that the IMF recommends the floating of exchange rates as a fundamental part of many reform packages, as this is a western capitalist notion which requires no capital expenditure by the IMF to achieve. However, what may work in developed western European and North American economies cannot be guaranteed to work in less developed economies or those undergoing structural reform. It is, then, little wonder that crises like the recent instabilities of the Russian rouble and Brazilian real occur. Once again the cart is before the horse.

There are lessons here for Europe, too, as it moves towards a single currency. In eastern Europe there are many new democracies with fledgling capitalist economies, some of them with floating exchange rates. Within the next decade it is likely that a number of them will be members of the European Union, although probably not the single currency. The recent Russian experiences, and the continued aftermath of German reunification, demonstrate what happens when economies move to floating exchange rates before the economic structure is reformed; you can put wheels on a car, but if the engine is missing it still won't go.

It may be that the 'classical strategy' for reform, particularly as regards exchange rate and trade liberalisation, is irretrievably flawed, and if this is the case the structural adjustment programmes of the IMF are likely to be harmful to the countries on which they are imposed. Thus it must be asked if there are theoretical alternatives to the 'classical strategy' and whether there are any models of a non-classical approach in operation.

The Republic of Ireland: an alternative to the classical strategy?

The economy of the Republic of Ireland may offer a good model. Here economic development has been unorthodox: high rates of personal taxation, generous social welfare payments, an ambitious industrial policy, managed trade as a member of the European Union and an exchange rate regime which has never been truly free-floating.

In the early years of the Irish Free State, much of Irish nationalism had shown a pronounced protectionist leaning, and with the election in 1932 of the nationalist Fianna Fail party, led by Eamon De Valera, this leaning was reflected in national policy. De Valera's dominance of Irish political life continued until the late 1950s, and he was committed to the creation of a Celtic utopia in Ireland based on its Gaelic, rural and Catholic traditions. Paradoxically, however, even though the Irish Free State introduced its own currency, the punt, it maintained the effective currency union with Britain that had existed since 1826.

As a means to ensure De Valera's ends, a policy of protectionism was introduced, and the passing of the Control of Manufacturers Acts (1932, 1934) severely limited foreign participation in Irish industry. In 1937, tariff levels of up to 40 per cent made Ireland the most trade-protected nation in western Europe, and this isolationism allowed Ireland to escape largely unscathed from the economic carnage of the Second World War. In the 1930s, trade declined by 30 per cent, and it fell by a further 50 per cent during the Second World War.

Although the 1950s did see some changes in manufacturing policy following the creation in 1949 of the Industrial Development Authority (IDA), the 1950s fully exposed the fallacy of Ireland's isolationist position: some 87 per cent of Irish exports were sold in the UK, and 80 per cent of Ireland's exports came from agriculture, compared to 7 per cent from manufactures. In short, import-substituting isolationism, if it had ever really existed, had failed to promote the sought-after indigenous industrial development. During the 1950s, Ireland's terms of trade worsened, and the import component of GNP rose. Ireland began to suffer balance of payments and inflationary problems and, as living standards fell, so emigration rose sharply.

Ireland's policy of isolationism began to fray in the mid-1950s, with Ireland joining the United Nations in 1955 and the World Bank and the International Monetary Fund in 1957. The 1958 publication, *Economic Development* (Department of Finance, 1958), highlighted the growing problems of the isolationist system and proposed a new focus on the encouragement of foreign participation and export enhancement.

In 1965, the Anglo-Irish Free Trade Agreement was signed, and membership of GATT was achieved in 1967. Perhaps most significant was Ireland's entry into the European Union in 1973. However, Irish indigenous industry was not capable of successfully competing in the wider European market, and so the Irish government sought to build Ireland's position as a base for foreign direct investment. The main mechanism for achieving this was the Export Profit Tax Relief (EPTR) scheme, introduced by the IDA in 1956 and modified in the 1960s. This allowed all profits generated by export transactions to be earned tax-free for a period of 15 years up to 1990, and allowed for 100 per cent repatriation of those profits. A European Community ruling on the 'opaque' nature of this incentive caused the EPTR to be replaced by a 10 per cent corporation tax in 1981. This is still one of the lowest in the European Union and thus continues to be a major incentive for multinational activity in Ireland.

The currency union with Britain was abandoned in 1979, when the Irish punt joined the newly established Exchange Rate Mechanism (ERM). The reason for abandoning the long-established link was the increased inflation of the 1970s which had seen Irish consumer prices rising by an average of 14 per cent a year. This figure was significantly higher than that of many of Ireland's industrial rivals, but closely mirrored inflation patterns in Britain. Ireland's dependence on Britain as a trading partner, combined with the punt/sterling exchange rate parity, was importing British inflation into Ireland.

Membership of the EU and the increase in multinational corporate activity in Ireland has led to a major expansion in Irish trade, and has also changed its composition and geographical parameters. Ireland's exports are now geared very much towards manufactured goods, and the historical dependence on the UK market as a destination for exports has been reduced.

The reform process in Ireland thus appears to have been highly successful, but it is clear that Ireland has followed a different path than that of Australia. In Australia, exchange rate reform was at the heart of the process and achieved early. In Ireland, however, successful reform has been achieved without making reform of the exchange rate regime a vital component part. Perhaps more importantly, in Ireland the exchange rate has never been free-floating. From 1826 until the late 1970s, the Irish punt shadowed sterling. After 1979, the punt became a member of the Exchange Rate Mechanism (ERM) of the European monetary system, another managed exchange rate regime.

The significant factor here is that the Irish exchange rate regime evolved naturally according to the circumstances of the time. Up to the late 1970s, the currency union with Britain appeared to serve the country well, offering as it did a firm anchor in the form of a link to a major reserve currency, the country's largest trading partner and an economically stable neighbour. Even after the currency parity was abandoned in favour of ERM membership, the punt continued to shadow sterling, benefiting from the lower inflation rates of the 1980s. Never in the Irish reform process was exchange rate reform a major plank.

Conclusion

The exchange rate, while important as a tool of both domestic economic policy and international trade policy, should perhaps not be the main focus of attention when it comes to economic reform. As Ireland and others demonstrate, factors such as education and training, and real structural reform are more important, as they create the conditions for an appropriate exchange rate regime. Free-floating exchange rates are not always a good thing, especially if the economic fundamentals are not in place, or are in the process of evolving. Get these fundamentals right, and the exchange rate will look after itself, whether managed or free-floating. But the exchange rate cart should always be behind the structural reform horse, and never in front.

References

Anderson, K. (1995), 'Australia's changing trade pattern and growth performance', in R. Pomfret (ed.), *Australia's Trade Policies*, Melbourne: Oxford University Press.

Department of Finance (1958), *Economic Development*, Dublin: The Stationery Office.

Edwards, J. (1996), *Keating: The Inside Story*, Ringwood, Victoria, Australia: Penguin Books.

Galligan, B., I. McAllister and J. Ravenhill (eds) (1997), *New Developments in Australian Politics*, Melbourne: Macmillan Education.

Halevi, J. and P. Kriesler (1993), 'Structural change and economic growth', in G. Mahony (ed.), *The Australian Economy Under Labor*, Sydney, Australia: Allen & Unwin.

Hawke, B. (1994), *The Hawke Memoirs*, London: Heinemann.

Hughes, H. (1991), 'Does APEC make sense?', ASEAN Economic Bulletin, 8.

IMF (1979), *Direction of Trade Statistics Yearbook*, Washington, DC: IMF.

IMF (1998), *International Financial Statistics Yearbook*, Washington, DC: IMF.

Krugman, P. (ed.) (1987a), *Strategic Trade Policy and the New International Economics*, Cambridge, MA: MIT Press.

Krugman, P. (1987b), 'New thinking about trade policy', in P. Krugman (ed.), *Strategic Trade Policy and the New International Economics*, Cambridge, MA: MIT Press.

Maddison, A. (1977), 'Phases of capitalist development', *Banca Nazionale del Lavoro Quarterly Review*, 30.

Mahony, G. (ed.) (1993), *The Australian Economy Under Labor*, Sydney, Australia: Allen & Unwin.

Ravenhill, J. (1997), 'Foreign economic policies', in B. Galligan et al. (eds), *New Developments in Australian Politics*, Melbourne: Macmillan Education.

Trood, R. (1997), 'Australia and Asia', in B. Galligan et al. (eds), *New Developments in Australian Politics*, Melbourne: Macmillan Education.

Villanueva, D. and A. Mirakor (1990), 'Strategies for financial reforms', *IMF Staff Papers*, 3.

Waterson, M. (1988), 'An outsider's view of the Button Plan for the car industry', *Economic Papers*, 17.

World Bank (1993), *World Tables,* Washington, DC: Johns Hopkins University Press.

CHAPTER SIX

Stabilisation and adjustment in Greece, 1990–99

Costas Karfakis

Introduction[1]

Greece has long had an unenviable reputation as an economic under-achiever. After the second oil shock its economic performance was particularly disappointing, with slow GDP growth and high inflation as it failed to adjust its production structures, despite sizable transfers from the Economic Community, refused to open up to the globalisation process and increased government intervention. In the late 1980s, the conditions of the economy gave even more than the usual grounds for concern, since developments were marked by the termination of the 1986–7 stabilisation programme and the subsequent relaxation of fiscal and income policies. Despite an exceptionally high gross fixed investment in 1988–9, which seems to have flattened out in 1990, real GDP growth fell from 4·1 per cent in 1988 to zero in 1990, the consumer price inflation jumped from 14·4 per cent in 1988 to 20·4 per cent in 1990, public finances were running out of control with the fiscal deficit-to-GDP ratio increasing from 11 per cent in 1988 to 16·1 per cent in 1990, and the public sector total debt-to-GDP ratio standing at 110·4 per cent in 1990, of which the foreign debt was close to 30 per cent. In addition the current account deficit had reached worrying proportions, increasing from 1·8 per cent of GDP in 1988 to 5·4 per cent in 1990. In this environment, the need for a radical adjustment was obvious with the aim of preparing the ground for Greece's participation in the process of the economic and monetary union (EMU). The Greek authorities responded to macroeconomic imbalances by launching four stabilisation programmes during the 1990s.[2] The philosophy of all programmes can be characterised by the Keynesian–Classical synthesis. There have been strong classical features, such as the importance attached to real wages in the inflation–output outcomes, the fiscal consolidation efforts, the extensive deregulation of the financial and labour markets and other structural reforms. On the other hand, the importance attached to tax policy as a means of fiscal consolidation and to centralised negotiations or collective settlements at the sectoral and firm levels, as distinct from allowing market forces to operate in the labour market, was consistent with the Keynesian thinking. On the monetary policy front, Greece followed a 'pragmatic' monetarist approach based on intermediate monetary or exchange rate targets to maintain price stability, while at the same time supporting economic growth, without prejudice to primary objectives.

It is only since 1996 that Greece made continuing progress in reversing most of the trends of long-standing macroeconomic imbalances, and in the time being has come to be regarded as a model of successful macroeconomic stabilisation.

In the light of these developments, this chapter examines the recent performance of the Greek economy, focusing on the disinflation process, and on the role of monetary and exchange rate policies in this adjustment.[3] The inflation performance since 1990 is summarised in the next section. The third section firstly contains a discussion about the role of monetary management in the adjustment and its impact on capital flows, and then examines the credibility of the exchange rate policy. The fourth section looks at the behaviour of fiscal and income policies during the disinflation process. The conclusion discusses the implications of the stabilization policies for the preparations Greece is making for a single currency regime.

Inflation trends

For several years, the Greek economy had a tendency towards high inflation as a result of nominal shocks to wages and imported prices, with a combination of lack of monetary credibility, loose fiscal policy and an inflation bias in the wage formation process. In the 1980s, the poor inflation performance was attributable to the excessively expansionary monetary and fiscal policies, coupled with a loose incomes policy and the inadequate operation of the markets. It is worth noting that the public sector borrowing requirement (PSBR) accounted for all the increase in the monetary base during the period 1984–9. Also there were some negative effects from the two successive oil crises in the 1970s. Consumer price inflation remained at the average level of about 20 per cent in the first half of the 1980s. During the stabilisation period 1986–7, inflation fell to 13·5 per cent. After the termination of the Stabilisation Plan, it remained subdued owing to the positive effects of the programme, but it jumped back to 20·4 per cent in 1990. The rebound in inflation was partly the consequence of fiscal measures taken in order to arrest the growth of PSBR by raising taxes. Structural deficiencies coupled with expansionary incomes policies also played a role.

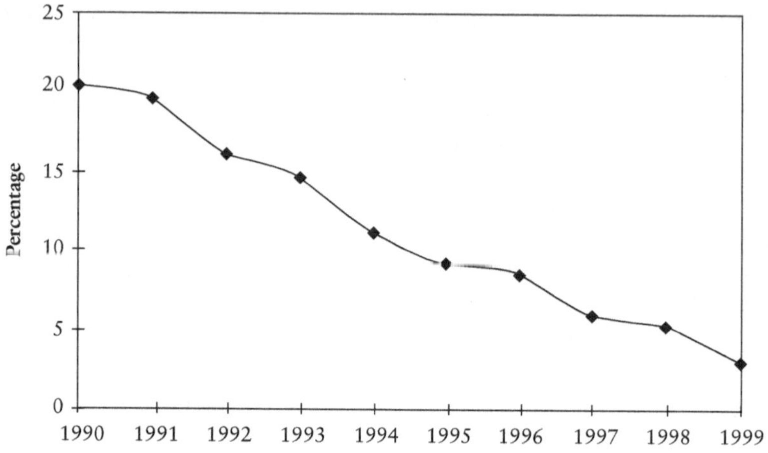

Figure 6.1 Consumer price inflation

The behaviour of inflation is the key feature of the improved performance of the Greek economy. The decline from 20·4 per cent in 1990 to 2·4 per cent in May 1999 is impressive (Figure 6.1).[4] The challenges, however, for macroeconomic policies still remain considerable in further reducing inflation towards the Maastricht targets. In 1998, the euro area inflation rate based on the harmonised index of consumer prices was 1·1 per cent, while the rate of the three best performing countries was 0·7 per cent.[5]

Monetary policy and exchange rates

Framework

The framework in which Greece's monetary policy operated in the 1990s is different from that in the 1980s in at least two respects: the objectives (ultimate and intermediate), and the techniques which were used to achieve them.

With the view of meeting the Maastricht inflation criterion, the principal goal of monetary policy was to reduce inflation gradually, while at the same time supporting economic growth. In order to achieve its ultimate goal, the Bank of Greece (BOG) uses a set of variables, called intermediate targets, which have a direct effect on inflation. Between 1990 and 1994, the design of monetary policy was based on the setting and attempted achievement of a monetary target for the broad monetary aggregate M3 (Table 6.1).[6] In September 1992, the BOG tightened the

Table 6.1 Intermediate targets and indicators

Year	*M3 (outcome)*	*M4 (outcome)*	*Drachma/ ecu-euro*[1]	*Domestic credit*	*Inflation*	*GDP*	*Nominal GDP*
1989	18–20 (24·2)			13–15	13·7	3·8	17·5
1990	19–21 (15·3)			15–16	20·4	0·0	20·4
1991	14–16 (12·3)			14	19·5	3·1	22·5
1992	9–12 (14·4)			14–16	15·9	0·7	16·6
1993	9–12 (15·0)			13–15	14·4	−1·6	12·8
1994	8–11 (8·8)			11	10·9	2·0	12·9
1995	8–11 (10·4)	11–13 (8·3)	3 (3)	6–8	8·9	2·1	11
1996	6–9 (9·3)	9–12 (12)	stable (1)	5–7	8·2	2·4	10·6
1997	6–9 (9·6)	8–11 (−1·6)	stable (1·7)	4–6	5·5	3·2	8·7
1998	(8·9)	(3·5)	±2·25% (5·4)	4–6	4·8	3·7	8·5

Notes: OECD country report, various issues.
[1]Numbers in parentheses indicate outcomes.
All figures denote percentages.

exchange rate policy by restricting the depreciation of the drachma against the ECU to less than would be needed to accommodate inflation differentials between Greece and the other member states of the European Union in an attempt to contain inflationary expectations and achieve a marked deceleration in the pace of inflation.[7] The removal of exchange controls on short-term capital movements in May 1994 made the monetary management based on controlling the aggregate M3 more difficult. Thus, in the context of the monetary programme of 1995, two intermediate targets of monetary policy were announced. They comprised a pre-announced 3 per cent annual depreciation of the drachma against the ECU, which was lower than the inflation differential and a target for M3. Also the BOG announced its intention of monitoring developments in the monetary aggregate M4 (M3 plus government bonds held by the private sector with a maturity up to a year) which constitutes a broader measure of total liquidity. Thus a target range of the growth rate of M4 was also announced. Even if the BOG announced formal monetary targets for M3 and M4, the role of these aggregates has been downgraded vis-à-vis their position in earlier years.

At the beginning of 1997, the BOG announced a new exchange rate policy to prevent short-term speculative capital inflows, according to which the exchange rate of the currencies that compose the ECU would remain approximately unchanged between the start and the end of the year, while permitting greater volatility within the year. A new monetary policy framework was introduced in 1998, comprising direct inflation targeting, central bank independence and the drachma's entry into the Exchange Rate Mechanism (ERM) with a central rate of 357 drachmas per ECU that represented a 13·8 per cent depreciation of the currency.[8] The BOG abolished the monetary targeting and adopted direct inflation targeting. The intermediate target of monetary policy is the drachma central rate against the ECU with a band of ±2·5 per cent.[9] However, the BOG introducing a new version of the 'hard drachma' policy allows the domestic currency to appreciate relative to its official parity in an attempt to contain the impact of imported inflation on domestic inflation. After the drachma's entry into the new ERM, with a central parity of 353 drachmas per euro, the same policy applied.

Along with a number of other financial and non-financial variables, monetary and credit aggregates play a role as information variables. In 1988, the variability of M3 and M4 was affected by portfolio shifts towards foreign exchange deposits and mutual funds. This compelled the BOG to introduce a new monetary aggregate, M4N, which represents a broader liquidity index and exhibits a more stable relationship with nominal GDP, since it is not affected by the substitution between different assets. The new aggregate comprises M4 plus residents' deposits in foreign exchange and the money market mutual funds units held by individuals.

The BOG has attempted to achieve its intermediate targets by manipulating other variables such as inter-bank interest rates, called operating targets, which are more responsive to its policy tools. In order to achieve its operating targets, the monetary authority has at its disposal a set of monetary policy instruments, such as open market operations, standing facilities and reserve requirements. In the early 1990s, the BOG was using administered interest rates, such as the savings rate and the Treasury bill rate, and was setting the interest rate on its overnight facility. In 1995, open market operations were mainly conducted through auctions of one-month fixed-term deposits with the BOG and auctions of 14-day repurchase agreements (repos). In 1997, the BOG announced that the principal intervention instrument was weekly auctions for 14-day repos and 14-day deposits. Standing facilities provide and absorb overnight liquidity and bear overnight interest rates. Two standing facilities are available to commercial banks on their own initiative: the deposit facility, with which a bank deposits with the BOG

Table 6.2 Interest rates

Year	*Interest rates of the BOG*			*Inter-bank interest rates*	
	O/N deposit facility[1]	*14 days deposit rate*	*Lombard facility*	*Overnight*	*1 month*
1997	10·9	12·75	19·0	11·0	18·0
1998	11·6	12·25	15·5	11·9	11·9
1999[2]	11·5	12·0	13·5	10·2	10·3

Notes: BOG, *Monetary Policy 1989–1999*, March 1999.
[1]First tranche.
[2]February 1999.
O/N = overnight.

overnight, and the marginal lending facility, with which a bank obtains overnight liquidity from the BOG against eligible assets. The interest rate on the deposit facility provides the floor and that of the marginal lending facility the ceiling for the overnight market rate (Table 6.2).[10] The BOG also applies reserve requirements to commercial banks at a rate of 12 per cent of their liabilities. Half of the reserve requirements are remunerated at a rate of 11 per cent.[11]

Developments

In order to evaluate the role of monetary policy in the disinflation process we use two indicators: the growth rate of real M3, and the real short-term interest rate. The results are shown in Figures 6.2 and 6.3. The striking feature of these figures is that both indicators point in the same direction of monetary tightness in the early 1990s in order to fight inflation by containing inflationary expectations and limit the depreciation of the drachma to somewhat less than the inflation differentials against trading partners. From Figure 6.2 we observe that the real growth rate of M3 became negative during the first half of the decade, with one exception in 1993, where the growth rate increased by half a percentage point. In addition, the tight monetary policy was also reflected in the behaviour of the growth rate of M3 velocity of circulation, which increased by about 6 per cent on average in 1990–92 compared with a drop of –6·7 per cent in 1989.

In Figure 6.3 we note that the real short-term lending rate remained very high, at about 14 per cent in 1993 and increased to more than 15 per cent in 1994 as inflation was declining. On the other hand, the real overnight interest rate reached its highest level (12·8 per cent) in 1992,

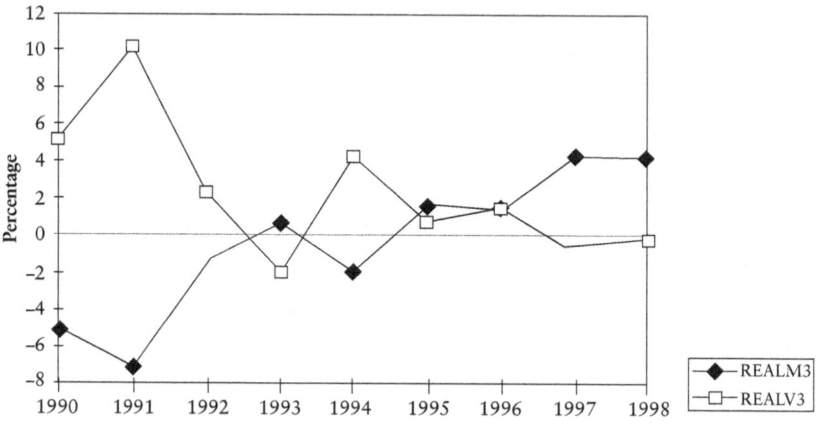

Figure 6.2 Real money and velocity growth

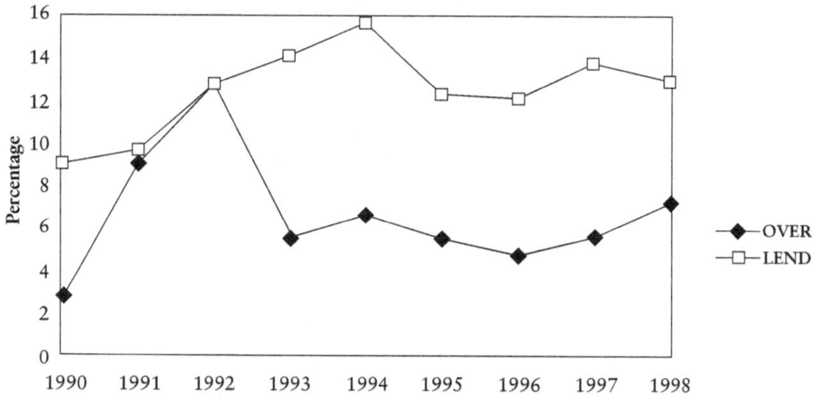

Figure 6.3 Real short-term interest rates

declining thereafter to 6 per cent on average in the period 1993–8. The nominal overnight interest rate remained very high, at the level of 28·7 per cent in 1992 in order to counteract the speculative pressures against the drachma which culminated in the financial turmoil of the European Monetary System.

Two additional indicators which measure the stance of monetary policy are also used: the yield curve, that is the difference between the long-term rate and the short-term rate, and the real exchange rate appreciation. When the yield curve slopes downward, this implies that the monetary authorities follow a restrictive monetary policy. Under fixed exchange rates, the discipline mechanism which ensures a

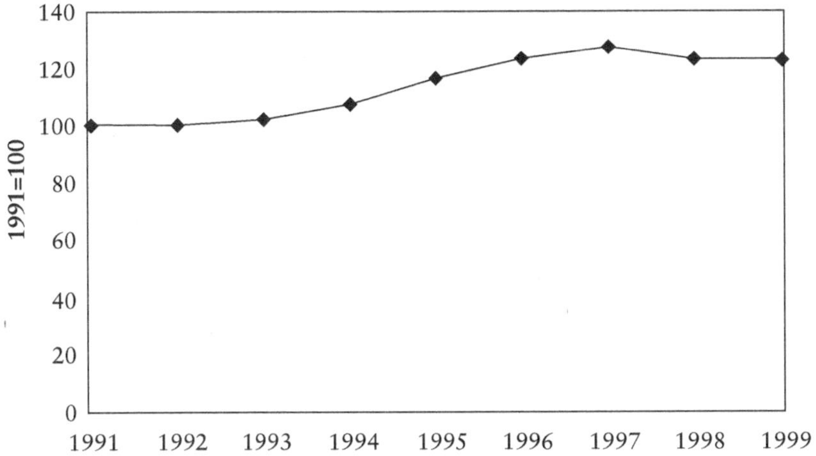

Figure 6.4 Real effective exchange rate

disinflation outcome is that the higher domestic relative to foreign inflation leads to a real exchange rate appreciation which brings a recession, which finally lowers domestic inflation. Since both indicators are influenced by other variables (for example, the yield curve is influenced by the expected change in the short-term rate, while the real exchange rate is affected by real shocks), their movements will be interpreted in conjunction with the previous two indicators.

The differential between the 10-year government bond yield and 12-month Treasury bills yield dropped from –0·7 per cent in 1997 to –3·4 per cent in 1998, suggesting that monetary policy was particularly tight.[12] From Figure 6.4, we note that the increase in the real effective exchange rate based on unit labour costs of the total economy was considerable during most of the 1990s, but decelerated in the last few years, revealing the strong disinflationary stance of the exchange rate policy.

In 1993, Greece went into a shallow recession with its GDP growth rate falling by 1·6 per cent as a result of previously implemented tight monetary policies (Table 6.3).[13] The deceleration in economic growth was mainly driven by a 3·5 per cent fall in gross fixed investment, a 0·8 per cent fall in consumption and a 3·4 per cent drop in net exports.

It is striking that, during the disinflation process, output growth continued to strengthen on the basis of a strong domestic demand, driven by business investment supported by declining financial costs and import prices which permitted firms to maintain their profitability, and by the prospect of joining the EMU (Figure 6.5), while the unemployment rate was rising.[14] Did the disinflation process contribute

Table 6.3 Aggregate expenditure

Year	*Private consumption*	*Public consumption*	*Private investment*[1]	*Final dom. demand*	*Net exports*[2]
1989	6·0	5·4	7·0	5·3	–5·9
1990	2·6	0·6	8·7	2·9	–12·8
1991	2·8	–1·5	2·0	3·7	–2·3
1992	2·4	–3·0	–6·3	–0·6	9·1
1993	–0·8	2·6	–5·0	–0·9	–3·4
1994	2·0	–1·1	–2·1	1·2	5·3
1995	2·7	5·6	2·0	3·9	–8·7
1996	1·9	1·0	9·9	2·9	–1·9
1997	2·5	–0·4	10·5	3·4	–0·1
1998	1·8	0·4	8·4	3·3	3·3
1999	2·1	–1·3	9·9	3·4	1·2

Notes: Annual percentage changes (in constant prices of pevious year).
[1]Gross fixed investment.
[2]Net exports = (exports of goods & services) – (imports of goods & services).

Source: Bank of Greece, *Monetary Policy 1998–1999*, March 1999.

to the increase in unemployment during the 1990s? In Figure 6.6, the behaviour present the evolution of the unemployment rate together with the inflation rate is shown. It can be seen that, whereas the inflation rate declined continuously, the unemployment rate experienced a significant increase until 1998. If unemployment is a supply-side phenomenon, it will be disconnected from the disinflation process and thus monetary policy will not affect it. This story, however, cannot explain the dynamics of the increase in unemployment, unless it is combined with the hypothesis that a demand shock triggered the increase in unemployment, but the inflexibility of the labour market perpetuated it. In particular, the recession of the early 1990s, which was mainly due to a decline in aggregate demand facilitated by a tight monetary policy, led to a decline in output growth and an increase in unemployment. The lack of labour market flexibility, on the other hand, prevented the unemployment rate from declining consequently. It is worth noting that the increase in the unemployment rate during the first half of the decade was associated with an increase in real unit labour costs. Therefore the flexibility of the labour market would not entail that it would reduce unemployment, but that, with each cyclical downturn, the unemployment rate would be brought to a lower level.

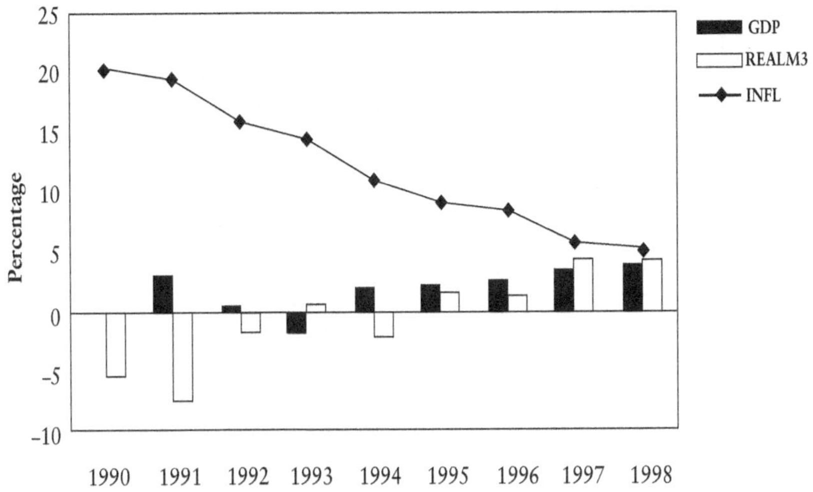

Figure 6.5 Inflation, output growth and real money

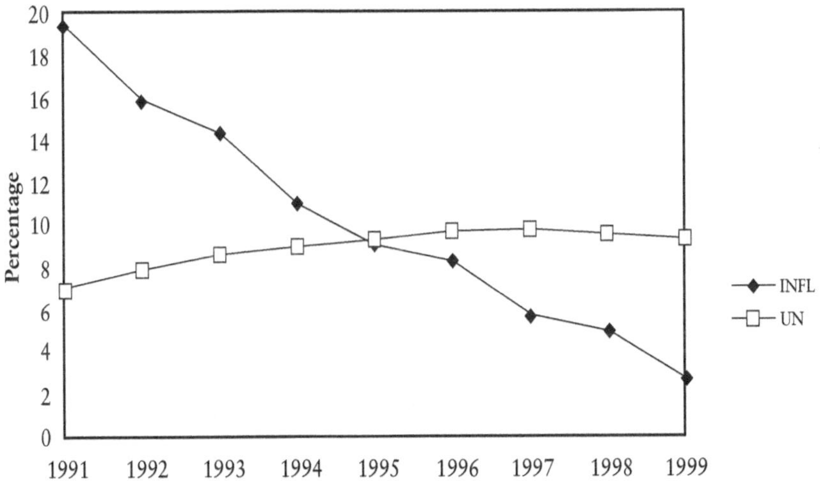

Figure 6.6 Inflation and unemployment

Compared with the situation at the beginning of the decade, economic stabilisation improved considerably in the second half of the 1990s, with the halving of inflation to less than 10 per cent and the acceleration of economic growth to more than 2 per cent. However, the disinflation process was slow because of inadequate support from policies other than monetary policy. In order to accelerate the pace of disinflation and reduce the impact of unit labour costs on domestic inflation, the authorities announced the use of the 'hard drachma' policy as the economy's nominal anchor. Inflation continued to decline at a moderate rate, accompanied by an increase in economic growth mainly driven by high private and public investment growth. Although the 'hard drachma' policy continued to pull down domestic inflation by lowering the cost of imported inputs, cost-push pressures worked in the opposite direction. Thus this policy mix, which remained unbalanced, led to a real exchange rate appreciation which adversely affected the current account deficit, which increased to 4·2 per cent in 1997.[15] On the other hand, the capital account surplus, mainly owing to large inflows of entrepreneurial capital, more than matched the current account deficit and thus induced an increase in foreign reserves. From Figure 6.2 we observe that the real growth rate of M3 became positive and higher than the output growth in 1997–8. The BOG had to sterilise the capital inflows in order to prevent them from increasing significantly the domestic money supply.

Sterilisation versus offsets: empirical analysis

Successful implementation of monetary policy requires an understanding of the way financial markets work and how they are linked both to each other and to the economy. The liberalisation of the international financial markets transferred resources to countries with low saving rates, thereby loosening the constraints imposed by self-finance and enabling increases both in the productivity of investment and in the smoothing of consumption. Also the surge in capital inflows helped many economies to reduce the cost of adjusting to various shocks and sustain the policy reform process. Difficulties in managing capital inflows may arise when the recipient economies are running near full capacity. The foreign capital inflows may lead to a large real exchange rate appreciation, fuel inflationary pressures through increased domestic liquidity and adversely affect the current account balance. If, at the time of a sudden capital inflow reversal, the monetary authority did not have sufficient reserves to cover all its liquid liabilities, this would create a liquidity problem in the domestic banking system, leading to a currency crisis. To deal with large reserve inflows, the recipient economies have at their disposal four policy options: (1) sterilised intervention, (2) fiscal policy restraint, (3) greater exchange rate flexibility, and (4) controls on capital movements. It is worth noting that the costs associated with these policy options can be substantial. The costs associated with sterilisation operations using government bonds refer to the spread between the higher interest rates paid on these securities and the rates from foreign assets acquired by the monetary authority. This interest rate differential attracts more reserve inflows. An increase in the reserve requirements is another instrument which could be used to mop up the excess liquidity from the inter-bank market. However, a rise in the reserve requirement may lead to higher lending rates, thereby inducing domestic firms to borrow internationally, thus further increasing capital inflows.

Monetary policy has played an important role in capital inflows that Greece has experienced for most of the past few years. The BOG used a tight monetary policy combined with a credible exchange rate target to contain inflation, but the resulting increases in interest rates attracted additional inflows. The structure in the period 1994–7 was characterised by substantial entrepreneurial capital inflows (Figure 6.7). Under these conditions, maintaining monetary independence with an exchange rate and an open capital account would become more difficult. The BOG reacted to resulting liquidity and liquidity-absorbing open market operations through auctions for 14-day repos and deposits which involved contracting domestic assets to offset increases in net foreign assets.[16] In addition, the BOG increased the reserve requirements to 12 per cent, introduced in March 1997 a new monetary management tool consisting of a two-tier window, and permitted greater exchange rate fluctuations of the drachma. The sterilisation operation in a situation of strong capital inflows implies that the net foreign and domestic assets will tend to move in opposite directions. This tendency can be seen in Figure 6.8, which presents the changes in the two components of the monetary base. The mirror-image path of changes in the net domestic and foreign assets is evidence of sterilisation in practice by the BOG.

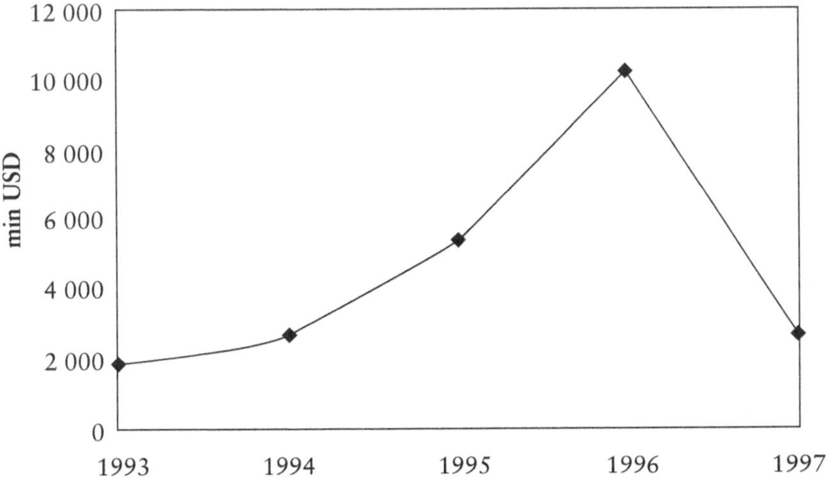

Figure 6.7 Entrepreneurial capital

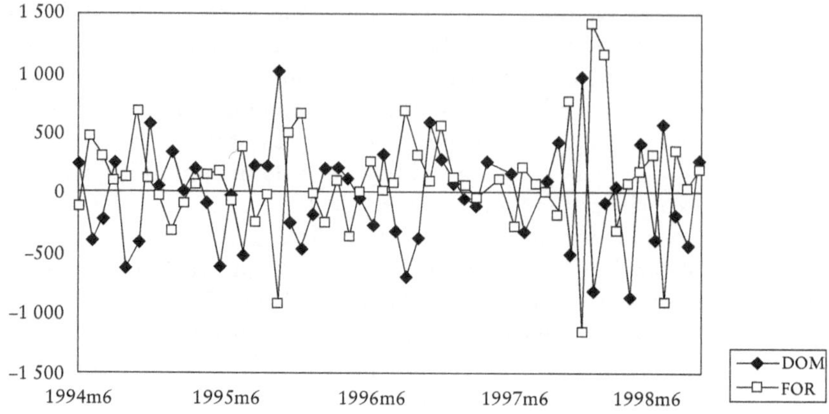

Figure 6.8 Changes in net domestic and foreign assets

To assess the role of monetary policy in capital inflows and the degree of sterilisation policies, we use an approach adopted by Kouri and Porter (1974) which is based upon a theoretical model viewing capital movements as a mechanism for eliminating excess supply or demand for money. The equation for net capital inflows is given by:

$$K_t = -\alpha\Delta NDA_t + f(z), \tag{6.1}$$

where ΔNDA denotes changes in net domestic assets and $f(z)$ is a function containing other variables, such as the current account, the foreign interest rate and the real income, which influence capital inflows. Using the balance of payments identity,

$$CAB + K = \Delta NFA, \tag{6.2}$$

where CAB denotes the current account balance and ΔNFA denotes changes in net foreign assets, equation (6.1) can be rewritten as

$$\Delta NFA = -\alpha\Delta NDA + f(z). \tag{6.3}$$

The offset coefficient α reflects the extent to which a change in the domestic component of monetary base is offset by a change in the foreign component. When α=1, a drop in net domestic assets to lower the monetary base will attract foreign capital through high domestic interest rates, thus increasing its foreign component, which will completely offset the contracting monetary policy.

Suppose that the sterilisation policy of the central bank is captured by the following reaction function:

$$\Delta NDA_t = -\phi \Delta NFA_t + g(x), \tag{6.4}$$

where $g(x)$ is a function which includes other variables, such as inflation and output growth. When $\phi=1$, an increase in net foreign assets is neutralized by a proportional fall in net domestic assets, and thus reserve inflows are sterilised completely. If $\phi<1$, sterilisation is incomplete. It is worth noting that, the greater is the degree of sterilisation, the greater is the instability of reserve flows and the less effective is sterilisation itself. To see this, substitute (6.4) into (6.3) which yields

$$\Delta NFA_t = \left(\frac{1}{1-\alpha\phi}\right)\Gamma(z,x) \tag{6.5}$$

The ratio $(1/(1-\alpha\phi))$ denotes the magnification effect associated with sterilisation of capital inflows. The closer the two coefficients are to unity, the larger the magnitude of capital inflows.

The empirical analysis is carried out using monthly data on net domestic and foreign assets of the BOG over the period May 1994 to March 1998.[17] The net domestic assets of the BOG is calculated after subtracting its net foreign assets from the monetary base.[18] The instrumental variables (IV) estimation results reported in Table 6.4 yield a statistically significant value of –0·58 for the offset coefficient, implying an important link between capital flows and movements in net domestic assets. During the period 1994–7, Greece accumulated a total of 21 billion drachmas of entrepreneurial capital. Of this amount, 12 billion drachmas, or 58 per cent, was due to a contraction in net domestic assets. In other words, the above figures indicate that, if monetary policy was passive and foreign exchange market intervention unsterilised, capital inflows would have reached a level of 9 billion drachmas.[19]

The IV estimation results yield a statistically significant value of –0·60 for the sterilisation coefficient, indicating that the BOG has neutralised a significant portion of the reserve flows.[20] The high values of both estimated coefficients indicate that the size of the magnification effect, which is equal to 1·54, is substantial.[21]

Nominal anchors and inflationary dynamics

Having discussed the role of monetary policy in the disinflation process and its impact on capital flows, we now investigate the degree of credibility of the 'hard drachma' policy on the persistence of inflation. The effectiveness of stabilisation programmes depends on the role of credibility factors. When policies implemented lack credibility, private agents will eventually recognise that government efforts to maintain a consistent set of policies over time will not be successful and the announced disinflation programme will not be sustainable in the long run. On the other hand, when the public is confident in the ability of policymakers to carry out a newly announced stabilisation programme, downward rigidities that characterise the inflationary process will be reduced by changing inflationary expectations. Since inflationary expectations have a significant effect on current wage and price decisions: a reduction in the actual inflation may result. The imperfect credibility of disinflation programmes depends on a variety of elements, such as internal inconsistency of the programme, reputational aspects of policymakers, incomplete or asymmetric information about the 'true' intentions of the authorities' commitment to disinflate, and an unstable political environment.

Table 6.4 Instrumental variable estimates

	Offset: dep. v/ble ΔNFA_t			*Sterilisation: dep. v/ble* ΔNDA_t		
Regressor	*Coeff.*	*St. error*	*T-ratio*	*Coeff.*	*St. error*	*T-ratio*
ΔNFA_t				–0·60	0·02	–2·42**
ΔNDA_t	–0·58	0·21	–2·70*			
Diagnostic tests						
R^2		0·48			0·46	
Sargan's test		$X^2(15)$=12·26[0.66]			$X^2(9)$=11·38[0·25]	
SC		$X^2(12)$=8·44[0.75]			$X^2(12)$=16·12[0·19]	
FF		$X^2(1)$=1·68[0.20]			$X^2(1)$=1·07[0·30]	
NO		$X^2(2)$=12·71[0.02]*			$X^2(2)$=0·26[0·88]	
HE		$X^2(1)$=0·31[0.58]			$X^2(1)$=0·25[0·62]	

Note: SC,FF,NO,HE denote tests for serial correlation, functional mispecification, normality and heteroscedasticity, respectively. Numbers in brackets are p-values. An asterisk indicates significance at 1%; two asterisks indicate significance at 5%. Instruments include 8 lagged values of each variable in the offset model and 5 lagged values of each variable in the sterilisation model.

Many developed and developing countries have adopted an exchange rate-based stabilisation programme as a way to bring down inflation. The speed with which this programme reduces inflation persistence is very important and depends on credibility factors. If private agents are able to evaluate how serious the authorities are about fighting inflation, inflationary inertia is likely to decline; otherwise, the inflation dynamics will be hardly affected. If inflation inertia declines very slowly, it will produce a real overvaluation that could jeopardise the programme.

Even though theory and public discussions have granted this role of policy credibility a degree of prominence, not much empirical work has been carried out to examine the empirical evidence pertaining to regime changes. Agenor and Taylor (1992) examine the existence of a credibility effect in the Cruzado stabilisation programme implemented in Brazil in 1986. The results suggest that, although the plan seems to have gained credibility rapidly, its impact on the inflationary process was less dramatic. Edwards (1996) analyses the effects of Chilean and Mexican exchange rate-based stabilisation programmes on inflation inertia. The results show that there is no evidence of a reduction in the degree of inflation persistence in Chile, whereas a decline in the degree of inertia is observed after the implementation of the programme in Mexico. Karfakis et al. (1999) examine the size and the diffusion effect of the credibility factors of the stabilisation programme implemented in Greece in 1985. An interesting aspect of the analysis is the evidence that the plan gained credibility rapidly, and its impact on the inflation dynamics was significant.

In order to examine the degree of credibility of the exchange rate-based disinflation programme implemented in Greece since 1995, we use a simplified version of a model employed by Edwards (1996). The model can be presented by the following set of equations:

$$\pi_t = b\,\pi_t^T + (1-b)\pi_t^N, \tag{6.6}$$

$$\pi_t^T = \pi_t^* + d_t, \tag{6.7}$$

$$d_t = \theta(\pi_{t-1} - \pi^*_{-1}), \tag{6.8}$$

$$\pi_t^N = w_t + m_t, \tag{6.9}$$

$$w_t = \pi_t^e = \pi_t, \tag{6.10}$$

where π, π^T, π^N, d, π^*, w, m are, respectively, the rate of change of the domestic price level, the rate of change of tradables prices in domestic currency, the rate of change of non-tradables prices, the rate of depreciation, the rate of world inflation, the rate of change in nominal wages, and the rate of change in the excess money stock. Equation (6.6) says that the domestic rate of inflation is a weighted average of tradables and non-tradables inflation. Equation (6.7) is the law of one price. Equation (6.8) states that the exchange rate is adjusted in a proportion θ of inflation differentials. If $\theta = 1$, the monetary authorities follow a real exchange rate target, whereas $\theta = 0$ implies a nominal exchange rate target. Equation (6.9) says that the non-tradables inflation depends on the rate of growth of wages and the rate of the excess money growth. Equation (6.10) states that workers, in order to maintain the real value of their wages, set nominal wages equal to the expected inflation which is assumed to be equal to the actual inflation under rational expectations. After manipulating the above equations, the dynamics of inflation are given by

$$\pi_t = \pi_t^* + \theta(\pi_{t-1}^* - \pi_{t-1}) + \left(\frac{1-b}{b}\right)m_t. \tag{6.11}$$

Suppose the authorities announce that the exchange rate policy will not accommodate price shocks; that is, $d_t = d = 0$. If private agents attach a probability $0 < \rho < 1$ to that announcement, the exchange rate policy rule (6.8) is written as

$$d_t = \rho d + (1 - \rho)(\pi_{t-1}^* - \pi_{t-1}), \tag{6.12}$$

where $(1-\rho)$ denotes the probability that the authorities will default. Then it is easy to show that the inflationary dynamics is given by

$$\pi_t = \pi_t^* + \rho d + (1 - \rho)(\pi_{t-1} - \pi_{t-1}^*) + \left(\frac{1-b}{b}\right)m_t. \tag{6.13}$$

According to equation (6.13), under full credibility ($\rho=1$) and monetary equilibrium, the inflation persistence will vanish, and in the long run the domestic inflation will converge to the world inflation.

In order to investigate empirically the way in which the adoption of a nominal exchange rate anchor affected the degree of inflation inertia, we estimated the following first-order difference equation:[22]

$$\pi_t = \alpha_1\pi_{t-1} + \alpha_2\pi_{t-1}^* + \alpha_3 m_t + v_t. \tag{6.14}$$

The behaviour of the coefficient α_1 reflects the inflation persistence. The empirical analysis is carried out using quarterly data on domestic and OECD-Europe consumer prices, and domestic money supply (M3) over the period 1986(1) to 1998(2).[23] The ordinary least squares (OLS) estimation results reported in Table 6.5 show that foreign inflation dominates movements in domestic inflation. The lagged rate of growth of M3 which was used as a measure of aggregate demand pressures has a significant influence on domestic inflation, although its magnitude is small. The high value of R^2 implies that the bulk of the variation of the inflation is explained by the model. The diagnostic tests reject the presence of serial correlation, functional misspecification and

Table 6.5 Inflation equation

	Dep. v/ble: π_t		
Regressor	*Coefficient*	*St. error*[1]	*T-ratio[p-value]*
π^t	0·83	0·05	18·13[0·00]*
π^t	0·44	0·18	2·38[0·02]**
m_{t-1}	0·05	0·02	2·12[0·04]**
	Diagnostic tests		
R^2	0·95		
SEE	0·99		
SC	$X^2(4)$=7·39[0·18]		
FF	$X^2(1)$=2·71[0·10]		
NO	$X^2(2)$=3·76[0·15]		
HE	$X^2(1)$=4·16[0·04]**		

Notes: $\pi_t = p_t - p_{t-4}$; $\pi_t^* = p^*_{t-4}$. SEE standard error of equation.
[1] OLS estimation based on White's heteroscedasticity adjusted SEs.
See notes to Table 6.3.

heteroscedasticity. Furthermore, the normality test suggests that the error process presents a random sample from a normal distribution.

We re-estimated the model (6.14) using recursive OLS. Figure 6.9 reports the recursive coefficient estimates of lagged domestic inflation. On inspection, it is observed that there is a reduction in the degree of inflationary inertia in the early 1990s where the point estimate of the coefficient dropped, from 0·92 in the fourth quarter of 1990 to 0·75 in the second quarter of 1992, and thereafter increased slightly, remaining at about 0·83 after the implementation of the nominal exchange rate anchor. The $X^2(15)$ statistic of the Chow predictive failure test, which is equal to 5·16 with a *p*-value of 0·99, indicates that the hypothesis of a structural break in 1995 in the inflationary equation is rejected. A likely explanation of this stubbornness of the inflation inertia is the somewhat low level of credibility of the 'hard-drachma' policy, associated with its internal inconsistency. In fact, the programme was not supported by fiscal and incomes policies. Also the large real appreciation of the drachma created expectations that the authorities would abandon the programme.

To sum up, the results presented above suggest that the adoption of a nominal exchange rate anchor was not a sufficient condition for reducing the degree of inflation inertia in the presence of expansionary fiscal and incomes policies.

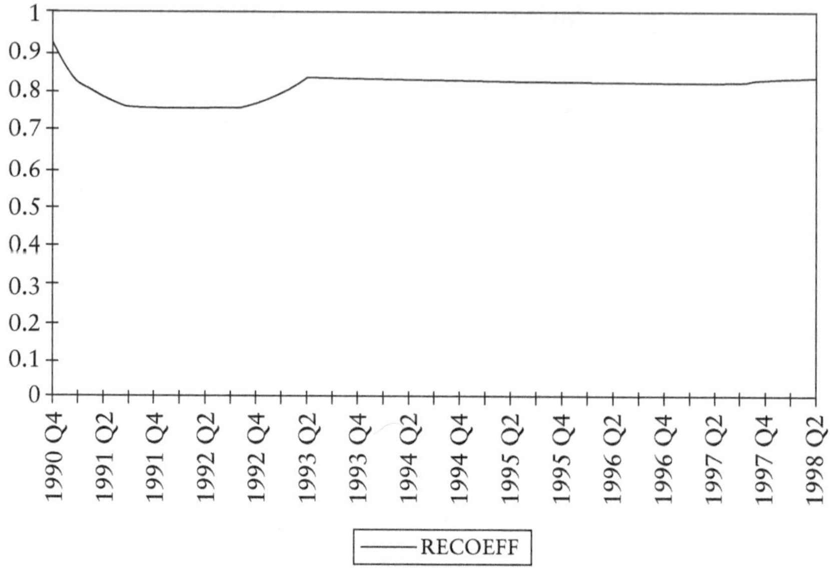

Figure 6.9 Inflation persistence

Other policies

The design of policy mix which was implemented during most of the 1990s was unbalanced as the disinflation strategy mainly relied on strict monetary policy without support from fiscal and income policies. In this section we analyse the stance of these two policies as reflected in the evolution of debt and deficit and real unit labour costs, respectively, during the disinflation process. Up to 1998, fiscal policy tried to achieve specific fiscal targets. The main instrument of fiscal policy was the introduction of a series of measures to increase public revenues, such as broadening of the tax base by imposing presumptive taxes on the self-employed, increasing the marginal tax rate and not adjusting income tax brackets for inflation. It is only in the 1999 government budget that fiscal policy is clearly aimed at price level stabilisation by reducing indirect tax cuts in selected items and tightening the incomes policy in the public sector. In Figure 6.10, we present the trends in the government deficit in Greece and the EU. As becomes evident, the deficit in Greece displays a persistent downward trend throughout the period, but exceeds the corresponding deficit of the EU. This impressive decline is largely attributable to the strengthening of the primary balance, which exceeds by far the corresponding EU ratio over the last four years. In particular, the primary balance increased from 4·1 per cent in 1994 to 6·9 per cent in 1999 (Figure 6.11).

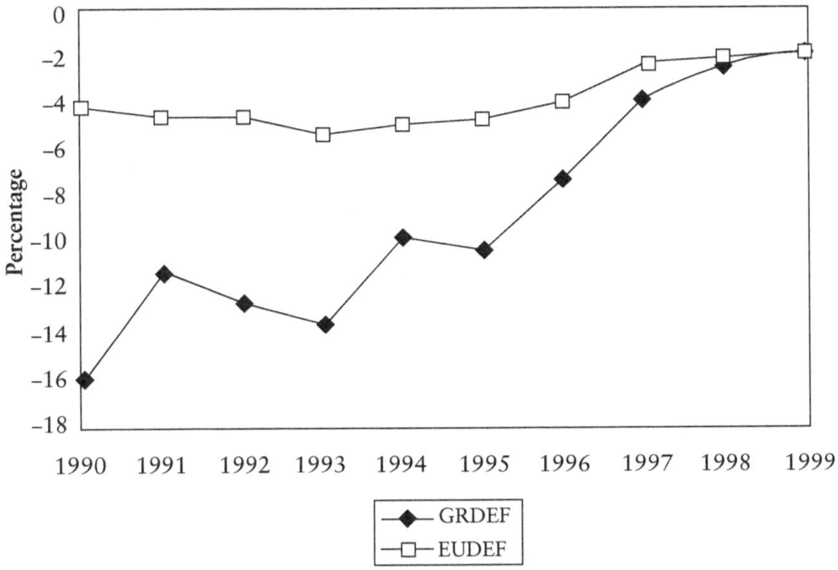

Figure 6.10 General government fiscal deficit

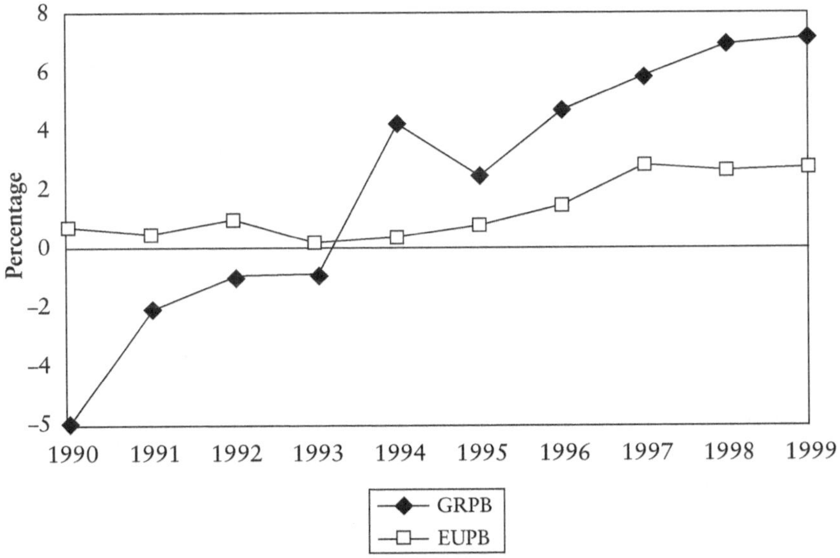

Figure 6.11 General government primary balance

Judging by the change in the government debt dynamics, the fiscal adjustment was sufficient to permit a drop in the debt-to-GDP ratio, from 112·2 per cent in 1996 to 107 per cent in 1999 (Figure 6.12). It

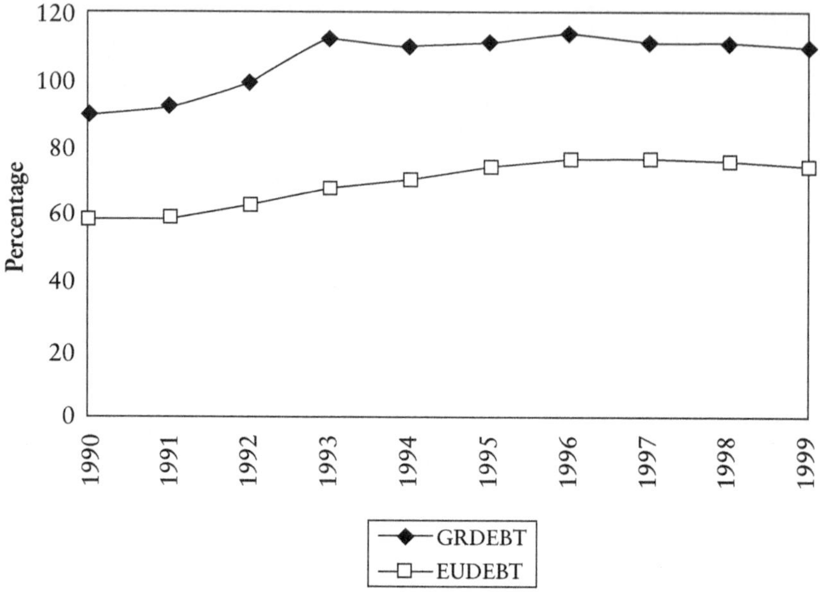

Figure 6.12 General government debt

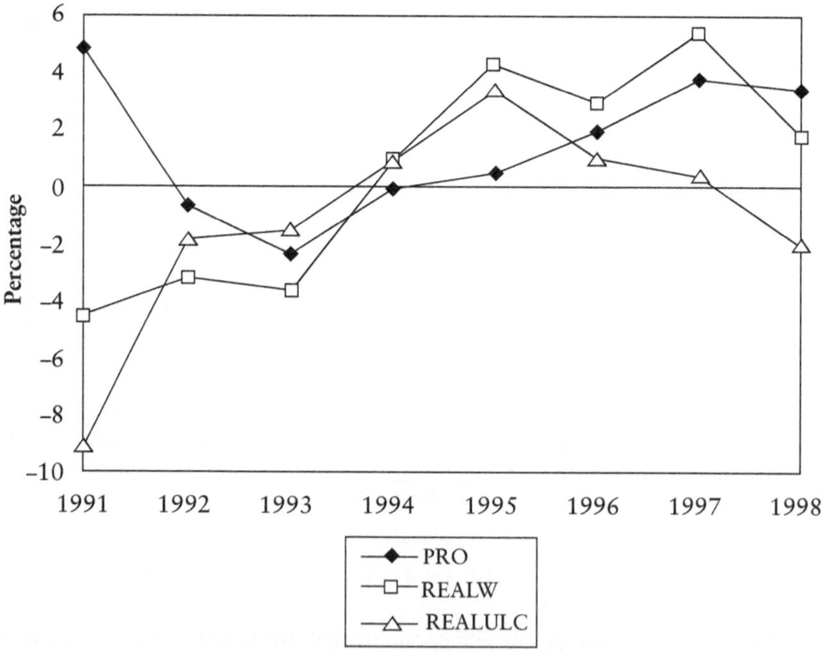

Figure 6.13 Productivity, real wages and real unit labour costs

should be noted that a further tightening of fiscal policy, by reducing primary outlays, is required not only to reduce fiscal debt and stabilise inflation, but also to deal with sudden reversals of capital flows and to support the adjustment of the exchange rate towards the central parity, before the drachma joins the euro, without jeopardising the price stability objective.

From Figure 6.13 we note that labour productivity growth was negative throughout the first part of the 1990s, followed by declining real wages growth rates and increasing real unit labour costs. The whole picture changed between 1995 and 1997, when productivity and real wages increased, but real unit labour costs exhibited a positive growth rate despite the slack in the labour market, indicating a fall in profit margins (Figure 6.14). These developments, however, delayed the disinflation process which gathered momentum again in 1998 when productivity improvements and restrained wage increases reduced real unit labour costs, thus further increasing the credibility of the exchange rate policy.

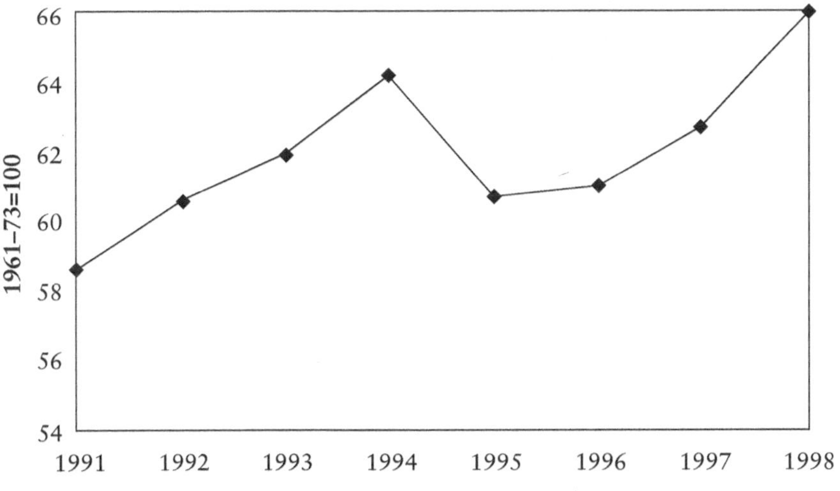

Figure 6.14 Profitability index

Summing up

With a view to meeting the Maastricht Treaty's convergence criteria – especially inflation and fiscal imbalances – and joining the single currency regime in early 2001, the Greek economy made solid progress in the 1990s. A number of factors contributed to the recent adjustment. The most important was the tight monetary policy, combined with a substantial decline in import prices facilitated by a 'hard-drachma' policy and a steady fall in real unit labour costs owing to a rapid growth in productivity relative to unit labour costs. This helped to contain inflation expectations and increase the pace of the disinflation process. The fiscal consolidation made progress in correcting the large fiscal imbalances. The deficit-to-GDP ratio fell below the Maastricht ceiling, while the debt-to-GDP ratio is on a downward trend and has dropped below the level of other member states of the euro zone. Further fiscal consolidation is needed to enhance the flexibility of fiscal policy, which will be the main instrument of aggregate demand management inside the euro area. While the macroeconomic adjustment that Greece has made for joining the single currency regime is considerable, the reversal of the economy's performance did not entail any radical restructuring of microeconomic policies. Major rigidities still persist in factor and product markets and there has been little reduction in the share of the public sector in the production process. The continued high level of unemployment points to the need for further measures to increase the flexibility of the labour market. All these problems need to be addressed in order to enhance efficiency and cost competitiveness, thus allowing the economy to cope with the challenges of the common currency.

Notes

1. I would like to thank, without implicating, Demetrios Moschos for his helpful comments and suggestions.
2. The New Democracy, which formed a government in April 1990, announced the '1991–93 Medium-term Adjustment Programme' aimed at correcting internal and external disequilibria by significantly tightening the stance of macroeconomic policy and bringing unit labour costs, which were running at about 20 per cent in 1990, under control. In addition, the government introduced institutional and structural reforms in order to enhance the efficient operation of the markets. Also the government presented the 1993–8 Convergence Programme with a view to meeting the Maastricht ceilings. On the other hand, the socialist government, which was appointed in October 1993 and in January 1996, announced the 1994–9 and 1998–2001 Convergence Programmes, respectively.
3. For an interesting analysis of the macroeconomic evolution of Greece from 1960 to 1990, see Alogoskoufis (1995).
4. The time-series data used in the plots were obtained from the following sources: INFL, M3 and output from OECD, various issues; OVER, LEND and CAPFLOW from the *Bulletin of Conjunctural Indicators*, BOG, April 1999; REALXR, UN, GRDEF, EUDEF, GRPB, EUPB, GRDEBT, EUDEBT, PRO, REALW, REALULC, PROFIT from European Commission (1998); DOM and FOR from the *Monthly Statistical Bulletin*, BOG, various issues; REALM3=M3–INFL. OVER and LEND constructed from nominal rates

after subtracting inflation; REALV3 constructed from nominal GDP after subtracting REALM3; FOR constructed after subtracting the foreign liabilities of the BOG from its foreign assets; DOM constructed after subtracting FOR from the monetary base.

5. For a detailed analysis of macroeconomic trends in Greece in 1998–9, see National Bank of Greece (1999).
6. The aggregate M3 consists of currency in circulation plus all private sector drachma deposits with commercial banks plus the bank bonds and repurchase agreements (repos).
7. Since the mid-1980s and substantially after the collapse of the stabilisation programme of 1986–7, the BOG has adopted a hard-drachma policy which allows the effective exchange rate to depreciate below the inflation differential between Greece and its main trading partners.
8. The Statutre of the BOG which was amended by Law 2548 on 12 December 1997 contains institutional, personal and functional independence. The decisions of monetary policy are taken by the Monetary Policy Council (MPC), consisting of six members: the governor, the two deputy governors and three other individuals, selected by the government and approved by presidential decree, and with a tenure of six years.
9. Although the official exchange rate target zone was set at ±15 per cent, the BOG announced that it will maintain a stable exchange rate within a range of ±2·25 per cent of the central parity to stabilise inflationary expectations.
10. The deposit facility of the BOG is a two-tier system, according to which it accepts one-day deposits of up to 300 billion drachmas from commercial banks with a large market share at a high interest rate, and all remaining funds at a lower interest rate. On the other hand, the marginal lending facility of the BOG employs two instruments: the Lombard, which was introduced in 1993 and aimed at covering temporary liquidity needs, and the overdraft facilities, which provide additional finance through the current accounts of banks with the BOG.
11. The liability base includes deposits and other liabilities in domestic and foreign (net of assets) currency, including repos.
12. The lack of available data for a longer period prevents us from plotting the government bond yield curve.
13. The recession prevailing among its European trading partners also affected the slowdown of economic activity.
14. Private investment jumped from 2 per cent in 1995 to almost 10 per cent in 1996 and thereafter flattened out. Public investment contributed a stimulus to total domestic demand, increasing from –4·7 per cent in 1994 to an average of about 9 per cent in the period 1995–8.
15. An additional determinant of the current account deficit was the large interest payments, dividends and profits reflecting heavy foreign currency-denominated borrowing from the business sector.
16. Additional measures to discourage capital inflows and facilitate outflows include (1) reduction from 4 per cent to 3 per cent of the tax levied on the value of all domestic loans, (2) introduction of the same tax for all domestic foreign currency-denominated loans, (3) reduction from 70 per cent to 12 per cent of the reserve requirements on foreign currency deposits of residents and non-residents, excluding Greek seamen and workers abroad, (4) reduction from 70 per cent to 60 per cent of the reserve

requirements on foreign currency-denominated deposits by Greek seamen and workers abroad.

17. For a discussion of the role of monetary policy with regard to capital flows in other countries, see Bond (1998), Oblath (1998), Durjasz and Kokoszczynski (1998).
18. The beginning of the sample coincides with the liberalisation of the short-term capital movements.
19. The estimated equation included other variables, such as the current account balance, the euro–dollar rate and the domestic real income, which were not statistically significant.
20. Gibson and Brissimis (1997) found that the offset coefficient for Greece was –0·65 during the period 1991–5.
21. The estimated equation also included the real GDP growth and inflation, which turned out to be insignificant.
22. To obtain (6.14), we assume that $E_{t-1}(\pi^*_t) = \pi^*_{t-1}$.
23. The beginning of the sample coincides with the implementation of the stabilisation programme of 1986–7. The OECD price level excludes high-inflation countries.

References

Agenor, P.R. and M. Taylor (1992), 'Testing the Credibility Effects', *IMF Staff Papers*, 39, 545–71.

Alogoskoufis, G. (1995), 'The two tales of Janus: Institutions, Policy Regimes and Macroeconomic Performance in Greece', *Economic Policy*, 147–92.

Bond, T.J. (1998), 'Capital Flows to Asia: The Role of Monetary Policy', *Empirica*, 25, 165–82.

Durjasz, P. and R. Kokoszczynski (1998), 'Financial Flows to Poland, 1990–96', *Empirica*, 25, 217–42.

Edwards, S. (1995), 'Exchange Rates as Nominal Anchors', *Weltwirtschaftliches Archiv*, 1–31.

Edwards, S. (1996), 'Exchange-Rate Anchors, Credibility, and Inertia: A Tale of Two Crises, Chile and Mexico', *American Economic Review Papers and Proceedings*, 86, 176–80.

European Commission (1998), *European Economy*, November.

Gibson, H. and S. Brissimis (1997), 'Monetary Policy, Capital Inflows and Deescalation of Inflation in Greece' (in Greek), *Economic Bulletin*, Bank of Greece, 9, 21–38.

Karfakis, C., M. Sidiropoulos and J. Trabelsi (2000), 'Testing the Credibility of Stabilization Programs: Evidence from Greece', *International Journal of Finance and Economics*, 5(2), 165–73.

Kouri, J.P. and M.G. Porter (1974), 'International Capital Flows and Portfolio Equilibrium', *Journal of Political Economy*, 443–67.

National Bank of Greece (1999), 'Greece, 1998–1999', *Annual Economic Review*, 2, Strategic Planning and Research Division, May.
Oblath, G. (1998), 'Capital Flows to Hungary in 1995–96 and the Accompanying Policy Responses', *Empirica*, 25, 183–216.

CHAPTER SEVEN

Riding the exchange rate roller-coaster: speculative currency markets and the durability of exchange rate regimes

Ross E. Catterall

Introduction

This chapter is concerned with several forms of competitive behaviour that affect nominal exchange rates and generate exchange rate volatility. This behaviour includes competition between monetary authorities and the currencies they control (especially the US dollar and the euro) to retain or establish prestige, credibility and usage: competition between economies, and industries within them, to sell internationally; and competition between commercial financial institutions, and their employees, to dominate the foreign exchange markets and reap individual and collective rewards. In this context it should be noted that the norms for the financial services sector are to reward successful traders with annual bonuses based on the profitability of their trades. These bonuses often exceed many times the annual salaries that traders are paid. In London, for example, annual bonuses exceeding £1 million are not unusual. In consequence aggressive traders seeking personal rewards via corporate profits have a vested interest in markets that move, or currency volatility.

This volatility can have profound impacts on the competitiveness of economies and a whole range of economic indicators. It can have significant effects on the real economy and the wealth and prosperity of 'Joe public', and it creates serious difficulties for policymakers in achieving their desired economic objectives. The latter part of this chapter concentrates on aspects of the political economy of exchange rate volatility, and in particular the impacts it may have on the sustainability of the euro zone's single currency.

The chapter attempts to address some critical policy issues for national governments and the European Union in a world of high volatility foreign exchange markets, utilising recent research evidence on exchange rate behaviour, and drawing out the implications for future policy.

The climate of exchange rate volatility

Exchange rates behave in perverse and volatile ways, and currency markets are notoriously unpredictable. This means that exchange rate movements can have profound effects on the trade competitiveness of nations, creating considerable problems for policymakers. These problems are heightened by the fact that there has been an enormous growth in speculation in currency markets, which renders government attempts to control exchange rates increasingly futile. It is far from certain that an intervention policy designed to move an exchange rate one way or another – such as that adopted by the G7 on 22 September 2000 (the first concerted support operation for the euro) – will actually work, or have a sustained impact. One consequence of this exchange rate turbulence is quite dramatic changes in trade competitiveness in very short time periods. This turbulence can have seriously dislocating effects on the export sectors of economies.

What factors underlie this volatility of exchange rates? Both supposedly fixed and floating exchange rate regimes are volatile. Floating rates fluctuate occasionally by large amounts on a day-to-day basis, but fixed rates may make sudden large jumps when the authorities are forced to give up the fight and devalue or depreciate. Substantial speculative attacks on fixed and floating rates are highly newsworthy events and intriguing to follow. Events like the ejection of sterling from the ERM, or the meltdown of the Mexican peso, the collapse of the Thai baht, or the demise of the Russian rouble in the autumn of 1998 received thousands of pages of coverage in the popular and the financial press. The extent of the collapses, and the futile attempt by the authorities to stem them, became major headlines. In the case of the rouble, after a devaluation of a third, the currency fell a further 14 per cent against the US dollar in a two-day period before trading was suspended. In the 48 hours prior to suspension, the Russian government had spent 25 per cent of an agreed IMF loan in support of the currency – even though this loan had not actually been received. Dramatic changes had taken place in Russian trade competitiveness in a very short period. But were these changes really justified by the lack of structural competitiveness of the Russian economy? If they were, why had it taken the foreign exchange markets so long to catch up with economic fundamentals?

In the preceding Asian crisis of 1997–8, currencies in the region lost 50–80 per cent of their values. Was such an excessive depreciation necessary to restore their competitive positions? If it was, it suggests currency markets had become seriously disconnected from economic fundamentals, and completely undermines the view that they are efficient markets. This of course assumes that economic fundamentals actually matter!

Against this dramatic foreground, there is also the ever-changing background scenery of floating exchange rates. Foreign Exchange (FX) markets are often highly volatile within the trading day, without there being clear evidence of changing national or international economic circumstances. This is where competition between banks and individual traders is critical. It is a world of big egos, big corporate players and big deals. Aggressive traders account for the enormous daily turnover of today's foreign exchange markets, where they are attempting to enhance the profits of the employing institutions (and their own bonuses). Large value trades are often made to exploit only small changes in nominal exchange rates, but because of the size of the trades, institutions can reap substantial profits by correctly anticipating the trend. The aggregation of these trades, where market participants leap on a bandwagon of increasing speed, often produces much more substantial pressure, causing major currency appreciations or depreciations. Often traders' bets on currency direction, because of herding behaviour, produce a self-fulfilling prophecy.

Many of the sharp movements of exchange rates that have taken place seem unwarranted at the time, and even more inexplicable in retrospect. For example, the appreciation of the US dollar in the mid-1980s or the yen in the mid-1990s seemed unrelated to economic fundamentals. Both had significant impacts on the trade competitiveness of the USA and Japan. Neither of these appreciations proved sustainable, with the market retreating sharply from previous highs. Equally mystifying has been the slide of the euro by almost 33 per cent against the US dollar in less than two years since its launch in January 1999. A continual upward movement of European Central Bank (ECB) interest rates was unable to halt the euro's decline. Towards the end of this period, US fundamentals were weakening at the same time as economies seem to have strengthened throughout Europe. Thus a central question to consider is to what extent markets rationally assess economic or other signals, or whether on many occasions, herding or over-tracking bandwagon movements are in place, or conceivably there are random walks. In the long-term, the issue is whether fundamentals do in fact reassert their influence, and currency markets recover from short-term aberrations.

Figures 7.1 and 7.2 below illustrate some of the oddities of foreign exchange market behaviour. In Figure 7.1 the almost continuous decline of the euro against the US dollar is apparent, during the first 18 months of the new currency's life. The ECB's concern about this was reflected in part in the upward movement of interest rates from the spring of 1999. There was also some concern about inflation, as Euroland began to recover from the low levels of economic activity experienced in 1998. Figure 7.2 shows the improved growth rates of the EU economies from

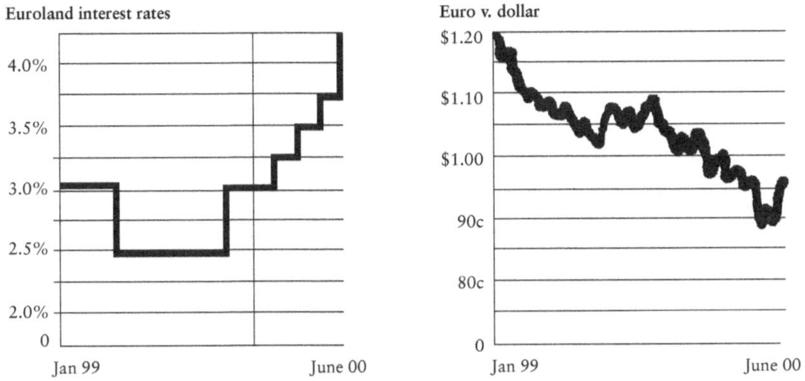

Figure 7.1 The first 18 months of the euro – eurozone interest rates and the USD value of the euro, January 1999–June 2000

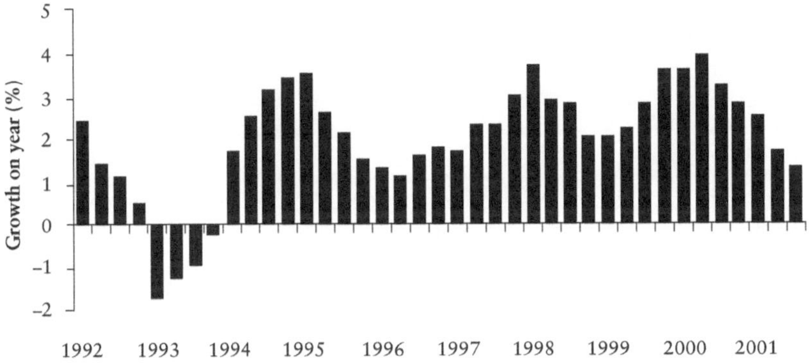

Source: Eurostar

Figure 7.2 Annual GDP growth rates for the EU, 1992–2001

the beginning of 1999 through to mid-2000. This was precisely the time the euro was declining most sharply against the US dollar. Interest rates alone failed to stem the euro's decline, and in the autumn of 2000, the ECB began a programme of intervention in the foreign exchange markets, with some support from other central banks.

Exchange rates and economic fundamentals

Standard explanations of exchange rate behaviour centre on Purchasing Power Parity (PPP) theory. According to the *absolute PPP* theory the exchange rate between two currencies is determined by the price levels of a comparable bundle of goods and services in the two countries under examination:

$$S = P/P^*$$

Where S is the exchange rate in terms of currency units per unit of foreign currency, P is the price of a bundle of goods expressed in the domestic currency, and P^* is the price of an identical bundle of goods in the foreign currency, expressed in its own currency units.

The weaker version of the *relative PPP*, brings the issue of inflation expectations into the estimation of future spot exchange rates. The assumption is that the future spot rate will reflect the expected future inflation rates in the country pair:

$$\%\Delta S = \%\Delta P - \%\Delta P^*$$

Alternatively this can be expressed as:

$$S = kP/P^*$$

where k is a constant parameter. In logarithmic terms this can also be written as:

$$s = \alpha + p - p^*$$

where s, p and p^* are the logarithms of S, P and P^*, and $\alpha = 0$, under the absolute version of PPP.

Whichever variant of PPP is applied, the conclusion is the same, that a change in the ratio of price levels implies an equal proportional change in the exchange rate, so that

$$\Delta s = \Delta p - \Delta p^*.$$

As Isard (1995) points out the 'relative PPP hypothesis has been regarded not only as a proposition in positive economics, but also as a policy guideline in normative economics'. He goes on to quote Balassa (1964), that PPP has proved especially useful to policymakers 'whenever existing exchange rates were considered unrealistic and the search began for the elusive concept of equilibrium rates'.

During the 20th century, policymakers found PPP an appropriate (if misguided) indicator for the restoration of the gold standard by the UK in April 1925, and for general realignments of exchange rates during the Bretton Woods period, as well as European realignments following the ERM crisis of 1992–3. If the theory is assumed to be valid, there is still an issue over what the proper indicators of prices and costs used in the analysis of PPP are. At the time of the return to gold, wholesale prices were used by Churchill's advisers. These were clearly inappropriate as they did not reflect the cost of finished goods and services. But there is still an ongoing debate over whether GNP deflators, consumer prices, prices of tradables, indices of labour costs or productivity are the most valid. Indeed the debate has extended to bring in very broad ranges of economic fundamentals. (For a discussion of various indicators, see Turner and Van't dack, 1993.) Often the use of PPP calculations by policymakers has seemed to be an attempt to justify *ex post* decisions on exchange rates taken for other reasons. Sayers, for example, reports that at the time of the return to gold, Montagu Norman's view of PPP calculations 'varied from day to day, characteristically, according to circumstances'. Likewise one of the Chancellor of the Exchequer's chief advisers at the time, Sir Otto Niemeyer, commented that 'over much importance should not be attached to any arguments based on precise interpretations of these figures'.

In fact, numerous research studies provide little support for the validity of PPP theory, at least in the short-run. This is especially true when the US dollar is one of the exchange rate pair, and another major currency is the other. Most available evidence suggests that deviations from PPP are both substantial and prolonged. Moreover exchange rates are much more volatile than the corresponding national prices levels. The latter point reinforces the destabilising nature of exchange rate movements, especially for economies with large export sectors.

Partly as a result of the poor performance of PPP, recent literature increasingly focuses on the asset market approach to exchange rate determination. The valuation of currencies via the exchange rate – or the assessment of the relative value of monetary assets – is analogous to the valuation of security (stock and bond) prices on financial markets. In principle it should be possible to establish fundamental values based on actual and expected fundamental economic data affecting the countries concerned. (To some extent this fundamental data may be considered as an extended data set of that used for PPP comparisons.) Obviously, subjective interpretation of these data plays a role, particularly when making an assessment of political factors that affect economic aggregates, but the process in principle is similar to the valuation of corporate securities through fundamental analysis. There will almost certainly be different expectations of future movements in fundamentals (for example, inflation rates, which provide a link with the relative version of the purchasing power parity theory). In practice all analysts will not agree on the precise currency valuation, but there will be a consensus range that is regarded as credible. Of course, this is not necessarily helpful in the real world as exchange rates may remain stubbornly outside the consensus range of credibility. Such is the case with the euro during 2000 and 2001, with most analysts, including the IMF, the G7 and, perhaps not surprisingly, the ECB, regarding it as undervalued (although largely on PPP grounds).

Assume, however, that a precise fundamental value for an exchange rate pair is not known, but that the open economies involved have stable macroeconomic circumstances. It might be expected that they would have stable exchange rate relationships, especially if there had been no recent exchange rate volatility and there were no new major dislocations elsewhere in the international economy, or expectations of them. If this is a valid argument, then unstable exchange rates would be anticipated only if there are unstable macroeconomic fundamentals. However, this is patently not the case when the empirical evidence is examined. (See, for example, Frenkel and Musa, 1980; Frenkel, 1981; Taylor, 1988; Wei and Kim, 1997; Flood and Rose, 1999). In part this may be the result of the difficulty of formally modelling the formation of expectations, and changes in them. To some extent this explains the widespread failure of econometric exchange rate models to explain the behaviour of nominal exchange rates. But another critical factor is certainly the ballooning of speculative currency flows as a result of the progressive deregulation of international financial markets.

As indicated by Balassa (1964), the concept of an 'equilibrium exchange rate' is an elusive one. In elementary economic theory an 'appropriate' exchange rate is assumed to be an equilibrium exchange rate. The concept here is that an equilibrium rate will in some time period balance the country's total international payments and receipts without any persistent inflow or outflow of gold stocks or exchange reserves and without abnormal capital movements. Such notions of equilibrium, still current in international trade texts, ignore a number of factors. Most important is that there may be an apparent equilibrium exchange rate, given the policy stance of the authorities. Put another way: high exchange rates can persist in the markets over long periods of time providing the authorities are willing and able to place sufficient deflationary pressure on the economy to force out exports and squeeze imports through high interest rates and the attraction of foreign money balances. However, at some point, a position will be reached where the policy becomes 'incredible': unemployment and/or the recession is too severe and the political situation becomes unstable, making inevitable a change in macroeconomic policy.

Such an approach explains both Britain's return to gold in 1925 and its exit from the system in the 1931 crisis, as well as the period of British membership of the ERM, 1991–2, culminating in sterling's enforced withdrawal from the mechanism (Fratianni and Artis, 1996; Eichengreen and Jeanne, 1998; Kitson and Michie, 2000). In a case like this, agents expect a speculative attack to bring about an abrupt change in macroeconomic policy (that is, lower interest rates and a lower parity) and act accordingly, causing a self-fulfilling attack on the currency. A so-called 'second-generation' currency crisis model of this kind suggests that anticipated instability in macroeconomic fundamentals leads to exchange rate instability. First-generation models concentrate on cases where excessive monetary growth makes the exchange rate peg increasingly inappropriate. A speculative attack occurs because the authorities increasingly deplete their reserves to support the exchange rate by direct intervention, with reserves also weakened by declining competitiveness and current account deficits. Again, macroeconomic policy is no longer credible and a speculative attack occurs.

Whilst competitiveness and trade performance may be critical in determining whether current macroeconomic policy can be sustained, trade performance is no longer the prime determinant of non-crisis day-to-day exchange rate volatility. Nor does research evidence suggest that the stability or otherwise, of other economic fundamentals affects short-run exchange rate fluctuations. Many textbooks, even relatively advanced ones, rather misleadingly continue to frame their explanations of exchange rate determination in terms of demand and supply of currencies for *trade* purposes, although they do recognise that there have been substantial increases in capital and speculative flows. However, this approach is a distortion of reality, in view of the massive increase in speculative currency flows since the breakdown of Bretton Woods and the global deregulation of financial markets. Teachers would do their students a great service by highlighting the overwhelming importance of speculative currency flows in exchange rate determination, and the day-to-day volatility of the foreign exchange markets.

It is often assumed that foreign exchange markets, because of their openness and relative accessibility compared to other kinds of financial market, will possess a high degree of efficiency in valuing currencies. Exchange rates will be driven to values that reflect economic fundamentals, and countries with stable economies can expect freedom from exchange rate volatility. In 1953, when making his famous argument in favour of flexible exchange rates, Milton Friedman contended that unstable exchange rates were only a reflection of economic instability and, 'a flexible rate need not be an unstable exchange rate' (Friedman, 1953, p. 151). This may once have been true, but the growth of speculation has changed the picture. An increasing number of researchers have shown that key macroeconomic variables such as money, output and consumption do not differ systematically between countries that have had very different exchange rate experiences. This has led Flood and Rose to conclude that, 'macroeconomics is an inessential piece of the exchange rate volatility puzzle' (Flood and Rose, 1999, F662). Their results lead to the conclusion that macroeconomic fundamentals *do not explain* exchange rate volatility.

Countries that have similar levels of macroeconomic stability have markedly different experiences in terms of exchange rate volatility. Quarterly data are the basis of the Flood and Rose tests, using standard deviations of exchange rates and macroeconomic fundamentals, including narrow money, real GDP and short interest rates for 18 industrialised countries. Germany is used as the comparator for the data, which relates to 1974–96. The exchange rate regimes range from deutschmark pegging in the Netherlands and Austria to free floating in Canada and Australia. Flood and Rose conclude that understanding exchange rate volatility remains 'a high-priority task for international finance scholars' (ibid., 1999, F671).

A more recent study by De Grauwe (2000) finds that there is overwhelming empirical evidence that the exchange rates of major currencies are generally unrelated to the fundamentals identified by economic theory. He finds that the decline of the euro against the US dollar during 1999–2000 was largely unrelated to observable news about underlying fundamentals. Again this corroborates the general findings from the empirical testing of exchange rate models that, in the short run at least, nominal exchange rate movements are disconnected from economic fundamentals.

The magnitude of speculative foreign exchange flows

It is instructive to ponder for a moment on the size of speculative flows that currently exist in the foreign exchange markets. It is not difficult to produce statistics of their gargantuan proportions and some are presented here. In the 1970s typical daily foreign exchange volumes were US \$10–\$20 billion. By 1983, daily turnover of \$60 billion had been reached. Survey data from the Bank for International Settlements (BIS) indicates that between April 1989 and April 1992, foreign exchange trading volume grew by 42 per cent to \$880 billion (880 000 000 000) a day. This was considerably faster than world trade and investment flows. A year later, FX trading exceeded \$1000 billion a day, or the equivalent of the entire monetary reserves of the 140 or so countries that belonged to the IMF (Roberts, 1995). By 1995 foreign exchange transactions of 26 countries amounted to $1230 billion daily, or $295 trillion (US) a year on the basis of 240 trading days a year. If currency derivatives (rights to acquire currencies) are included, *daily turnover* was probably $1300 billion, $312 trillion annually. Compare this with the annual value of global trade in goods and services at $4300 billion or the annual value of equity market transactions at $210 billion (Halifax Initiative, 1996, p. 3). BIS figures show that by 1998, currency turnover was at $1500 billion daily, approximately equivalent to the total annual output of the German economy. Since 1970 world trade has grown at around 5 per cent per annum, yet FX transactions have been growing at 20–25 per cent per annum in recent years (Lietaer, 2001, p. 312). However, there has been some respite. Following the introduction of the euro in 1999 there has been a reduction in daily turnover, reported by the BIS to be $1210 billion daily during April 2001 (BIS, 2001). This is unsurprising given that euro deposits (rather than the national currencies of the eurozone) were increasingly used after 1999 in international transactions ahead of the formal launch of euro notes and coins at the beginning of 2002. It is likely that the creation of the euro has only produced a short pause in the growth of speculation and FX turnover will again increase, especially if the euro itself continues to be volatile.

It is hardly surprising that in the wake of the enormous increase in speculative activity in the last 30 years of the 20th century, central bank intervention in support of exchange rates has lost its effectiveness. Of course it is true that central banks do not need to possess market power equal to all speculative forces, but if they are to turn exchange rates the way they want and keep them there, it is arguable that IMF members are collectively and individually under-reserved. This point is amply demonstrated by the experience of the events surrounding the ejection of the Italian lira and sterling from the ERM in September 1992. In the early phases of this crisis, Finland, Norway and Sweden came under severe speculative pressure. Finland's entire foreign exchange reserves were swept away, Norway lost 46 per cent of hers in a two-day period and Sweden suffered an outflow of $26 billion in a six-day period (even with 500 per cent overnight interest rates). This outflow was equivalent to forty days lost output or 11 per cent of GDP.

Twenty-five years ago about 80 per cent of foreign exchange transactions were related to trade or investment, hence the focus in older textbooks on them as determinants of exchange rates. To quote Lietaer, 'the "real" economy (that is, transactions relating to the purchase and sale of real goods and services abroad, including portfolio investments) has now been relegated to a sideshow of the global casino of the speculative monetary exchange game' (Lietaer, 2001, p. 314).

The latest BIS estimates suggest that perhaps as much as 98 per cent of all currency transactions are speculative, and the real economy share (trade and investment) is down to only 2 per cent of daily turnover. Even if allowance is made for the fact that some FX transactions may be double-counted in the BIS figures, these percentages change little in significance. If it is assumed all transactions are double-counted, the share of real economy transactions only rises to 4 per cent, with 96 per cent of the trading volume being speculative.

Financial deregulation bringing in new institutions as players and technological development facilitating fully integrated 24-hour global currency markets have made FX trades the big game in global financial markets. Transaction costs are low, and the market is now deep and highly liquid because of the big institutional players involved. The growth and size of the FX market has enormous implications for economic policy. Superficially at least, it could be seen as an attractive argument for a global single currency. In the EU, where a single currency has existed since 1 January 2002 amongst 12 member states, exchange rate volatility remains a critical factor for the success of the whole endeavour (and possibly for the EU itself).

Implications for the EU: euro dream or eurosclerosis?

Currency speculators are having profound effects on international price competitiveness. They are driving exchange rate movements and determining the degree to which countries can compete in export markets. In the new Euroland, where the European Central Bank is committed to proving the strength of its currency, and aggressive speculators may be trying to destabilise it to boost trading profits, the level of European reserves may become a critical issue. The ECB is able to intervene, but in reality how much power does it have to ward off speculative attack? Total EU central bank reserves are less than 20 per cent of *daily* trading volume. Frequent unsuccessful ECB interventions could quickly erode the limited reserves available, setting the scene for a speculative currency crisis of the first generation type. Moreover, each ECB foray into the market so far appears to provide only limited and short-lived relief. Initial rallies of the euro have been followed by a retreat to or below the pre-intervention level. The coordinated G7 intervention of 22 September 2000 achieved a value for the euro of almost 90 US cents, but three subsequent interventions by the ECB alone in October and November 2000, resulted in lower peaks with the currency trading below 83 US cents (even with support). There then followed some improvement to above the 90 US cent level, but largely as a result of uncertainty about the US economy in the wake of 11 September 2001, and the poor performance of the Dow (especially the New Economy, IT and telecommunications sectors). Fortunately for the ECB, 2003 brought a new resurgence for the euro, although again a rather puzzling development given the weaknesses of the main eurozone economies (see Figures 7.3 and 7.4).

Only completely fixed exchange rates eliminate speculation. Bretton Woods did not achieve this, nor did the gold exchange standard of 1925–31. Nor will the euro achieve this as it will only eliminate foreign exchange trading of European currencies, and exchange rates between the euro and other currencies will continue. Furthermore, if the single monetary policy of EMU becomes increasingly 'incredible' and the break-up of the single currency becomes a possibility, speculators may be merciless in their attempts to bring about that end. EMU provides no guarantee of enduring, completely fixed, exchange rates. The seeds for a second-generation crisis may exist.

Consider the mechanics of membership of the euro zone. To qualify for membership EU countries had to pass a convergence test, enshrined in the Maastricht Treaty. This convergence test was meant to align macroeconomic aggregates of total public sector deficits, annual budget deficits, inflation rates and interest rates, on the assumption that their convergence would also have led to stable membership of the ERM (a precursor to monetary union). Not only were these convergence criteria extremely 'broad-brush' and imprecise, but it is now recognised that several countries did not in reality attain them, and the final test for membership was fudged. Progress in the right direction was taken as passing the test.

In addition, despite the attainment of Maastricht style convergence, the EU is characterised by economic diversity. This diversity can be a threat to euro stability. Convergence *at a point in time* is also very different to convergence *through* time. Moreover, the whole picture is further complicated by the desire of the EU to undertake further enlargement to include some much weaker eastern European economies. An EU of 15 has become an EU of 25 in May 2004, with Bulgaria, Romania and even Turkey being future candidates for inclusion from 2007 onwards. With the anticipation that some new members will progress quickly to single currency membership, the asymmetric nature of the existing monetary union is being further increased. There is an obvious tension between EMU, convergence and the early EU timetable for further enlargement. (Table 7.1 shows the 'tests' that the first 12 countries had to meet for membership of EMU. New members are expected to have to meet a modified version of these hurdles.)

Some Euroland members, such as Greece, already have severe

Table 7. 1 Maastricht tests for EMU membership

CRITERION: price stability
STANDARD: over the past year the member state has inflation which does not exceed by more than 1½ percentage points the average of the three best performing states. The fall in inflation to this level should be sustainable.

CRITERION: budgetary policy
STANDARD: the Commission should not have judged that the state has an 'excessive deficit' in its budget. Ideally, the government deficit will be running at less than 3 per cent of national output and outstanding government debt will represent less than 60 per cent of output. If the actual figures have fallen substantially and 'come close' to these values, this may be sufficient.

CRITERION: ERM membership
STANDARD: The membership state should have maintained its currency within a narrow band for at least two years 'without severe tensions' and without initiating a devaluation.

CRITERION: long-term interest rates
STANDARD: In the year prior to the entry request, average long-term interest rates should not exceed by more than 2 percentage points the average for the three best performing member states in terms of price stability.

structural problems and high unemployment. As Costas Karfakis shows in Chapter 6 of this book, in recent years strong monetary and fiscal disinflation have been the key elements in achieving its Euroland membership. However, the achievement of eurozone membership in 2001 has brought with it significantly lower interest rates compared to recent years, creating favourable expectations of future growth. This optimism has been reinforced by investment taking place in the run up to the 2004 Athens Olympic Games and an inflow of European structural funds. These inflows have been associated with a consumer boom (retail sales have been growing at 5–6 per cent annually since 2001, underlying the 4 per cent growth of GDP). But despite government assurances, inflationary pressures are a worry despite labour market slack, and with low ECB interest rates present a threat to Greece's international competitiveness. A strong euro might force Greece's industrial sector to upgrade, but if the euro grows too strong, it could spell disaster for Greek manufacturing (*The Times*, 2003).

Ireland coped with boom conditions in 1999 and 2000 (experiencing an 11.5 per cent increase in GDP in 2000), but has been adversely affected by the global technology slowdown. GDP growth in 2001 and 2002 has slowed to 6·2 per cent and 6·9 per cent respectively although still remaining well above the dismal record of the larger eurozone economies. Despite this reduction in growth rates, inflationary pressures remain strong (consumer prices increasing by just under 5 per cent in 2001 and 2002) and the authorities would have preferred a significantly higher interest rates in the early years of the 21st century.

The weakness of the euro and the threat of higher inflation forced the ECB to increase interest rates after May 1999, peaking at 4·75 per cent by the end of 2000. But the danger of checking the weak recovery especially in the dominant economies of Germany (with only a 0·6 per cent GDP increase in 2001) and France was a key factor in the ECB's decision to intervene in currency markets rather than push up interest rates further in 2000. Reductions in interest rates began in April 2001, largely reflecting lower interest rates in the USA, as the Fed tried to combat the slide into recession, compounded by the economic after-effects of 11 September 2001. Although the requirements of individual EU countries differ, due to their collective weakness since 2001 (see Figure 7.4) there has been greater consensus on a eurozone-wide interest rate policy than there was in 2000. At that time Ireland's boom conditions, juxtaposed with very low growth and high unemployment in the three major economies of Germany, France and Italy, highlighted the tensions of the 'one-size-fits-all' monetary policy. The greater symmetry of experience since 2001 has reduced (although not alleviated completely) these tensions. The 'big 3' eurozone economies have continued to suffer sustained unemployment in excess of 9 per cent, whilst Ireland has unemployment around 4 per cent. Several other smaller EU economies – the Netherlands, Spain, Portugal and Greece – have also had inflation rates around or in excess of 4 per cent (against an ECB target of 2 per cent). These economic asymmetries highlight the difficulties presented by operating a single monetary policy. Such difficulties (and disputes over asymmetric governmental policy preferences) can only intensify as the EU is enlarged, although the hope is that through time genuine convergence of the eurozone economies will occur.

The diversity of performance in the Euroland economy is apparent from disparities in terms of economic aggregates. Table 7.2 indicates the range of diversity for inflation, growth and measures of economic structure. It underlines the fact that what is appropriate for Euroland as a whole, may have adverse effects on individual sectors and particular

Table 7.2 The range of differences across the EU countries (percentages)

	Inflation 1999 (2001)	*GDP growth 1999 (2001)*	*Share of manufs (agric/ construc) 1997**	*Share of exports in GDP 1998*	*Labour share 1997***
Maximum	2·5 (4·5)	8·3 (5·5)	0·253 (0·051/0·106)	0·844	0·526
Minimum	0·6 (1·7)	1·4 (0·6)	0·178 (0·011/0·069)	0·239	0·413

Notes: *Construction includes mining, electricity, gas and water.
**Compensation of employees/GDP.

Table 7.3 EU countries' position on the world competitiveness scoreboard (International Institute for Management Development Rankings)

Ranking in the 'WCS': 2002	*(2001)*	*Country*	*Competitiveness score (2002)*	*Competitiveness score (2001)*
1	1	USA	100·00	100·00
2	**3**	**Finland**	**84·33**	**83·38**
3	**4**	**Luxembourg**	**84·26**	**82·81**
4	**5**	**Netherlands**	**82·77**	**81·46**
5	2	Singapore	81·14	87·66
6	15	Denmark	80·41	71·79
10	**7**	**Ireland**	**76·20**	**79·20**
11	8	Sweden	75·31	77·86
13	**14**	**Austria**	**74·64**	**72·54**
15	**12**	**Germany**	**70·90**	**74·04**
16	19	UK	68·90	64·78
18	**17**	**Belgium**	**66·69**	**66·03**
22	**25**	**France**	**61·56**	**59·56**
23	**23**	**Spain**	**61·42**	**60·14**
28	*27*	*Hungary*	*56·65*	*55·64*
29	*35*	*Czech Republic*	*55·29*	*46·68*
32	**32**	**Italy**	**51·79**	**49·58**
33	**34**	**Portugal**	**49·26**	**48·36**
36	**30**	**Greece**	**46·90**	**49·96**
38	*39*	*Slovenia*	*45·44*	*42·49*
45	*47*	*Poland*	*30·18*	*32·01*

Notes: Countries in **bold** are the 12 euro members. Countries in *italic* are countries within the European geographic zone that are expected to be part of the 2004 EU enlargement.

Source: Extracted from IMD (2002).

national economies. These growth and inflation disparities remain sizeable.

Table 7.3 uses data from the IMD in Geneva to illustrate the competitive position of the 12 Euroland members relative to the USA score of 100 in 2001 and 2002. Current EMU members break down into three groups. In 2002, the most competitive group of Finland, Luxembourg and the Netherlands are second, third and fourth countries respectively in the IMD's top 100 most competitive countries, having scores between 82 and 85. Ireland, Austria and Germany form the second eurozone group with scores in the 70s. A third group of eurozone economies (Belgium, France and Spain) had scores in the 60s. The least competitive group of Italy, Portugal and Greece, have scores between 46 and 52. These scores reflect the considerable differences that exist in national competitiveness in Euroland. They signify a eurozone characterised by marked disparities in competitive attainment and suggest the need for considerable structural reform to raise the productivity levels of those countries with the lowest scores. It is also noteworthy that some of the new transition economy aspirants to EU membership have higher scores than the least competitive of current members. Also, Poland, which is due to enter in 2004, has a score of only 30. The 2002 Euroland average score is nearly 68 (67·56). The 2001 scores and rankings are broadly similar. The picture is one of some highly competitive economies in international terms, linked together through EMU with others that have serious structural, environmental and productivity handicaps.

All this leads to reflection on what kind of future growth scenarios can be expected in a Europe joined together in economic and monetary union, and theoretically isolated from the world of volatile exchange rates. One possibility is the 'euro dream' scenario. This envisages growth accelerating steadily in the mid-term to around its sustainable trend of 2·25–2·5 per cent. Inflation would remain relatively low, helped by a stable euro that is strong, but not excessively so. This would also encourage weaker economies to upgrade. The ECB would inherit the Bundesbank's mantle as a guarantor of price stability and this would foster the rapid growth of integrated European product and financial markets. Relatively strong steady growth rates would keep benefit payments down and tax receipts up, with budget deficits below the 3 per cent of GDP level specified in the Stability Pact.

Euroland does not appear to have been on course for this dream scenario. Until 2003, the weakness of the euro, looser monetary policy as reflected in the reduction of ECB interest rates to combat the slide into recession in the bigger economies, and the possibility of renewed rises in oil prices was threatening the ECB's 2 per cent inflation target. Since early 2003 the strong (and somewhat mysterious) resurgence of the euro against the US dollar and sterling has threatened the competitiveness of the eurozone and intensified deflationary tendencies in the major economies (which have experienced either negative or only marginally positive growth rates since the last quarter of 2002). European economies, despite the existence of the single currency, are indeed at the mercy of the exchange rate roller-coaster. Moreover there is evidence from the Bundesbank that Germany and France, the eurozone's largest and second largest economies, are becoming increasingly reliant on USA, British and other export markets outside the eurozone for their exports (*The Business*, 2003). This increases the significance for them of the volatile nature of FX markets. In addition these countries in 2003 are in breach of their Stability and Growth Pact obligations with budget deficits well in excess of the 3 per cent level and likely to remain so in 2004. Both have managed to flout the German inspired rules, which may have signalled a significant nail in the coffin of the Stability Pact arrangements. These arrangements were introduced to give credibility to the eurozone as a low inflation area and to increase the stability of the euro itself. This major breach of the Stability Pact rules, may tend to enhance the future volatility of the euro. However, given the levels of unemployment in Germany and France in 2003 and 2004, a tightening of fiscal policy from a domestic perspective is inappropriate as it would further increase the stagnation of the economies.

While a rise in interest rates might be welcomed in Ireland to counter inflation, economies where unemployment is high (and the 'big 3' of Germany, France and Italy have unemployment rates in excess of 9 per cent) are unlikely to have similar reactions, especially in an environment of subdued global growth. Such rate increases might threaten structural reform designed to improve productivity and competitiveness in poorly performing economies by discouraging investment and depressing growth even more. As well the euro might strengthen further, increasing the eurosclerosis tendencies. Figure 7.3 illustrates the poor growth performance of the EU economies between 2000 and 2003, where in many of the eurozone members, eurosclerosis is becoming a reality.

Disputes over the single monetary policy are a potential threat to the longer-term sustainability of the single currency. When the bigger economies recover (possibly aided by the upswing in the USA which appeared to be gathering pace from mid-2003), interest rates could rise again, further strengthening the euro. This strengthening of the currency might proceed so far that weaker countries faced with reduced competitiveness and mounting unemployment could threaten exit. Alternatively, they might force strong countries to lessen their inflation vigilance. Currency turmoil or a reduction in the size of the euro club might be an

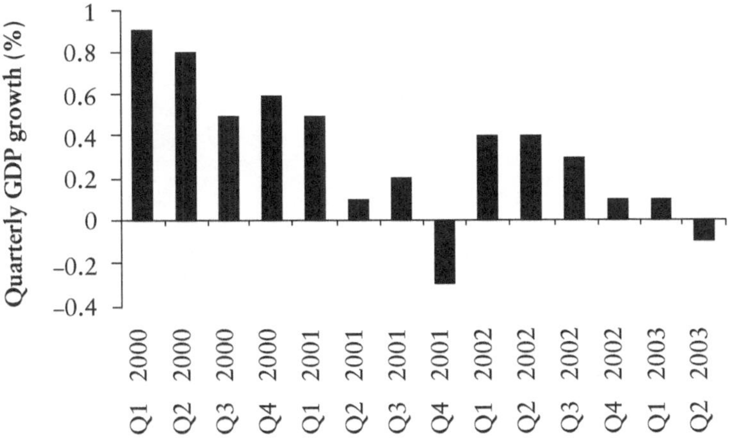

Source: Adapted from Eurostat.

Figure 7.3 EU growth rates, quarter 1, 2000–quarter 2, 2003

outcome. These tension possibilities and outcomes become increasingly likely as the size and asymmetry of the eurozone increases.

The sustainability of the single currency: some pessimistic conclusions?

The fluctuation of exchange rates can lead to substantial changes in the price competitiveness of trading nations in short time periods, producing profound effects on their economies (Catterall 2000). Witness the case of the UK during 1999 and much of 2000. For more than a year after the introduction of the euro the pound continuously appreciated against it. The reasons for this appreciation were unclear, especially as the continental European economy appeared to be moving into a recovery phase. One of its effects was to reduce the competitiveness of UK products in European markets. This may have encouraged upgrading, but for weaker firms (particularly in manufacturing) the effects were serious.

The strengthening of sterling showed the destructive effects that exchange rate appreciation can have on countries and industries. Europe, under the euro regime is certainly not free from such movements. In 2003 the tide for the euro has turned and there has been strong appreciation against the US dollar. A continuing appreciation of this kind would not be beneficial to Greek, Italian or Portuguese economic development, nor would it facilitate the assimilation of new economies

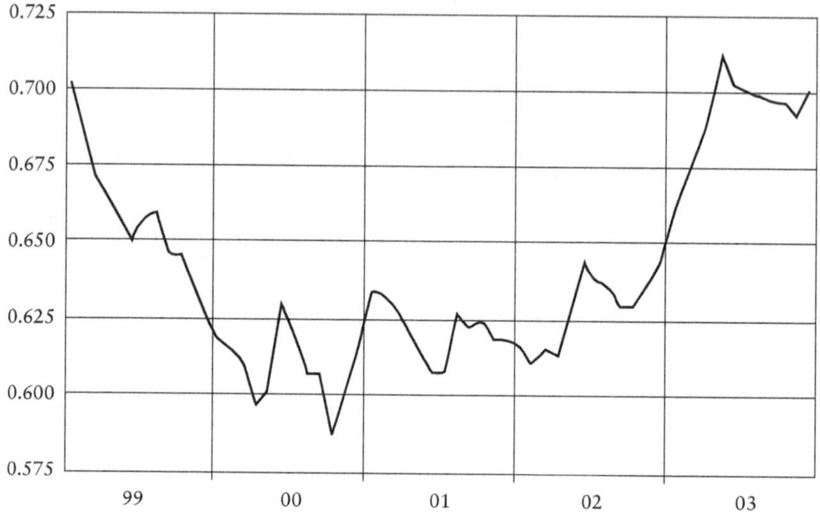

Source: Pacific Exchange Rate Service – Copyright 2003 Professor Werner Antweiler, University of British Columbia, Vancouver BC, Canada

Figure 7.4 British pounds per euro, January 1999–December 2003

into an enlarged EU. Upgrading of firms could prove impossible, with it more likely they would go out of business. In such circumstances of a substantial currency appreciation, the euro regime itself might be under threat with the club being torn apart over the competitive impacts on the weak.

There are many cases of substantial currency appreciation, which have significantly eroded the ability of countries to compete internationally. Periods of sustained exchange rate change of whatever form, disturb competitive relationships in the global economy and can cause the liquidation of sectors of an economy that are no longer price competitive. Arrangements where countries link their currencies to those of another (usually stronger) partner have often proved problematic from the point of view of competitiveness. For example, in Asia several currencies were effectively pegged to the US dollar during the 1990s. The sharp appreciation of the dollar relative to the yen and European currencies between mid-1995 and mid-1997 caused these Asian currencies to appreciate along with the dollar. This led to significant trading difficulties and loss of competitiveness for the Asian economies. It was worst for Thailand, Malaysia, Indonesia and the Philippines, whose currencies appreciated 25 per cent in real terms between 1990 and early 1997. For Korea, the real exchange rate appreciation was less as it allowed some nominal exchange rate depreciation to take place (Burnside et al., 1999, pp. 36–7). The real exchange appreciation in Thailand, Malaysia, Indonesia and Korea caused a significant deceleration in the trend rate of growth of exports in 1996. The existence of overvalued currencies in the region and faltering export performance for several economies, with hindsight, was regarded as one of the triggers for the currency crisis of 1997–8, although few had acknowledged the problem prior to the crisis.

A key reason for establishing a single currency in a customs union is to remove exchange rate fluctuations that hamper the growth of trade and investment between union members (Currie, 1997). But there are many difficulties as well, especially in establishing the parities of the former national currencies to the new currency unit. Because of speculative noise, a market test of exchange rates, especially in the short run, may be misleading. On the other hand the record of governments or monetary authorities in picking exchange rates is poor. Yet, in establishing rigid parities between national currencies and the euro, this is exactly what governments and monetary authorities have attempted to do, basing their formula on market signals in the form of the exchange rates that existed between national currencies as at 31 December 1998 (with some adjustments to ensure 'appropriateness'). These 'market rates' were themselves influenced by the policy stances of the various governments and monetary authorities. If these relativities prove unworkable over time (just as Bretton Woods parities did), obvious tension will be created within the eurozone, with some of its members facing the prospect of increased unemployment as their tradables become uncompetitive, and price level adjustments are forced upon them. With a single monetary policy, it is likely that these price level adjustments will occur through unemployment and labour market pressure. The question then arises as to whether some parts of Euroland might reach levels and durations of sustained unemployment which make a break-up of the monetary union a possibility, particularly if fiscal harmonisation proceeds, removing the use of a fully independent national tax policy. The view of the first ECB President, Wim Duisenberg, is that the Bank's priority is the control of inflation and the stability of the euro, not addressing the structural problems of the EU or its members (Duisenberg, 1999). In November 2003, Duisenberg was succeeded for an eight-year term by Jean-Claude Trichet, previously Governor of the Bank of France and a former deputy governor with the International Monetary Fund (IMF) and World Bank. Trichet has a long record as an inflation fighter in France, and his background at the IMF suggests he will continue Duisenberg's approach. He was an architect of the French 'franc fort' (strong franc) policy to combat inflation in the second half of the 1980s and early 1990s. He has indicated to the European Parliament that he believes price stability is a pre-condition for sustainable growth and creation of jobs. Despite the difficulties experienced by France and Germany in 2002–3 he has fiercely opposed any relaxation of the EU's tight budget rules, enshrined in the European Stability and Growth Pact. A lively debate over the future of the Stability Pact is in prospect.

Greece was the 12th member to be admitted to the euro club in January 2001. It is relevant to note what Greece agreed to: an 'irrevocable' locking together of the value of the drachma and the euro, at the exchange rate of EUR 1 = GDR 340·750. There is no 'wiggle' room here. An allegedly irrevocable fixed rate of conversion has been set. Greece has to live with this conversion rate no matter what happens to its level of productivity or inflation relative to its Euroland partners, or its level of internal unemployment. If it becomes politically unacceptable to live with this rate, Greece has only one realistic option, and that is abandoning the euro. In this context, it is often not appreciated that monetary unions are not only created, but they can also be destroyed (and there are several historical precedents for this).

Previous exchange rate crises have demonstrated that the level of unemployment calls into question the credibility of an exchange rate. This explanation was important in determining Britain's withdrawal from the gold exchange standard in 1931, and her exit from the ERM in 1992. This explanation also fits Sweden's experience during the ERM crisis. In September 1992, her authorities successfully resisted the first wave of speculative attack against the krona by temporarily increasing the inter-bank rate to the 500 per cent level (annualised). The breathing space was short-lived: renewed speculative pressure was encountered in November, when the currency was finally floated. Given the level of unemployment, the cost of the peg was too high, and the policy stance had become 'incredible' (FRBSF, 1996).

Certainly, EMU looks much more robust than ERM because national currencies have been replaced by the euro. But that does not guarantee that countries could not withdraw from EMU, reconstituting a national currency. Undoubtedly the administrative complexities are legion, but where the fixed parity is wrong and it is clearly reducing the competitiveness of an economy and creating sustained and mounting unemployment, withdrawal is a possibility (and perhaps a political imperative). History provides many examples of countries that have completely restructured their currency systems in the face of serious distortions of them (a prime example is that of Germany in 1924 following the ravages of hyperinflation). Indeed Romano Prodi (European Commission president) conceded that 'certainly it's possible' for countries to leave the euro and go back to their old money (*The Times*, 2000). Once speculators begin to sense that a national government's commitment to a single currency is weakening, they could be merciless in their attacks on the euro, and the ECB would have little power to resist. Alternatively the apparently rigid Stability Pact setting a framework of fiscal rectitude for eurozone members could be renegotiated and loosened to allow weaker economies more scope to inflate. Germany, once Europe's powerhouse, has breeched the Pact rules (as have Portugal and France as well). The German Finance Minister, Hans Eichel, has already argued for relaxing the rules, which were a German inspired framework for keeping countries like Italy closer to fiscal discipline. The new ECB governor takes the opposite view and the resultant outcome is uncertain. However, any relaxation of the rules to cope with cyclical deficits would be likely to have an impact on the euro, making it appear less of a hard currency. This perhaps would not be without benefit for European competitiveness, but it could lead to destabilising volatility over time. It may lack the credibility that the Pact was meant to underpin.

Euro gyrations are unlikely to be beneficial to the expansion of the European economy. Growth may come in fits and starts and a strong euro may harm the weaker economies of the possibly enlarged European periphery, whilst a weak euro may threaten the inflation rate. European currency games for speculators may not be over. The lack of symmetry between the national components of the enlarged EU creates opportunities for speculators to try to destabilise single currency arrangements. One possibility is that a flight from the currency might cause core nations to impose stronger rules for fiscal rectitude, contrary to the short-term interests of the weaker economies. Another is that speculation in favour of the currency, might also cause some of the periphery to wish to exit. Professor Buiter, a strong supporter of common currency arrangements in a world of financial turmoil, is over-optimistic in regarding the break up of the EMU as a result of speculative attacks as an impossibility. However, like the European Commission President, he does concede voluntary exits as being a (remote) possibility (Buiter, 1999). On the other hand, Eltis (1997), Dooley (1998), and Calomiris (1999), regard the possibility as much less remote. There is at least a door ajar.

Speculators have the power to determine the price competitiveness of nations and this power is not used to further international economic interdependence or foster national economic growth. There is little evidence that their influence is benign, or that they keep exchange rates closely in line with economic fundamentals. Governments, whether they fix, float or join in formal or informal currency unions, are at their mercy, and they have only small reserves to fight back.

In order to prevent speculative attacks dislocating international trade and commerce, the tax on speculative activity (the so-called 'Tobin Tax'), put forward in 1978 by the Nobel Laureate James Tobin (see Tobin, 1978, 1996), has considerable merit. The tax would be placed on spot foreign exchange transactions, many of which are short-term and designed to exploit small rate differentials. The effect on normal business transactions would be small as these are generally hedged through forward contracts tailored to specific contractual payment dates. The tax would not deter destructive speculation where massive profit potential existed, but it could deter speculation on small profit margins that often builds into major speculative crises. The Canadian government gave its support to the tax in 1999 (although subsequently appears to have dragged its feet), and an international effort is underway to create a consensus on the proposal. Support for the proposal has come from a wide range of non-governmental organisations (NGOs), who see the revenue from the tax as a means to provide financial assistance to poor countries of the world. The tax has also been endorsed by the French National Assembly, and is being explored as a possibility by several EU nations. In Britain, support has come from the Chancellor of the Exchequer, Gordon Brown. Opposition, however, has come from the financial services sector, particularly in the USA, where little governmental enthusiasm seems to exist for the proposal. Supporters claim the tax could be used to stabilise an important aspect of global competitive relationships, while at the same time helping to promote competitiveness in the poor countries of the south.

When Milton Friedman argued persuasively for floating exchange rates in the 1950s, he assumed that there was an underlying pattern of stable, equilibrium exchange rates between economies, which would be reached by the operation of impersonal free market forces. If this was so, speculation would lead to a speedy return of exchange rates to this underlying pattern, and prevent their future deviation from it. But if his assumption was wrong, floating exchange rates would not lead to an outcome reflecting economic fundamentals, and speculation could seriously distort economic relationships between countries. As discussed here, evidence from recent years suggests that Friedman was indeed wrong and that FX markets are characterised by unwarranted upward or downward spirals which may persist for long periods of time with potentially damaging effects. The enormous expansion of this speculative activity, which forms the bulk of FX transactions, has increased the size of these spirals and warrants corrective action of the kind proposed by Tobin.

If the tax were able to reduce significantly incidence of speculative attack, it would allow firms a more stable demand prospect and the opportunity to focus on productivity rather than currency hedging.

Governments have an equally important role. While the Tobin Tax might dampen speculative activity, sound domestic policies are an integral part of reducing the opportunities for speculation and allowing opportunities for business expansion. There is thus a strong argument for Stability Pact type arrangements, providing the arrangements are not so rigid that governments are precluded from addressing problems of cyclical unemployment and serious structural imbalance. As the period since the break up of Bretton Woods has shown, sound domestic policies alone do not guarantee freedom from exchange rate volatility. Speculator-generated gyrations of the exchange rate roller-coaster are likely to remain a threat both to international economic stability and the diverse and potentially expanding Euroland club. The Tobin Tax could be a useful counterweight, with the possibility of increase in times of severe turbulence.

Europe's economic and monetary union has as much to do with politics as it does with economics. Political issues dominate even more the case for further European enlargement. Europe should be wary of threatening the economic success of EMU with the hurried rush to integrate further countries into an already diverse monetary union. The existing EU needs to digest EMU first, to establish the credibility of the euro. Central to this is establishing a workable long-term revision of the Stability Pact, which does not threaten the cohesiveness or credibility of the eurozone, before extending the single currency area further. Alongside this both inside and outside the EU, the Tobin Tax needs to be seriously considered as part of a global initiative to respond to the rapid growth of potentially destabilising currency market speculation. A monetary union that is far from Mundell's ideal of an Optimum Currency Area could be at the mercy of destabilising speculative spirals. But as always, there will be a complex interplay between economics and politics in determining the way forward.

References

Bank for International Settlements (2001), *Central Bank Survey of Foreign Exchange and Derivatives Market Activity in April 2001*, October, www.bis.org

Balassa, B (1964) 'The Purchasing-Power Parity Doctrine: A Reappraisal', *Journal of Political Economy*, 72, 584–96.

Buiter, W. (1999), 'Alice in Euroland', CEPR Policy Paper No.1, Centre for Economic Policy Research, London.

Burnside, C., M. Eichenbaum and S. Rebelo (1999), 'What Caused the Recent Asian Currency Crises?', in W. Hunter, G. Kaufman and T.

Krueger (eds), *The Asian Financial Crisis: Origins, Implications and Solutions*, Boston: Kluwer Academic Publishers.

Calomiris, C.W. (1999), 'The Impending Collapse of the European Monetary Union', *Cato Journal*, 18 (3), Winter.

Catterall, R.E. (2000), 'International Competitiveness and speculative foreign exchange markets', in L. Lloyd-Reason and S. Wall, *Dimensions of Competitiveness: Issues and Policies*, Cheltenham, UK and Northampton, MA, USA: Edward Elgar.

Currie, D. (1997), *The Pros and Cons of EMU*, London: HM Treasury.

De Grauwe, P. (2000), 'Exchange Rates in Search of Fundamentals: The Case of the Euro-Dollar Rate', Discussion Paper Series No. 2575, Centre for Economic Policy Research, London, October.

Dooley, M.P. (1998), 'Speculative Attacks on a Monetary Union?', *International Journal of Finance and Economics*, 3(1), January, 21–6.

Duisenberg, W.F. (1999), 'EMU: Growth through Stability', speech to the Global Economy Conference organised by the Economic Strategy Institute, Washington DC, 27 April.

Eichengreen, B. and O. Jeanne (1998), 'Currency Crisis and Unemployment: Sterling in 1931', Discussion Paper Series No. 1898, Centre for Economic Policy Research, London, May.

Eltis, W. (1997), 'The Creation and Destruction of the euro', Policy Study No. 155, Centre for Policy Studies, August.

Flood, R.P. and K.R. Rose (1999), 'Understanding Exchange Rate Volatility without the Contrivance of Macroeconomics', *Economic Journal*, 109, F660–F672, November.

Fratianni, M. and M. Artis (1996), 'The Lira and the Pound in the 1992 Currency Crisis: Fundamentals or Speculation?', Working Paper Series in Economics, 96-022, Indiana University, July.

FRBSF (1996), 'Models of Currency Speculation: Implications and East Asian Evidence', FRBSF Economic Letter, 96–13, Federal Reserve Bank of San Francisco, 19 April.

Frenkel, J.A. (1981), 'The collapse of purchasing power parities during the 1970s', *European Economic Review*, 16, 145–65.

Frenkel, J.A. and M. Musa (1980), 'The efficiency of foreign exchange markets and measures of turbulence', *American Economic Review*, 70, 374–81.

Friedman, M. (1953), 'The Case for Flexible Exchange Rates', in *Essays in Positive Economics*, Chicago: University of Chicago Press.

Halifax Initiative (1996), 'Currency Speculation Control Options', discussion paper, December.

Isard, P. (1995), *Exchange Rate Economics*, Cambridge Surveys of Economic Literature: Cambridge University Press.

IMD, (2001), *World Competitiveness Yearbook*, Lausanne, Switzerland: International Institute for Management Development.

Kitson, M. and J. Michie (2000), *The Political Economy of Competitiveness*, London: Routledge.

Lietaer, B. (2001), *The Future of Money: Creating New Wealth, Work and a Wiser World*, London: Century.

Mayes, D.G. and M. Virén, M. (2000), 'Asymmetry and the Problem of Aggregation in the Euro Area', Bank of Finland Discussion Papers, 11/2000, Helsinki.

Roberts, J. (1995), *$1000 Billion a Day: Inside the Foreign Exchange Markets*, London: Harper-Collins.

Taylor, M.P. (1988), 'An empirical examination of long-run purchasing power parity using co-integration techniques', *Applied Economics*, 20, 1369–81.

The Business (2003), 'Single currency fails to boost eurozone trade', 297, 9–10 November.

The Times (2000), 'Britons could learn to love the euro, says Prodi', 26 May.

The Times (2003), 'The race for survival after the Games', 3 December.

Tobin, J. (1978), 'A Proposal for International Monetary Reform', *Eastern Economic Journal*, 4 (July–Oct), 153–9.

Tobin, J. (1996) 'Prologue', in M. ul Haq, I. Kaul and I. Grunberg, *The Tobin Tax: Coping with Financial Volatility* (Oxford: Oxford University Press).

Turner, P. and J. Van't dack (1993), 'Measuring International Price and Cost Competitiveness', *BIS Economic Papers*, 39.

Wei, S-J. and J. Kim (1997), 'The Big Players in the Foreign Exchange Market: Do They Trade on Information or Noise?' *NBER Working Papers*, 6256, Cambridge, MA: National Bureau of Economic Research, November.

CHAPTER EIGHT

The elusive case for flexible exchange rates

George Zis

Introduction

Is the European Union an optimum currency area? In posing this question as the basis for the assessment of the viability and the desirability of membership of the European Monetary Union, what is effectively being asked is which, if any, of the intra-European Union exchange rates should be fixed. In other words, the question as to whether or not the European Union is an optimum currency area is an alternative way of debating the relative merits of exchange rate flexibility. But addressing the issue of fixed versus flexible exchange rates in terms of optimum currency area considerations reflects a significant change of emphasis in the case for flexible exchange rates. Stating the case in these terms involves the concession that, in principle, exchange rate fixity may be the economically appropriate choice under certain circumstances. No such qualification featured in the original case for flexible exchange rates.

In what follows, the post-1950 evolution of the case for exchange rate flexibility will be discussed. First, the background to the development of the arguments for flexible exchange rates will be described. Next, the case for flexible exchange rates as presented prior to 1973 will be considered. This will be followed by a discussion of the way flexible exchange rates actually behaved after 1973 and the validity of the predictions of those who advocated exchange rate flexibility will be evaluated. Fourth, how the case for flexible exchange rates evolved after 1973 will be described. The final section will present conclusions relating to the evolution of the case for flexible exchange rates during the last half-century.

Post-1973 exchange rate flexibility: the background

Economic rivalry among countries has played and continues to play a significant role in the determination of national economic policies. The significance of nationalism as a determinant of economic policy has varied over time and across countries. For example, in the immediate post-1945 period, the economic policies required for the potentially successful conduct of the Cold War and the 'containment' of Soviet 'expansionist' ambitions were assigned a higher priority than the pursuit of narrowly defined national economic objectives. The protection of the 'market economy' as a politico-economic system on a world scale emerged as the principal objective of the countries of the 'free world'. The elevation of the system's survival as the binding constraint on the design of national economic policies, in contrast to the inter-war years when economic nationalism determined countries' economic policies, involved western governments in a compromise that implied that domestic economic objectives were assigned a supporting rather than a leading role.

But this compromise, while on a world scale involving the self-destructing economic nationalism of the inter-war years giving way to an ill-defined internationalism, was a reflection of the particular balance of power among the capitalist countries that prevailed in the aftermath of the Second World War. It reflected the world dominance of the USA, in both economic and military terms. Thus the compromise committing capitalist countries to assigning to the 'defence of the free world' a priority higher than narrowly defined national economic interests did not prevent the USA from eventually, in the 1960s, adopting economic policies in an aggressively nationalistic pursuit of domestic objectives.

The exchange rate regime in place, at any moment in time, largely determines the ability of any individual country to pursue narrowly defined national economic objectives independently of the rest of the world. The international monetary system agreed upon at Bretton Woods in July 1944 envisaged a world monetary order which would facilitate economic cooperation among countries rather than allow the re-emergence of economic nationalism in its extreme inter-war years form. The Bretton Woods system was a compromise between British and American views as to what could potentially constitute a durable international monetary system. But it was an uneasy compromise. It mainly reflected the White Plan rather than the principal features of the Keynes Plan which was largely inspired by a determination to allow the pursuit of full employment to be only loosely constrained by the balance of payments.

The fragility of the agreement reached at Bretton Woods is, perhaps, best reflected by the provision in the IMF Articles of Agreement that member countries would be allowed to change their exchange rate only if they developed a 'fundamental disequilibrium' in their balance of payments. The concept of 'fundamental disequilibrium' was not defined. Thus sharply contrasting interpretations of the concept were presented on either side of the Atlantic. In the British House of Commons the concept was praised as evidence of the compatibility of the new international monetary system with the rigorous pursuit of the full employment objective. In the US Senate the 'fundamental disequilibrium' clause was interpreted as an acceptance by IMF member countries of the principle that national macroeconomic policies would be subject to a binding balance of payments constraint so that exchange rate changes would occur only rarely. Thus the ambiguity of the concept of 'fundamental disequilibrium' ensured that both legislatures ratified the Bretton Woods agreement to establish the IMF.

The durability of the Bretton Woods system was never tested. It was effectively abandoned even before it came into operation. The system which disintegrated in March 1973 was not the international monetary system agreed upon in July 1944. The Bretton Woods compromise embodied the principle of equality of status for all currencies. A reserve currency international monetary system was rejected as incompatible with the objective of multilateralism. Hence the US pressure on Britain to phase out the reserve currency role of sterling. However, the onset of the Cold War resulted in a radical reordering of the priorities of the capitalist world. The 'containment' of the Soviet Union's sphere of influence became the principal policy objective for the western world. For the USA, the pursuit of this objective was possible only if both the military and the economic dimensions of its foreign policy were completely purged of the ideology of isolationism which, despite the Second World War, had not ceased to exert some influence on post-1945 America attitudes towards the rest of the world.

Thus, in March 1947, the Truman Doctrine was declared as a principal feature of America's foreign policy. Three months later, George Marshall argued the political case for a significant increase of American economic aid to Europe. The funds for the implementation of the Marshall Plan were approved by Congress in April 1948. Isolationism had been abandoned. But isolationism determined the price the USA was to exact from its allies for committing its economic and military resources to the 'resistance' of Soviet 'expansionism'. America judged international institutions, designed during the war on the assumption that cooperative solutions to post-1945 international economic problems would be sought and preferred, to be an undesirable constraint on its ability to provide an effective leadership for the western world. Bilateral agreements, rather than those concluded during the war, were deemed to provide a better environment for the conduct of the Cold War. The institutions established by decisions while the war was still on were to be assigned a different role, namely, that of providing American actions and policies with legitimacy.

The USA extended economic aid under the Marshall Plan on condition that the recipient country would not make use of the resources of the IMF. This feature of the Marshall Plan resulted in the marginalisation of the IMF until 1956 when, after the Suez crisis, Britain sought IMF aid despite US objections. But by that time the gold exchange standard was not only in place but also signs of its inherent instability were becoming evident. In 1968, under the force of speculative pressures, the price of gold in the private market ceased to be fixed and was allowed to be freely determined by market forces, while the official price of the metal remained fixed at its 1934 price of \$35·00 per ounce. The separation of the official from the private market for gold signalled the end of the gold exchange standard and the move onto a dollar standard. The Bretton Woods agreement did not envisage either a gold exchange standard or a dollar standard. The system that disintegrated in March 1973 was not the international monetary system agreed upon at Bretton Woods in July 1944.

The discarding of the Bretton Woods system and the imposition of the gold exchange standard in its stead simply reflected the balance of power within the western world and the onset of the Cold War. Keohane (1994, p. 59) has observed:

> The beginnings of the Cold War in 1947 reoriented American foreign policy and profoundly changed the relationship between the United States and Europe, and soon thereafter, the relationship between the United States and Japan ... The Cold War was therefore one of the props of the Bretton Woods system, along with the capability and willingness of the United States to provide side payments. Indeed, the willingness of the United States to help other democracies and the willingness of the countries of Europe and the Pacific Rim to defer to the United States are both hard to imagine in the absence of the Cold War.

Inevitably, therefore, as the international political conditions, the onset of the Cold War and the balance of power prevailing at the time within the western alliance that gave rise to the post-war international monetary system could not endure, the system put in place by America was inherently unstable. America had the military capacity to 'protect' Europe from Soviet 'armed aggression'. However, the effectiveness of America's military 'protection' depended on economic developments in Europe. America's military might could not defend Europe's market economies from the potential political implications of socially destabilising conflicts that would inevitably follow a re-emergence of the inter-war economic conditions. Therefore the rapid and sustained recovery of the western European economies was necessary for the successful resistance of the Soviet 'threat'. Economic rather than military warfare would ultimately determine the fate of Europe's market economies.

Hence the decision of the USA to provide, through the Marshall Plan, resources for the economic reconstruction of Europe on a scale that it would not even consider during the negotiations leading to the Bretton Woods agreement. But a rapid and sustained European economic recovery would necessarily involve a change in the balance of power within the western alliance that initially allowed the USA to force the abandonment of the Bretton Woods international monetary system. In other words, the successful defence of the market economy was inconsistent with the long-run survival of the gold exchange standard that was put in place after 1947.

The inherent instability of the post-war international monetary system was not associated only with the political origins of the system. Its very characteristics were also a source of instability. As Johnson (1973, p. 510) explained:

> A gold reserve standard is inherently an unstable standard, in a sense in which a pure gold standard at least theoretically is not, because of the use of a national currency (or possibly several national currencies) as a provisional substitute for non-existent gold.

However, such use of a national currency need not necessarily undermine the durability of a gold reserve standard. How countries respond to the redundancy problem largely determines whether or not the use of a national currency as a substitute for non-existent gold will jeopardise the longevity of the gold reserve standard. Mundell (1969, pp. 36–7) defined the redundancy problem and the questions that it raises as follows:

> Only n-1 countries in an n-country world need achieve balance-of-payments equilibrium (because of Cournot's Law). Which country, if any, should be the nth country that is spared a balance-of-payments constraint? And if all countries are required to share in the adjustment, what institutional means can be explored to exploit the extra degree of freedom for world employment or price stability? The problem is closely related to the problem of determining the distribution of the burden of adjustment between countries.

It follows, therefore, that if the extra degree of freedom/extra policy instrument is employed to promote price stability in the reserve currency country and, consequently, across all the countries on the standard, the destabilising potential of using a national currency as a substitute for gold will be limited. Confidence in the reserve currency will be maintained and the gold exchange standard would endure, especially if a mechanism for the orderly growth of international liquidity were collectively agreed upon and operated.

Large-scale economic aid by the USA resulted in the rapid and sustained economic recovery of Europe's market economies. US policies ensured that a dollar shortage did not materialise and, therefore, governments successfully pursued the objective of full employment. International trade grew at highly impressive rates. These developments occurred against a largely non-inflationary background. Except for the Korean War period, inflation rates were controlled at relatively low levels. Social welfare expenditures were significantly increased, thus reducing the potential risks of social conflict. US foreign economic policies smoothly transformed the wartime anti-fascist alliance into an anti-communist alliance in which the former enemies, Germany, Japan and Italy, emerged, particularly the first two, as strategically significant players in the economic conduct of the Cold War.

In brief, then, America provided a highly successful economic leadership of the western alliance. But the framework within which this leadership was exercised could not survive the success of US foreign economic policies. As a result of the increasingly impressive performance of western Europe and Japan, the economic balance of power within the capitalist world was continuously changing against the USA. In absolute terms, America's economic power was unrivalled; in relative terms, it continuously declined.

The North Atlantic Treaty Organisation (NATO), established in 1949, provided the institutional framework for America's military leadership of the anti-Soviet alliance. In contrast, America's economic leadership of the alliance was not judged to require the creation of a new international institution. The Bretton Woods agreement was to provide the legitimisation of US policy decisions. The IMF Articles of Agreement, the outcome of a compromise between American and British views, with the former predominating, were sufficiently ambiguous to be consistent with the postwar international monetary system evolving in US-determined directions which were diametrically opposite to those envisaged by the authors of the Bretton Woods agreement. The condition imposed on countries receiving economic aid under the Marshall Plan, that they were not to use IMF resources, relegated the Fund to a marginal role in international monetary relations, in sharp contrast with the vision of the architects of the Bretton Woods system, of the IMF providing a framework for collective decision making by member countries. The USA used its voting power at the IMF to veto any revision of countries' IMF quotas until 1959.

Thus what was envisaged as a mechanism with the potential of ensuring the orderly and systematic growth of international liquidity was ignored. The outcome of the decisions to forbid countries in receipt of Marshall Aid from using IMF resources and to freeze member countries' IMF quotas was the emergence of US balance of payments deficits as the principal source of increases in international liquidity. Thus the gold exchange standard came into existence in total contradiction to the

Bretton Woods agreement, which aimed at establishing an international monetary system that did not rest on any national currency evolving into a reserve asset within the system.

A corollary of the emergence of the gold exchange standard as a consequence of unilaterally taken decisions by the USA, rather than of an international agreement, was that America imposed itself as the *n*th country in the system which, in turn, allowed it to take advantage of the system's extra degree of freedom/extra policy instrument to render redundant the balance of payments constraint. In other words, the USA was not to share the burden of adjustment. This was to be borne entirely by the rest of the world.

As early as in 1959, Triffin (1960) argued that it was only a matter of time before the prevailing international monetary arrangements would collapse. His firm prediction rested on the diagnosis that the system lacked the capacity to resolve its internal contradictions. If America corrected its balance of payments deficit, a shortage of international liquidity would develop with deflationary implications for the world economy; if the deficit was ignored, the ratio of US liabilities/US gold holdings would continuously increase, thus undermining confidence in the dollar and, consequently, generating ever-increasing speculative flows of capital.

US balance of payments deficits, having significantly assisted the postwar economic recovery of the world's principal capitalist economies, by the end of the 1950s, because of the path along which the international monetary system had evolved, had become a threat to the sustainability of the performance of the market economies. The use of the dollar as a provisional substitute for non-existent gold had emerged as a source of instability.

Triffin's conviction that the collapse of the international monetary system was inevitable rested on an analysis of the system's economic characteristics. But the end of the 1950s also coincided with a fundamental change in the political relations within the western alliance. De Gaulle's ascent to power in 1958 marked the beginning of a sustained challenge to America's hegemony, on all three (political, economic and military) fronts. France's new intentions became evident very soon. Fleming (1961) in his discussion of the preparations of the USA, Britain and France for their summit meeting with the Soviet Union, scheduled for May 1960, concluded: 'it was plain that President Eisenhower had lost his campaign when he let the Western Summit Meeting in Paris, in December 1959, pass without asserting his leadership as the head of the Western coalition over President de Gaulle' (p. 989).

Eisenhower was prepared to reach an accommodation with the Soviet Union, even if that were to involve significant concessions by the west over Berlin. For West Germany this was not an acceptable prospect. De

Gaulle exploited these German concerns to impose the condition that no fundamental agreement was to be reached with the Soviet Union: otherwise, France would not attend the Summit meeting with the Soviet Union. Further, he extracted the agreement of America and Britain that the Summit meeting be held in Paris and, in a demonstration of determination to assert his independence, France exploded its first A-Bomb in February 1960. It was not much later that France withdrew from NATO's military command structures, having meanwhile forged a close relationship with West Germany with the explicit objective of establishing continental Europe as a force independent of the Anglo-Saxon world and capable of negotiating with the Soviet Union from a position of relative strength.

In the area of international monetary relations, France's challenge concentrated on vigorously disputing the desirability and the right of America's exploitation of the system's extra degree of freedom to impose itself as the system's *n*th country that is spared the balance of payments constraint. In 1966, Giscard d'Estaing (1969, p. 11), after characterising the existing international monetary system as 'senseless', went on to explain:

> There is no relation between the reserve needs of the world and the foreign deficits of the reserve currency countries. This is quite obvious, and nowadays everybody knows it. Yet I am always impressed by the fact that, as obvious as this is, there are still some theories to back this system which has no corrective mechanism for the reserve currency countries or, at least, only a very weak one. For instance, compare the United States and Italy in 1963 and 1964. The deficits of the United States started much before the Italian deficits. Italy had to adopt a very hard and very exacting internal economic policy which made its employment, its growth and its foreign trade suffer, all because it had to return to equilibrium within strict time limits. And Italy did return to equilibrium. Yet, in the same time period, the corrective mechanism for the reserve currency countries did not work as hard, if at all. It is a one-sided system: the non-reserve currency countries acquire the currencies of others, but not vice versa. And it is an unstable system; past a certain limit, there is a feeling of uncertainty concerning its development in the future.

Having questioned the survival prospects of the system, d'Estaing proceeded to advance what he described as a 'fundamental' suggestion, indicative of France's strategic objectives. He argued that at the same time as discussions were taking place aimed at the reform of the international monetary system,

> the six Common Market countries should begin preliminary work on a monetary union. Apart from the fact that these countries may have their own reasons for achieving this – reasons which are linked to the good functioning of the Common Market itself – the present

> structure of world payments and reserves makes the absence of a single monetary instrument appear an anomaly. The figures speak for themselves; as of June 13, 1966, out of a total volume of world liquidity estimated at 70 billion dollars, the United States held 14.9 billion, the United Kingdom 3.2 billion, and the Common Market countries 23.7 billion. To deal with the problem of international settlements on the basis of only two currencies would be to ignore the contemporary facts. We can see that the debate would be made clearer by the emergence of a third monetary unit which would be the common medium for the external monetary action of the Six.
>
> (Ibid., pp. 17–18)

Triffin's diagnosis and prediction were, initially, judged to be unduly pessimistic. The US authorities would not concede the case that the international monetary system was seriously flawed and in need of radical reform, if it were to survive in a form resembling, even remotely, that which it had acquired by the end of the 1950s. America unequivocally rejected an increase in the price of gold in terms of all currencies. Such an initiative was justified in economic terms and was permissible under the IMF Articles of Agreement. America was equally adamant in its opposition to a devaluation of the dollar against continental Europe's stronger currencies. Indeed, quite remarkably, US policymakers argued that neither measure was technically feasible.

America was originally successful in resisting the pressures for the reform of the international monetary system largely because its policies had facilitated Europe's rapid economic recovery in the 1950s in a non-inflationary environment. But as the signs of the fragility of the system increased in the early 1960s, America agreed to discussions with its principal allies on how the system could be reformed so as to become more speculation-resistant and gave vague hints that it would introduce measures aimed at the reduction of its balance of payments deficit. It is interesting to note that these discussions were not conducted under the umbrella of the IMF. The Group of Ten and, to a lesser extent, the OECD were the fora for these deliberations.

The discussions on the reform of the international monetary system were soon to be deprived of any rationale. The decision by the Johnson administration in the mid-1960s to finance the rapid escalation of America's war in Vietnam and the introduction of domestic social programmes by increasing the US money supply rather than by raising domestic taxes, resulted in a sharp deterioration of the country's balance of payments and the generation of worldwide inflationary pressures which persisted well into the 1970s. Inevitably, speculative pressures intensified. Sterling was forced to devalue in November 1967, and in March 1968 the gold reserve stand was abandoned, with the capitalist world moving to a dollar standard through the separation of the official from the private market for gold, with the price of the metal in the latter rising steeply. The 1968 Special Drawing Rights (SDR) scheme, scheduled to become operational in January 1970, failed to moderate the intensity of the speculative pressures on the dollar. Their persistence forced the USA to announce, in August 1971, the suspension of the dollar's convertibility into gold.

The ensuing crisis was 'resolved' by the December 1971 Smithsonian Agreement on a new set of exchange rates which involved the dollar's devaluation against both gold and some national currencies and, quite bizarrely, the revaluation of the German mark and the Japanese yen against gold. This Agreement, too, failed to generate confidence. Severe speculative pressures in March 1973 finally forced the disorderly abandonment of the principal features of the international monetary order which America had put into place in the late 1940s. The capitalist world collapsed into exchange rate flexibility. No international agreement preceded the decision of countries to abandon their commitment to particular exchange rates and allow the price of their currency, in terms of other currencies, to be determined by the free interaction of demand and supply in foreign exchange markets. Indeed, it was nearly three years before the post-March 1973 exchange rate practices were legitimised through the Second Amendment to the IMF Articles of Agreement, adopted at the 1976 annual meetings of the IMF in Jamaica.

The sequence of developments during the terminal stage of the postwar international monetary system was largely determined by America's economic status within the capitalist world. In absolute terms, America was sufficiently powerful to adopt highly nationalistic monetary policies which ensured that the war in Vietnam and the newly introduced social expenditures were partly financed by the rest of the world economy. But, in relative terms, the USA no longer had the economic power to extract from the other capitalist countries acquiescence to its monetary policies that could, perhaps, have prolonged the system's precarious existence. The USA by the end of the 1960s could no longer threaten the other major capitalist economies with economic sanctions. Military sanctions were the only potentially effective means for America to exert pressure on Europe, as its military supremacy was as absolute in the late 1960s as it was in the late 1940s. The following quotation from Bergsten (1973, pp. 287–8) accurately reflects America's position within the western alliance as it had evolved by the early 1970s:

> It is virtually certain that major economic conflict between Europe and America would decisively undercut the ability of any US administration to maintain any significant (let alone the present) level of U.S. troops in Europe. Senator Mike Mansfield bizarrely saw the monetary crisis of May 1971 as an 'attack on the dollar', and

> used it in the Senate to mobilise support for legislation requiring an immediate 50 percent cut in those troops. He lost by only eight votes, and only after the most intensive lobbying carried out by the Nixon administration on any single issue. Pressures for cuts in the defense budget, especially abroad, are already very severe. U.S. economic interests that would be hurt by U.S.–European economic conflict would surely seek to retaliate on issues of security, even if the administration were wise enough not to try to use its leverage on those issues to extract economic concessions ... Such a result would obviously have a major impact on overall U.S. foreign policy. The broad foreign policy costs of economic conflict were, of course, also demonstrated vividly in late 1971, when British Prime Minister Edward Heath refused to meet President Nixon to discuss the president's forthcoming trips to Peking and Moscow until the United States called a meeting of the Group of Ten (which took place in Rome) to negotiate a solution to the deepening international economic crisis.

Evidently, then, by the end of the 1960s the Bretton Woods spirit of cooperation had given way to intensely antagonistic rivalries.

By the time of the collapse of the international monetary system in March 1973, there had developed a strong consensus, at least among academic economists and policy commentators, in favour of exchange rate flexibility. Indeed, since June 1972, Britain had ceased to support the price of sterling in terms of other currencies in the foreign exchange market. What, then, was the case for flexible exchange rates prior to 1973? The next section addresses this question.

The case for flexible exchange rates

The principal statements of the case for flexible exchange rates prior to the 1973 collapse of the international monetary system are to be found in Friedman (1953), Meade (1955), Sohmen (1961) and Johnson (1969). The discussion which follows concentrates on the studies by Friedman and Johnson. The former is chosen because of its profound influence in identifying the issues that had to be addressed when assessing the relative merits of alternative exchange rate regimes. It effectively determined the framework within which the viability, desirability and potential for reform of the postwar international monetary system were debated. But Friedman's study went further. He argued that exchange rate flexibility was desirable in its own right and not only as a solution to the problems facing the capitalist world of the 1950s. In so doing, Friedman provided a framework for the analysis of exchange rate determination which endured well into the 1970s, rich in its predictions of the way flexible exchange rates would actually behave. The Johnson essay is chosen as it enables an assessment of the evolution of the case for flexible exchange rates between the publication of Friedman's study and the last days of the postwar international monetary system.

Friedman (1953) explained that his paper 'had its origin in a memorandum written in the fall of 1950 when [he] was a consultant to the Finance and Trade Division of the Office of Special Representative for Europe, United States Economic Cooperation Administration' (p. 157). This is, perhaps, worth noting for an appreciation of the way Friedman motivated his arguments in favour of exchange rate flexibility. He began by asserting that the exchange rate fixity, provided for by the IMF Articles of Agreement, was 'ill suited to current economic and political conditions' and, therefore,

> These conditions make a system of flexible or floating exchange rates – exchange rates freely determined in an open market primarily by private dealings and, like other market prices, varying from day to day – absolutely essential for the fulfillment of our basic economic objective; the achievement and maintenance of a free and prosperous world community engaging in unrestricted multilateral trade.
>
> (Ibid.)

Friedman then proceeded to list a number of problems, including the 'promotion of rearmament', that would 'take on a different cast and become far easier to solve in a world of flexible exchange rates and its corollary, free convertibility of currencies' (pp. 157–8). Thus 'The sooner a system of flexible exchange rates is established, the sooner unrestricted multilateral trade will become a real possibility' (p. 158). Friedman characterised 'unrestricted multilateral trade' as 'one of the basic freedoms we cherish' (ibid.) and concluded by stating that the 'prompt establishment' of a system of flexible exchange rates was 'the fundamental prerequisite for the economic integration of the free world through multilateral trade' (p. 203).

Friedman's emphasis on the need for unrestricted multilateral trade and how this would be satisfied by the establishment of a system of flexible exchange rates is not surprising given the economic and political uncertainties generated by the Korean War, the numerous wartime controls still in force and the rapidly warming Cold War. However, more than 15 years later, Johnson (1969) when explaining the merits of exchange rate flexibility, though his focus was different from Friedman's, did highlight the potential implications of a system of flexible exchange rates for international trade. He maintained that such a system would allow 'maximum possible freedom of trade', at the same time recognising what had been achieved during the 1950s and early 1960s in terms of the liberalisation of international trade. He observed:

> While the post-Second World War period has been characterised by the progressive reduction of the conventional barriers to international trade and payments – tariffs and quotas, inconvertibility and exchange controls – the recurrent balance-of-payments and international monetary crises under the fixed rate system have fostered the erection of barriers to international economic integration in new forms – aid-tying, preferential governmental procurement policies, controls on direct and portfolio international investment – that are in many ways more subtly damaging to efficiency and growth than the conventional barriers.
>
> (Ibid., p. 210)

Friedman identified support for flexible exchange rates with an enlightened commitment to the price system. He attributed opposition to flexible exchange rates partly to 'a questionable interpretation of limited historical evidence' and partly to the fact that market determined exchange rates had been

> condemned alike by traditionalists, whose ideal was a gold standard that either ran itself or was run by international central bankers but in either case determined internal policy, and by the dominant strain of reformers, who distrusted the price system in all its manifestations – a curious coalition of the most unreconstructed believers in the price system, in all its other roles, and its most extreme opponents.
>
> (Friedman, 1953, p. 203)

Johnson, like Friedman, identified exchange rate flexibility with the efficient functioning of the price mechanism. He argued: 'The case for flexible exchange rates derives fundamentally from the laws of demand and supply, in particular, from the principle that, left to itself, the competitive market will establish the price that equates quantity demanded with quantity supplied and, hence, clear the market' (1972, p. 207).

Friedman's claim of an association between support for the price system and support for exchange rate flexibility, though not particularly convincing, is understandable given the origin and timing of his study. What is more difficult to rationalise is the insistence of later statements of the case for flexible exchange rates on identifying exchange rate flexibility with economic liberalism. All advocates, without exception, of exchange rate flexibility also prescribed that national governments' monetary policy should be based on an unambiguous rule rather than on discretion. However, the policy prescription involving both exchange rate flexibility and a rule-determined monetary policy is inconsistent with the proposition that adherence to the principles of economic liberalism necessarily implies support for flexible exchange rates. Mundell (1969a, p. 635) explained:

> The argument against fixed exchange rates is sometimes put as one of opposition to government price fixing: a liberal (or 'libertarian') is by tradition opposed to government price-fixing and therefore fixed exchange rates. But this is a false presentation of the case for liberty and should be scrapped. The real choice is between price-fixing and quantity-fixing. A country can fix the price of its currency to the international standard and allow the quantity to adapt, as under a properly-run fixed exchange rate system; or it can fix the quantity of its currency (or its rate of increase) and allow the price of it to adapt, as under a flexible exchange system. Quantity-fixed is not necessarily more 'liberal' than price-fixing.

In brief, then, by the end of the 1960s Friedman's assertion that the adoption of a system of flexible exchange rates was 'absolutely essential' for the development of multilateral trade had not been vindicated, even if we allow for Johnson's observations regarding the erection of a variety of non-tariff barriers to international transactions during the 1950s and 1960s. Further, the link between economic liberalism and support for exchange rate flexibility was exposed as logically flawed. But as neither of these two ingredients of the case for exchange rate flexibility was central to the assessment of the relative merits of a system of flexible exchange rates, essentially their role being that of evidence of the ideological correctness of those who employed them when arguing for such a system, when Johnson urged the adoption of market-determined exchange rates in 1969, he was largely preaching to the converted. A general consensus had emerged that the international monetary system was beyond reform, with a large majority of economists persuaded that, under the prevailing circumstances, exchange rate flexibility offered the best way out of the rapidly deteriorating international monetary crisis. What, then, were the principal arguments for a system of flexible exchange rates?

Friedman (1953, p. 200) argued that

> flexible exchange rates are a means of combining interdependence among countries through trade with a maximum of internal monetary independence; they are a means permitting each country to seek for monetary stability according to its own lights, without either imposing its mistakes on its neighbours or having their mistakes imposed on it.

The policy autonomy associated with exchange rate flexibility was forcefully emphasised by Johnson (1969, p. 199):

> The fundamental argument for flexible exchange rates is that they would allow countries autonomy with respect to their use of monetary, fiscal and other policy instruments, consistent with maintenance of whatever degree of freedom in international

> transactions they chose to allow their citizens, by automatically ensuring the preservation of external equilibrium.

Therefore

> Flexible rates would allow each country to pursue the mixture of unemployment and price trend objectives it prefers, consistently with international equilibrium, equilibrium being secured by appreciation of the currencies of 'price stability' countries relative to the currencies of 'full employment' countries.
>
> (Ibid., p. 210)

Friedman clearly recognised that 'governments of "advanced" nations [were] no longer willing to submit themselves to the harsh discipline of the gold standard or any other standard involving rigid exchange rates' (1953, p. 179). But if countries assigned priority to their domestic economic objectives over their exchange rate commitments, there would necessarily exist an incentive for countries to resort to trade controls whenever there developed a conflict between the full employment objective and the need to maintain balance of payments equilibrium. Flexible exchange rates, by reconciling potentially conflicting policy objectives would, therefore, remove one source of pressures for the retention of wartime barriers or the introduction of new trade barriers. Thus Friedman urged that 'we had best recognise the necessity of allowing exchange rates to adjust to internal policies rather than the reverse' (ibid., p. 180). As this necessity would be satisfied under a system of flexible exchange rates, the ability of any individual country to determine its domestic economic policies independently of its economic partners emerged as the 'fundamental' argument for such a system.

As already noted, the focus of Johnson's study was different from that of Friedman's essay. Johnson was mainly addressing the problems associated with the worldwide inflationary pressures emanating from US policies, while Friedman was interested in prescribing a framework of international monetary relations conducive to the growth of 'unrestricted multilateral trade'. Johnson (1969) described the end of the 1960s as follows:

> a great rift exists between nations like the United Kingdom and the United States, which are anxious to maintain high levels of employment and are prepared to pay a price for it in terms of domestic inflation, and other nations, notably the West German Federal Republic, which are strongly averse to inflation. *Under the present fixed exchange-rate system, these nations are pitched against each other in a battle over the rate of inflation that is to prevail in the world economy, since the fixed rate system diffuses that rate of inflation to all the countries involved in it.*
>
> (Ibid., pp. 209–10, emphasis added)

Therefore, for Johnson, 'the adoption of flexible exchange rates would have the great advantage of freeing governments to use their instruments of domestic policy for the pursuit of domestic objectives' (p. 209).

Both Friedman and Johnson, in presenting the freedom of countries to determine their domestic economic policies as dictated by their domestic economic objectives as the principal argument for a system of flexible exchange rates, were in effect accepting that a conflict between internal objectives and exchange rate commitments could emerge as the outcome of policies with economic justification. In terms of Friedman's study, this is understandable as his thesis was consistent with mainstream thinking. There were still fears that a dollar shortage could develop with potentially severe deflationary implications for the European market economies. If that were to occur, these economies were not going to abandon their full employment objective so that they could successfully defend their exchange rate. Only a system of flexible exchange rates was consistent with priority being assigned to domestic objectives over exchange commitments. Therefore such a system had to be preferred.

Johnson, on the other hand, developed his thesis in terms of the unemployment–inflation rate trade-off and the observation that countries were not all equally inflation-averse. For Johnson, then, exchange rate flexibility had to be preferred as it allowed countries to be on different points on their Phillips curve. There is no real difference between Friedman and Johnson in their perception of the nature of the policy conflict that only exchange rate flexibility could resolve. This is somewhat surprising. The above quotation unambiguously implies that Johnson accepted the existence of a long-run trade-off between unemployment and inflation rates. It is the existence of such a trade-off that allows Johnson to define the potential conflict between a country's mixture of unemployment and price trends, on the one hand, and external equilibrium, on the other hand, a conflict that only flexible exchange rates can resolve.

But, by 1969, Johnson's thesis that divergent national preferences, reflected in countries choosing different combinations of inflation and unemployment rates from the set presented by their respective stable long-run Phillips curve, generate a conflict between external and internal equilibrium was sustainable only if the presence of money illusion was assumed. Friedman (1968) had demonstrated that, in the absence of money illusion, the long-run Phillips curve was vertical, with deviations from the 'natural' rate of unemployment being only a short-run phenomenon, lasting for as long as was necessary for the expected rate of inflation to adjust to its new equilibrium value. Any attempt to maintain unemployment below or above its 'natural' rate would simply result in the acceleration or deceleration of the rate of inflation. The presence or otherwise of money illusion is, of course, an empirical issue. The statistical studies of the determinants of the inflation rate were increasingly contradicting the hypothesis of a stable long-run trade-off between unemployment and inflation rates. The apparent breakdown of the Phillips curve in the second half of the 1960s gave rise to a variety of cost-push and sociological hypotheses of the determinants of inflation, all of which denied a significant role to excess aggregate demand in the generation of inflationary pressures and, therefore, provided the rationale for the adoption of price and incomes policies.

Johnson, not surprisingly, was totally dismissive of these hypotheses. However, he does not appear to have been persuaded by the empirical relevance of the natural rate hypothesis and, therefore, presented the 'fundamental argument' for flexible exchange rates, the policy autonomy which they endow countries with, implicitly assuming the existence of a stable long-run trade-off between inflation and unemployment rates. Without such an assumption the conditions that would lead to a conflict between external and internal equilibrium cannot be defined. It is a necessary implication of the natural rate hypothesis that external equilibrium cannot be defined independently of internal equilibrium. A conflict between external equilibrium and domestic economic objectives may arise only if the latter are not consistent with internal equilibrium. But if domestic policies are set in pursuit of unsustainable internal objectives, the inconsistency between domestic policies and internal equilibrium becomes significantly more costly under flexible than under fixed exchange rates.

For example, suppose that a country's government wishes to maintain a rate of unemployment below the natural rate and determines its policies accordingly. In the short run, for any given deviation of the actual from the natural rate of unemployment, the increase in the rate of inflation will be larger under flexible than under fixed exchange rates. The short-run Phillips curve, other things equal, is steeper when exchange rates are flexible than when they are fixed. Now, if the government were to persist with its employment objective, then, in the absence of money illusion and assuming flexible exchange rates, the inflation rate would accelerate and the domestic currency would depreciate at an increasing rate. This, of course, would not occur if exchange rates were fixed. Therefore, under fixed exchange rates, the conflict that may arise is not between internal and balance of payments equilibrium, but between domestic policies, on the one hand, and domestic and external equilibria, on the other hand. Exchange rate flexibility cannot resolve such a conflict. In brief, then, as Laidler, a firm advocate of flexible exchange rates, explained (1982), what exchange rate flexibility does, in the absence of money illusion, is to 'confer on a country the ability to choose its own long-run rate of inflation independently of that ruling in the rest of the world' (ibid., p. 155) and he conceded that it was 'difficult to attach too much importance' (ibid.) to this property of flexible exchange rates.

It may be objected that the assessment of Johnson's case for a system of flexible exchange rates is unfair. It may well be argued that the implications of the natural rate hypothesis for the theory of economy policy in an open economy had not been fully appreciated by 1969 and the empirical studies had not yet unambiguously established the absence of money illusion. However, even if such a defence were accepted, it is still possible to question the consistency, in terms of economic theory, of Johnson's thesis that the 'fundamental argument' for flexible exchange rates is that they allow the individual country to determine its policies independently of those in the rest of the world by ensuring that the exchange rate automatically adjusts so as to equate the demand for a supply of this country's currency in the foreign exchange market. Johnson, himself, in his path-breaking studies of the nature of balance of payments equilibrium (Johnson, 1958a; 1958b), refuted the possibility of defining external equilibrium independently of internal equilibrium Thus, for example, Johnson (1958b, p. 18) argued:

> no matter what problems a country may have, their manifestation as a balance-of-payments problem is always a consequence of governmental policy; though it must be recognised that in many cases a balance-of-payments problem is easier to endure than the alternative problems the country could have.

In summary, as the postwar international monetary system entered its terminal stage, the claim that the principal benefit of a system of flexible exchange rates being put into place would be that such a system would allow the resolution of the conflict between domestic economic objectives and exchange rate commitments was, in terms of economic theory, ill-founded. This, not surprisingly, was not sufficient to deter the UK government in June 1972 from unilaterally deciding to cease supporting the price of sterling in terms of other currencies. Barber (1972), the Chancellor of the Exchequer at the time, explained: 'it is neither necessary nor desirable to distort economies to an unacceptable extent in order to maintain unrealistic exchange rates ... I do not believe there is any need for this country ... to be frustrated on this score in its determination to sustain economic growth and to reduce unemployment.' The consequences of that decision have been well documented.

As already noted, America's economic assistance, military aid and investment in Europe's market economies and Japan, all combined to ensure rapid growth rates throughout the capitalist world and the continuous expansion of international trade on a multilateral basis during the 1950s. Countries successfully pursued their objective of full employment and, highly significant, these achievements occurred against a non-inflationary background. In the economic environment of the 1950s, the case for flexible exchange rates was not particularly convincing. The international monetary system was not an obstacle either to the rapid expansion of multilateral trade across the capitalist world or to the successful pursuit of the full employment objective. For countries' policy decision makers, there were no obvious economic benefits to be gained from acquiring the ability to determine domestic economic policies independently of the rest of the world through the adoption of flexible exchange rates. And, of course, such independence was unacceptable, particularly to America, as incompatible with the requirements of the conduct of the Cold War. Countries' policies were ultimately determined by a common objective, namely, the survival of the market system on a world scale.

There were, of course, balance of payments crises during the 1950s, but they were not either severe or prolonged enough to undermine confidence in the viability of the international monetary system. What the system needed, it was felt, to meet the demands of a rapidly growing and increasingly interdependent world economy, was judicious fine-tuning rather than radical reform. This judgment was ill-founded. By focusing on the impressive performance of the world economy, it ignored the profound implications of the continuously changing nature of the growing international economic interdependence. By the end of the 1950s, the relationship between America and the other capitalist countries was hardly comparable to that of the immediate postwar period. The latter countries were no longer dependent on America's direct or indirect economic assistance. Economic relations among western European countries were rapidly becoming as important for these countries' economic performance as their relations with America. Further, these countries no longer perceived domestic economic conditions as a threat to their social system and, consequently, they were no longer prepared to continue subserviently acquiescing to America's policies. The external 'threat', Soviet 'expansionist ambitions', could no longer sustain the relationship between Europe and America which characterised the immediate aftermath of the outbreak of the Cold War. By the end of the 1950s, the ground on which the Cold War was being fought was moving away from Europe to other areas of the world, particularly south-east Asia and Africa.

Further, the judgment that occasional fine-tuning was all that was needed for the international monetary system to endure was ill-founded as it perceived the growing economic interdependence of capitalist economies during the 1950s as principally the outcome of the rapid expansion of world multilateral trade and ignored the developing short-term capital mobility as a significant feature of the evolving world economy.

As the frequency and severity of foreign exchange market crises escalated, the case for flexible exchange rates attracted increasing support during the 1960s, particularly among economists. The policy autonomy argument now had a relevance that it lacked a decade earlier. Exchange rate flexibility was now advocated as a means by which the individual country could insulate its economy from the inflationary pressures generated by US monetary policies, rather than as means of escaping the deflationary impulses associated with exchange rate fixity. Flexible exchange rates would allow countries to choose their preferred levels of employment and implied rates of domestically generated inflation without having to import American inflation. But equally significant for the increasing attractiveness of exchange rate flexibility was the conventional wisdom as to how exchange rates would actually behave if they were market-determined.

Friedman (1953, p. 159) noted that:

> Changes affecting the international trade and the balance of payments of various countries are always occurring. Some are in the 'real' conditions determining international trade, such as the weather, technical conditions of production, consumer tastes, and the like. Some are in monetary conditions, such as divergent degrees of inflation or deflation in various countries.

He then went on to explain:

> Under flexible exchange rates freely determined in open markets, the first impact of any tendency towards a surplus or deficit in the balance of payments is on the exchange rate. If a country has an incipient surplus of receipts over payments – an excess demand for its currency – the exchange rate will tend to rise. If it has an incipient deficit, the exchange rate will tend to fall.
>
> (Ibid., p. 161).

Equilibrium in the foreign exchange market will emerge following an exchange rate change because

> A rise in the exchange rate produced by a tendency towards a surplus makes foreign goods cheaper in terms of domestic currency, even though their prices are unchanged in terms of their own currency, and domestic goods more expensive in terms of foreign currency, even though their prices are unchanged in terms of domestic currency.
>
> (Ibid., p. 162)

It followed, therefore, that in response to a change in the real or monetary conditions of a country, changes in the exchange rate would '*occur rapidly, automatically, and continuously and so tend to produce corrective movements before tensions can accumulate and a crisis develop*' (p. 163, emphasis added).

This property of a market-determined exchange rate was emphasised by Friedman as a principal advantage of a system of flexible exchange rates when he asserted that

> if Germany had had a flexible exchange rate in 1950, the crisis in the fall of that year would never have followed the course it did. The exchange rate would have been affected not later than July and would have started to produce corrective adaptations at once. *The whole affair would never have assumed large proportions and would have shown up as a relatively minor ripple in exchange rates.* As it was, with a rigid exchange rate, the warning of impending trouble was indirect and delayed, and the government took no action until three months later, by which time the disequilibrium had grown to crisis dimensions, requiring drastic action at home, international consultation, and help from abroad.
>
> *The recurrent foreign-exchange crises of the United Kingdom in the post-war period are perhaps an even more dramatic example of the kind of crises that could not develop under a system of flexible exchange rates. In each case no significant corrective action was taken until large disequilibriums had been allowed to cumulate, and then the action had to be drastic. The rigidities and discontinuities introduced by substituting administrative action for automatic market forces have seldom been demonstrated so clearly or more impressively.*
>
> (Ibid., p. 163, emphasis added)

This theme, not surprisingly, was also a prominent feature of Johnson's statement of the case for flexible exchange rates. He observed:

> if economic changes or policy changes occurred that under a fixed exchange rate would produce a balance-of-payments surplus or deficit, and ultimately a need for policy changes the flexible exchange rate would *gradually* either appreciate or depreciate to preserve equilibrium. The movement of the rate would be *facilitated* and *smoothed* by private speculators, on the basis of their reading of current and prospective economic developments and governmental policy.
>
> (Johnson, 1972, pp. 208–9, emphasis added)

Therefore

> *a rate that is free to move under the influence of changes in demand and supply is not forced to move erratically*, but will instead move only in response to such changes in demand and supply – including

> changes induced by changes in governmental policies – *and normally will move only slowly and fairly predictably.*
>
> (Ibid., p. 213, emphasis added)

To appreciate why Friedman's study has had such a profound and enduring influence on the debate on fixed versus flexible exchange rates, it is worth recalling his prediction of how a market-determined exchange rate would approach its new equilibrium value in a world of zero capital mobility and following a 'real' external disturbance. Such a disturbance would induce a variety of adjustments which would differ in terms of their rapidity. He maintained:

> It is clear that the initial change in exchange rates will be greater than the ultimate change required, for, to begin with, all the adjustment will have to be borne in those directions in which prompt adjustment is possible and relatively easy. As time passes, the slower-moving adjustments will take over part of the burden, permitting exchange rates to rebound towards a final position which is between the position prior to the external change and the position shortly thereafter ... *the actual path of adjustment may involve repeated overshooting and undershooting of the final position, giving rise to a series of cycles around it or to a variety of other patterns.*
>
> (Friedman, 1953, p. 183, emphasis added)

Nearly a quarter of a century later, the combination of perfect exchange rate flexibility and short-run price-level rigidity was necessary, though not sufficient, for the Dornbusch (1976) model to generate the prediction that the exchange rate may, in response to a disturbance, overshoot its new equilibrium value.

If market-determined exchange rates behaved as predicted by those who advocated them, exchange rate flexibility would remove the sources of the deepening international monetary crisis of the 1960s. The Bellagio Study Group identified 'three major problems':

> (1) the problem of payment adjustment, deriving from the need for correcting persistent imbalances in the payments positions of individual countries;
> (2) the problem of international liquidity, connected with the need for long-term adaptation of the total volume of world reserves to the full potentialities of noninflationary economic growth; and
> (3) the problem of confidence in reserve media, implied in the need for avoiding sudden switches between different reserve media.
>
> (Machlup and Malkiel, 1964, p. 24)

Now, if in response to 'incipient' balance of payments surpluses and deficits, exchange rates were to change 'rapidly, automatically ...

continuously' and 'fairly predictably', then exchange rate flexibility, by preventing the development of 'persistent imbalances', would solve 'the problem of payment adjustment'. In terms of the second 'problem', exchange rate flexibility, by ensuring continuous equilibrium in the foreign exchange market, would, at worst, reduce the problem of international liquidity to manageable proportions and, at best, eliminate it. It followed, therefore, that exchange rate flexibility, by solving the international liquidity problem, would automatically eliminate the 'confidence' problem as defined by the Bellagio Study Group. In brief, exchange rate flexibility was potentially a simple but effective cure for the capitalist world's monetary ills.

Flexible exchange rates: performance

It was not long after the collapse of the international monetary system in March 1973 that the predictions of those who advocated flexible exchange rates were shown to be ill-founded. For example, Mussa (1976, p. 139) conceded:

> Concerning the desirability of a return to fixed exchange rates, I have been forced to modify my views in the light of recent experience. A number of the arguments in favour of flexible exchange rates which I had previously accepted now appear to be either invalid or irrelevant. The principal argument in favour of flexible exchange rates is that they permit individual countries to pursue independent monetary policies and, to some extent, insulate national economies from disturbances originating abroad. Recent experience does not suggest that the way in which independent monetary policies have actually been used has contributed to greater stability of most national economies. The phenomenon of world inflation followed by world recession does not suggest that the degree of insulation provided by flexible exchange rates, as they actually function, is very great. Further, the short term movements of exchange rates which have occurred, given the actual functioning of the exchange markets, appear to have generated greater costs than were usually envisioned in arguments in favour of flexible rates.

As already emphasised, advocates of exchange rate flexibility had maintained that market-determined exchange rates would respond to disturbances rapidly, continuously, automatically and fairly predictably. If flexible exchange rates were to behave in this manner, it followed that changes in *real* exchange rates would be small, gradual and predictable. This was not how flexible exchange rates actually behaved after 1973. The IMF (1984a), after observing that nominal exchange rate changes after 1973 sometimes were as large as 2–3 per cent on a daily basis when averaged over a few quarters and that real effective exchange rates had on a number of occasions changed by 30 per cent or more over a period of two to three years, presented a number of conclusions relating to exchange rate volatility:

> (1) By almost any measure, exchange rate variability has been much greater during the period of floating rates (1973–82) than it was during the last decade of the adjustable par value system (1963–72).
> (2) Within the period of floating rates itself, there has *not* been a sustained tendency for exchange rate variability to decline over time ...
> (3) The variability of nominal exchange rates under floating rates has been substantially *greater* than implied by inflation differentials across countries, thereby yielding sizeable changes in *real* exchange rates as well.
> (4) ... the variability of nominal exchange rates under floating rates has still been considerably *smaller* than the variability of some other assets.
> (5) ... for making the transition from exchange rate variability to exchange rate uncertainty, most exchange rate changes under floating rates appear to have been *unexpected*.
>
> (IMF, 1984a, pp. 5–8)

In another IMF (1984b) study, it was calculated that the weighted average of monthly changes in nominal effective exchange rates among the major industrial countries was 0·2 per cent during the period 1961–70 but 1·2 per cent over the period 1974–83. Quarterly changes in nominal exchange rates had also increased sixfold between these two periods while real exchange rate changes were '2½–3 times greater in the period 1974–83 than in the decade of the 1960s' (p. 12).

The most significant aspect of post-1973 exchange rate behaviour, however, is that exchange rate changes, regardless of their magnitude and volatility, have been unpredicted. Frenkel (1981) concluded that the 'key fact' which emerged from his empirical analysis was that 'predicted changes in exchange rates account for a very small fraction of actual changes' (p.673) while Mussa (1979) had identified as one of the empirical regularities of the post-1973 international monetary experience that 'Over 90 percent of month-to-month or quarter-to-quarter changes in exchange rates are attributable to unexpected exchange rate changes and under 10 percent are attributable to expected changes' (p. 21).

Exchange rate flexibility was advocated as a solution to the international liquidity problem. Williamson (1976), when assessing this argument, was led to 'the paradoxical conclusion that reserve use actually increased following the adoption of floating' (p. 198). Further, as the IMF (1984a) study showed, contrary to what was predicted, exchange rate flexibility did not improve the adjustment process, with trade account imbalances being slow to respond to exchange rate changes and persisting for significant periods of time. It is, therefore, not surprising that Mussa (1979) concluded:

> Looking at the totality of our experience with floating exchange rates, there is no sound basis for the belief that exchange rates will adjust slowly and smoothly to correct 'fundamental disequilibria' that would otherwise develop between national economies. Of course, the magnitude of fluctuations may increase or decrease with the magnitude of disturbances to the world economy, but the *smoothly adjusting exchange rate is, like the unicorn, a mythical beast.*
>
> (Mussa, 1979, p. 9, emphasis added)

Exchange rate flexibility was perceived as a means of containing international economic conflict, if not actually enhancing mutually beneficial cooperation among capitalist countries. However, the decision to establish the European Monetary System in March 1979 was explained by the Commission of the European Communities (1984) as follows: 'The EMS was set up as a result of a defensive reaction against the disorderly movements of the dollar and against the danger of economic deterioration in the community if uncoordinated behaviour continued' (p. 2). This motivation was emphasised by Bilson (1979) who welcomed the establishment of the EMS as 'the first step back from the rugged individualism and national self-interest that lay behind the formal acceptance of flexible exchange rates at the Jamaica meetings of the International Monetary Fund in January 1976' (p. 154).

But, indicative of how the balance of power had changed against the USA and of America's attitudes was the judgment in the 1982 Economic Report of the President that, 'as a general proposition, one way to achieve compatibility of policies is for countries *voluntarily* to adopt the monetary rule of a large country whose avowed goal is to stabilise prices' (p. 169).

Developments in the case for exchange rate flexibility

Why were advocates of exchange rate flexibility so wrong in their predictions of how exchange rates would behave if they were freely determined by market forces? There is a consensus that they were grossly misled by the exchange rate determination model which they employed when generating their predictions. McKinnon (1981) defined the 'insular economy' as one 'with limited financial and commodity arbitrage with the outside world but one not closed to foreign trade' (p. 531). In a world of insular economics exchange rates would be determined by the interaction of the demands for and supplies of currencies arising from the demands for and supplies of imports and exports. But the very nature of the economic interdependence among insular economies implied that, if exchange rates were market-determined, the exchange rate changes required for foreign exchange market equilibrium to be maintained would, as Friedman and Johnson argued, occur rapidly, automatically and continuously. Therefore exchange rate changes would be small and predictable. This perception of how the foreign exchange market functioned was shared by economists of all persuasions. However, while elasticity optimists, including the advocates of exchange rate flexibility, argued that an exchange rate change would be necessary and sufficient for an incipient balance of payments disequilibrium to be corrected, elasticity pessimists asserted that such a change would magnify the trade imbalances among countries.

The case, then, for flexible exchange rates rested on a model in which the equilibrium exchange rate equates the flow supply of the domestic currency, arising from the domestic demand for imports, with the flow demand for the domestic currency, arising from the foreign demand for domestic exports. Mussa (1976) after analysing the post-1973 exchange rate behaviour, reached 'the fundamental conclusion ... that the flow market model is not notably successful in explaining any of the empirical regularities that have characterised the behaviour of floating exchange rates and, hence, that *this model of the foreign exchange market is essentially useless and devoid of empirical content*' (p. 9, emphasis added).

The abysmal failure of the flow foreign exchange market model can ultimately be traced to the assumed principal characteristics of the nature of the interdependence among what McKinnon (1981) termed 'insular economies'. What distinguished them from closed economies was that they engaged in trade among themselves. This interdependence rested on three assumptions. First, only a small fraction of the insular economy's GDP was assumed to be associated with foreign trade and, therefore, exchange rate changes could have only negligible effects on its price level. Second, it was hypothesised either that there was no integrated international capital market or that exchange controls were effective in restricting the international mobility of private capital so that capital flows could not finance current account disequilibria. Third, it was assumed that the insular economy could sterilise balance of payments disequilibria and, consequently, determine its own money supply growth rate independently of the rest of the world. But by the mid-1960s, if not earlier, no major capitalist economy remotely resembled the insular economy and, therefore, inevitably the flow foreign exchange market model which rested on the insularity assumption was exposed after 1973 to be 'useless and devoid of empirical content'.

To suggest, however, that the deficiencies of the flow model were revealed only after the world economy collapsed into exchange rate flexibility in March 1973 would be grossly erroneous. An early expression of dissatisfaction with the flow model can be found in Johnson (1958a), where it is argued that 'a balance-of-payments deficit implies *either* dishoarding by residents, *or* credit creation by the monetary authorities', thus asserting the monetary character of balance of payments disequilibria. But the most radical departures from the prevailing orthodoxy are to be found in Mundell's work during the 1960s. His studies, collected in Mundell (1968) and (1971), trace the progressive replacement of the insular economy with the open economy and paved the way for the highly influential Johnson (1977) essay on the monetary approach to the balance of payments. The central proposition of the approach is that balance of payments disequilibrium is a manifestation of domestic excess demand for/supply of money and, therefore, unless recreated by the monetary authorities, is self-adjusting. Johnson (1977) explained that 'deficits and surpluses represent phases of stock adjustment in the money market and not equilibrium flows, and should not be treated within an analytical framework that treats them as equilibrium phenomena' (p. 235), and, therefore, 'domestic monetary policy does not determine the domestic money supply but instead determines only the division of the backing of the money supply the public demands, between international reserves and domestic credit' (p. 238).

For a monetary disturbance to generate a self-correcting balance of payments disequilibrium the necessary condition is that the demand for money function is stable. Frenkel and Johnson (1976) emphasised that 'the essential assumption of the monetary approach, like the restated quantity theory of money according to Friedman, is that there exists an aggregate demand function for money that is a function of a relatively small number of aggregate economic variables' (p. 24), which led Johnson (1977) to assert that 'A proper test of the monetary approach must be essentially a test of the stability of the demand for money, in Friedman's terminology' (p. 263).

The monetary approach to the balance of payments was easily transformed into the monetary theory of exchange rate determination. The early statements of the latter can be found in Herin et al. (1976) and Frenkel and Johnson (1978). The exchange rate is by definition the relative price of two monies. Therefore, if the excess demand for/supply of money in one country changes *relatively* to the excess demand for/supply of money in another country then the relative price of the two countries' currencies, the exchange rate, will alter. Again, for this prediction to hold, the money demand functions of both countries must be stable, in the Friedmanite sense that the demand for money is systematically and predictably related to a few variables, usually taken to be real income and the rate of interest. The original formulation of the monetary approach to exchange rate determination assumed perfect price flexibility, the continuous clearing of money markets and that purchasing power parity held continuously. Some early empirical studies yielded results that were consistent with this formulation. However, by the end of the 1970s, the simple monetary approach could not explain observed exchange rate behaviour. This is not surprising. As already noted, nominal exchange rate variability was significantly larger than the variability of inflation rate differentials, thus inducing large and persistent deviations from purchasing power parity. Under these circumstances, the poor performance of the original monetary model which assumed a constant real exchange rate was inevitable.

From the perspective of the original monetary model of exchange rate determination, what was at issue was how the observed post-1973 deviations from purchasing parity were to be interpreted. If they reflected changes in equilibrium real exchange rates, the monetary model was theoretically deficient and empirically irrelevant. If, alternatively, these deviations were a short- to medium-term phenomenon, then what the monetary model provided was a theory of exchange rate determination in the long run which had to be modified so as to generate predictions of exchange rate behaviour in the short run which did not rest on the assumption that purchasing power parity held continuously. By introducing price stickiness into the original monetary model, Dornbusch (1976) was able to demonstrate how the nominal exchange rate would overshoot its new long-run, purchasing power parity-consistent, equilibrium value following a monetary disturbance. In the long run, with prices having fully adjusted, purchasing power parity is restored with the equilibrating change in prices being equal to the change between the original and the new equilibrium nominal exchange rate. In other words, the simple monetary model and the Dornbusch model yield identical long-run results, with the latter involving a more complex process of adjustment. Be that as it may, the Dornbusch model is not significantly more successful than the basic monetary model in explaining either the magnitude or the direction of exchange rate changes since 1973. But it is interesting to note that the Dornbusch model undermines the case for flexible exchange rates. Overshooting exchange rates by definition imply excessive exchange rate changes. But if exchange rate changes are excessive, then intervention in foreign exchange markets by monetary authorities is justifiable.

The original formulation of the monetary approach highlighted relative demands for/supplies of money as the principal determinant of exchange rates. However, this formulation is consistent with a different focus, namely, with assigning to expectations a dominant role in the determination of exchange rates. To clarify matters, let domestic and foreign monetary equilibrium be defined as follows:

$$m = p + gy - hi \tag{8.1}$$

and

$$m^* = p^* + gy^* - hi^*, \tag{8.2}$$

where

m is the logarithm of the money supply;
p is the logarithm of the price level;
y is the logarithm of real income;
i is the nominal rate of interest;
g is the income elasticity of the demand for money;
h is the interest rate semi-elasticity of the demand for money; and
$*$ denotes the variables of the foreign country.

Subtracting (8.2) from (8.1) yields

$$m - m^* = p - p^* + g(y - y^*) - h(i - i^*). \tag{8.3}$$

Next assume purchasing power parity so that

$$\varepsilon = p - p^*, \tag{8.4}$$

where ε is the logarithm of the exchange rate, E. Now combine (8.3) and (8.4) to derive the exchange rate equation of the monetary approach:

$$\varepsilon = (m - m^*) - g(y - y^*) + h(i - i^*). \tag{8.5}$$

If, when interpreting equation (8.5), the emphasis is to be confined to relative demands for/supplies of money as the principal determinant of ε, then, as Frenkel (1983) has observed, it is necessary to assume that *uncovered* interest rate parity holds. In other words, it is necessary to assume that domestic and foreign assets are perfect substitutes and, therefore, asset holders are indifferent as to the composition of their portfolios, provided that the expected rates of return on domestic and foreign assets are equalised when expressed in any common denominator. Uncovered interest rate parity implies that the interest rate differential, $i - i^*$, in equation (8.5) equals the *expected* exchange rate change. Therefore equation (8.5) may be rewritten as follows:

$$\varepsilon_t = (m - m^*) - g(y - y^*) + h(\varepsilon^{\varepsilon}_{t+1} - \varepsilon_t), \tag{8.6}$$

where $\varepsilon^{\varepsilon}_{t=1}$ is the expected spot rate at time t+1 and ε_t is the spot rate at t. Now supose that $Xt = (m - m^*) - g(y - y^*)$, so that

$$\varepsilon_t = Xt + h(\varepsilon^{\varepsilon}_{t+1} - \varepsilon_t), \tag{8.7}$$

or

$$\varepsilon_t = \frac{1}{1+h} Xt + \frac{h}{1+h} \varepsilon^{\varepsilon}_{t+1}. \tag{8.8}$$

Equation (8.8) implies that today's exchange rate, ε_t, depends on today's values of the variables which influence the determination of the exchange rate and are embodied in Xt, plus the spot exchange rate expected to prevail in the next period, t+1. But equation (8.7) implies that $\varepsilon^{\varepsilon}_{t+1}$ will depend on $\varepsilon^{\varepsilon}_{t+2}$, which will in turn depend on $\varepsilon^{\varepsilon}_{t+3}$ and so on. Therefore it follows that

$$\varepsilon_t = \frac{1}{1+h} \sum_{n=0}^{\infty} \left(\frac{h}{1+h}\right)^n X^e_{t+n}. \tag{8.9}$$

In words, equation (8.9) states that today's exchange rate depends on economic agents' current expectations of all the variables incorporated in X from now into the indefinite future. Equation (8.9), which is adapted from Levich (1985), views the exchange rate as analogous to the current price of any security that reflects the discounted value of all future cashflows. That is, the exchange rate emerges as the relative price of two durable assets (moneys). Frenkel (1983, pp. 11–12) has argued as follows:

> The central insight of the modern approach to the analysis of exchange rates is the notion that the exchange rate, being the relative price of two durable assets (moneys), can best be analyzed within a framework that is appropriate for the analysis of asset prices. The volatility and the unpredictability of price changes are key characteristics of auction and organised asset markets. In such markets current prices reflect expectations concerning the future course of events, and new information, which induces changes in expectations, is immediately reflected in corresponding changes in prices, thus precluding unexploited profit opportunities from arbitrage.

Equation (8.9) implies that any observed exchange rate change may potentially be split into two components: an anticipated and an unanticipated. At time t, economic agents employ all the available information relating to current and future monetary conditions to formulate their expectations of the spot rate at $t + 1$, ${}_t\varepsilon^e_{t+1}$. If no new information becomes available between t and $t + 1$, then

$$\varepsilon_{t+1} - \varepsilon_t = {}_t\varepsilon^e_{t+1} - \varepsilon_t. \qquad (8.10)$$

That is, the exchange rate change is fully anticipated. But suppose some new information becomes available between t and $t + 1$. This information is not reflected in ${}_t\varepsilon^e_{t+1}$ as it became available after ${}_t\varepsilon^e_{t+1}$ had been determined. The new information leads to a change in expectations which will have an immediate and equiproportionate effect on the current and expected future spot rates. But this implies that some of the change in the exchange rate between t and $t + 1$ will be unanticipated. That is,

$$\varepsilon_{t+1} - \varepsilon_t = ({}_t\varepsilon^e_{t+1} - \varepsilon_t) + N, \qquad (8.11)$$

where N denotes 'news' or new information and represents the unanticipated change in the exchange rate, while ${}_t\varepsilon^e_{t+1} - \varepsilon_t$ represents the anticipated change.

At this stage it is necessary to emphasise that, in deriving equation (8.7), two assumptions were implicitly made: first, that the foreign exchange market is efficient, and, second, that expectations are rationally formed.

The asset approach to exchange rate determination suggests that exchange rate behaviour should exhibit certain characteristics. First, the expected component of an exchange rate change should be a small fraction of the aggregate change. If this is not the case, the implication is that the foreign exchange market is inefficient, in the sense that all available information is not utilised and, therefore, opportunities for large profits would exist. As already noted, post-1973 exchange rate changes have been largely unexpected.

Second, the perception of the exchange rate as the relative price of two durable assets by assigning a dominant role to expectations implies that exchange rates may well be highly volatile. Equation (8.9) suggests that the exchange rate is highly sensitive to expectations regarding future events and policies. Any change in expectations reflecting new information has an immediate impact on the current and expected future spot rates. Therefore volatile expectations will result in volatile exchange rates. But, as exchange rates promptly respond to new information, it necessarily follows that actual exchange rate changes cannot be accurately predicted. That is, volatile expectations will lead to large and unpredictable exchange rate changes. Again, high volatility has characterised post-1973 exchange rate behaviour.

Third, the asset approach to exchange rate determination is perfectly consistent with deviations from purchasing power parity featuring as a prominent characteristic of exchange rate behaviour. This follows naturally from the second characteristic. If there is a persistent flow of new information, expectations will be continually raised and, given the extreme sensitivity of exchange rates to changes in expectations, exchange rates will be highly volatile. But, as Frenkel (1983, p. 14) has emphasised, this highlights the following:

> An intrinsic difference thus exists between exchange rates and national price indices. Exchange rates do not reflect only current circumstances but also reflect expectations concerning the *future*. In contrast, the prices of national outputs reflect to a large extent *present* and *past* circumstances as they are embedded in existing contracts. Consequently, when there are large and frequent changes in expectations, it is likely that the future will be expected to differ greatly from the present and the past.

But if exchange rates respond differently and more rapidly to new information than the prices of non-durable goods and services then, inevitably, deviations from purchasing power parity will occur, which is exactly what happened after 1973.

In brief, highly volatile expectations will induce large and unpredictable *real* exchange rate changes which will primarily reflect the volatility and unpredictability of nominal exchange rates. As volatility, unpredictability and significant deviations from purchasing power parity have been characteristic of post-1973 exchange rate behaviour, Frenkel (1983) was led to maintain that the foreign exchange market had in fact 'behaved as an efficient asset market and that much of the volatility of exchange rates reflected frequent and large changes in expectations concerning the future' (p. 12). Frenkel based his efficiency conclusions on the evidence existing at the time that forward exchange rates are the best, in the sense of being unbiased, though highly inaccurate, predictors of future spot rates. He attributed the volatility of exchange rates to 'the volatile character of the 1970s, which witnessed great turbulence in the world of economy, large swings in government policy and great uncertainties about the future course of economic and political events' (p. 12).

The study of international monetary issues had abandoned the insular economy in favour of the open economy, suggesting a radically different and deeper interdependence among capitalist economies, before actual exchange rate behaviour had revealed the total inadequacy of the flow foreign exchange market model as the basis on which the case for flexible exchange rates could rest. What are, then, the implications for the case for exchange rate flexibility of the emergence of the asset approach to exchange rate determination as the new orthodoxy?

Central to the restatement of the case for exchange rate flexibility is the judgment that the foreign exchange market is efficient and, therefore, that the exchange rate behaves consistently with equation (8.9). But if the exchange rate exhibits the characteristics of an asset price determined in an efficient market, then the observed post-1973 exchange rate fluctuations may not be considered as excessive (as is the case in the Dornbusch overshooting model) and, thus, provide an argument against market-determined exchange rates. Instead, Frenkel and Mussa (1980) argued that these fluctuations reflect 'adjustments to new information about equilibrium, exchange rates' (p. 379) and that, consequently, any government attempt to frustrate them through foreign exchange market intervention is economically undesirable.

Frenkel and Goldstein (1986) strongly disputed the validity of the assessment that post-1973 exchange rate volatility was excessive. They argued that, as the exchange rate is intrinsically different from wages and the prices of non-durable goods, it is illegitimate to compare exchange rate volatility with the volatility of wages and goods prices. The appropriate yardstick for an evaluation of the former is the volatility of other asset prices. In the highly turbulent post-1973 world economic conditions, when the volatility of all asset prices increased, Frenkel and Goldstein pointed out that exchange rate changes were in fact 'smaller than changes in prices of other assets, e.g. national stock market prices, changes in short-term interest rates, changes in commodity prices' (ibid., p. 643). Pressing the distinction between the exchange rate, as an asset price, and the prices of non-durable goods and wages, they suggest that 'it is precisely because wages and prices are so slow to adjust to current and expected economic conditions that it is desirable to allow for "excessive" adjustment in exchange rates' (ibid., p. 14).

For proponents of market-determined exchange rates, the unpredictability of the post-1973 exchange rate changes is an argument for, rather than a weakness of, exchange rate flexibility. Frenkel (1983) argued that 'since the foreign exchange market is a market in which risk can easily be bought and sold, it may be sensible to concentrate disturbances in this market rather than transfer them to the other market, such as labor markets, where they cannot be dealt with in as efficient a manner' (p. 18). These arguments in defence of exchange rate flexibility rest on the proposition that the foreign exchange market is efficient. In principle, this is an empirical issue. However, Levich (1985,

p. 1022) in his excellent survey of the empirical literature, when identifying the difficulties in testing foreign exchange market efficiency, observed:

> The critical point ... is that all tests of market efficiency are testing a joint hypothesis – first, the hypothesis that defines market equilibrium or expected returns as some functions of the [information set assumed to be fully reflected in the price under consideration], and second, the hypothesis that economic agents can set actual prices or returns to conform to their expected values.

To clarify matters, recall that, in equation (8.7),

$$X = (m - m^*) - g(y - y^*).$$

Failure of the exchange rate to behave as predicted by equation (8.7) could reflect either a misspecification of the underlying exchange rate determination model, in the sense that X does not include all the relevant exogenous variables, or that economic agents do not utilise all the available information. If, instead, it was assumed that the exchange rate did behave as implied by equation (8.7), it could still be maintained that current and expected relative excess demands for money in the domestic and foreign economies are not the 'correct' determinants of exchange rates and, therefore, that unusual profit opportunities do exist in the foreign exchange market. But efforts extending over the last quarter of a century to isolate the principal determinants of exchange rates have not met with success. After highlighting the superiority of the monetary models over the flow foreign exchange market model, Mussa (1979) concluded that there remained 'a great deal of exchange rate variability that has not been adequately explained by any model of the foreign exchange market' (p. 51). Levich (1985), in his survey of the empirical studies of exchange rate determinants observed that no consensus had emerged as to which of the various foreign exchange market models was the appropriate one. In a later survey, Frenkel and Rose (1995) reached the 'dispiriting conclusion' that the models that had been estimated were found to have 'relatively little explanatory power' and contained 'little forecasting ability compared to very simple alternatives' (p. 1705).

Taylor (1995) described the uncovered interest rate parity condition as the 'cornerstone parity condition for testing foreign exchange market efficiency' (p. 14), if economic agents are assumed to be risk neutral. Now, if risk neutrality and rational expectations are combined, uncovered interest rate parity implies that the expected exchange rate change is equal to the interest rate differential. Or, in other words, the forward rate is the expected future spot rate, with the forward discount being the expected exchange rate change. That is, the risk premium is assumed to be zero. The empirical evidence, surveyed by Taylor (ibid.), does not support the foreign exchange market efficiency hypothesis that rests on the risk neutrality version of the uncovered interest rate parity condition. This result may reflect either that economic agents are risk-averse or that expectations are not rational. If economic agents are risk-averse, they will demand a risk premium on forward contracts and, therefore, the forward rate will no longer be the expected future spot rate and the forward premium will be equal to the expected exchange rate change plus the risk premium. As Levich (1985) notes, risk aversion is not incompatible with foreign exchange market efficiency. The efficiency hypothesis adapted for the presence of a risk premium, too, has lacked the support of empirical evidence. In summary, then, the forward rate emerges as a biased predictor of the future spot, with the risk premium remaining as the explanation of this forward rate bias. This raises the question of what determines the risk premium. The empirical evidence has provided no satisfactory answer to this question. Levich (ibid.) was, therefore, led to maintain:

> it is difficult to test whether investors efficiently set the actual spot exchange rate equal to its equilibrium value unless there is some agreement on what the equilibrium value is. Similarly, it is difficult to test whether risk-bearing is efficiently rewarded if there is no agreement on the fundamental nature of foreign exchange risk, no adequate measure of it, and no model that determines the equilibrium fair return for bearing it.
>
> (Ibid., p. 1024)

He went on to conclude: 'In the absence of agreement on a hypothesis about the equilibrium exchange rate, it is not possible either to prove or disprove the efficiency hypothesis in the foreign exchange market' (ibid., p. 1025). But this conclusion ignores the possibility that the failure to isolate systematic empirical evidence in support of the hypothesis that the foreign exchange market is efficient may reflect a failure of the hypothesis that expectations are formed rationally. Taylor (1995) draws attention to empirical studies which contradict the rational expectations hypothesis.

In summary, such is the empirical evidence that the case for flexible exchange rates cannot rest on the argument that the foreign exchange market is efficient.

Monetary policy autonomy and currency substitution

Under flexible exchange rates, each country is free to determine its money supply growth rate so as to achieve its preferred long-run inflation rate.

This is perceived to be a major advantage of exchange rate flexibility. Suppose that exchange rate flexibility does enable, say, the UK to determine the sterling supply growth rate and that achieving its preferred long-run inflation does involve significant economic benefits. Ignoring legitimate objections to both of these assumptions, the question arises whether the ability to control the sterling supply growth rate is sufficient for the UK to achieve its preferred long-run inflation rate. The widely accepted answer is that, if the UK demand for money function is stable, the control of the sterling supply growth rate is sufficient to ensure that the UK achieves its chosen long-run inflation rate. This line of reasoning implies that the sterling demand function is the UK money demand function.

The proposition that exchange rate flexibility enables the individual country to choose its long-run inflation rate, independently of other countries' choices, suggests that the transition from the insular to the open economy has yet to be completed. The insular economy could control its money supply growth rate even under fixed exchange rates through the sterilisation of balance of payment disequilibria. For the open economy this is not possible except, perhaps, in the very short run. Exchange rate flexibility restores control of the monetary supply to the domestic authorities. In terms, then, of the monetary supply process of determination, the open economy is radically different. However, as McKinnon (1981) has observed, the specification of the demand for money function has remained the same for the open economy as it was for the insular economy.

Whether in theoretical analyses or in empirical investigations, the commonly adopted assumption is that the domestic demand for money depends on domestic variables. Recall that this assumption was employed in the discussion of the monetary approach to exchange rate determination. This Friedmanite specification of the money demand function makes no allowance for the openness of economies, as it implies that UK residents hold only sterling balances. Therefore the UK demand for money is identical to the demand for sterling. If the former is stable then it is assumed that the demand for sterling is necessarily also stable. The Friedmanite assumption that UK residents hold only sterling balances, residents in France hold only French francs, and so on, has been challenged in the currency substitution literature. For example, Miles (1978a) described it as 'quite dubious'. He argued that one of the consequences of the ever-deepening interdependence among capitalist economies was the generation of strong incentives for economic agents to diversify the currency composition of their cash balances. This composition may alter even if the aggregate demand for cash balances remains unchanged. But if economic agents hold portfolios of currencies, the composition of which they may alter by substituting between currencies, then it is possible to distinguish between a country's demand for money and the demand for its currency. This distinction has a highly significant implication. Since it is no longer valid to identify a country's demand for money with the demand for its currency, instability of the latter is perfectly compatible with stability of the former. Therefore, if the demand for sterling was unstable, control of the sterling supply growth rate would not be sufficient for the UK authorities to achieve their preferred long-run inflation rate, even if the UK demand for money function were stable.

Diversified currency portfolios imply that inflationary pressures generated in one country will be transmitted across the rest of the world economy even under flexible exchange rates. Suppose that dollars are held by economic agents in countries other than the USA and that the latter increases the supply of dollars. Conventional thinking would predict an equiproportionate rise in the American price level and devaluation of the dollar. However, as Miles (1978b) argued, if dollars are held outside America, then the US price level will rise proportionately less that the increase in the supply of dollars, while countries in the rest of the world will also experience increases in their price level. In other words, national inflation rates will at least be partially determined by foreign money supply growth rates. Thus there will not exist a systematic relationship between national money supply growth rates and domestic rates of inflation. This was one of the findings presented by McKinnon (1982), who also presented evidence of correlation between the world money supply growth rate and the world rate of inflation.

Equally relevant for the case for exchange rate flexibility, McKinnon (ibid.) and Boyer and Kingston (1987), in their analyses of currency substitution, drew attention to the possibility of negative transmission of inflation. Suppose that the foreign country's money supply growth rate increases and, as a result, economic agents' preferences alter in favour of the domestic currency: that is, the demand for the domestic currency increases and the demand for the foreign currency decreases. The foreign rate of inflation would rise above what it would have been had the demand for the foreign currency remained unchanged, while the increase in the demand for the domestic currency would lead to a reduction of the domestic rate of inflation.

To summarise, in the presence of diversified currency portfolios, exchange rate flexibility does not enable the individual country to choose its long-run rate of inflation. Therefore its ability to control its money supply yields no economic benefits.

Concluding remarks

The process of transition from the insular to the open economy had begun well before 1973. Progress was slow, largely because developments in macroeconomics were primarily determined by the work of American economists. Given the size of the US economy, in absolute as well as relative terms, the *closed* economy assumption was central to analyses of economic phenomena which reflected the openness of economics. This was the case, for example, with the debate on the causes of inflation. The overwhelming majority of economists perceived world inflation as a series of national problems, while a few argued that it could not be explained unless it was treated as an international monetary phenomenon, with the focus of analysis being world, rather than national, macroeconomic aggregates. Be that as it may, it is interesting to note that the case for flexible exchange rates remained essentially the same and was hardly influenced by the development, albeit very slow, of open economy macroeconomics. The arguments advanced by Johnson at the end of the 1960s were not significantly different from those put forward by Friedman in the early 1950s. Post-1973 exchange rate behaviour had a profound impact on the theory of exchange rate policy. The flow foreign exchange market model was rapidly discarded in favour of the perception of the exchange rate as an asset price.

In terms of the theory of economic policy, it is beyond dispute that this perception marks a highly significant improvement in the approach to the study of interdependent economies' policy problems. However, the transition to the open economy has yet to be completed. As the currency substitution literature emphasises, the Friedmanite specification of the demand for money function, which effectively assumes that economies are closed, is entirely inappropriate for the analysis of open economy macroeconomic issues, including the relative merits of exchange rate flexibility. In other words, the case for flexible exchange rates was ill-founded prior to 1973 and continues to be so. Therefore it may be argued that economists' attempts to explain short-to-medium-term exchange rate movements, by utilising increasingly high-frequency data, not only are misplaced but also have disoriented research.

It is equally significant that the case for flexible exchange rates has consistently lagged behind international political developments and, therefore, has never developed a political rationale. Prior to 1973, the advocacy of exchange rate flexibility was void of political credibility as it implied the voluntary surrender by the USA of its dominant position. Since 1973, the defence of flexible exchange rates invariably takes the form of a justification of a choice made by governments. But exchange rate flexibility was not chosen in 1973. The world economy collapsed into flexible exchange rates when international political conditions could no longer sustain the international monetary system that had been created by America and which was dependent on US absolute dominance. One of the consequences of the relative economic decline of the USA was the international monetary conditions. The response could not but be political.

However, just as the evolving balance of power among the major capitalist countries could not prevent the complete breakdown of the international monetary order in 1973, so, inevitably, it could not provide the basis for an international agreement on a new world monetary system of whatever variety. The 1976 Second Amendment to the IMF Articles of Agreement allows countries to do as they please when deciding their exchange rate policy. But if the international balance of power was such as to make an international political agreement on a new system impossible, it could not prevent regional solutions to the post-1973 international monetary chaos. The European Union principal member countries, France and Germany, took the *political* decision to create the European Monetary System in March 1979 independently of and without consultation with the USA. They were able to compel the acquiescence of the other member countries. Subsequently, a series of *political* decisions culminated in the establishment of the European Monetary Union in 1999.

Proponents of exchange rate flexibility, particularly in Britain, misjudged the entire process. First, they predicted the collapse of the European Monetary System; then, they dismissed the Delors Report; and, when the Maastricht Treaty was agreed upon, they confidently forecast that it would not be implemented. These errors of judgment simply reflect a lack of appreciation of the *political* nature of the exchange rate policy decision making.

In brief, a case for flexible exchange rates which is consistent with economic theory and actual exchange rate behaviour and explicitly allows for the political character of exchange rate policy decision making has yet to be articulated.

References

Barber, A. (1972), 'Budget Statement', *Hansard*, vol. 833, col. 1354, London: HMSO.

Bergsten, C.F. (1973), 'Comments', in L.B. Krause and W.S. Salant (eds), *European Monetary Unification and its Meaning for the United States*, Washington, DC: The Brookings Institution.

Bilson, G.F.O. (1979), 'Why the Deutschmark could trouble the EMS', *Euromoney*.

Boyer, R.S. and G.H. Kingston (1987), 'Currency substitution under finance constraints', *Journal of International Money and Finance*, 6, 235–50.

Dornbusch, R. (1976), 'Expectations and exchange rate dynamics', *Journal of Political Economy*, 84, 1161–76.

European Communities (1984), *Five Years of Monetary Cooperation in Europe*, COM (84), final, Brussels.

Fleming, D.F. (1961), *The Cold War and its Origins 1917–1960*, London: George Allen and Unwin.

Frenkel, J.A. (1981), 'Flexible exchange rates, prices and the role of the "news": Lessons from the 1970s', *Journal of Political Economy*, 89, 665–705.

Frenkel, J.A. (1983), 'Turbulence in the foreign exchange markets and macroeconomic policies', in D. Bigman and T. Taya (eds), *Exchange Rate and Trade Instability: Causes, Consequences and Remedies*, Cambridge, MA: Ballinger.

Frenkel, J.A. and M. Goldstein (1986), 'A guide to target zones', *International Monetary Fund Staff Papers*, 33, 633–73.

Frenkel, J.A. and H.G. Johnson (eds) (1976), *The Monetary Approach to the Balance of Payments*, London: George Allen and Unwin.

Frenkel, J.A. and H.G. Johnson (eds) (1978), *The Economics of Exchange Rates*, London: Addison-Wesley.

Frenkel, J.A. and M.L. Mussa (1980), 'The efficiency of foreign exchange markets and measures of turbulence', *The American Economic Review*, 70, 374–81.

Frenkel J.A. and A.K. Rose (1995), 'Empirical Research on Nominal Exchange Rates', in G.M. Grossman and K. Rogoff (eds), *Handbook of International Economics*, Vol. 3, Amsterdam: Elsevier Science B.V.

Friedman, M. (1953), 'The Case for Flexible Exchange Rates', *Essays in Positive Economics*, Chicago: University of Chicago Press.

Friedman, M. (1968), 'The role of Monetary Policy', *The American Economic Review*, 58, 1–17.

Giscard d'Estaing, V. (1969), 'The international monetary order', in R.A. Mundell and A.K. Swoboda (eds), *Monetary Problems of the International Economy*, Chicago: University of Chicago Press.

Herin, J., A. Lindbeck and J. Myhrman (eds) (1976), *Flexible Exchange Rates and Stabilisation Policy*, London: Macmillan.

IMF (1984b), 'Exchange Rate Volatility and World Trade', Occasional Paper 28, Washington, DC: IMF.

IMF (1984a), 'The Exchange Rate System: Lessons of the Past and Options for the Future', Occasional Paper 30, Washington, DC: IMF.

Johnson, H.G. (1958a), 'Towards a General Theory of the Balance of Payments', *International Trade and Economic Growth*, London: George Allen and Unwin.

Johnson, H.G. (1958b), 'The Balance of Payments', *Pakistan Economic Journal*, VIII, 16–28; reprinted in *Money, Trade and Economic Growth*, London: George Allen and Unwin.

Johnson, H.G. (1969), 'The Monetary Approach to Balance of Payments Theory', *Further Essays in Monetary Economics*, London: George Allen and Unwin.

Johnson, H.G. (1972), 'The Case for Flexible Exchange Rates', *Further Essays in Monetary Economics*, London: George Allen and Unwin.

Johnson, H.G. (1973), 'Secular Inflation and the International Monetary System', *Journal of Money, Credit and Banking*, V, 509–19.

Johnson, H.G. (1977), 'The monetary approach to the balance of payments: a nontechnical guide', *Journal of International Economics*, 7, 289–98.

Keohane, R.O. (1994), 'Comment', in P.B. Kenen (ed.), *Managing the World Economy: Fifty Years After Bretton Woods*, Washington, DC: Institute for International Economics.

Laidler, D. (1982), 'The case for flexible exchange rates in 1980', in M. Sumner and G. Zis (eds), *European Monetary Union: Progress and Prospects*, London: Macmillan.

Levich, R.M. (1985), 'Empirical studies of exchange rates', in R.W. Jones and P.B. Kenen (eds), *Handbook of International Economics*, Vol. 2, Amsterdam: Elsevier Science B.V.

Machlup, F. and B.G. Malkiel (eds) (1964), *International Monetary Arrangements: The Problem of Choice – Report on the Deliberations of an International Study Group of 32 Economists*, Princeton, NJ: Princeton University Press.

McKinnon, R.I. (1981), 'The exchange rate and macroeconomic policy: changing postwar perceptions', *Journal of Economic Literature*, 19, 531–57.

McKinnon, R.I. (1982), 'Currency substitution and instability in the world dollar standard', *The American Economic Review*, 72, 320–33.

Meade, G. (1955), 'The Case for Variable Exchange Rates', *Three Banks Review*, 3–27.

Miles, M.A. (1978a), 'Currency substitution, flexible exchange rates and monetary independence', *The American Economic Review*, 68, 428–36.

Miles, M.A. (1978b), 'Currency substitution: Perspective implications and empirical evidence', in B.H. Putnam and D.S. Wilford (eds), *The Monetary Approach to International Adjustment*, New York: Praeger Publishers.

Mundell, R. (1968), *International Economics*, London: Macmillan.

Mundell, R. (1969a), 'Towards a Better International Monetary System', *Journal of Money, Credit and Banking*, I, 625–48.

Mundell, R.A. (1969b), 'Problems of the International Monetary System', in R.A. Mundell and A.K. Swoboda (eds), *Monetary Problems of the International Economy*, Chicago: University of Chicago Press.

Mundell, R. (1971), *Monetary Theory*, Pacific Palisades, CA: Goodyear Publishing Company.

Mussa, M. (1976), 'Our Recent Experience with Fixed and Flexible Exchanges: A Comment', in K. Brunner and A.H. Meltzer (eds), *Institutional Arrangements and the Inflation Problem*, Carnegie–Rochester Conference Series on Public Policy, vol. 3, Amsterdam: North-Holland.

Mussa, M. (1979), 'Empirical Regularities in the Behaviour of Exchange Rates and Theories of the Foreign Exchange Market', in K. Brunner and A.H. Meltzer (eds), *Policies for Employment, Prices and Exchange Rates*, Carnegie–Rochester Conference Series on Public Policy, vol. 11, Amsterdam: North-Holland.

Sohmen, E. (1961), *Flexible Exchange Rates*, Chicago: University of Chicago Press.

Taylor, M. (1995), 'The Economics of Exchange Rates', *Economic Literature*, XXXIII, 13–47.

Triffin, R. (1960), *Gold and the Dollar Crisis*, New Haven: Yale University Press.

Williamson, J. (1976), 'Exchange-rate Flexibility and Reserve Use', in J. Herin, A. Lindbeck and J. Myhrman (eds), *Flexible Exchange Rates and Stabilisation Policy*, London: Macmillan.

CHAPTER NINE

Unilateral euroisation in transition countries: the case of southeastern Europe

Angelos Kotios

Introduction

The integration of the transition economies of central and east European countries (CEECs) into the European Union (EU) structure is one of the most important national goals of these countries.[1] In this context practical policy and economic analysis, since the beginning of the transition process, has been focusing mainly on integration aspects like political dialogue, trade, investment, the adoption of acquis communautaire and European financial and technical assistance. Recently, the choice of an exchange rate regime after the introduction of the euro, and the monetary integration of the CEECs with the EU, have emerged as new policy and research topics (Köhler and Wes, 1999; Masson, 1999; Kopits, 1999; Corker, et al., 2000; DeGrauwe and Lavrac, 1999; Schweickert, 2001). Increasing trade and monetary integration between the EU and the CEECs, and progress in market reforms and external liberalisation, as well as in the accession process, have intensified the debate about the proper exchange rate policy in transition countries and the path of their monetary integration into the EU's new monetary order. Most of the proposals recommend the introduction of a form of fixed exchange rates against the euro, usually in the form of a currency board (Gulde et al., 2000; Freytag, 1998).

The countries of southeast Europe (SEE) form a special part of the CEE group of countries. For several reasons, these countries are still coping with serious political tensions and regional conflicts, highly fragmented markets, adjustment rigidities and transition deficiencies, low growth and a vicious circle of poverty and underdevelopment (Petrakos, 2001a; 2001b). The recent conflict in Kosovo has shown not only the magnitude of the adjustment problems in the region, but also its importance for European stability and prosperity (Kotios, 2001a). The consequence of this has been the introduction by the international community, after initiation by the EU, of a regional approach for the reconstruction and stability of the Balkan region (Stability Pact) and its integration into Europe (Kotios, 2001b). In order to achieve the aims of the Stability Pact, a set of national, regional and international policies and initiatives must be implemented (World Bank, 2000).

Many strategic analysis papers concerning this region include the monetary aspect in their approach (Gligorov, 2000; Gligorov et al., 1999; EastWest Institute, 2000; CEPS, 1999; Gross, 1999). In these papers the formulation of a proper exchange rate policy is viewed as an important instrument for stabilisation, development, regional cooperation and integration of the Balkan countries into the EU. The complete integration into the payments system, money and capital markets of the euro area through the euroisation of the national monetary systems of SEE countries is also recommended by some authors as a proper strategy (CEPS, 1999; Gross, 1999; Emerson, 2000; Nuti, 2000). On the basis of mainstream thinking concerning the choice of exchange rate regimes in the increasingly integrated world economy (about this discussion, see Williamson, 1999; IMF, 2000; Velasko, 2001), they reject many forms of an adjustable peg, as well as free floating for small, open, undeveloped economies with shallow foreign currency markets, which by definition are vulnerable to international shocks. Instead, they advocate the introduction of a hard peg in the form of a currency board or a unilateral euroisation (Lewis and Sevic, 2000). The euroisation proposals recommend different paths of implementation (Steil and Woodward, 1999). Some of the analysts propose the immediate introduction of Deutschmark/euro, as in Kosovo and Bosnia-Herzegovina, or as a parallel currency, as in Montenegro. Others suggest the establishment, starting now, of a euro-denominated currency board national regime, with the use of the Deutschmark for parallel cash money, and, from 1 January 2003, the introduction of full euroisation, including euro banknotes.

The aim of this chapter is to analyse the theoretical and practical aspects of the unilateral euroisation approach. The next section focuses on the degree of integration between the transition Balkan countries and the EU and its implications for monetary and exchange rate policy. The analysis of the third section concentrates on the concept of unilateral euroisation and especially the changes in national monetary order it implies. The potential benefits and costs for the countries of the SEE region are discussed in the fourth and fifth sections, respectively. Next, a comparison between euroisation and currency board arrangement is attempted. The seventh section discusses the EU position regarding unilateral euroisation by non EU-members, and in the eighth section, attention is given to the potential paths for implementing euroisation. The concluding section summarises the main findings and attempts to answer the question whether the Balkans should euroise.

The EU–Balkans economic integration

The degree of economic integration between two economic areas is decisive for the choice of the proper bilateral exchange rate regime. Economic theory and policy have long maintained that, the more integrated are two economic areas, the better it would be to establish a bilateral fixed exchange rate regime or a monetary union (Mundel, 1961; McKinnon, 1963; Rose, 2000). In this context, the question which arises is: how integrated are the EU and southeastern Europe economic areas?

Regarding contractual relations and institutional integration, in the 1990s the EU and the countries of the SEE region shaped a network of bilateral relations composed of different agreements (see Table 9.1) which reflect a different pace of integration for each transition country (Kotios, 2001b). The differences in the stage of contractual relations between the EU and the countries of the SEE reflect divergences in the political and economic adjustment process in the SEE transition countries, assuming that the rapprochement of a transition country to the EU depends on a rigorously defined political and economic conditionality. For example, Bulgaria and Romania have signed (in 1993) accession agreements with the EU in order to promote political dialogue, to establish a free trade area, to develop economic cooperation and to encourage the gradual adoption of EU rules, policies and practices. Since 2000, Bulgaria and Romania have been negotiating their accession to the EU, and have been enjoying the benefits of the support mechanisms of the EU pre-accession policies.

After the war in Kosovo, the EU adopted a new regional approach for the countries of the western Balkans, the so-called 'Stabilisation and Association Process'. This approach aims at the protection of peace and stability, and fosters economic development in the region. It also seeks to improve the conditions for the integration and accession of the western Balkan countries into European structures. The main components of the Stabilisation and Association Process are the Association Agreements, similar in content to the European Agreements signed with the accession candidates Bulgaria and Romania. The signing of the Agreements between the EU and each of the five eligible Balkan countries presupposes the fulfilment of well-defined political and economic terms. Failure to adopt the Stabilisation and Association Agreement, however, does not deprive the countries of the area of the ability to enjoy, even to a lesser extent, the benefits of the Community preferential trade treatment through autonomous trade preferences, the receipt of financial, technical, economic and critical aid, political cooperation and political dialogue, even when they do not fully comply with the political and economic conditions. In 2001, the EU signed Stabilisation and

Table 9.1 The EU–Balkans contractual relations

	Trade and cooperation agreement and/or tariff preferences	*Stabilisation and association process*		*Europe agreement*	*Accession partnership (accession negotiations)*	*Potential member of EU*
		Stabilisation and association agreement (SAA)	*Candidates for SAA*			
Albania	+		+			+
Bulgaria				+	+	+
Bosnia and Herzegovina	+		+			+
Croatia	+	+	+			+
FYR Macedonia	+	+				+
Romania				+	+	+
Yugoslavia, FR	+		+			+

Source: Kotios (2001b).

Association Agreements with the former Yugoslav Republic of Macedonia (FYROM) and Croatia. Under consideration is the signing of such agreements with the other three countries of the western Balkans. Also the EU has improved the existing autonomous trade preferences and provided autonomous trade liberalisation for more than 90 per cent of the western Balkan exports to the EU.

Regarding trade integration, Table 9.2 shows that, in 2000, the EU was the most important trade partner for the SEE countries (Petrakos, 2001a; Kirkilis, 2001). With the exception of Bosnia-Herzegovina and the former Republic of Yugoslavia, owing to special conditions, more than 50 per cent of the total trade of the SEE countries was carried out with the EU. Since the beginning of the transition process (1989) this tendency has been steadily increasing, thus a further increase is to be expected in the near future. The same tendency can be observed in the field of foreign direct investments. The biggest part of these investments flows from the euro zone countries (see Risopoulos, 2001).

In addition to the increasing trade orientation of the SEE countries to the EU, a similar tendency can be observed in monetary integration. In many countries the Deutschmark/euro has experienced an extensive use as deposit and asset nominator. According to Bishev (2000) the currency and asset substitution rates in the seven SEE transition countries are very high in comparison to other transition countries. In 1998, the average rate of currency substitution defined as the percentage of foreign currency deposits to M1 was 107·6 per cent (see Table 9.3). The leading currency substitution countries were Bosnia-Herzegovina (423 per cent) and Croatia (265 per cent) and the countries with the lowest rates of currency substitution were Albania (45 per cent) and FYR of Macedonia (45·8 per cent). The average rate of asset substitution (foreign currency deposits to M2, 1998) was 42·5 per cent. The rate of asset substitution ranges between 20·9 per cent (Albania) and 80·3 per cent (Bosnia and Herzogovina). The foreign currencies used most to substitute for national currencies in the SEE region were the Deutschmark and, after its circulation, the euro. This high rate of currency substitution occurs mainly because of political and economic instability and lack of credibility, characterising, to a greater or lesser degree, all of the SEE transition countries. Also, despite the differences in exchange rate regimes (Table 9.4) the euro serves as the anchor currency for four SEE countries. Bulgaria, Bosnia-Herzegovina, FYR of Macedonia and Croatia pursue an exchange rate targeting monetary strategy, which means they have subordinated their monetary policies to the exchange rate objective, and hence (since 1 January 1999) to the monetary policy of the European Central Bank (ECB). The other three countries follow monetary targeting strategies that are less dependent on monetary developments in the euro zone (Bishev, 2000).

Table 9.2 SEE external trade, 2000

	Trade with EU		*Intraregional trade (8 countries)*	
	Exports as % of total	*Imports as % of total*	*Exports as % of total*	*Imports as % of total*
Albania	93.4	75.6	2.1	6.1
Bulgaria	51.2	44.0	12.6	4.4
Bosnia and Herzegovina	47.6	33.2	30.5	21.4
Croatia	50.5	54.3	12.0	2.0
FYR Macedonia	46.1	49.4	30.9	19.8
Romania	60.6	63.0	2.3	0.7
Yugoslavia, FR	37.7	40.9	28.2	20.9
Greece	43.6	58.7	15.9	3.3

Source: WIIW Database.

Table 9.3 Monetary integration with the EU, 1998

	Foreign currency deposits to M1 in % (12 month average)	*Foreign currency deposits to M2 in % (12 month average)*	*Dm/euro as anchor currency for monetary policy*
Albania	45·0	20·9	
Bulgaria	107·9	42·1	+
Bosnia and Herzegovina	423·6	80·3	+
Croatia	264·9	64·2	
FYR Macedonia	45·8	27·3	+
Romania	127·9	29·7	
Yugoslavia, FR	463·7[1]	347·8[1]	+
Total	107·6[2]	42·5[2]	

Notes: [1] Including frozen (blocked) foreign currency deposits.
[2] Average is calculated without including Yugoslavia.

Source: Bishev (2000) and own calculations.

Table 9.4 Exchange rate regimes in SE Europe

	Exchange rate regimes			
Countries	*Currency board arrangement*[1]	*De facto peg arrangement under managed floating (against a single currency)*[2]	*Managed floating with no pre-announced path for exchange rate*[3]	*Independently floating*[4]
Albania				X
Bulgaria	X			
Bosnia and Herzegovina	X			
Croatia			X	
FYR Macedonia		X		
Romania			X	

Notes: 1 Currency board arrangement (CBA): A monetary regime based on explicit legislative commitment to exchange domestic currency for a specific foreign currency at a fixed rate. Domestic currency can be issued only against foreign exchange. The monetary base is fully backed by foreign assets. No place for discretionary monetary policy.

2 De facto peg arrangement under managed floating (against a single currency): the country pegs de facto (not formally) its currency at a fixed rate to a major currency, where the exchange rate fluctuates within a narrow margin (e.g. of at most ±1%) around a central rate. The monetary authority stands ready to maintain the parity through intervention. The degree of monetary policy discretion is limited, however greater relative to CBAs.

3 Managed floating with no pre-announced path for exchange rate: the monetary authority influences the movements of the exchange rate through active intervention in the foreign exchange market without specifying a pre-announced path for the exchange rate.

4 Independently floating: the exchange rate is market-determined, without any intervention. The monetary policy is in principle independent of exchange rate policy.

Source: IMF, *Annual Report 2001*, pp. 124–5.

The stage of integration achieved between the EU and the SEE region, as well as the implementation policies and the market dynamics which will enforce it further, confirm that currency stability in the framework of a fixed exchange rate system is necessary to promote economic integration between the two regions. But greater economic and financial integration is a necessary but not sufficient precondition for euroisation. The decision to euroise indicates the political will of a country to introduce enormous institutional reforms and disciplines in order to improve and consolidate its political and economic image and transform the commitment to euroise into a virtuous circle between structural reform and market performance.

In the following, the analysis turns to the question of whether the proper exchange rate and monetary policy for the Balkan countries vis-à-vis the euro and the euro zone is unilateral euroisation.

The regime of unilateral euroisation

The monetary regime of euroisation (like dollarisation) can take two forms: de facto and de jure euroisation (Berg and Borensztein, 2000; United States Senate, 1999; Horvath, 2001). De facto euroisation means that market agents and people in their economic activities increasingly prefer to use the euro instead of the national currency. Owing to high current inflation, inflationary or devaluation expectations, people's distrust of national economic policy or political instabilities, national money cannot fulfil its functions. In these cases, a stable foreign currency progressively substitutes for national money without a formal decision or a policy intervention by monetary authorities. But national currency still circulates as a parallel currency, and national monetary authorities continue to exist.

De jure (or unilateral) euroisation is based on a formal political decision and implies constitutional changes in the national monetary order. It includes the elimination of national currency and its complete replacement by the euro. In the case of unilateral euroisation, the national monetary base is converted into ECB notes and the euro constitutes the sole legal tender and sole unit of account. A further implication is the disestablishment of the national central bank and of national monetary policy. Through the adoption of the ECB's monetary policy, the constellations of money demand and supply in the national market are self-regulated. The national central bank or a follow-up institution would merely undertake the surveillance of the national financial system. Under the regime of unilateral euroisation there is no need for foreign currency reserves, for intervention on the exchange rate markets or for covering foreign balance deficits. The national monetary space of euroising countries becomes a passive part of Euroland on which are registered all the monetary developments of Euroland itself.

The question that arises is why a country would prefer to give up its monetary sovereignty and monetary flexibility. It is well known that national currency is not only a crucial economic component and policy instrument but also a symbol of national independence and sovereignty, which is of vital psychological importance for the new SEE democracies. The answer could be that rational politicians consider that the expected advantages of establishing euroisation will be more than the expected costs. The following two sections refer to this question.

The potential benefits of euroisation

The replacement of a national currency by the euro eliminates the exchange risk that exists (Bratkowski and Rostowski, 2000; Nuti, 2000). The positive impact on trade and investments is correlated with the degree of trade and capital market integration between the euroising country and the EU. But it does not eliminate the currency risks against other currencies (such as the dollar, the yen or the pound). A first positive impact of eliminating currency risk leads to a reduction of the risk premium and to a consequent lowering of interest rates (Table 9.5). What remains is default or country risk, which continues to depend on factors such as political stability, level of public debt, budget financing or macroeconomic situation. Lower interest rates would result in a lower cost of servicing public debt and also in a higher level of investments and economic growth. The higher the currency risk, the higher the interest rate differences between the euro zone and the euroising SEE country and, consequently, the higher the expected positive growth effects of adopting the euro.

A further effect of euroisation has to do with the reduction of foreign exchange transaction costs. The more integrated a Balkan economy with Euroland, the more important this reduction will become. Lower transaction costs could lead to more intensive bilateral trade and to lower export and import prices.

Direct price linkages, inherent in a currency area, mean that price level and price movements in a euroising Balkan economy, as a price taker, will be bound to price developments in Euroland. The higher the degree of openness of the euroising country and the higher its trade with Euroland, the closer will be these price linkages. According to Maastricht rules, the ensuring of price stability and low inflation rates (for example, up to 2 per cent) is the only policy goal of the ECB. If price stability in

Euroland is assured, then the same will apply to a euroising Balkan economy (Table 9.5). This link would result in lower inflation (similar to that of Euroland) that could improve business and investment conditions in the euroising economy.

Euroisation could also encourage fiscal consolidation and permanent fiscal discipline because there would be no central bank monetisation of the budget deficit. Financing of such deficits would be possible only through financial markets. In the case of an increase in public debt, the result would be a decrease in credibility and worse borrowing conditions. It could also promote financial sector reform and stability owing to the lack of a lender of last resort. It could eliminate currency risk and, consequently, currency and maturity mismatches, and also bring a closer integration with international banking and financial systems.

The loss of a national monetary policy and restraints on the flexibility of fiscal policy emphasise the importance of income and structural policies for macroeconomic management. In the case of asymmetric shocks, prices of goods and production factors have to react in both directions flexibly. If not, the real costs of adjustment will be very high. In order to improve market flexibility, the euroising country could enforce labour market and other institutional and structural reforms (Eichengreen, 2001).

The recent financial crisis has made it clear that small, open economies with liberated capital markets cannot be protected from contagion episodes, regardless of whether they have fixed or flexible exchange rate regimes. The most important consequences of these crises are banking crises, the collapse of national payment systems, the loss of foreign reserves, the abandonment of the peg or the overshooting of depreciation (in the case of flexible exchange rates), a decline in economic activity and social conflicts. These effects are much less significant in large developed countries or in economic unions because of their strong banking systems, deep and wide financial and exchange rates markets, better crisis management abilities and so on. In the event of an international financial crisis, a monetary union protecting its participating economies is like a public good. The crisis can also be 'absorbed' passively, via euroisation, by participating member countries. The conclusion is that euroisation would tend to limit the incidence and magnitude of crisis and contagion episodes.

All the above-mentioned effects of euroisation may drive the process of economic integration with the EU, as well as intraregional integration. Trade integration can be promoted especially by lower transaction costs and the elimination of exchange rate risks. The (passive) participation in Euroland could boost European and other direct investments in the

Table 9.5 Selected economic indicators, 2000

	GDP (change in %, real)	*Consumer prices, %*	*Current account (US$ mn)*	*Average interest rates (discount rates)*	*Gross foreign reserves (excl. gold in US$ mn)*
Albania	7·8	–0·2	–151	8·5[c]	481
Bulgaria	5·8	9·9	–701	4·7	3155
Bosnia and Herzegovina	5·0	2[a] 15[b]	–963	1·4	455
Croatia	3·7	6·2	–800	5·9	3525
FYR Macedonia	5·1	10·5	–320	7·9	429
Romania	1·6	45·7	–900	35·0	2470
FRY	6·4	85·6	–1298	26·3	505
Euroland (12)	3·4	2·3		4·4	

Notes: [a] Federation.
[b] Srpska Republica.
[c] 1999.

Sources: calculated from WIIW Database, IMF, EU.

euroising country, as well as the establishment of foreign banks and other financial corporations. If the whole SEE region were to euroise, then intraregional trade and capital transactions would be easier, more transparent and less costly. Intraregional trade competition would be based on real economic factors and not on competitive devaluations. The impact of participation on political integration in the monetary union only, and not in the European Economic Union, is less obvious. But a common currency is a matter of common interest and could influence positively the attitudes of people in both areas towards better and deeper cooperation.

The potential costs and risks

The establishment of the euroisation regime could result not only in the above-mentioned benefits; it could also produce costs and risks (Wójcik, 2000). The most common disadvantage is the loss of seigniorage revenues accruing from the issue of legal tender. Seigniorage is frequently measured as the increase in the volume of the monetary base, which is equivalent to the resulting central bank profits in present discount value terms. For all SEE transition countries the seigniorage revenues are a significant percentage of GDP, and an important source of financing of the public budget. The loss of this revenue would cause serious problems in public finance because of limited alternative sources. Low GDP, inefficient tax systems and a limited tax base characterise transition economies and especially the economies of the SEE region. Consequently, these countries are still dependent on other sources of state financing such as seigniorage revenues, import tariffs, public loans, privatisation revenues and indirect taxation. But the loss of seigniorage revenues and its effect on public finance could be compensated or overcompensated by the potential decrease in interest rates, as mentioned above.

The replacement of the national currency by the euro would mean the purchase of domestic currency (the outstanding monetary base) against the euro by the national central bank. It presupposes the existence of sufficient foreign reserves (Table 9.5). If these reserves cannot cover the necessary amount then there are other possibilities, such as loans and contributions by the EU.

A further risk of euroisation has to do with the management of the national banking system. In the case of bank crises it could impair the lender of last resort function of the national central bank. In order to prevent this risk, central banks, or a new institution, could create a special emergency fund. The introduction of high-quality requirements as in Euroland could also act preventively. The privatisation of national commercial banks and the openness of national money and capital markets has led to the establishment in the SEE transition countries of many foreign banks. These banks practise modern management and carry out, more or less, the control or surveillance of the home country's monetary authorities. It could be expected that, after euroisation, more foreign banks will extend their branches into the euroised countries. The dominant presence in the local banking system of dynamic foreign banks would diminish the risk of banking crises and the need for a lender of last resort.

The adjustment to large asymmetric shocks might be the most important policy challenge in a monetary union (Schweickert, 2001). The appearance of such shocks is more probable when there are different economic structures, reverse economic cycles and different foreign trade structures among the members of the monetary union. Because of the loss of important instruments of adjustment policy, the euroising economy would need flexible wages and prices. Otherwise, such shocks could cause depression, an increase in unemployment and social conflicts.

Euroisation and currency board arrangements: a comparison

The successful implementation of currency boards in some transition economies (for example, Bulgaria, Bosnia-Herzegovina and Estonia) has encouraged suggestions for an introduction of this regime in the other SEE countries. The establishment of currency boards have been viewed as the route to euroisation. The question that arises is whether a currency board is similar to euroisation and whether such a regime is superior to the formal replacement of national money by the euro.

There is no doubt that a currency board arrangement (CBA) constitutes a hard peg version, and has impacts similar to unilateral euroisation. But there are a lot of differences between the two regimes (on the deficiencies of CBA, see Roubini, 1998; Enoch and Gulde, 1998). First, the introduction of a CBA would imply strong commitments and obligations regarding coverage of the monetary base, convertibility, exchange rates and economic policy. But national currency, foreign reserves, the central bank and other monetary authorities would continue to exist. This would mean that an exit option would always be possible. On the other hand, euroisation is essentially irreversible and therefore more credible than a CBA.

In a CBA, devaluation cannot be excluded. Hence speculative attacks and destabilising capital flows could occur. In the case of euroisation, these phenomena would be possible only against other currencies and would involve the whole euro area, which has more effective means than a small country to introduce counter-measures.

Because of devaluation risk in a CBA, interest rate differentials against the anchor currency would be higher than in the case of euroisation. Current account deficits could cause capital exports, reduction of money supply and higher interest rates in the country implementing a CBA. Eventually, increased interest rates could counterbalance capital export and might also lead to a repatriation of exported capital or to additional capital imports. If the cause of current account deficits was the increase in domestic prices then the result would be a real appreciation of the national currency. But increased interest rates and real appreciation of a national currency, very probable in the case of a CBA, would cause competitiveness losses and a severe recession.

In the event of large fluctuations of the monetary base and abrupt interest rate changes, the domestic banking and financial system could be highly destabilised. This means that, in a CBA, the lack of a lender of last resort has a stronger negative impact on the financial system than would occur under the regime of unilateral euroisation. A currency board could collapse if an attack on the domestic currency were to occur, as total domestic financial assets would be much higher than foreign reserves. In the best case foreign reserves could cover only the national monetary base. In the case of unilateral euroisation, such a collapse could not occur.

A further difference between the two regimes has to do with transaction costs. In a CBA these costs would still exist and hence would be higher than in the case of euroisation.

This short analysis could lead to the conclusion that euroisation is superior to a CBA as regards transaction costs, currency risk, a country's credibility and economic stability and growth. But for some countries the elimination of their national currency and the potential high costs of exiting from the euro could be regarded as a disadvantage of euroisation in comparison to a currency board arrangement.

The EU's position regarding euroisation

Following the circulation of euro banknotes, an unbroken expansion of their use in countries highly integrated into the EU economy (such as EFTA countries, central and east European countries, Mediterranean partner countries, and the African, Caribbean and Pacific partners) and the emergence of a broad euro area (like the dollar area) can be observed. This means that a strong expansion of de facto euroisation is an expected natural process (Heise, 2002) and de jure euroisation in the periphery of

Euroland is a very probable scenario. The more stable the euro and the more successful the EMU, the more attractive it would be to use the euro in other countries. Under these conditions, in an increasingly integrated European and world economy with free capital movement, Euroland governments or the European System of Central Banks could not prohibit this tendency.

Euroisation, in general, could have some positive economic impacts on the EU. The first expected benefit could be an increase in the seigniorage revenues of the EU's member states. These kinds of 'windfall profits' would depend on the number and value of euro banknotes that would circulate in other countries. Should the euro become an attractive currency, these revenues could be a very important financing source for member states (HypoVereinsbank, 1999, p. 15). In the case of the USA, the state realises an annual $12–15 billion as additional revenue inflows resulting from the circulation of dollar banknotes abroad (Cohen, 2001).

A second benefit could result from the reduction of transaction costs and the elimination of currency risks in Euroland's trade and investment activities within the euroising countries (or region). The size of these 'denomination rents' (Swoboda, 1968) for exporters, importers, investors, insurance companies, tourists and so on, in the country of issue would depend on the intensity and magnitude of economic relations between the EU and SEE regions. A higher import demand for European goods and services and an improved environment for European foreign investment could be important benefits for European companies. In any case, the benefits for the EU are unlikely to be considerable, since the economic relations between the EU and the SEE transition countries are not significant for the EU. An extensive use of the euro as a parallel currency abroad could also be important from a political point of view: it could be an indicator of the success of the euro and the economy of the euro zone.

The main risk for the EU following an extended euroisation would be an increase in the volatility of Euroland's monetary aggregates and a stronger pressure on ECB's monetary policy. For example, if money demand in euroising countries were to be subject to sudden or frequent shifts, net flows would be generated that could increase the short-term volatility of Euroland's monetary aggregates. In the case of a massive or frequent currency substitution in euroising countries (for example, dollar for euro), depreciation of the euro, or an increasing volatility in exchange rate markets, could be expected. From a theoretical point of view, these risks seem to be important. But the experience of the growing use of the dollar outside the borders of the USA (55–70 per cent of the total outstanding stock of US banknotes – see Porter and Judson, 1996) or other currencies (such as the Deutschmark or the British pound) shows that it has very little or no evident impact on practical monetary policy. The use of the euro as a national currency abroad would influence the aggregate demand in the euroising countries and not in Euroland. Also the euro monetary base in SEE countries would be a very small part of the total. The movement of the euro exchange rate against other currencies will depend on the monetary and real economic conditions and policy decisions in Euroland, and not on what happens in the small euroising countries, which are 'recipients' of the EU monetary policy.

In the euroisation debate, the EU's institutions (ECOFIN and the Commission) have responded negatively (see Bratkowski and Rostowski, 2000). Their main argument is mainly of an institutional nature: 'it should be made clear that any unilateral adoption of the single currency by means of "euroization" would run counter to the underlying economic reasoning of the EMU in the Treaty, which foresees the eventual adoption of the euro as the endpoint of a structured convergence process within a multilateral framework'; and 'the introduction of the euro will ensure equal treatment between future Member States and the current participants in the euro area' (ECOFIN, 2000). According to ECOFIN's statement, all candidate states can gain access to Euroland only after fulfilling the Maastricht convergence criteria and according to the prescribed procedures. The recommended path to the EMU is accession to EU, at least two years' participation in the European Exchange Rate Mechanism (ERM II), and fulfilment of nominal convergence criteria. As the ECOFIN Council pointed out, during the pre-accession stage the candidate states need to meet the Copenhagen economic criteria and ensure progress on real convergence and macroeconomic stability. In this context, the exchange rate would be an important instrument of the convergence policy, as well as 'a yardstick of success in adjustment' (Deutsche Bundesbank, 2000, p. 99).

As Bratkowski and Rostowski (2000) have argued, the EU's opposition to unilateral euroisation is based on many misunderstandings. These could be summarized as follows.

1. Unilateral euroisation would mean a passive adoption of the euro and not admission into the EMU. This implies that the unilaterally euroising countries would not participate in the EMU's institutions and hence could not influence their monetary decisions.
2. Through unilateral euroisation the equal treatment between EMU member states and the new or future members would not be violated because euroising countries would not be coequal members of the EMU, and because unilateral euroisation would 'provide a better test of a country's commitment to price stability than the traditional route does, partly because it makes it harder for a country to

temporarily repress inflation through nominal appreciation' (ibid., p. 14).

3. A new member state of the EU which had adopted the euro unilaterally would be admitted to the EMU after satisfying the public finance, inflation and interest rate criteria. The exchange rate stability criterion would be regarded as already having been fulfilled.
4. Unilateral euroisation would not imply any legal obligation for the European Central Bank to act as a 'lender of last resort'.
5. Euroising countries could not be considered as 'free-riders' on the euro, because they would have to buy it, paying seigniorage to EMU members.
6. Unilateral euroisation, as well as de facto euroisation, would mean an increase in demand for the euro, and hence an improvement in its international reputation, which is a desirable outcome for the EMU authorities.

Implementing unilateral euroisation: a potential path

If a country should decide to euroise, it must create a route-map to attain this goal. For a unilaterally euroising country there would be different paths of implementation. The following discussion concentrates on some important technical aspects concerning preconditions, accompanying policies, implementation phases, institutional reforms and so on.

First of all, it must be emphasised that the decision to euroise is primarily a momentous political act and secondarily an economic and technical issue (Frieden, 2000). Euroisation would be an 'imposed' monetary order and not a spontaneous one. It would presuppose a collective decision and enforcement by the state. This decision must be rational and accepted by the national society and economy, as well as by other cooperating countries. On this basis, the main steps towards euroisation are considered below.

Analysis of costs and benefits

This analysis in the form of an ex ante evaluation should be made to include all potential economic, social and political effects of unilateral euroisation. It should be considered that euroisation generates winners and losers, and that it would change entirely the function of economic policy and the structure of the economy.

Negotiation with the EU on the feasibility of a monetary association agreement

Notwithstanding that the adoption of the euro as a national currency would be attained unilaterally, that is, without previous acquiescence by the EU, there are many reasons for negotiating this step with the EU. The most important reason is that the SEE countries are highly asymmetric in their dependence on EU markets, foreign direct investments, financial and technical assistance and political support. While all countries of this region are intended to become full members of the EU, they would have to accept and implement the acquis communautaire, according to the EU enlargement tradition. Since the EU insists that the Maastricht EMU criteria and procedures must be fulfilled before accession to the euro zone, the candidate states have to follow that path, unless the EU changes its position against unilateral euroisation in the sense discussed above.

Development of the basis for a broad national consensus

As mentioned, euroisation is a fundamental decision, which should not be taken solely on the basis of economic and technical considerations. It is critical that a country considering unilateral euroisation should achieve a strong political and social consensus. This requires a serious, open and broad discussion of the pros and cons, and support by the business community, the financial sector, labour organisations and civil society.

Announcement of the euroisation decision and of a reform plan

The policy reform programme should try to consolidate public finance, ensure the sustainability of monetary stability, modernise the financial sector, liberalise the factor markets and introduce labour market reforms, which will improve its ability to cope with asymmetric real shocks without recourse to monetary, exchange rate or even fiscal policy.

Implementation of the reform plan in four or five years

Only after a successful implementation of the reform plan and after achieving the mentioned consensus should a country consider unilateral euroisation. During that period the country could introduce a currency board arrangement as an instrument supporting the reform programme and as an 'antechamber' to full euroisation.

Assurance that the central bank has sufficient euro reserves

A new role must be defined for the central bank (surveillance of banking system, lender of last resort) or a new institution established for banking sector surveillance and liquidity.

Development of a timetable

A timetable must be drawn up for the date on which the exchange rate with the euro will be set, for the date on which the euro will become legal tender, for rules for the conversion and reinterpretation of old contracts, and so on. An 'up-front' competitive devaluation should be avoided because it could cause an increase in imported inflation and a loss of competitiveness. It could also cause tensions with EU and other third countries. Also, an 'up-front' revaluation could cause serious damage to the competitiveness of the euroising country.

Should the Balkans euroise?

The above analysis has shown that the debate about unilateral euroisation for SEE countries raises a lot of complicated theoretical and political questions. The answer to the question of whether transition countries like those in the SEE, which are highly integrated into the EU, should euroise cannot be answered unequivocally. The process of euroisation in the SEE region poses both economic and political benefits and costs, few of which can be estimated in advance with any degree of precision. The estimation is very complex and, in most aspects, inherently subjective.

From a purely economic point of view, it would seem that the expected advantages of unilateral euroisation would more than compensate for the potential costs and risks (for an opposite view, see Wójcik, 2000). But the results of the ex ante calculus must be interpreted under the presupposition that the new monetary regime would change the performance of economic policy and the structure of the economy in significant ways and with uncertain results. This uncertainty leaves much room for debate and disagreement.

The decision to euroise or not would be determined by political economy considerations (about this aspect, see Frieden, 2000). A state willing to euroise would have to make a very fundamental political and economic decision. It would be a decision with uncertainties, which, after implementation, could be reversed only with extremely high costs. Therefore the final decision on euroisation would be dependent on the following political and economic criteria.

First, the political aspects involve, among others, the EU position, the national political and social consensus, government strength and stability, the existence of strong cross-border investing/financial interests and import and export competing producers. If the EU continues to oppose unilateral euroisation, and insists on Maastricht procedures, it seems unlikely that a transition country of the SEE region could proceed to such a decision. All these countries are dependent on the EU market and financial assistance, and intend to become full members in the future. Under these circumstances a tension in their relations with the EU due to unilateral euroisation would produce additional costs and risks for SEE countries. Strong governments with a pro-European public opinion would be able to choose a commitment to euroisation, and might use it in elections. But, also, it might be easier for a new government coming to power at a time of hyperinflation or chronic high inflation to make such a fundamental decision. At the domestic level, strong EU-oriented economic agents and interest groups (such as financial institutions, international firms and borrowers) are more likely to want euroisation. Producers of international tradable goods and import competitors are more likely to oppose it.

Second, economic aspects include trade openness and the degree of economic integration with the EU, correlation of economic conditions and the business cycle with those of the EU, inflation rate and inflationary expectations, level of foreign reserves, flexibility of markets and so on. The greater the commercial and financial integration and the greater the synchronisation of the national business cycle with that of the EU, the greater would be the likelihood of euroisation. The will to break the inflationary dynamic and to bring discipline into economic policy might also influence this decision positively. Also a positive impact could be expected should there be sufficient foreign exchange reserves and flexible factor markets and, especially, labour markets.

Politicians will make the ultimate decision about euroisation after considering all the above-mentioned political economy aspects. The SEE transition countries are characterised by divergent political and economic structures and, therefore, political economy considerations concerning the euroisation decision will vary. The economic effects of unilateral euroisation would vary across SEE countries, as would their evaluation among individuals and groups. Hence further analysis would be needed to estimate the special economic and political conditions which would favour or counter euroisation in each SEE transition country.

Notes

1. The paper on which this chapter is based is part of a research project on 'Monetary Integration of Southeastern Europe – Alternative Approaches and Their Economic and Integration Implications', financed by the Greek State Scholarships Foundation, Programme for the Promotion of the Exchange and Scientific Cooperation Between Greece and Germany, Programme IKYDA 2001.

References

Berg, A. and E. Borenszstein (2000), 'The Pros and Cons of Full Dollarization', *IMF Working Paper*, 50.

Bishev, G. (2000), 'Monetary Policy and Transition in South-East Europe', in Vl. Gligorov (ed.), *Balkan Reconstruction,* LSE-WIIW Balkan Studies, Vienna, pp. 11–36.

Bratkowski, A. and J. Rostowski (2000), 'The EU Attitude to Unilateral Euroization: Misunderstandings, Real Concerns and Ill-designed Admission Criteria', CASE Institute, Warsaw.

CEPS (1999), 'A System for Post-War South East Europe', Working Document no. 131, Brussels.

Cohen, B. (2001), 'U.S. Policy on Dollarization: A Political Analysis', <www.polsci.ucsb.edu/faculty/cohen/working/dollarization.html>.

Corker, R., C. Beaumont, R. van Elkan and D. Iakova (2000), 'Exchange Rate Regimes in Selected Advanced Transition Economies – Coping with Transition, Capital Inflows, and EU Accession', *IMF Policy Discussion Paper,* no. 3.

DeGrauwe, P. and V. Lavrac (1999), 'Challenges of European Monetary Union for Central European Countries', in P. DeGrauwe and V. Lavrac (eds), *Inclusion of Central European Countries in the Monetary Union,* Boston, Dordrecht and London: Kluwer, pp. 1–12.

Deutsche Bundesbank (2000), 'Annual Report', Frankfurt.

EastWest Institute (2000), *Task Force on Economic Strategy for South Eastern Europe, Final Report,* New York: EastWest Institute.

ECOFIN (2000), 'Council Conclusions', 2301st Council Meeting, Brussels, 7 November 2000, 12925/00 (Presse 417).

Eichengreen, B. (2001), 'What Problems Can Dollarization Solve?', *The Journal of Policy Modeling*, 23(3), 267–77.

Emerson, M. (2000), Perspective for the Balkans and a wider Europe, Vl. Gligorov (ed.), *Balkan Reconstruction,* LSE-WIIW Balkan Studies, Vienna, pp. 321–47.

Enoch, Ch. and A.-M. Gulde (1998), 'Are Currency Boards a Cure for All Monetary Problems?', *Finance and Development*, 35(4).

Freytag, A. (1998), 'Getting Fit for the EU: A Currency Board for Poland', Institut für Wirtschaftspolitik an der Universität zu Köln, Cologne.

Frieden, J.A. (2000), 'The Political Economy of Dollarization: Domestic and International Factors', Department of Government, Harvard University, Cambridge, MA.

Gligorov, Vl. (ed.) (2000), *Balkan Reconstruction*, LSE-WIIW, Vienna: Balkan Studies.

Gligorov, Vl., M. Kaldor and L. Tsoukalis (1999), *Balkan Reconstruction and European Integration*, The Hellenic Observatory, The European Institute, LSE, The Centre for the Study of Global Governance, LSE and The Vienna Institute for International Economic Studies, London School of Economics.

Gross, D. (1999), 'An Economic System for Post-War-South Europe', companion paper to the CEPS Working Document no. 131, CEPS, Brussels.

Gulde, A.-M., J. Kähkönen and P. Keller (2000), 'Pros and Cons of Currency Board Arrangements in the Lead-up to EU Accession and Participation in the Euro Zone', IMF Policy Discussion Paper, PDP/00/1.

Heise, P.A. (2002), 'Gresham's Law and the Euroization of the Central and Eastern European Countries', Department of Political Science and Economics, Lebanon Vallege, Annville (heise@lvc.edu).

Horvath, J. (2001), The Costs and Benefits of Euroization (mimeo), ACE Phare Project no. P98 1061 R, Central European University, Budapest.

HypoVereinsbank (1999), 'Von der Dollarisierung zur Euroisierung? Potentiale der Verwendung des EURO außerhalb der EWU', Strategie and Trend Research, Munich.

IMF (2000), 'Exchange Rate Regimes in an Increasingly Integrated World Economy', Occasional Paper 193, Washington, DC.

Kirkilis, D. (2001), 'Regional Integration in South Eastern Europe', paper presented at the International Conference on 'Restructuring, Stability and Development in Southeastern Europe', South and East European Development Center (SEED-Center), University of Thessaly, Volos, 1–3 June.

Köhler, H. and M. Wes (1999), 'Implications of the Euro for the Integration Process of the Transition Economies in Central and Eastern Europe', EBRD, Working Paper no. 38.

Kopits, G. (1999), 'Implications of EMU for Exchange Rate Policy in Central and Eastern Europe', IMF Working Paper 9, Washington, DC.

Kotios, A. (2001a), 'European Policies for the Reconstruction and Development of the Balkans', G. Petrakos and Stoyan Totev (eds), *The Development of the Balkan Region,* Aldershot: Ashgate, pp. 235–80.

Kotios, A. (2001b), 'The European Union's Balkan Development Policy', *INTERECONOMICS, Review of European Economic Policy*, 36, July/August, 196–207.

Lewis, M.K. and Z. Sevic (2000), 'The Political Economy of Currency Boards in the Balkans', *MOCT-MOST 3–4*, Kluwer Academic Publishers, pp.285–310.

Masson, P. (1999), 'Monetary and Exchange Rate Policy of Transition Economies of Central and Eastern Europe after the Launch of EMU', IMF Policy Discussion Paper no. 5.

McKinnon, R. (1963), 'Optimum Currency Areas', *American Economic Review*, 53, 717–25.

Mundell, R. (1961), 'A Theory of Optimum Currency Areas', *American Economic Review*, 51, 657–65.

Nuti, D.M. (2000), 'The Costs and Benefits of Euroisation in Central–Eastern Europe Before or Instead of EMU Membership', paper presented at the Sixth Dubrovnik Economic Conference, 29–30 June.

Petrakos, G. (2001a), 'Fragmentation or Integration in the Balkans? Strategies of Development for the 21st Century', in G. Petrakos and Stoyan Totev (eds), *The Development of the Balkan Region*, Aldershot: Ashgate, pp. 219–34.

Petrakos, G. (2001b), 'The Balkans in the New European Economic Space: Prospects of Adjustment and Policies of Development', paper presented at the International Conference on 'Restructuring, Stability and Development in Southeastern Europe', South and East European Development Center (SEED-Center), University of Thessaly, Volos, 1–3 June.

Risopoulos, G. (2001), 'Foreign Direct Investments and Western Firms' Internationalisation Strategies in the Balkan Countries', in G. Petrakos and Stoyan Totev (eds), *The Development of the Balkan Region*, Aldershot: Ashgate, pp. 75–111.

Rose, A.K. (2000), 'One Money One Market', *Economic Policy*, 15(30), 7–46.

Roubini, N. (1998), 'The Case Against Currency Boards: Debunking 10 Myths about the Benefits of Currency Boards' (www.stern.nyu.edu/~nroubini/asia/CurrencyBoardsRoubini.html).

Schweickert, R. (2001), 'Assessing the Advantages of EMU-Enlargement for the EU and Accession Countries: A Comparative Indicator Approach', Kiel Working Paper no. 1080, Kiel Institute of World Economy, Kiel.

Steil, B. and S.L.Woodward (1999), 'A European "New Deal" for the Balkans', *Foreign Affairs*, 78, 95–105.

Swoboda, A. (1968), 'The Euro-Dollar: An Interpretation', *Essays in International Finance*, 64, International Finance Section, Princeton, NJ.

United States Senate, Joint Economic Committee (1999), 'Encouraging Official Dollarization in Emerging Markets', Staff Report, April.

Velasko, A. (2001), 'The Impossible Duo? Globalization and Monetary Independence in Emerging Markets', Harvard University and NBER.

Williamson, J. (1999), 'Crawling Bands or Monitoring Bands: How to Manage Exchange Rates in a World of Capital Mobility', IIE, *International Economics Policy Briefs, Number 99–3,* Washington, DC.

Wójcik, C. (2000), 'A Critical Review of Unilateral Euroization Proposals: The Case of Poland', *Focus on Transition* 2/2000, Vienna: Austrian National Bank, 48–76.

World Bank (2000), 'The Road to Stability and Prosperity in South Eastern Europe: A Regional Strategy Paper', Washington, DC.

Index

Anglo-Saxon countries 19
Anti-export bias (AXB) 137–44
Argentina 8, 116
Asia Pacific Economic -Cooperation 181–2, 191–4
Asian crisis (1997–98) 229, 246–7
Asymmetric currency management (1930s) 30–33
Australia 50, 51
  composition of trade 189
  consumer price inflation 176
  deregulation of financial services 181, 186
  discount rates 196
  economic policy 172–4, 183
    assessment of 183–97
    classical strategy 197
    reform of 174, 188
  exchange rate liberalisation 179
  exchange rate policy 177–8
  exports 181
  GDP growth 175
  industrial production 187
  manufacturing 188
  monetary policy 179
  share prices 186; exchange rate movements 183
  tariff reform 180; protection 179–80
  terms of trade 190, 191
  trade patterns 181–2, 190–2, 194
  unemployment rates 175

Balkan countries 299, 300, 301
  contractual relations 299
  exchange rate regimes 303
  monetary integration with EU 302
  selected economic indicators 307
  trade shares 301
  see also South-eastern Europe
Baltic States 54
Bank for International Settlements (BIS) 45–6, 55, 94, 236–37, 238
Bank of England 35, 36, 124
Bank of Greece 204, 205, 206, 213
Belgium 22
Bellagio Study Group 275
Brazil 8
Bretton Woods 6, 10–11, 58–9, 103–7, 117, 233, 239, 251, 257–64
  Bretton Woods Conference (1944) 10
  Bretton Woods system 255, 256, 257, 258
British Dominions 17, 34, 35
British Empire Currency Declaration 36
Brown, Gordon 258
Brown, W. A. 27
Buiter, W. 249

Canada 54
Cassel, G. 26
China 8
Clarke, S. V. O. 47
Clearing agreements 41
  extent of 41, 56
Cold War 256, 257, 265, 272
Common Agricultural Policy (CAP) 13, 123
Competitiveness 134, 230, 315
Convergence 2, 15, 108, 120, 131–2, 233, 239, 241, 312
Corner solutions 4, 7
Credibility (of policy) 15, 57, 91–4, 109, 122–7, 203, 215–24, 228, 234, 239, 244, 248–9, 251, 300, 310
Currencies (in 1920s) 17–18
  debate on 18
Currency boards 4, 67, 116, 296–97, 309–10
Currency crisis 212, 235, 238, 247–8
Currency management in 1930s 44
  range of fluctuations under 30–33
Currency stabilisation (in 1920s) 17–19, 20–22
  types of 19–20

Currency zones 33–4
Czechoslovakia 22, 49, 53

Delors Report 121, 292
Denmark 2
Deregulation 172, 195–96, 228
financial 179, 182–6, 202, 234, 238
Deutschmark 13, 114, 119
Devaluation 8, 10–12, 30, 33, 176, 229, 240, 262, 290, 304, 308, 310, 315
interwar years 37–57, 73–100
Disinflation 203, 240
in Greece 203, 240
Dollar depreciation (under Roosevelt) 82–7
Dornbusch, R. 275, 281–6
Duisenberg, Wim 247

Economic asymmetries 241
Economic recovery (1930s) 49
comparison of European countries 50–1, 52–3
under alternative exchange rate regimes 49–57
Eichel, Hans 249
Eichengreen, B. 4, 19, 33, 35, 40, 52–3, 56, 122, 235, 306
Einzig P. 34
Equilibrium exchange rate 234
Ethiopia 8
Euro 1, 2, 14, 15
launch of 2, 3
performance of 2, 15
prospects for 14, 15
value of 246
Euro-dream scenario 238, 243
Euroland 2, 230, 241, 243, 251, 311
see also eurozone
Euroisation unilateral 304–305, 310–15
Europe 18
exchange rate discipline in 116–23
inflation (in 1920s) 19–21
reconstruction of 22–6
recovery (in 1920s) 19, 20–22, 23–4, 26, 27
recovery (in 1930s) 49–57
European Central Bank 14, 15, 117, 120–21, 220, 234, 238, 240, 241, 243, 247, 249, 300, 304, 305, 311, 313
European Common Margins Agreement 118
European Currency Unit (ECU) 6, 120
European Economic Community (EEC) 11–12
European Economic and Monetary Union 2–5, 13–14, 120–22, 202, 209, 239–40, 243, 248, 249, 251, 311–14
European Exchange Rate Mechanism, *see* Exchange Rate Mechanism (ERM)
European Monetary System (EMS) 12, 104, 116, 120, 121, 122, 123, 278
European Monetary Union (EMU) 3, 13, 15, 130, 117, 239, 240, 248, 251, 312
macroeconomic issues relating to membership 131
microeconomic gains from 132–3
European Union (EU) 14, 230, 238, 239, 254, 300, 302, 306
additional members 239
and euroisation 310–13
competitiveness scores 242–3
diversity of experience in 241, 242
growth rates in 231, 245
prospects for 243–4
Eurosclerosis 121, 238, 243–4
Eurozone 228, 230, 231, 237, 239–40, 244, 248, 300, 304–305, 311, 314
inflation in 241–4
interest rates in 231
Exchange control 30–7, 38–41, 59, 177, 195, 205, 266, 279
Exchange control countries 39–4
disadvantages of 40
effects of 40
German influence 41
members 39
motives for 39–40
multiple exchange rates 40
overvaluation of currencies 40
Exchange Equalisation Account 42–4
effects of 43, 44
objectives of 42–3

Exchange rate flexibility (post-1973) 251
  background to 254–64
Exchange Rate Mechanism (ERM) 6, 12–13, 104, 113, 120, 121, 122, 123, 139, 198–9, 206, 312
  crisis in (1992–93) 13, 123, 233, 235, 237, 248
  Greece 206
  Ireland 198–9
  UK membership 113
Exchange rate models 105–10
Exchange rate regimes 3, 4–7, 9, 17–59, 117, 229, 236, 264, 297, 300, 306
Exchange rate targets 5, 11, 104, 108–109, 116, 122, 126, 203
  experience with 126–7
Exchange rate volatility 4, 228, 229, 230
Exchange rates 17
  exchange rate risks 140–1
  free floating of in 1920s 18–19
  impact of economic fundamentals on 231–6
  instability of 30, 32
  stability of 55
  trade barrier effects of 139–40, 147–9
Exchange stabilisation funds 42–4
  effects of 44
Exports 24, 50, 181

Financial crisis (1931) 8, 17, 29, 35, 49, 235
Finland 22, 237
Fixed exchange rates 6–9, 10, 11, 17, 28, 47, 58, 111, 116, 122, 124, 187, 208, 239, 267, 270, 276, 289, 296
Fleming-Mundell model 105–107
Flexible exchange rates 9, 10, 263
  case for 264–76, 278
  determination of 277–88
  monetary policy under 288–90
  performance under 276–8
Floating exchange rates 9, 10, 17–22, 57–9
  desire to avoid 33
Foreign exchanges 235
  speculation in 18, 38, 236–7, 238, 239
France 20, 22, 37, 49
Fraser, Malcolm 180, 192
Free float (in 1920s) 17–22, 57–9
French franc 92
  flight from 43
  stabilisation of 29
Friedman, Milton 28, 49, 87, 105, 115, 125, 235, 250–51, 264–9, 273–5, 275, 280
Fundamental disequilibrium 10, 256–8

General Agreement on Tariffs and Trade (GATT) 179
Germany 12, 104, 105, 114, 115, 116, 119, 249
  monetary union 3
Gold bloc 37–9, 90
  disadvantages of 38, 53
  disintegration of 28–9, 36
  members of 37
Gold exchange standard 9, 26, 36, 72, 232–3
  associated with depression 28, 29
  disintegration of 28–9
  economic performance under 23–9
  gold reserves under 28
  trade and currency movements under 26–7
  views on 26–8
Gold panics (in 1930s) 87–100
Gold standard 8, 17–18, 108, 258, 266
  and unemployment 28
  attempts to restore 8
  disintegration of 28–9
  effects of war on 8
  extent of 8
  models of 72–5
  new 22–9
  return to (1925) 17, 235
Great Depression (1929–1933) 10, 17, 22, 81, 100
Greece 2, 13, 21, 49, 52, 240, 248
  aggregate expenditure 210
  capital assets 214
  disinflation 209, 211
  economic performance (postwar II) 202–3, 204
  economic stabilisation 211, 212–15, 216, 217–20

exchange rate appreciation 212
exchange rate policy 204–6
exchange rates 204–5
fiscal deficits 221
fiscal policy 220–21
government debt 222
government primary balance 221
inflation trends 203, 210, 211, 220
interest rates 207, 208, 209, 213, 214
monetary policy 204, 207–8, 209, 213, 214–15
monetary targets 205, 206
money supply 208
productivity 222, 223
profitability 223
real wages 222, 223
Stabilisation Plan 203
sterilisation 212–15
unemployment 210
Gross domestic product (GDP) 23
fluctuations in 50
Gulf Cooperation Council (GCC) 3–4

Hague, William 15
Hawke, Robert 172, 173, 174, 178, 181, 182, 187, 190
Hyperinflation 19–27, 248, 316

India 8
Industrial production 51
fluctuations in 51
Inflation 5–11, 13, 20–22, 78–80, 103, 111–14, 131, 134, 192, 248, 273, 277, 304, 306, 313, 315
(in 1920s) 11, 13, 19, 20–1
and convergence 240
and purchasing power parity 232–4
and trade-off with unemployment 269–72
and US policies 268
Australia 176–84
Eurozone 241–44
Greece 203–204, 211
Inflation targets 104–5, 109–10, 123–6
Institute for Management Development, Geneva (IMD) 242–3
International monetary cooperation 44–8
International Monetary Fund (IMF) 6–7, 10, 108, 112, 172, 174, 186, 196–8, 229, 237, 247, 255–9, 260, 263, 275, 276–7, 292
International monetary management (in 1930s) 30–33
currency fluctuations under 30–33
International monetary system 57
assessment of interwar regimes 57–9
collapse of 264
instability of 258
Intervention in exchange markets (1930s) 41–4
Intervention (in FX markets) 236–8, 241–4
Ireland, Republic of, 197–9, 241, 244
economic strategy compared with Australian 198–9
Italy 21

Johnson H. C. 29
Johnson, H. G. 29, 112–13, 258, 264, 266, 267, 268–71, 274, 289

Keating, Paul 172, 173, 174, 177, 179, 181, 182, 187, 190
Keynes, J. M. 4, 18, 22, 113–114

Latin America 8, 32
Lawson, Nigel 13
League of Nations 33, 47, 55

Maastricht Treaty 204, 223, 239–40, 292, 305, 312
convergence criteria 2, 223–4
tests for EMU membership 240
Managed float 7, 9, 11, 57, 59, 303
Marshall Plan 256
McKinnon, R. I. 12, 289–90
Mexico 8, 116, 229
Microeconomic gains 132–4
Monetary policy 180
in Australia 179
in Greece 204–12
in UK 112–13
Monetary targets 103, 106–16
experience with 110–16
Monetary unions 3–5, 16, 117–18, 121, 306

Multiple exchange rates 40
Mundell, R. A. 132, 251, 258, 266–7, 280

Netherlands 20, 22, 37
Niemeyer, Otto 233
Norman, Montagu 36, 45, 233
North American Free Trade Area 3, 15, 123
North American Monetary Union (NAMU) 3
North Atlantic Treaty Organisation (NATO) 259, 261
Norway 237

Optimum Currency Area 132, 251, 254
Ottawa Conference (1932) 35

Persia 8
Peru 8
Plaza-Louvre Accords 12
Portugal 54
Protection, rates of 135–7;
  effective rates of 137–9
  investment disincentives 137–9
  simulation tables 151–71
  simulations of effective rates of 141–4
Purchasing Power Parity (PPP) theory 74, 131, 231–3, 281–2, 285

Reichsmark bloc 41
Return to gold standard (1925) 17, 235
Royal Institute of International Affairs (RIIA) 44
Russia 229

Scandinavia 20, 22
Single currency, 2, 7, 14, 15, 121, 228
  problems of 244–6
Silver standard 8
Single European Act (1986) 121–2
Smithsonian Agreement 263
Snake, the 11–12, 117–18
South American republics 32
South-eastern Europe 296–7
  costs and risks of euroisation 308–9
  economic integration in 293–300
  euroisation compared with currency boards 309–10
  euroisation in 304
  exchange rate regimes in 303
  implementation of unilateral euroisation 313–15
  monetary integration with EU 300, 302
  potential benefits of euroisation 305–8
  selected economic indicators 307
  should the Balkans euroise? 315–16
  trade orientation towards EU 300, 301
  trade shares of Balkan countries 301
Spain 54
  Civil War in 54, 55
Special Drawing Rights (SDRs) 61, 263
Speculative attacks 9
Speculators 6, 9, 42, 73, 123, 176–78, 239, 249, 274
Sprague, O. M. W. 26
Stabilisation of currencies 18
  need for after first war 18
Stability and Growth Pact 244, 248–9, 251
Statistical data
  aggregate expenditure 210
  bank deposits 75
  capital 213
  commodity prices 83
  competitiveness scores 242
  currency fluctuations 31, 32
  dollar price 83
  domestic assets 214
  exchange rates 183, 209, 231, 303, 246
  exports 24, 50, 181, 189, 242
  external trade 301
  fiscal deficits 221
  foreign assets 214
  general government debt 222
  government primary balance 221
  gross domestic product 23, 50, 126, 175, 211, 231, 242, 245
  industrial production 51, 75, 187
  inflation 125, 176, 204, 211, 220, 242

interest rates 196, 207, 208, 231
labour shares 242
manufacturing production 25, 51
manufacturing shares 188, 242
monetary gold stocks 73, 75
monetary targets 125, 126, 205
money supply 185, 208, 211
profitability
real unit labour costs 22
real wages 222
selected economic indicators 307
share prices 78, 83, 186
simulation tables for selected variables 151–71
terms of trade 190
trade shares 34, 299, 300, 301
unemployment 175, 211
velocity growth 208
Sterling area 34–6
coverage 34
role of 35–6
success of 36
Suez crisis 257
Sumner, S. 28, 29
Sweden 2, 237
Switzerland 20, 115

Thatcher, Margaret 14, 112, 192
Tobin, James 250
tax proposals of 250–1
Trade barriers 136
measures of 137–40
Trade policy 134
theory of 135–9
Trading blocs 33–4
breakdown of 34
effects of 34, 56
Trichet, Jean Claude 247
Triffin, R. 260–62
Tripartite Agreement 39, 46–8, 90
impact of 47–8
role of 46–7
Truman Doctrine 256
Turkey 21, 22

United Kingdom 2, 8, 13–14, 20, 54, 125, 264
departure from gold (1931) 29
devaluation (1931) 90
floating of sterling (1972) 112
inflation 112
monetary policy 112–13
United States 3, 9–10, 12, 43, 104, 230, 241, 250, 255, 258, 259, 260, 263, 272
anti-inflation programme 91
commodity prices 100
decline in output 71
devaluation 73
dollar panics 75–82, 87–99
gold panics 87–99
gold purchase policy 86
relationship between variables 75, 78, 83
Roosevelt's dollar depreciation policy 82–7
share prices 76–82, 83; 100
Upgrading of firms 245–6
Uruguay 8

Werner Plan 117, 121
Whitlam, Gough 180
World Economic Conference (1931 London) 33, 37, 45, 46
World liquidity 29
World monetary gold stocks 73